CONVERGING PERSPECTIVES ON CONCEPTUAL CHANGE

D1615263

Conceptual change, how conceptual understanding is transformed, has been investigated extensively since the 1970s. The field has now grown into a multifaceted, interdisciplinary effort with strands of research in cognitive and developmental psychology, education, educational psychology, and the learning sciences. *Converging Perspectives on Conceptual Change* brings together an extensive team of expert contributors from around the world, and offers a unique examination of how distinct lines of inquiry can complement each other and have converged over time.

Amin and Levrini adopt a new approach to assembling the diverse research on conceptual change: the combination of short position pieces with extended synthesis chapters within each section, as well as an overall synthesis chapter at the end of the volume, provide a coherent and comprehensive perspective on conceptual change research.

Arranged over five parts, the book covers a number of topics including:

- the nature of concepts and conceptual change
- representation, language, and discourse in conceptual change
- modeling, explanation, and argumentation in conceptual change
- metacognition and epistemology in conceptual change
- identity and conceptual change.

Throughout this wide-ranging volume, the editors present researchers and practitioners with a more internally consistent picture of conceptual change by exploring convergence and complementarity across perspectives. By mapping features of an emerging paradigm, they challenge newcomers and established scholars alike to embrace a more programmatic orientation towards conceptual change.

Tamer G. Amin is Associate Professor in the Department of Education, and Director of the Science and Mathematics Education Center at the American University of Beirut, Lebanon.

Olivia Levrini is Associate Professor in Physics Education and History of Physics at the University of Bologna, Italy.

CONVERGING PERSPECTIVES ON CONCEPTUAL CHANGE

Mapping an Emerging Paradigm in the Learning Sciences

Edited by Tamer G. Amin and Olivia Levrini

Routledge
Taylor & Francis Group

LONDON AND NEW YORK

First published 2018
by Routledge
2 Park Square, Milton Park, Abingdon, Oxon OX14 4RN

and by Routledge
711 Third Avenue, New York, NY 10017

Routledge is an imprint of the Taylor & Francis Group, an informa business

British Library Cataloguing-in-Publication Data
A catalogue record for this book is available from the British Library

Library of Congress Cataloging-in-Publication Data
A catalog record for this book has been requested

ISBN: 978-1-138-20539-0 (hbk)
ISBN: 978-1-138-20540-6 (pbk)
ISBN: 978-1-315-46713-9 (ebk)

Typeset in Bembo
by codeMantra
Printed and bound by CPI Group (UK) Ltd, Croydon, CR0 4YY

Cover image: Fausto Melotti
Tema e variazioni I (Theme and Variations I)
1968
Ottone
40 x 33 x 14 cm.
Milano, Collezione privata
Courtesy the Estate of Fausto Melotti and Hauser & Wirth

For Lina
For Lella and my students

CONTENTS

ACKNOWLEDGMENTS

The idea for this book grew out of our experience co-chairing the *9th International Conference on Conceptual Change* in Bologna, Italy in 2014. This was the 9th biennial meeting of the Special Interest Group on Conceptual Change (SIG 3) of the European Association for Research on Learning and Instruction (EARLI). The contributions to this conference and the conversations we had with its participants convinced us that there was a need to begin an effort to bring diverse strands of research on conceptual change together.

We are grateful to Clark Chinn, Mariana Levin, Bruce Sherin, Carol Smith, and Marianne Wiser for agreeing to contribute to this book as section editors. We greatly appreciate our discussions in the early stages of the design of the book. Their enthusiasm for the project was a very important motivator for us as we embarked on it and helped us see this book through to completion. Given its scope, we could not have considered editing this book without their participation. We thank them for the time they devoted to our discussions over Skype (coordinating schedules at multiple time zones), careful reading and editing of contributions to their sections, and the feedback they shared on chapters in other parts of the book.

We are also very grateful to Nahed El-Oud, Laura Fontanesi and Nessrine Machaka for their help in preparing the index.

Tamer Amin gratefully acknowledges the European Institutes for Advanced Study (EURIAS) Fellowship Programme/Marie-Curie Actions, 7th Framework Program and the Hanse-Wissenschaftskolleg (HWK) (Institute for Advanced Study), Delmenhorst, Germany for a 2016–17 fellowship during which a large portion of the work on this book was completed. The HWK is a wonderful environment in which to work and leaves its mark on this book.

Olivia Levrini wishes to thank the research group in Physics and Mathematics Education of the University of Bologna, for inspiring and thoughtful discussions on draft chapters of the book. Thanks also to Franco Righi for his continuous and strong support.

CONTRIBUTORS

Tamer G. Amin
American University of Beirut, Lebanon

Leema K. Berland
University of Wisconsin-Madison, USA

Pablo Brocos
Universidade de Santiago de Compostela, Spain

David E. Brown
University of Illinois, Urbana-Champaign, USA

Pinar Seda Cetin
Abant Izzet Baysal University, Turkey

Michelene T. H. Chi
Arizona State University, USA

Clark A. Chinn
Rutgers, The State University of New Jersey, USA

Eliza L. Congdon
Bucknell University, USA

Nicolas Décamp
LDAR, Université Paris Diderot, UCP, UPEC, Univ. d'Artois, Univ. de Rouen., France

Jasmine M. DeJesus
University of Michigan, USA

Andrea A. diSessa
University of California, Berkeley, USA

Sibel Erduran
University of Oxford, UK & University of Limerick, Ireland

Paola Fantini
Liceo "A. Einstein", Rimini, Italy

Susan A. Gelman
University of Michigan, USA

Susan Goldin-Meadow
University of Chicago, USA

James Greeno
University of Pittsburgh, USA

David Hammer
Tufts University, USA

J. Bryan Henderson
Arizona State University, USA

Einat Heyd-Metzuyanim
Technion—Israel Institute of Technology, Israel

Barbara K. Hofer
Middlebury College, USA

María Pilar Jiménez-Aleixandre
Universidade de Santiago de Compostela, Spain

Shulamit Kapon
Technion—Israel Institute of Technology, Israel

Ebru Kaya
Bogazici University, Turkey

Frank C. Keil
Yale University, USA

Elon Langbeheim
Weizmann Institute of Science, Israel

Richard Lehrer
Vanderbilt University, USA

Mariana Levin
Western Michigan University, USA

Olivia Levrini
Alma Mater Studiorum—Università di Bologna, Italy

Doug Lombardi
Temple University, USA

Cecilia Lundholm
Stockholm University, Sweden

Ananda Marin
University of California, Los Angeles, USA

Felicity McLure
Curtin University, Australia

Douglas Medin
Northwestern University, USA

Miriam A. Novack
Northwestern University, USA

bethany ojalehto
Northwestern University, USA

Rosemary S. Russ
University of Wisconsin-Madison, USA

Roger Säljö
University of Gothenburg, Sweden

William A. Sandoval
University of California, Los Angeles, USA

Geoffrey B. Saxe
University of California, Berkeley, USA

Leona Schauble
Vanderbilt University, USA

Bruce Sherin
Northwestern University, USA

Gale M. Sinatra
University of Southern California, USA

Carol L. Smith
University of Massachusetts, Boston, USA

David F. Treagust
Curtin University, Australia

Laurence Viennot
*LDAR, Université Paris Diderot, UCP, UPEC, Univ.
d'Artois, Univ. de Rouen., France*

Stella Vosniadou
*The Flinders University of South Australia, Australia &
National and Kapodistrian University of Athens, Greece.*

Elizabeth M. Wakefield
Loyola University Chicago, USA

Marianne Wiser
Clark University, USA

Mihye Won
Curtin University, Australia

INTRODUCTION

Tamer G. Amin and Olivia Levrini

Research on conceptual change is a multidisciplinary endeavor that examines how conceptual structures in specific domains of knowledge are transformed. These processes of knowledge transformation have been explored in the history of specific disciplines like science and mathematics, in communities as they interact with others and develop new practices, and in individuals as a result of informal and formal learning experiences. This volume is primarily concerned with conceptual change in individual learners (including children and adults), although some attention is given to connections with historical and sociohistorical knowledge transformations. More specifically, researchers investigate the content and structure of early conceptions; how conceptual knowledge is represented in learners and experts; and the factors and processes that drive change in conceptual understanding. They also examine the implications all this has for designing effective formal instruction and enhancing the public understanding of disciplinary knowledge.

The origins of research on conceptual change in individuals can be traced back to the early 1970s and, by the mid-1980s, this research endeavor took shape as several disciplines—including science education, cognitive psychology, developmental psychology, history and philosophy of science—jointly contributed to our understanding of how people learn scientific concepts (see Amin, Smith, & Wiser, 2014). A substantial amount of empirical and theoretical research has been carried out since and conceptual change is now being investigated in other disciplines like mathematics (e.g. Vosniadou & Veschaffel, 2004) and the social sciences (e.g. Lundholm & Davies, 2013).

The last five decades has seen the accumulation of a rich body of research. Five decades is not much in the history of a discipline, however, and areas of inquiry in their early stages of development are typically characterized by the proliferation of different perspectives and analytical methods (Kuhn, 1962). In these early stages, engagement between researchers mostly takes the form of a confrontation between perspectives: proponents of one perspective emphasize the distinctiveness of their own view and put forward meta-theoretical arguments for why their preferred perspective and methodological preferences are likely to be more fruitful than those of others. Research on conceptual change illustrates this well. Researchers investigate the transformation of knowledge in individuals from many distinct theoretical perspectives, sometimes grounded in assumptions that seem to be squarely at odds with one another. Sometimes similar constructs are proposed but it is not always clear how to translate across perspectives. Conversely, the same terminology is sometimes used to refer to different constructs. The methods of investigation used also vary, and it is sometimes argued that these are grounded in fundamentally different epistemological assumptions. This diversity can be gleaned from edited compilations of research on conceptual change published over the years, notably in a recent authoritative volume, the *International Handbook of Research on Conceptual Change* (Vosniadou, 2013). This handbook provides a comprehensive picture of key theoretical perspectives, how conceptual change has been investigated in learners across a range of disciplinary domains and in the history and philosophy of science, and the progress that has been made in instruction and curriculum design oriented to conceptual change.

Theoretical and methodological pluralism can be celebrated on the grounds that different perspectives can help make sense of different aspects of a complex and unwieldy whole. However, extensive theoretical and methodological diversity does not serve the goal of cumulative knowledge construction. By "cumulative knowledge construction" we mean a more mature stage of inquiry that emerges out of early exploratory stages. In this more mature stage, researchers working on different problems know how their work contributes to a larger whole; they agree on what the community of researchers "has learned so far" and should pass on to the next generations of researchers; and broadly agree on important next steps. This kind of cumulative knowledge construction depends on at least a minimal shared theoretical vocabulary and agreement about what kind of knowledge certain methods can and cannot provide; for it is this common ground that makes precise model construction and theory-building and evaluation possible. Stated broadly, we need a shift in our approach to research on conceptual change that is more programmatic.

We believe this is an appropriate moment for such a shift. Abstracting away from differences between perspectives on concept learning in science, Amin, Smith, and Wiser (2014) were able to outline a three-phase story of progress in the field: from replacing Piaget's stage theory with accounts of restructuring the content of student conceptions in specific domains (Phase One); to identifying the different aspects of the process of change (e.g. ontology, personal epistemologies, modeling and social interaction) (Phase Two); and on to the characterization of concept representation and the process of conceptual change as systemic phenomena (Phase Three). By stepping back from the details and adopting this bird's-eye view of the field, we see individual researchers (possibly adhering to

different theoretical perspectives) at each phase, making similar and/or complementary contributions to our understanding. Moreover, we can discern a degree
of consensus in the current phase in which we find the field. This is a promising
starting point from which to initiate a more programmatic effort at building
knowledge about conceptual change.

There is also a more pragmatic reason for a shift in orientation. There is
increasing pressure on academic research to make contributions to improving
education, as reflected in many international reports (e.g. Rocard et al., 2007).
Addressing these reports' recommendations requires that scholars move their research closer and closer to the reality of schools and classroom practice. Given
the complexities of classrooms and schools and, indeed, the learners themselves,
synthetic and well-articulated frameworks are needed. In other words, it is of
great practical value to be able to see how distinct lines of research contribute to
a larger whole. Attempts to draw on conceptual change research for the purposes
of curricular and instructional innovation require establishing clear links between the many different aspects of conceptual change. However, until quite recently, research has mainly conceptualized and studied these aspects in isolation.

This book implements such a shift in orientation by exploring convergence
and complementarity in conceptual change research. The book's structure and
the process of its preparation were designed accordingly. The book has been
organized into five parts, each addressing an aspect of the larger whole that constitutes research on conceptual change.

Part I, "The nature of concepts and conceptual change," edited by Bruce
Sherin, deals with foundational issues of concept representation and the processes
of change. It engages with key tensions in the literature such as stability versus
contextual variation in conceptualization; universal constraints on concept development versus variability due to sociocultural contexts; individual versus sociocultural mechanisms of change; and differences between concepts and the process
of change across domains such as science, mathematics, and the social sciences.

Part II, "Representation, language, and discourse in conceptual change,"
edited by Tamer Amin, addresses the format in which conceptual knowledge
is represented and how representations of various kinds figure in the process of
conceptual change. Contributions to this part of the book consider external representations such as language, visual representations and simulations, equations,
and gesture and how these interact with internal mental representations such as
imagery, image schemas, mental models, and the essentialist assumption.

Part III, "Modeling, explanation, and argumentation in conceptual change,"
edited by Clark Chinn, examines how the process of conceptual change is related
to key reasoning and epistemic practices. This part examines how changes in
learners' concepts are often part of a process of change in the kinds of explanations they give to phenomena; how representing concepts and constructing novel
understanding in any domain often involve processes of modeling; and how concept and belief revision can require the evaluation of claims in light of evidence,
a process that is realized discursively through argumentation.

Part IV, "Metacognition and epistemology in conceptual change," edited by Carol Smith and Marianne Wiser, explores learners' ideas about, and implicit orientations to, the nature of knowledge, understanding, and learning. Importantly, this part examines how these ideas and orientations affect conceptual change in specific domains of knowledge as well as their ability to engage in the reasoning and epistemic practices needed to construct more sophisticated understanding of technical concepts.

Part V, "Identity and conceptual change," edited by Mariana Levin and Olivia Levrini, is concerned with how learner identity interacts with the learning of the conceptual content of various disciplines. Bidirectional influences are explored: how, on the one hand, identity affects the processes of conceptual change and, on the other, instruction inspired by models of conceptual change affects the construction of students' identity.

Each part includes a number of short chapters, written by key contributors to the field, followed by a synthesis. The goal of each part is to provide the reader with concise descriptions of important strands of research dealing with a particular aspect of conceptual change and to consider ways in which these different lines of research converge and complement one another. Authors of the short chapters were asked to prepare relatively short, up-to-date position statements that clarify their perspectives on the theme of that part of the book. They were provided with guidelines that would help the authors of the syntheses compare and contrast distinct lines of work with respect to common themes. The syntheses at the end of each part adopt a reflective stance and explore the possibility of synthesis: they evaluate potential obstacles to synthesis, describe common themes that cut across the contributions, and when relevant point out ways in which the different lines of research contribute to a larger program of investigation.

Given the synthetic goals of this book, we invite the reader to treat each contribution as part of an integrated whole: each short chapter as contributing to a larger project exploring an aspect of conceptual change addressed by a part; each part contributing to the larger project of understanding conceptual change more broadly. In a final overall synthesis, we reflect on the broader picture of conceptual change research emerging from the five parts of this volume. We offer a number of readings of the content of the book as a whole. We examine *how* the authors of the syntheses approached their task, noting and comparing the different strategies they used. We also present what we call a "Synthetic Narrative," which we see as a road map of the research landscape that weaves together an overall picture of conceptual change research emerging from the different strands. We also discuss how challenges to synthesis were addressed in this volume and what we view as some of the remaining challenges to programmatic research on conceptual change that we still face moving forward. We view this book as the *beginning* of a *process* to shift our research orientation. We do not, of course, claim to offer a finalized synthesis of this diverse field. Instead, we suggest that such a synthesis should be the goal to which we strive as a research community and that that goal should influence how we each build on the work of others. This book is intended as an invitation to embrace this common goal.

References

Amin, T. G., Smith, C., & Wiser, M. (2014). Student conceptions and conceptual change: Three overlapping phases of research. In N. Lederman & S. Abell (Eds.), *Handbook of research on science education* (vol. 2, pp. 57–81). New York: Routledge.

Kuhn, T. (1962). *The structure of scientific revolutions.* Chicago, IL: University of Chicago Press.

Lundholm, C., & Davies, P. (2013). Conceptual change in the social sciences. In S. Vosniadou (Ed.), *International handbook of research on conceptual change* (2nd ed., pp. 288–304). New York: Routledge.

Rocard, M., Csermely, P., Jorde, D., Lenzen, D., Walwerg-Henriksson, H., & Hemmo, V. (2007). *Science education now: A renewed pedagogy for the future of Europe.* European Commission. Community Research. http://ec.europa.eu/research/science-society/document_library/pdf_06/report-rocard-on-science-education_en.pdf.

Vosniadou, S. (Ed.) (2013). *International handbook of research on conceptual change* (2nd ed.). London: Routledge.

Vosniadou, S., & Verschaffel, L. (2004). Extending the conceptual change approach to mathematics learning and teaching. *Learning and Instruction, 14,* 445–451.

PART I

The nature of concepts and conceptual change

Editor: Bruce Sherin

Orientation

This section addresses the nature of concepts and conceptual change. As such, this section is very important to the larger endeavor undertaken in this book, which is to work toward a convergence in research on conceptual change. As a microcosm of the larger volume, the chapters here illustrate some of the tensions to be negotiated, as well as the prospects for synthesis.

The first three chapters in this section represent a trio of voices that have been very prominent in research on conceptual change in the context of school science learning. The first chapter, from Andrea diSessa, describes the knowledge-in-pieces (KiP) theoretical perspective. diSessa illustrates this theoretical perspective in a discussion of his models of two types of knowledge, *phenomenological primitives* (p-prims), and *coordination classes*. In the second chapter, Stella Vosniadou lays out her own theoretical perspective. She argues that, in response to phenomenal and cultural experience, people develop what she calls *framework theories*. Then, when students encounter formal instruction, the existence of the framework theory leads to the formation, by individuals of "synthetic" conceptions. Vosniadou summarizes a range of empirical work that supports this theoretical perspective, and she also responds to a range of criticisms. In the third chapter, J. Bryan Henderson, Elon Langbeheim, and Michelene Chi ask the question: What makes some misconceptions robust? Their answer is that misconceptions tend to be robust when they involve ontological miscategorization. They argue, in particular, that many robust misconceptions result from the miscategorization, by students, of *emergent* processes as *sequential* processes. Furthermore, learning is complicated by the fact that learners generally lack the emergent process category.

The remaining three chapters broaden the discussion, each in a different manner. Cecilia Lundholm extends the discussion of conceptual change to school learning in the social sciences. She argues that conceptual change in the social sciences involves many of the same challenges as in disciplines that have been the traditional focus of research. But there are, in addition, challenges that are somewhat unique. Students' values and identities are relevant factors in conceptual change in the social sciences. Also, social science disciplines tend to include value-laden and contestable assumptions. In the next chapter, Ananda Marin, Douglas Medin, and bethany ojalehto argue that concepts should be treated as embedded within epistemological orientations, which can differ across cultural communities and contexts. As an illustration, they look at how an underlying view of the relationship between humans and nature influences conceptual organization. To support their points, they draw on research on the organization of folkbiological knowledge. The final chapter, by Geoffrey Saxe, broadens the discussion still further, to look at the conceptual change of communities. Saxe looks at the changing meaning of a word, "fu," used by the Oksapmin of Papua, New Guinea.

Clearly, the chapters here are divergent in many respects. The broad nature of the phenomena understood differs dramatically. Some of the chapters, for example, look at learning in response to formal science instruction, while others look at developmental and community-level phenomena. Furthermore, the theoretical perspectives employed are diverse. Nonetheless, as discussed in the synthesis by Bruce Sherin, it is possible to view the larger body of work as complementary; we can see the work conducted as small parts of the same larger endeavor. Furthermore, the chapters contain some of the seeds of a theoretical synthesis.

1

KNOWLEDGE IN PIECES

An evolving framework for understanding knowing and learning

Andrea A. diSessa

Empirical focus

Instead of providing a scholarly setting for the Knowledge in Pieces (KiP) perspective, it is briefer and as insightful to observe that my studies of conceptual change emerged from a passionate and sustained personal interest in how people (students, children, adults) naturally think about situations that might also be construed from the viewpoint of professional science. I have been enchanted by the richness, flexibility, great nuance, and often wonderful insightfulness of everyday thinking. I have systematically sought topics to discuss, situations that are accessible, but also somewhat problematic, so as to engage extended thinking and reflection. "Explanation" is at the center of this; "problem-solving" is peripheral. Problem-solving in school often entails students grasping at straws conceptually and just juggling the combinatorics of variables in equations. Understanding mathematics and its use in science is a worthy topic, but I believe it is secondary to deep qualitative, conceptual understanding.

Focusing on reasoning about less technical situations has proved immensely enlightening of schooled learning. Of course, there is a lot that is new in school, but the assumption that learning is substantially a recrafting of naïve conceptual resources has been among the most robust and productive assumptions in the history of learning studies.

Early on, I learned that just talking with people was a superior way of "seeing" their thinking. I learned a few lessons from this, which I think still escape the attention of many conceptual change researchers: (1) People have a vast repertoire of ways to think about many scientific situations; it might be that requiring them to engage with the most inscrutable ones (often forced on them in school) is mainly beside the point. (2) Their thinking is subtly tied to circumstances and frames of mind; slight shifts of perspective can induce dramatic changes. (3) Every person with whom I've engaged seems to be one-of-a-kind. Hence, there is not only a variety in how individuals can consider a given situation, but there's great variation across individuals.

The technical version of "just talking with people" is *clinical interviewing*, which has been a mainstay of my work. Of course, as someone with a deep professional and personal commitment to education, instruction and learning are also important foci, even if overt instruction almost never enters the clinical context. I see the following connections between just "talking with people" and instruction:

1   *Input to conjectures and expectations*: Knowing how people think within their zone of felt competence provides important, general and often very specific conjectures about how they can learn from instruction.
2   *Input to design*: Some of the insights from item 1, above, can instigate new avenues of instruction based on using powerful but underexplored and undervalued intellectual resources. This means that such research affects the very goals of instruction (what and when topics should be taught, and how they should be construed), in addition to instructional strategies.
3   *Input to observation*: Looking at learning-from-schooling shows indelible earmarks of both the productive and sometimes less productive roles of pre-instructional knowledge.

Recent work of our group exemplifies all these: (1) From studying students' ideas, we conjectured that it would be possible for middle school students to learn about an exotic topic, *dynamical systems theory*—and with substantially increased enthusiasm compared to traditional topics. (2) We conjectured that teaching about equilibration could be based on a prominent but often maligned intuitive idea. (3) Results of the instructional design validated that conjecture. But with the help of a prior and parallel clinical study, we observed many details not evident in our conjecture, which would have been unrecoverable from classroom observation, student work, and test data alone (diSessa, 2014).

Theoretical orientation

KiP theory involves problematizing the concept of *knowledge*, gradually developing a modern, detailed, and empirically supported replacement for previous commonsensical, inexplicit, philosophical, or other views of knowledge that are not up to deeply engaging the specifics of learning (diSessa, 2016). In particular, the concept of "concept" has too often evaded critical consideration, or versions of the idea have shown no purchase on designing or understanding instruction. The technical concepts of science and mathematics turn out to behave very differently from everyday concepts, such as "bird" or "animal," which have been a mainstay of psychological study. Traditional concepts of "concept" also turn out to be completely ineffective in understanding the form and function of intuitive ideas and their powerful roles in learning.

The KiP approach involves two strategies. First, *divide-and-conquer*—looking to define, elaborate, and validate a variety of new knowledge terms that enfold different aspects of knowing, such as everyday intuitive understanding, or, in contrast, full-blown professional concepts. I will exemplify KiP approaches to both such kinds of knowledge.

The second strategy is an incremental *modeling approach* to developing a science of knowledge. We need to develop new theory slowly and with due respect for how much we do not know. This entails two characteristics. *Explicit and consequential*—We seek to articulate specific models of various kinds of knowledge, models that have clear consequences and can be thoroughly tested against the realities of learning and instruction. *Continuous improvement*—We must simultaneously cultivate an understanding of the limits of these models, which constitute a frontier for future development.

KiP as a whole, then, aims to provide a coherent global empirical and theoretical framework in which to design and continuously improve a family of models of various kinds of knowledge, models with strong empirical tractability and powerful consequences.

Focal themes

I highlight two KiP themes in this chapter.

Integrated analyses at multiple time-scales: Conceptual change research (and KiP in particular) is distinguished by a strong focus on learning that can embrace an extended learning trajectory (years) with many difficulties for students and challenges for teachers. What is more distinctive of KiP is a focus on process data and analyses. We seek high-resolution accounts of thinking-and-learning-in-the-moment. Evident long-term changes in understanding must be happening *sometime*, and we embrace the task of saying exactly when something is being learned, how that is happening, and how such events accumulate over the long term. The complementary "micro" focus is rare in conceptual change work, especially within the tradition of developmental psychology. In education, also, before-and-after studies of learning are rarely augmented with process data and analyses. In sum, KiP accepts the challenge to integrate short and long time-scale descriptions and explanations.

Encompassing Diversity in Learning: I mentioned that I felt that every subject in my clinical interviews thought differently. If true—which I expect—this has strong consequences for learning, especially given that many theories of conceptual change emphasize (1) generic views of before-and-after states ("*the* naïve theory" vs. an assumed-to-be uniform "normative science"), and (2) generic paths to understanding to the point of severely marginalizing individual differences.

Two models: illustrative data and analysis

The remainder of this chapter concentrates on concretizing and exemplifying the generalizations above, both with respect to theory development and with respect to phenomenological focus and empirical methods. I will use the two best-developed and best-known KiP models of knowledge types. Descriptions here, of course, are necessarily bare bones, giving only hints about model details and the breadth of empirical support.

Intuitive knowledge

P-prims are elements of intuitive knowledge that constitute people's "sense of mechanism," their sense of what happenings are obvious, which are plausible, which are implausible, and how one can explain or refute real or imagined possibilities. Example glosses of p-prims are as follows: (1) increased effort begets greater results; (2) the world is full of competing influences for which the greater "gets its way," even if accidental or natural "balance" sometimes exists; and (3) the shape of the situation determines the shape of action within it (e.g., orbits around a square planet are nearly square).

We must develop a new model for this kind of knowledge because, empirically, it violates presumptions of standard knowledge types, like beliefs or principles. First, classifying p-prims as true or false (like beliefs or principles) is a category error; p-prims are unclassifiable by standard scientific norms. They work—prescribe verifiable outcomes—in typical situations but always fail in others. Indeed, when they will even be brought to mind is a very delicate consequence of context (both internal: "frame of mind"; or external: the particular sensory presentation of the phenomenon). So, for example, it is inappropriate to say that a person "believes" a p-prim, as if it would universally be brought to mind, when relevant, and as if it would always dominate other ways of thinking. Furthermore, students simply cannot *consider and reject* p-prims (a commonly prescribed learning strategy for "misconceptions"). Blocks to "consideration" are severe—there are no common words for p-prims, and people are in general not even aware that they have such ideas; "rejection" does not make sense for ideas that usually work!

Data and analysis: J, a subject in an extended interview study (diSessa, 1996), was asked to explain what happens when you toss a ball into the air. J responded fluently with a completely normative response: There is only one force in the situation, gravity, which slows the ball down, eventually to reverse its motion and bring it back down. Then the interviewer asked a seemingly innocuous question, "What happens at the peak of the toss?" Rather than responding directly, J completely reformulated her explanation of the toss. She first implicated "air resistance" as a second force that is competing with gravity to influence the ball's motion, but quickly decided that it really is only gravity that is acting against the upward motion. Finally, restarting her explanation once again, she imputed "a force that you gave the ball with your hand," which gradually dies out, leaving gravity to pull the ball downward.

The key to understanding these events so far is that the interviewer "tempted" J to apply an intuitive idea of balancing and overcoming; he asked about the peak because the change of direction there looks like one influence is getting weaker and is overcome by another. J "took the bait" and reformulated her ideas to include conflicting influences: the downward influence is gravity, but she struggled a bit (first trying air resistance) to find an upward one.

Over the next four sessions, the interviewer continually returned to the tossed ball, providing increasingly direct criticism. "But you said the upward force is gone at the peak of the toss, and also that it balances gravity there. How can it both be zero and also balance gravity?" Over the last two sessions, the interviewer broke clinical neutrality and provided a computer-based instructional sequence on how force affects motion, including the physicist's one-force model of the toss. At the end of the instructional sequence, J was asked again to describe what happens in the toss. Mirroring her initial interview but with greater precision and care, she gave a pitch-perfect physics explanation. But, asked to avoid an incidental part of her explanation (energy conservation), J reverted to her two-force model. After the interviewing sessions were over, J reflected that she knew that it would appear to others that she described the toss in two different ways, and the two-force (balancing) model might be judged wrong. But she felt both were really the same explanation.

Salient points: The dominant description of intuitive physics in the 1990s was that it constituted a coherent theory, and the two-force explanation of the toss was a perfect example. External agents (the hand) supply a force that overcomes gravity, but is eventually balanced by it, and finally overcome. The KiP view, however, was that the "theory" only appears in particular situations (e.g., when overcoming is salient). J's case is particularly dramatic since she never relinquished her intuitive ideas, even while she improved her normative ones. Instead, situation-specific saliences continued to cue one or the other "theory" of the toss.

Another subject in the same study, K, started by asserting the two-force model of the toss. However, this subject reacted to very modest suggestions to rethink her explanation by completely reformulating her description to the normative model. She then observed that she had changed her mind and explained the reasons for doing so. The two-force model was then gone from the remainder of her interviews.

Ironically, a standard assessment (employing first responses) would classify J as normative, and K as "maintaining the naïve theory." Rather, K was a very different individual who could autonomously correct and stabilize her own understanding. J, in contrast, alternated one-and two-force explanations, and didn't really feel they were different.

Lessons learned: The knowledge state of individuals is complex, and assessments cannot presume first responses will coherently differentiate them. The assumption of coherence in students' understanding is plainly suspect, since J consistently maintained both the correct view and the "misconception," even in the face of direct instruction. The interviewer, knowing that fragile knowledge elements like p-prims are important, primed one (balancing, at the peak), and saw its dramatic influence. Finally, p-prims explain a lot about the differences and similarities between J and K, but not everything. We must be modest in our claims for the power of any one model in understanding the complex conceptual ecology of students.

P-prims behave very differently from normative concepts. We need a different model to understand substantial, articulate, and context-stable scientific ideas.

Scientific concepts

Coordination classes are a model aimed at central properties of expert concepts.

According to the coordination class model, the core function of scientific concepts is to read out particular attributes of the concept reliably, across a wide range of circumstances, unlike the slip-sliding activation of p-prims. Figure 1.1 explains.

Figure 1.2 shows the primary difficulty in creating a coherent, scientific concept. All possible paths from world to concept attributes must result in the same determination.

Dufresne, Mestre, Thaden-Koch, Gerace, and Leonard (2005) provided an accessible example. They showed two groups of university students, engineering and social science majors, various simulated motions of a ball rolling along a path that dipped down, but ended at the original height. They asked which motion looked most realistic. Subjects saw the motions in two contexts: one that showed only the focal ball, and another that also showed a simultaneous and constant ball motion in a parallel, non-dipping path. The social scientists' judgments of the realism of the focal motion remained nearly the same from one-ball to two-ball situations. But, the engineers showed a dramatic shift, from preferring the correct motion to one that literally no one initially believed to be realistic. In the two-ball case, engineers performed much worse than social scientists.

Using clinical interviews, the researchers confirmed that the engineers were looking at different things in the different situations. Relative motion became

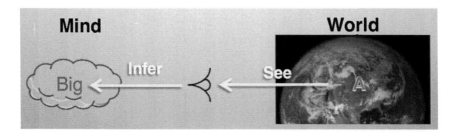

FIGURE 1.1 Coordination classes allow reading out attributes of concepts, here illustrated by "size," from the world. The readout happens in two stages. (1) "See" involves extracting *any* concept-relevant information: "The 'A' covers a goodly part of North America." (2) "Infer" draws conclusions specifically about the attribute (size) using what has been seen: "That 'A' must be huge!"

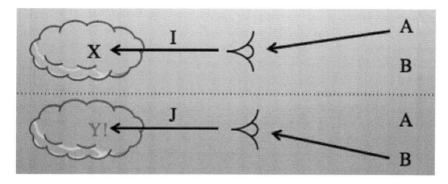

FIGURE 1.2   In situations where multiple features are available (A, B), different choices of what to observe may lead to different inferences (I, J) and potentially contradictory determinations (X, Y) of the "same" information.

salient with two balls, changing the aspects of the focal motion that were attended to. In the two-ball presentation, a kind of balancing, "coming out even" dominated their inferences about realism. The very same motion that they had resoundingly rejected as least natural became viewed as most realistic.

Lessons learned: Scientific concepts are liable to shifts of attention, and thus different (incoherent) determinations of their attributes. This is an easily documentable feature of learning concepts such as "force." So, people must learn a variety of ways to view particular concepts in the world, fitting what can be seen in various conditions, yet all determinations must "align."

It is only mildly surprising that the "culprit" inference, here, is a kind of balancing, as implicated in J's case. Balancing is a core intuitive idea, but it also becomes a powerful principle in scientific understanding. In this case, engineering students have elevated the importance and salience of balancing compared to social scientists, but have not yet learned very well what exactly balances out, and when balancing is appropriate. Certain p–prims have thus been learned to be powerful, but they have not yet taken their proper place in understanding physics. Thus, p–prims and coordination classes are nicely complementary models. Within coordination class theory, p–prims turn out to account for certain problems, but they also lie on good trajectories of learning.

The future

What are the most important coming advances in conceptual change research? With respect to the field as a whole, the continued fragmentation, infighting, and inability to come to a consensus about the basic nature of conceptual change is unsettling. Whether and how a better field-wide understanding can emerge is too complex a topic to engage here.

With respect to the KiP work, the frontier is clearer, owing to the fact that the modeling perspective requires attention to shortcomings, as well as convincing accomplishments. For example, the existence of p-prims and their gradually changing roles in understanding seems manifest. But I know of no "observation" of their very origins. And, although changes in individual p-prims' roles in student thinking can be observed, understanding the underlying processes sufficiently well to predict, rather than just observe, is not yet in place.

References

Core reference

diSessa, A. A., Sherin, B., & Levin, M. (2016). Knowledge analysis: An introduction. In A. diSessa, M. Levin, & H. Brown (Eds.), *Knowledge and interaction: A synthetic agenda for the learning sciences* (pp. 30–71). New York: Routledge.

References for examples

diSessa, A. A. (1996). What do "just plain folk" know about physics? In D. R. Olson & N. Torrance (Eds.), *The handbook of education and human development: New models of learning, teaching, and schooling* (pp. 709–730). Oxford: Blackwell Publishers, Ltd.

diSessa, A. A. (2014). The construction of causal schemes: Learning mechanisms at the knowledge level. *Cognitive Science, 38*(5), 795–850.

Dufresne, R., Mestre, J., Thaden-Koch, T., Gerace, W., & Leonard, W. (2005). When transfer fails: Effect of knowledge, expectations and observations on transfer in physics. In J. Mestre (Ed.), *Transfer of learning from a modern multidisciplinary perspective* (pp. 155–215). Greenwich, CT: Information Age Publishing.

2

INITIAL AND SCIENTIFIC UNDERSTANDINGS AND THE PROBLEM OF CONCEPTUAL CHANGE

Stella Vosniadou

Theoretical presuppositions

I use the term *conceptual change* to refer to major changes that happen in our knowledge system with learning and development, focusing in particular on changes that take place after exposure to counter-intuitive science and mathematics concepts. These changes may require the reorganization of existing knowledge structures and the acquisition of new concepts and new forms of reasoning. A conceptual system describes all our knowledge about the world that can be manipulated under conscious control. It includes all linguistic and cultural knowledge but also experiential and observational information that we can have access to. I am interested in understanding the nature of these changes and the learning mechanisms that make them possible.

Empirical research

Over the years I have used various methodologies and experimental designs in my research. These include cross-sectional developmental studies using interviews and open questions (Vosniadou & Brewer, 1992, 1994), closed questionnaires (Vosniadou, Skopeliti, & Ikospentaki, 2004), categorization experiments (Vosniadou & Skopeliti, 2014), reaction time studies (DeWolf & Vosniadou, 2015), and text comprehension experiments (Vosniadou & Skopeliti, 2014; Vosniadou & Skopeliti, submitted). I have also created innovative learning environments and curricula for science education and investigated the long-term effects of these interventions on student learning (Vosniadou, Ioannides, Dimitrakopoulou, & Papademetriou, 2001). The populations I have studied range from four-year-old children to adults.

My first empirical work in this area investigated elementary school children's ideas about the Earth and explanations of astronomical phenomena such as the day/night cycle and seasons, using a cross-sectional developmental methodology (Vosniadou & Brewer, 1992, 1994). The results of a series of studies, some of them cross-cultural (Diakidoy, Vosniadou, & Hawks, 1997; Samarapungavan, Vosniadou, & Brewer, 1996), showed that young children form initial conceptions based on phenomenal experience, while older children, who have been exposed to science instruction, provide synthetic or fragmented conceptions that are in-between the phenomenal and the scientific. These hybrid responses were interpreted to result from students' attempts to reconcile counter-intuitive scientific information with initial conceptions based on phenomenal experience. Synthetic conceptions were considered responses which although scientifically incorrect had some explanatory value and were used consistently in the context of the interviews. For example, a synthetic model of the day/night cycle is to think that night happens when the sun moves down to the other side of a spherical Earth and the moon moves up. Fragmented or mixed conceptions were considered the responses that exhibited no explanatory adequacy and internal consistency of use. For example, children sometimes said that night happens when the sun goes behind clouds and some other times they referred to the movement of the Earth.

The presence of initial conceptions and their gradual change into synthetic and fragmented responses, which combined initial understandings with scientific information, was subsequently confirmed by additional studies conducted in my lab regarding the composition and layering of the Earth's interior (Ioannidou & Vosniadou, 2001), children's understanding of the meaning of "force" (Ioannides & Vosniadou, 2002), and plant nutrition (Kyrkos & Vosniadou, 1997). It was also observed in studies conducted by other authors, such as children's developing understanding of matter (Smith & Wiser, 2008; Wiser & Smith, 2008), changes in children's biological thinking (Inagaki & Hatano, 2008), and theory of evolution (Evans, 2008) among many others.

The framework theory

The framework theory approach to conceptual change was developed on the basis of the results of the above-mentioned empirical studies (Vosniadou, 2003; Vosniadou & Skopeliti, 2014; Vosniadou, Vamvakoussi, & Skopeliti, 2008). The most important tenets of this approach are the following:

1   Before they are exposed to systematic science instruction, children have already formed a naïve physics, based on their experiences and in the context of lay culture;

2   Naïve physics forms a loose but relatively coherent explanatory system, a framework theory;

3   Learning science requires many conceptual changes in the framework theory, such as changes in categorization, in representation and in epistemology
and the creation of new concepts and new reasoning processes.
4   The achievement of these conceptual changes does not happen overnight; it
is a slow process during which fragmented and synthetic conceptions can be
created.

A "framework theory" is not a well-formed, explicit and socially shared scientific theory. Rather, it is a skeletal conceptual structure that grounds our deepest
ontological commitments and causal devices in terms of which we understand a
domain (see also Wellman, 1990; Wellman & Gelman, 1992). Although it lacks
the consistency, explanatory power and systematicity of a scientific theory, we
consider it a "theory" because it is a principle-based system that can give rise
to explanation and prediction. There can be different framework theories and
a distinction can be made, for example, between a framework theory of physics
and a framework theory of psychology. Research with infants has shown that
they make categorizations and form ontological distinctions based on everyday
experience in the context of lay culture, such as the distinction between physical objects and psychological beings, which seems to be initially based on the
detection of self-initiated movement (Baillargeon, 1995; Carey & Spelke, 1994).
This system is generative and can lead to prediction. For example, when an
entity like the Earth is categorized as a physical object, because of its phenomenal lack of self-initiated movement, it inherits all the characteristics of physical
objects, such as solidity, need for support, up/down organization of space, up/
down gravity, etc.

The conceptualization of initial understandings as a framework theory, rather
than as singular and isolated units, explains why conceptual change is not a
sudden replacement of intuitive conceptions with scientific ones, but a slow and
gradual process during which fragmented and synthetic conceptions are formed.
This is the case because scientific theories are very different from the framework
theory and require the creation of new concepts, new ontological categories,
new representations and new forms of reasoning. These are difficult conceptual
changes and need a great deal of time to be achieved.

The framework theory approach is a constructivist approach that assumes that
students use constructive learning mechanisms to connect new information to
their existing knowledge base. The creation of synthetic or fragmented conceptions can result from the operation of the same learning mechanisms in situations where the new, scientific, information is very different and cannot be easily
bridged with prior knowledge. On these occasions, only some of the beliefs and
presuppositions of the framework theory change, creating hybrid conceptions
which can be characterized as synthetic or fragmented. A synthetic conception
is an erroneous hybrid of initial and scientific understandings, but is nevertheless characterized by some explanatory power and internal consistency. Internal
consistency is determined by examining students' protocols to see if they use the

same explanation in an internally consistent manner throughout the interview. For example, the misconception that day/night happens because the Earth revolves around the sun every 24 hours is obviously wrong but it does have some explanatory adequacy and when used consistently it counts as a synthetic model. Mixed, internally inconsistent and ad hoc responses are considered fragmented.

It must be clear from the above that synthetic conceptions are not unitary, faulty and unchanging "specific theories," but are malleable mental models, adaptable to contexts and situational changes and often constructed on the spot. Their presence is not to signify that students form coherent alternative theories but that students are sensitive to issues of consistency and explanatory power and strive to provide responses that are as much as possible internally consistent and explanatorily adequate.

The predictions of the framework theory were put to the test in a series of studies in the domain of mathematics that examined children's difficulties in understanding rational number. We argued that the learning of mathematics can be seen from a conceptual change point of view because (a) children's early knowledge of mathematics develops around a concept of number that resembles the mathematical concept of natural number; (b) natural number knowledge can be conceptualized as a framework theory of number; and (c) natural number knowledge can inhibit the acquisition of more advanced mathematical concepts, such as the concept of rational number, causing fragmented and synthetic conceptions, similar in kind to those found in science (Vosniadou & Verschaffel, 2004).

A number of studies confirmed these predictions, showing that students' difficulties with rational number are located exactly in the areas where the rational number concept differs from natural number, such as their symbolic representation, ordering and discreteness vs. density (Stafylidou & Vosniadou, 2004; Vamvakoussi & Vosniadou, 2010). They also showed that the development of the rational number concept is slow and gradual and characterized by fragmented and synthetic conceptions produced by the gradual modification of the framework theory as students are exposed to instruction, producing hybrid conceptions. For example, many students interpret the symbolic notation of a fraction to consist of two independent natural numbers (the numerator and the denominator), or they consider it possible that there is an infinite number of numbers between decimals but not between fractions and/or they think that only decimals exist between decimals, and fractions between fractions (Vamvakoussi & Vosniadou, 2010).

To sum up, the framework theory approach to conceptual change addresses all the criticisms of the approach to conceptual change originally described by Posner, Strike, Hewson, and Gertzog (1982), and usually known as the *classical approach* (see also McCloskey, 1983), and can also account for fragmentation (Smith, diSessa, & Roschelle, 1993). First, we are not describing unitary, faulty and rigid "specific theories," but a dynamic knowledge system consisting of many different elements organized in complex ways. Second, we make a distinction between initial understandings prior to instruction and those that result after instruction, some of which are synthetic conceptions. Synthetic conceptions are not stable but fluid and constantly changing as children's developing knowledge systems evolve. Our theoretical position is a constructivist one that shows how constructive types of mechanisms can create fragmentation and synthetic conceptions when scientific information is built on existing but incompatible knowledge structures. Finally, we argue that conceptual change is not a sudden replacement of an inadequate naïve physics with a correct scientific theory, but a slow and gradual process that involves the creation of new ontological categories in the context of continuous representational and epistemological growth.

Responses to criticism

In 2004, diSessa and his colleagues published an article entitled "Coherence versus fragmentation in the development of the concept of force" (diSessa, Gillespie, & Esterly, 2004; hereafter dG&E), which criticized Vosniadou's theory of conceptual change, based on what the authors called a "quasi-replication" of a study by Ioannides and Vosniadou (2002; hereafter I&V). I&V investigated the meanings young students assign to the word "force" and found that 93 out of 105 (88 percent) participants, ranging in age from 5 years and 5 months to 14 years and 8 months, consistently used four basic meanings of force, which combined in seven distinct patterns. These seven patterns showed sensitivity to context, local consistency in their application, and developmental effects. However, dG&E's so-called replication found that only 10 out of 21 (48 percent) participants had internally consistent meanings of force similar to those identified by I&V. dG&E therefore concluded that their results supported the "fragmentation" point of view compared to the "coherence" one.

If dG&E truly wanted to replicate the I&V study, they should have asked the same questions, in the same order, and they should have used the same coding scheme as I&V. However, they did not. dG&E eliminated some of the I&V questions, added others and combined and ordered the questions differently. They did not use the I&V phrasing "*Is there a force exerted on....*," but instead the words *push/pull* in addition to the word *force* and, furthermore, they coded their data on the basis of the participants' Yes/No responses without taking into consideration the content of these responses. I&V had clearly shown that a yes/no response could be consistent with more than one of the meanings of force and additional information from the subjects' explanations was necessary to make a distinction.

In order to give a small example of how these changes might explain the differences in the results, it suffices to mention three of the four basic meanings that I&V found their participants assigned to the word "force": *internal force*, according to which force is an internal property of stationary objects related to their size and weight; *acquired force*, according to which force is an acquired property of moving objects when they have been pushed or pulled; and *push/pull*, where force is interpreted as the interaction between an (animate) agent and a (usually inanimate) object. It is clear that by changing the phrasing of the question from "*is there a force exerted on ...*" to "*is there a force/push-pull exerted on...*" dG&E

confused their subjects and destroyed any chance of finding consistent differences between these three meanings of the word "force."

There are some other studies that have criticized the framework theory by arguing that there is much less coherence in children's responses than Vosniadou and colleagues have argued for and that the frequency of synthetic models compared to fragmented conceptions is lower than that identified by the original Vosniadou experiments. We are disturbed by these differences and we have defended our position by pointing out the methodological differences between the original studies conducted by our team and the so-called "quasi-replications" of our critics (see Brewer, 2008; Vosniadou & Skopeliti, 2014; Vosniadou, Skopeliti, & Ikospentaki, 2004). We claim that it is much easier to destroy internal consistency of the participants' responses by asking confusing questions, as in the dG&E case, than to create internal consistency and systematization.

However, beyond these methodological issues there are more important theoretical issues that need to be resolved. Our critics, and particularly dG&E have not accurately interpreted the I&V theoretical position and have failed to understand the important theoretical differences between the framework theory approach and other approaches to conceptual change. Most importantly, they have failed to understand that the framework theory approach does not claim that students are always "coherent" or that the synthetic models are stable, faulty and singular conceptions that are like "specific theories." Our position on fragmentation and coherence is as follows.

First, we do not, in principle, exclude the possibility that knowledge elements such as p-prims might be present in our (sub)conceptual knowledge system. From the framework theory's point of view, however, such knowledge elements should be organized in conceptual structures from very early on. Let us take, for example, the well-known Ohm's p-prim, according to which more effort leads to more effect and more resistance leads to less effect (diSessa, 1993). This p-prim might serve to schematize a phenomenological experience but could only be formulated in a conceptual system where a distinction has already been made between animate and inanimate objects, where it is known that effort is usually exerted by animate agents when they push or pull animate or inanimate objects, that forces are implicated, that the size and weight of the agents and objects in question are important, etc. (Ioannides & Vosniadou, 2002). In other words, the very generation of a p-prim presupposes the presence of a skeletal conceptual system together with other, more fundamental distinctions and categorizations, as well as the operation of certain fundamental learning mechanisms, such as categorization and generalization.

Second, the framework theory system is not a rigid and unchanging theory but a loose conceptual structure that constantly evolves as more information comes in. As mentioned earlier, this system has certain constraints but also some degrees of freedom that allow for variation in the kinds of explanations it generates. For example, some may consider the explanations "the sun goes behind the mountains" different from "the sun goes behind clouds." But we consider these two explanations to be consistent with a single framework theory because they all obey some fundamental constraints that stem from the categorization of the Earth as a stationary and supported physical object, and of the sun and moon as solar objects that move in the sky and/or hide behind mountains or clouds.

Third, the framework theory does not claim that the process of conceptual change involves a sudden replacement of one coherent conception with another. Rather, we argue for a slow and gradual process of change during which constructive learning mechanisms produce fragmentation and/or synthetic conceptions when students are exposed to scientific information. As mentioned earlier, this is the case because scientific theories are very different from the framework theory and require the acquisition of new concepts and new forms of reasoning. As a result, constructive learning mechanisms produce hybrid conceptions, which can be fragmented or synthetic. Synthetic conceptions are dynamic and sometimes situation-specific structures produced when only some of the beliefs and presuppositions of the framework theory are altered. Their presence is important in our theory, not because we claim that students are always "coherent" but because it shows that students *are sensitive* to issues of internal consistency and explanatory adequacy.

Our main difference with diSessa (2008) is not the "coherence" or "fragmentation" of pre-scientific conceptions, but *the search for coherence and explanatory adequacy*. Unlike diSessa (1993, 2008), who argues for a learning process that proceeds from fragmentation to coherence under the influence of instruction, where it is posited that top-down coherence is triggered by students' exposure to symbolic and verbal knowledge, presented via instruction and texts, we believe that the need and search for coherence is more an initial condition of the cognitive system. If, as we propose, initial instruction can destroy the loose coherence of the framework theory, we should expect that students should be bothered by conceptual inconsistencies, to the extent that they can understand them, and that they will try to remedy the situation by creating synthetic conceptions. This is why the presence of synthetic conceptions is important in our theory. Not because it shows that students are always coherent, but because it demonstrates that even very young children are sensitive to issues of coherence and empirical adequacy of explanation.

References

Baillargeon, R. (1995). A model of physical reasoning in infancy. In C. Rovee-Collier & L. P, Lipsitt (Eds.), *Advances in infancy research* (Vol. 9, pp. 305–371). Norwood, NJ: Ablex.

Brewer, W. F. (2008). Naïve theories of observational astronomy: Review, analysis and theoretical implications. In S. Vosniadou (Ed.), *The international handbook of conceptual change* (pp. 155–204). New York: Routledge.

Carey, S., & Spelke, E. (1994). Domain-specific knowledge and conceptual change. In L. A. Hirschfeld & S. A. Gelman (Eds.), *Mapping the mind: Domain specificity in cognition and culture*. Cambridge: Cambridge University Press.

DeWolf, M., & Vosniadou, S. (2015). The representation of fraction magnitudes and the whole number bias reconsidered. *Learning and Instruction, 37,* 39–49. doi:10.1016/j.learninstruc.2014.07.002.

Diakidoy, I. A., Vosniadou, S., & Hawks, J. D. (1997). Conceptual change in astronomy: Models of the Earth and of the day/night cycle in American-Indian children. *European Journal of Psychology of Education, XII*(2), 159–184.

diSessa, A. A. (1993). Toward an epistemology of physics. *Cognition and Instruction, 10*(2/3), 105–225.

diSessa, A. A. (2008). A bird's-eye view of the "pieces" vs. "coherence" controversy (from the "pieces" side of the fence). In S. Vosniadou (Ed.), *International handbook of research on conceptual change* (pp. 35–60). New York: Routledge.

diSessa, A. A., Gillespie, N., & Esterly, J. (2004). Coherence vs. fragmentation in the development of the concept of force. *Cognitive Science, 28,* 843–900.

Evans, M. (2008). Evolutionary biology and conceptual change: A developmental perspective. In S. Vosniadou (Ed.), *The international handbook of research on conceptual change* (pp. 205–239). New York: Routledge.

Inagaki, K., & Hatano, G. (2008). Conceptual change in naïve biology. In S. Vosniadou (Ed.), *The international handbook of research on conceptual change.* New York: Routledge.

Ioannides, C. & Vosniadou, S. (2002). The changing meanings of force. *Cognitive Science Quarterly, 2*(1), 5–62.

Ioannidou, I., & Vosniadou, S. (2001). The development of knowledge about the composition and layering of the Earth's interior. *Nea Paedia, 31*(in Greek), 107–150.

Kyrkos, Ch., & Vosniadou, S. (1997). Mental models of plant nutrition: A study of conceptual change in childhood. Poster presented at the *Seventh European Conference for Research on Learning and Instruction,* Athens, Greece.

McCloskey, M. (1983). Intuitive physics. *Scientific American, 248*(4), 122–130.

Posner, G. J., Strike, K. A., Hewson, P. W., & Gertzog, W. A. (1982). Accommodation of a scientific conception: Towards a theory of conceptual change. *Science Education, 66,* 211–227.

Samarapungavan, A., Vosniadou, S., & Brewer, W. F. (1996). Mental models of the Earth, Sun, and Moon: Indian children's cosmologies. *Cognitive Development, 11,* 491–521.

Smith, J. P., diSessa, A. A., & Roschelle, J. (1993). Misconceptions reconceived: A constructivist analysis of knowledge in transition. *The Journal of the Learning Sciences, 3,* 115–163.

Smith, C., & Wiser, M. (2008). Learning and teaching about matter in the elementary grades: What conceptual changes are needed? In S. Vosniadou (Ed.), *International handbook of research on conceptual change.* New York: Routledge.

Stafylidou, S., & Vosniadou, S. (2004). The development of students' understanding of the numerical value of fractions, in L. Verschaffel and S. Vosniadou (Guest Editors), Conceptual Change in Mathematics Learning and Teaching. Special Issue of *Learning and Instruction, 14*(5), 503–518.

Vamvakoussi, X., & Vosniadou, S. (2010). How many decimals are there between two fractions? Aspects of secondary school students' reasoning about rational numbers and their notation. *Cognition and Instruction, 28*(2), 181–209.

Vosniadou, S. (2003). Exploring the relationships between conceptual change and intentional learning. In G. M. Sinatra & P. R. Pintrich (Eds.), *Intentional conceptual change* (pp. 377–406). Mahwah, NJ: Lawrence Erlbaum Associates.

Vosniadou, S., & Brewer, W. F. (1992). Mental models of the Earth: A study of conceptual change in childhood. *Cognitive Psychology, 24,* 535–585.

Vosniadou, S., & Brewer, W. F. (1994). Mental models of the day/night cycle. *Cognitive Science, 18,* 123–183.

Vosniadou, S., Ioannides, C., Dimitrakopoulou, A., & Papademetriou, E. (2001). Designing learning environments to promote conceptual change in science. *Learning and Instruction, 11,* 381–419.

Vosniadou, S., & Skopeliti, I (2014). Conceptual change from the framework theory side of the fence. *Science and Education, 23*(7), 1427–1445.

Vosniadou, S., & Skopeliti, I. (submitted). *Children's erroneous inferences in the comprehension of counter-intuitive science text.*

Vosniadou, S., Skopeliti, I. & Ikospentaki, K. (2004). Modes of knowing and ways of reasoning in elementary astronomy. *Cognitive Development, 19,* 203–222.

Vosniadou, S., Vamvakoussi, X. & Skopeliti, I. (2008). The framework theory approach to the problem of conceptual change. In S. Vosniadou (Ed.), *International handbook of research on conceptual change* (pp. 3–34). New York: Routledge.

Vosniadou, S., & Verschaffel, L. (2004). Extending the conceptual change approach to mathematics learning and teaching. In L. Verschaffel & S. Vosniadou (Guest Editors), Conceptual change in mathematics learning and teaching, Special Issue. *Learning and Instruction, 14*(5), 445–451.

Wellman, H. M. (1990). *The child's theory of mind.* Cambridge, MA: MIT Press.

Wellman, H. M., & Gelman, S. A. (1992). Cognitive development: Foundational theories of core domains. *Annual review of psychology, 43,* 337–375.

Wiser, M., & Smith, C. L. (2008). Learning and teaching about matter in grades K-8: When should the atomic-molecular theory be introduced? In S. Vosniadou (Ed.), *International handbook of research on conceptual change.* New York: Routledge.

3

ADDRESSING ROBUST MISCONCEPTIONS THROUGH THE ONTOLOGICAL DISTINCTION BETWEEN SEQUENTIAL AND EMERGENT PROCESSES

J. Bryan Henderson, Elon Langbeheim, and Michelene T. H. Chi

What makes a misconception robust?

It has been known for several decades now that, while certain misconceptions can be easily overcome through proper instruction, other misconceptions seem to persist even after instruction that specifically targets naïve ideas (Chi, 2005; Confrey, 1990; Reiner, Chi, & Resnick, 1988). What makes these latter misconceptions so *robust*? It has been theorized that at the root of these robust misconceptions is an *ontological miscategorization* of a concept, and hence an *ontological shift* is necessary in order to overcome the robust misconception (Chi, 2005; Chi & Slotta, 1993). Keil (1979) defined an *intuitive ontology* as "one's conception of the basic categories of existence, of what sorts of things there are" (p. 1). More specifically, Keil (1983) describes the concept of *predicability*, which concerns the language *predicates* (i.e., verbs and adjectives) that can be sensibly combined with *terms* (i.e., nouns). According to Keil, two categories are *ontologically distinct* when the predicates of one category cannot be sensibly combined with the terms of another category. Nonetheless, learners have been observed to combine the predicates of one ontological category with the terms of a different, ontologically distinct category. For example, learners have been observed to confuse the assignment of terms to the ontologies of *entities* and *processes* (Chi, Slotta, & De Leeuw, 1994).

When a concept is perceived as having an *entity* ontology, appropriate predicates include attributes such as mass, size, weight, and color. A human being is an entity, for example. In contrast, *processes* are events that occur over time, and hence predicates which pertain to time are appropriate. The biological evolution of human beings is an example of a process. When students encounter a concept they are not familiar with, they conceive of that concept with an ontology, such as an entity or a process. In doing so, they proceed to think of the concept as having the kind of predicates consistent with the perceived ontology. If a concept is perceived with an incorrect ontology, learners will remain committed to that ontological classification. For example, some learners describe an object losing heat as the loss of "hot particles," where the object cools down over time as its total number of "hot particles" decreases. In such a case, trying to convince learners by presenting contradictory or refuting information would be futile for achieving conceptual change. When attempting to refine their understanding, the learners would be looking for ideas that belong to a specific ontological category, and will reject ideas belonging to a different ontological category, for example, that heat is a *process* (Chi, 2013). Hence, according to the *ontological shift* theory of conceptual change (Chi, 1997), what makes misconceptions *robust* is the lack of cognitive access to appropriate ontologies.

However, when studying student explanations of heat transfer, it was discovered that overcoming robust misconceptions is not as straightforward as an ontological shift between entities and processes. When learners describe an object losing heat as the loss of "hot particles," this thinking is not as simple as mistaking a process (i.e., heat transfer) as an entity (i.e., "hot particles") (Slotta, Chi, & Joram, 1995). After all, the explanation described "hot particles" being lost *over time*, and time is characteristic of a *process*. Hence, while the "hot particle" view suggests an entity ontology, the explanation suggests the presence of a schema for processes as well. If what makes misconceptions robust is the lack of familiarity with appropriate ontologies, then what makes the heat transfer misconception robust if the learner possesses schemas for both entities and processes? The answer lies in the fact that learners tend to be much more familiar with one type of process than another. More specifically, there is a tendency for learners to assign predicates to a *sequential* process ontology when they should be conceiving of these attributes with an *emergent* process ontology instead.

Distinguishing sequential and emergent processes

In order to thoroughly distinguish sequential and emergent processes, let us first delineate some important aspects shared by all processes. We can then explain how sequential and emergent processes differ with respect to these aspects. First, processes can be conceived to involve both an *agent* level (i.e., the micro level) and a *pattern* level (i.e., the macro level). Agents can be thought of as the individuated, micro-level elements of a process. For example, in the case of a flock of birds in flight, each bird can be thought of as an individual agent. In contrast, the *pattern level* of a process is the collective, macro-level result of all the individuated activity at the agent level. For a flock of birds, the familiar V-formation in which the birds collectively fly would be a pattern-level observation of the process of bird flight over time. Second, the behavior at the agent level is different from the behavior at the pattern level. While the behavior of a flock of birds appears to take a coordinated V-formation at the pattern level, at the agent level there is no macro-scale coordination, but rather, individual birds are interacting with other birds in their vicinity as they each try to find pockets of air that minimize air resistance.

When we see a flock of birds flying in V-formation, it is tempting to think that the formation is the collective intent of the entire flock. It is tempting to think that the birds are actively communicating with each other as they assume their proper positions toward the ultimate goal of establishing a V-formation, perhaps even paying close attention to the directives of "leader birds" that help orchestrate the collective effort. Such thinking would be a misconception, of course, for two reasons: (1) the process is not coordinated by a central leader, and is therefore *decentralized*; and (2) the process emerges and continues according to a single mechanism, not as a series of events with different mechanisms. Chi, Roscoe, Slotta, Roy, and Chase (2012) claim that the availability of a *Direct Schema* (the term was later replaced with the term *Sequential Schema*—see Chi, 2013), as evidenced by people's ability to comprehend story narratives as well as everyday scripted events, helps explain why it is so tempting for us to interpret the V-formation flocking of birds in a linear, sequential, and goal-driven fashion. A Sequential Schema is what compels us to view the V-formation of the flock as an end goal of the birds, and that a series of interactions between the birds was carried out in accordance with the goal of achieving the V-formation. More specifically, since a Sequential Schema typically involves some sort of triggering event, central characters (e.g., protagonists/antagonists), and a series of actions carried out in accordance with the goals of the central characters, this would explain our temptation to think of the V-formation as the result of a *sequential* process, that is, a series of events that were preplanned and organized by a central command.

In reality, a proper explanation for why a flock of birds appears to fly in V-formation at the pattern level requires an understanding of a process ontology that is NOT sequential. Interactions with a single bird or subgroup of birds does not cause, control with special status, or necessarily correspond to the V-formation observed at the pattern level. There is no intent on the part of birds at the agent level to achieve V-formation at the pattern level, nor does our recognition of the V-formation in its final pattern form require us to recount, one by one, the sub-events leading up to the V-formation. Rather, the interactions of each and every bird in the flock must be considered, both collectively and simultaneously, in order to understand why a V-formation occurs at the pattern level of the flocking process. Such an understanding requires a different and less familiar process ontology—understanding of *emergent* processes.

In addition to living agents such as flocking birds, the sequential/emergent distinction can be applied to processes involving non-living agents as well. For example, if we place a droplet of ink in a container of water, it will diffuse and ink will move to the other end of the vessel. When interpreting the motion of the ink in the water, students often say that the ink particles have a tendency to move to an area of lower concentration because "there are too many particles crowded into one area, therefore they move to an area with more room"

(Odom & Barrow, 1995, p. 52). This type of reasoning represents a misconceived ontological categorization of the diffusion process as sequential, because the explanation aligns the agent-level behavior with the observed macro-level behavior of the pattern. This sequential interpretation also reflects thinking that a subgroup of agents directs the pattern, because the pattern seems to be driven by the ink particles, and not by the water molecules that are also part of the system. As diffusion is in actuality an emergent phenomenon, sequential thinking about the diffusion process is likely to remain robust to change if the less familiar, emergent ontology for processes is not made available.

Clarifications of the ontological shift view

The ontological categorization framework has been used as a guide in several studies (e.g., Jacobson, Kapur, So, & Lee, 2011). However, some aspects of the framework have been subject to critique. In light of that criticism, this update puts forth three clarifications to the ontological shift view.

A. Ontological categorization of process mechanisms is not ambiguous. In many cases, expressions of students' categorization of processes seem to contain emergent features alongside sequential ones. For example, in response to the question "How is it that birds form flocks?" a student wrote, "Cause there is leader in the flock to guide them, also due to survival reasons" (Jacobson et al., 2011, p. 774). The first part of the student response (*there is a leader in the flock to guide them*) suggests that this student thinks one bird has controlling status over an observable pattern, which suggests a *sequential* process categorization of how the pattern is formed. However, the second part of the student response (*due to survival reasons*) might suggest an *emergent* process categorization with respect to the intention of the agents who pursue local goals (i.e., survival) without any intention of creating the V-shape pattern. Such an interpretation might imply a "mixed" or "hybrid" ontological categorization of the process—in one respect the process is categorized as sequential, whereas in another respect the process is categorized as emergent.

Gupta, Hammer, and Redish (2010) claim that such examples suggest that the ways in which people ontologically categorize concepts is often not fixed, but rather, quite flexible. They use several examples of reasoning from informal, classroom, and professional contexts to demonstrate that both experts and novices dynamically move across ontologies as they reason about a given concept. In other words, as opposed to describing conceptual change as a clear ontological shift from one category to another, their examples suggest that experts and novices can utilize multiple ontologies in a flexible manner. More specifically, their examples suggest that perceived ontologies can be sensitive to context, and hence vary from moment to moment. Gupta et al. interpret these findings as inconsistent with the ontological shift view, which they interpret as characterizing a learner to only perceive one ontology at a time.

While we completely agree that experts can shift across ontologies flexibly (Chi, 1997), this is because experts have access to both kinds of ontologies.

Experts may indeed use expressions that suggest an ontological miscategoriza-tion, but do so with full awareness that their usage of terms and predicates do not align ontologically (e.g., for instructional purposes). However, whether a process is *emergent* or *sequential*, by our definition, refers to the inter-level causal rela-tion between the micro- and macro-levels. This does not preclude novices from knowing that interactions at the agent level can be intentional and goal-directed. Thus, novices can misrepresent the formation of the V-shaped pattern as caused by a controlling leader bird, and yet at the same time recognize that individual birds may wish to fly in the least exhausting locations for survival reasons. An alternative interpretation for expressions that represent mixed or ambiguous cat-egorizations by novices is that they may represent a transient state in the forma-tion of a sequential process ontology. In this transitional state, the differentiation between emergent and sequential processes is still malleable and the categorical shift has not yet reached its final point.

B. *Some emergent processes can be explained entirely at the macroscopic or microscopic level.* While the sequential/emergent distinction made above is predicated on how micro (i.e., *agent*) levels relate to macro (i.e., *pattern*) levels of phenomena, for many systems, one can use models of processes that rely on macro-level variables without referring to the constituents at the micro-agent level. Such explanations can be categorized as sequential when the focus is exclusively on macro-scale properties. For example, diffusion can be described using Fick's laws as a consequence of a macro-level *concentration gradient* in the system (Fick, 1855). Such an explanation is legitimate despite the micro-level interactions between particles not being men-tioned at all. In this case, as in many others (e.g., heat conduction, electric current, and transitions between different phases of matter), an entirely macro-level rep-resentation or an entirely micro-level explanation can provide a legitimate descrip-tion of the process mechanism as sequential. This is because the only aspect of a process that is emergent is the inter-level mechanism of how the macro-level arises from the micro-level interactions. Hence, if a learner focuses exclusively on either the macroscopic or microscopic level of a phenomenon, the notion of whether an inter-level mechanism is sequential or emergent would be moot, as inter-level thinking requires consideration of *both* the pattern and agent levels.

C. *Building upon students' prior knowledge cannot replace a clear definition of the novel ontological category of emergent processes.* Our theory does not frame students' knowledge as rigid or static, nor does it contradict the framework that describes knowledge as a dynamic web of ideas that are based on experiential encounters and intuitions (diSessa, 1993). Rather, it provides tools for educators to analyze student thinking and support their construction of proper reasoning. Indeed, building upon students' prior knowledge can be fruitful for explaining natural processes, but must be done with caution. For example, students may know that in some communal animal species, such as a pack of wolves, the alpha male often leads the pack and hence leads the hunt. Thus, a wolf hunt should be described as a sequential process, since the process is coordinated by a central leader. In this case, if an instructor attempts to build upon students' knowledge of the wolf hunt as analogous to bird migration, it may lead students to conclude that the V-shape formation of the bird flock suggests a "leading alpha bird." This result would be a misconceived sequential process categorization of bird-flocking predicated on intuitive knowledge about wolf hunting. Hence, the awareness and care that instructors should exercise in deciding when it is appropriate to build upon students' prior knowledge.

This is not to say that our approach should not build upon students' prior knowledge. However, we build upon students' prior knowledge as a contrast to what we intend students to learn. That is, our approach is to help students build knowledge of an *Emergent Schema* by directing students' attention to the contrastingly different characteristics of emergent and the more familiar sequential processes. Our evidence suggests that after exposure to differences in the characteristics of emergent and sequential processes, 8th and 9th grade students seemed to have transferred some knowledge of emergence to facilitate their understanding of a science concept prone to robust misconceptions—diffusion. See Chi et al. (2012) for a review of this evidence.

Discussion

This chapter served as an update to the ontological shift view of conceptual change that pertains to certain *robust* misconceptions. These misconceptions do not stem from a confusion between entity and process ontologies, but rather, are rooted in the ontological categorization of different types of processes that learners may be more or less familiar with. Robust misconceptions are resistant to targeted instruction if a schema with the appropriate ontology is not available to the learner. Pointing to a "narrative-like," *Sequential Schema* that develops from our familiarity with storytelling and everyday scripts, we argue that learners are more apt to intuit a concept with a *sequential ontology* for processes than they are an *emergence ontology* for processes. A sequential ontology is predicated by agents with special status that are goal-driven and carry out a series of intentional steps to achieve that goal at the pattern level. In contrast, an emergence ontology is predicated by all agents being on an equal footing, where the simultaneous consideration of local interactions manifests in a macro-scale pattern that was by no means intentional. We suggest this important sequential/emergent distinction can help overcome notoriously robust misconceptions in the sciences. In addition, we clarified three aspects of the ontological shift view. First, the ontological shift view does not consider student thinking to be an inflexible set of ideas. Second, the ontological shift view accepts that emergent processes can be explained using an entirely macro-level or an entirely micro-level representation. Third, the ontological shift view purports that a proper distinction between categories must be presented to students, and that instructors cannot necessarily rely on analogizing and refining prior student knowledge.

We close by suggesting a few open questions regarding the ontological shift framework. Since developing an emergent ontological categorization for processes is difficult, future research should explore which descriptive characteristics make emergent process ontologies more distinguishable to learners than others. It should also gauge more closely the observed paths of change that students demonstrate as they learn to distinguish between emergent and sequential processes. This will enable us to design better scaffolds for building the bridge that will lead to appropriate categorization and analysis of emergent processes. Finally, the descriptive characteristics that we have identified to differentiate emergent from sequential processes do not address the mechanism that shows how the pattern level emerges from the agent level interactions. Students need to understand this mechanism in order to generate scientifically appropriate causal explanations.

References

Chi, M. T. H. (1997). Creativity: Shifting across ontological categories flexibly. In T. B. Ward, S. M. Smith, & J. Vaid (Eds.), *Conceptual structures and processes: Emergence, discovery and change* (pp. 209–234). Washington, DC: American Psychological Association.

Chi, M. T. H. (2005). Commonsense conceptions of emergent processes: Why some misconceptions are robust. *The Journal of the Learning Sciences, 14*(2), 161–199.

Chi, M. T. H. (2013). Two kinds and four sub-types of misconceived knowledge, ways to change it, and the learning outcomes. In *International handbook of research on conceptual change* (pp. 49–70). New York: Routledge.

Chi, M. T. H., & Slotta, J. D. (1993). The ontological coherence of intuitive physics. *Cognition and Instruction, 10*(2–3), 249–260.

Chi, M. T. H., Roscoe, R. D., Slotta, J. D., Roy, M. & Chase, C. C. (2012). Misconceived causal explanations for emergent processes. *Cognitive Science, 36*(1), 1–61. http://doi.org/10.1111/j.1551-6709.2011.01207.x.

Chi, M. T. H., Slotta, J. D., & De Leeuw, N. (1994). From things to processes: A theory of conceptual change for learning science concepts. *Learning and Instruction, 4*(1), 27–43. http://doi.org/10.1016/0959-4752(94)90017-5.

Confrey, J. (1990). A review of the research on student conceptions in mathematics, science, and programming. *Review of Research in Education, 16*, 3–56.

diSessa, A. A. (1993). Toward an epistemology of physics. *Cognition and Instruction, 10*(2–3), 105–225.

Fick, A. (1855). V. On liquid diffusion. *The London, Edinburgh, and Dublin Philosophical Magazine and Journal of Science, 10*(63), 30–39.

Gupta, A., Hammer, D., & Redish, E. F. (2010). The case for dynamic models of learners' ontologies in physics. *The Journal of the Learning Sciences, 19*(3), 285–321.

Jacobson, M. J., Kapur, M., So, H.-J., & Lee, J. (2011). The ontologies of complexity and learning about complex systems. *Instructional Science, 39*(5), 763–783.

Keil, F. C. (1979). *Semantic and conceptual development: An ontological perspective* (Vol. 1). Cambridge, MA: Harvard University Press.

Keil, F. C. (1983). On the emergence of semantic and conceptual distinctions. *Journal of Experimental Psychology: General, 112*(3), 357–385. http://doi.org/10.1037/0096-3445. 112.3.357.

Odom, A. L., & Barrow, L. H. (1995). Development and application of a two-tier diagnostic test measuring college biology students' understanding of diffusion and osmosis after a course of instruction. *Journal of Research in Science Teaching, 32*(1), 45–61.

Reiner, M., Chi, M. T. H., & Resnick, L. (1988). Naive materialistic belief: An underlying epistemological commitment. In *Proceedings of the tenth annual conference of the cognitive science society* (Vol. 10, pp. 544–551). Hillsdale, MI: Erlbaum.

Slotta, J. D., Chi, M. T., & Joram, E. (1995). Assessing students' misclassifications of physics concepts: An ontological basis for conceptual change. *Cognition and Instruction, 13*(3), 373–400.

4

CONCEPTUAL CHANGE AND THE COMPLEXITY OF LEARNING

Cecilia Lundholm

Introduction

This chapter addresses the process of conceptual change in general and in the social sciences specifically. In the conceptual change process students come to identify differences between conceptions generated through everyday experiences, perceptions and explanations prevalent in society, and those concepts and theories which have been developed by academic communities or disciplines (Driver & Easley, 1978; Solomon, 1983). The process can be described in terms of creating relationships between the "bits and the whole":

> It is reasonable to argue that learning is not a linear process which proceeds from small bits of information towards a coherent whole nor is it vice versa; instead learning should be regarded as a compounded process where the cognitive activity oscillates between interpretations of isolated bits of information and reflections about a coherent whole.
>
> *(Halldén, 1993, p. 324)*

The way the process of conceptual change is described in this chapter implies that learners hold various perspectives on concepts simultaneously, and do not need to abandon an everyday understanding in favour of the "scientific" (Solomon, 1983). Importantly though, this further implies that learners need to develop an awareness concerning when different explanations or descriptions are appropriate to use, thus understanding the context of applicability (Halldén, 1999; Lundholm, 2004; Shtulman & Varcarcel, 2012).

In addition, research on conceptual change in the social sciences, in particular, has shown that student values and identities need to be addressed to better understand the challenges they face in the conceptual change process (Lundholm & Davies, 2013; Lundholm, Hopwood, & Rickinson, 2013). Meta-levels in social science disciplines include value-laden and contestable assumptions. Further, social science is generally characterized by competing bodies of thought about how societies and economies *should* be organized (Davies & Lundholm, 2012; Lundholm & Davies, 2013).

The process of change

Constructivist research since the 1970s (Driver & Easley, 1978) has emphasized that teachers need to know the ways that students view the phenomena they encounter in everyday life. As argued by Goldwater and Schalk (2016, p. 16), "(Students) come to the learning task with a pre-existing conceptual system (even if relatively incoherent) that conflicts with the material to be learned." Following Piaget (1936), the conceptual change tradition examines the *process* of conceptual development in terms of assimilation and accommodation. In consequence, conceptual change means integrating and differentiating (assimilating and accommodating) between a range of concepts, the physical phenomena, representations, and not least the appropriate framework or theory, and finally, acknowledging the cultural setting and situation (see Halldén, Scheja, & Haglund, 2008). In the words of Halldén et al. (2008, p. 522), "ultimately this meaning making process, involving the connection of disparate pieces of information to one another in an attempt to make sense of the world, is an essential ingredient in learning and understanding."

For example, young children develop their understanding of the Earth as spherical, being both flat (immediate surroundings) and round at the same time, in a process that includes both integration and differentiation of already acquired information and a process of reorganization (Larsson & Halldén, 2010). Initially, children view the "earth" as two separate places: as a spherical body in the sky and the surroundings where we live. These different views are then integrated into a compounded model. However, an additional step in this process is one of differentiation. This means that the children eventually separate and distinguish between different contexts of applicability of explanations. Two things are important to highlight: first, the process is one of re-structuring; and second, a range of relations is being created and established: between objects (house, moon), between representations (maps, terrestrial globe) and finally, between conceptual ideas and contexts of "relevance."

The process of change: an activity of acquiring disciplinary knowledge

Scholars have argued that a concept gains its meaning from the web of concepts in which it itself is a part. Researchers in conceptual change are broadly agreed that "scientific" concepts are embedded in large conceptual systems (cf. Goldwater & Schalk, 2016), which presume ontological and epistemological standpoints as well as theories and modes of representation (Vosniadou, 1994, 2008). Caravita

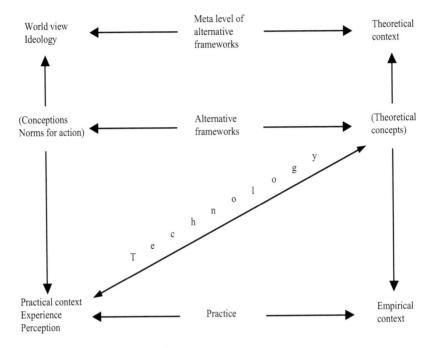

FIGURE 4.1 Different contexts for interpretation.

Source: Reproduction with permission from Elsevier of Figure 1, p. 108, from Caravita, S. and Halldén, O. (1994). Reframing the problem of conceptual change. *Learning and Instruction*, 4(1), 89–111.

and Halldén (1994), as well as Tiberghien (1994), suggested that the understanding of a concept may be in relation to three different levels: a theoretical,
a conceptual and an empirical (see Figure 4.1). This relates quite closely to
the learning paradox as it was stated in Plato's Menon, where Menon says to
Socrates that if we know what justice is we do not have to make any investigations about it and, on the other hand, if we do not know anything about justice,
how do we know when we have found it. The paradox has been discussed by
Bereiter (1985) and also by Halldén (1994, 1997) who proposed a solution that
involves a simultaneous processing of the concepts forming a new conceptual
structure; "the successful learning of something entirely new is the case when
reflection at the theoretical level and temporary interpretations at the level of
field of reference become on par with one another and create a new Gestalt"
(Halldén, 1997, p. 209).

Meta level

At a meta level, a discipline is comprised of theoretical explanations and descriptions of processes and phenomena in the world. However, if we think

of disciplinary knowledge as an understanding of what kinds of causal explanations are relevant and acceptable, yet another level above the meta level would be appropriate, and be fruitful to explore through empirical research. In the social sciences and history, explanations of causal relations typically assume more complex relationships (than everyday reasoning) between structure and agency (Torney-Purta, 1994) and a structural perspective on society and the economic, political and social world is challenging for students because their value positions come into play (Murstedt, Jansson, Wendt, & Åse, 2014). Moreover, causality is not only understood in the strict and more scientific sense prescribed (e.g. in Newton's Laws), it also includes intentional causality. For example, studies in economics show that the concept of price is challenging to learn, partly because of the multidirectional causality involved, feedback loops, and the ways in which these are conventionally represented (see Figure 4.2; Lundholm & Davies, 2013). These challenges are compounded by their association with the way in which the discipline handles causal relationships between individual preferences and intentions and outcomes at the system level. System outcomes are treated as products of individuals' intentions, but they may not conform with individuals' expectations. Lundholm and Davies (2013, p. 292) write, "[T]he way in which 'steady states' and 'equilibria' can emerge from systems with feedback loops is critical in economic thinking."

Another example is provided by Halldén (1990). He discusses how students struggle with coming to a theoretical understanding of evolution in biology, which requires a change from teleological explanations of evolution to mechanistic explanations of evolution. These examples illustrate that learning in a discipline can be challenging at a *meta level* as students need to understand causality and the ways it is used in various disciplines (see Figure 4.3). However, importantly, the "data" level can be equally challenging as students need to understand "what is data?" and "what counts as data in *this* discipline?" (e.g. Halldén, 1994, on learning history) (see Figure 4.3).

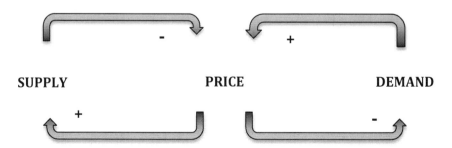

FIGURE 4.2 Multidirectional causality and feedback loops.
Source: Adapted from Figure 3 in Wheat (2007).

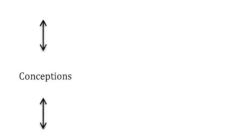

Common sense context   **Subject context**

1. Descriptions and explanations: 1. Descriptions and explanations:
theories of change   *Meta level*   theories of change
2. Causality (unidirectional causal   2. Causality (multidirectional
relation)   feedback loops in economics)
3. Ideology (values)   3. Values

Conceptions   Price

Practical context   Empirical context
Experience   Data
Perception   Applicability

FIGURE 4.3   Different contexts for interpretation and aspects concerning the meta
            level.

Source: Developed from Figure 1 in Caravita and Halldén (1994, p. 108).

On "relational categories" and causality

In a review of the literature in cognitive psychology and educational psychology
addressing conceptual change, Goldwater & Schalk (2016, p. 2) argue for the
benefit of considering *relational categories* when researching learning in education,
with the interest of knowing what concepts are most challenging for students to
learn. Relational categories, such as "gift" or "divorce", stand in contrast to categories that concern the intrinsic features of individual entities, and which have
until recent years dominated the focus in cognitive psychology.

Goldwater and Schalk (2016) also point to the importance of understanding
the nature of the relations, for example, in terms of "positive feedback systems"
(Goldstone & Sakamoto, 2003) thus focusing on causal structures. Goldwater and
Schalk (2016) conclude, "to become expert in a scientific domain, learners need
to acquire a highly interrelated set of concepts and principles that classify phenomena, problems, and situations by their deep (common) relational structure
and not (only) by superficial features" (p. 5). Rottman, Gentner, and Goldwater
(2012) present results on learning climate change and economics and discuss
how learning in each domain supports the learning of the other, as complex
systems are central to both disciplines. Further, Rehder and Ross' (2001) work

on relational categories points out that social science concepts like *divorce* and *revolution* belong to a relational category. Importantly, the list could be expanded to core concepts in political science such as *freedom*, *power* and *rights*.

Acknowledging students' everyday experiences and conceptions—what do we know?

The literature on conceptual change in the social sciences is very limited. The work of Lundholm and Davies (2013) is one notable exception. They present a summary of existing research on common-sense or everyday understandings of children (up to 12 years) and undergraduates in economics. Given the discussion above about causality and relational categories, an important question is the extent to which students hold lay or common-sense theories of how the economic and political, or other "social worlds", work. Philip (2011), using "an ideology in pieces approach" to conceptual change, studied "naturalized axioms", which are axioms prevalent in society about the social world and are socially constructed. Although there is often nothing "inherently natural" about them, they nonetheless come to be taken as common sense, within particular historical, cultural and social contexts, and are used as if they were natural, inevitable, universal and ahistorical (p. 302). For example, naturalized axioms pertaining to schooling include "the harder you try, the more likely you are to succeed", "some kids are just smart", "inequality will always exist" or "competition is good" (p. 302). Interestingly, some of these axioms, such as "the harder you try, the more likely you are to succeed", are theory-like and can be classified as a relational category, as they state causal links.

Conceptual change research has often focused on the learning of concepts that are challenging, because they seem counterintuitive, as in physics. So is there something counterintuitive in social science? Results from a current research project (Ekström & Lundholm, in press) on conceptual change in political science show a strong influence of everyday understandings. After a semester, students can provide scientific definitions, but explanations still include the use of everyday reasoning and connotations.

Another important matter to consider is the relationship between everyday experience and conceptual change in the social sciences. For example, recent findings on the development of understanding the concept of *price*—a relational concept or phenomenon—suggest students do have experiences of price but not the price mechanism. In particular, they do not have access to the decision-making processes of sellers, or the processes by which decisions are coordinated. Thus, in contrast to *force*, there is no one-to-one relation between the concept and the experience. Students explained production (supply) as the single cause of price, and after one year were still "struggling to integrate their thinking about productivity and their thinking about consumer preferences", and no firm steps of stronger integration were made (Ignell, Davies, & Lundholm, 2017, p. 28).

Procedural knowledge and representations

Finally, conceptual change in social science—as in the learning of science more generally—also requires students to acquire procedural knowledge that is characteristic of a discipline, and to understand how representations are used. This means developing a sense for the practice of the discipline and "coming to think like an economist" or like a social scientist more generally (Davies & Mangan, 2013, p. 1). Important skills in political science, and arguably in the social sciences in general, are to be able "to problematize" and to develop "analytical thinking" (Wendt & Åse, 2014). In research on learning history, scholars have argued for the existence of "second order" concepts, pointing to learning that encompasses procedural knowledge beyond the "mere" facts, and as being an important part of historical understanding (Lee, 2005; cf. Sandahl, 2015, on social science learning).

Davies and Mangan (2013) present important findings on economics students' learning difficulties with graphs; however, research on learning about representations in the social sciences is scarce. A recent finding (Jägerskog, 2015) suggests that representations are mostly used in textbooks with the purpose of being illustrative (e.g. a picture of a divan when describing Freud's theory).

Values and sense of self

Lundholm and Davies (2013) and Lundholm, Hopwood, and Rickinson (2013) provide empirical insights into the various ways that learning in economics and environmental studies evoke students' values and their sense of self, and challenge conceptual change. Recent findings (Ekström & Lundholm, in press) are in line with these findings, which could suggest that learning in the social sciences has two inherent components; both the value dimension of the discipline (Ekström & Lundholm, 2017) and the values and emotions that students hold (cf. Sinatra & Mason, 2013).

Future research

In Lundholm and Davies (2013, p. 291) we argue that structure and agency is critical throughout social science, and needs further research attention. This suggestion is still, we believe, relevant. Furthermore, our understanding of the process of conceptual change, especially in the social sciences, would benefit from including aspects such as students' emotions and values. Finally, in order to improve our understanding of students' learning of causality and complex systems and of values *in* the discipline, as well as representations, it is important to acknowledge students' epistemological thinking.

References

Bereiter, C. (1985). Toward a solution of the learning paradox. *Review of Educational Research,* 55, 201–226.

Caravita, S., & Halldén, O. (1994). Re-framing the problem of conceptual change. *Learning and Instruction, 4,* 89–111.

Davies, P., & Lundholm, C. (2012). Students' understanding of socio-economic phenomena: conceptions about the free provision of goods and services. *Journal of Economic Psychology, 33,* 79–89.

Davies, P., & Mangan, J. (2013). Conceptions of graphs and the progression of students' understanding. *Korean Journal of Economics Education, 4,* 189–210.

Driver, R., & Easley, J. (1978). Pupils and paradigms: A review of literature related to concept development in adolescent science students. *Studies in Science Education, 5,* 61–84.

Ekström, L., & Lundholm, C. (in press). What's positive about "positive rights"? Students' everyday understandings and the challenges of teaching political science. *Journal of Political Science Education.*

Ekström, L., & C. Lundholm (2017, 27 April–3 May). How much politics is there? Students' understandings of the role of values in political science teaching. *American Education Research Association Conference,* San Antonio, Texas.

Goldstone, R. L., & Sakamoto, Y. (2003). The transfer of abstract principles governing complex adaptive systems. *Cognitive Psychology, 46,* 414–466. http://dx.doi.org/10.1016/S0010-0285(02)00519-4.

Goldwater, M. B., & Schalk, L. (2016). Relational categories as a bridge between cognitive and educational research. *Psychological Bulletin, 142*(7), 729–57. http://dx.doi.org/10.1037/bul0000043.

Halldén, O. (1990). Questions asked in common sense contexts and in scientific contexts. In P. L. Lijnse, P. Licht, W. De Vos, & A. J. Waarlo (Eds.), *Relating macroscopic phenomena to microscopic particles. A central problem in secondary science education* (pp. 119–130). Utrecht: CD-b Press.

Halldén, O. (1993). Learners' conceptions of the subject matter being taught: A case from learning history. *International Journal of Educational Research, 19,* 317–325.

Halldén, O. (1994). Personalization in historical descriptions and explanations. *Learning and Instruction, 8,* 131–139.

Halldén, O. (1997). Conceptual change and the learning of history. *International Journal of Educational Research, 27*(3), 201–210.

Halldén, O. (1999). Conceptual change and contextualization. In W. Schnotz, S. Vosniadou, & M. Carretero (Eds.), *New perspectives on conceptual change* (pp. 53–65). Amsterdam: Pergamon.

Halldén, O., Scheja, M., & Haglund, L. (2008). The contextuality of knowledge: An in-tentional approach to meaning making and conceptual change. In S. Vosniadou (Ed.), *Handbook of research on conceptual change* (pp. 509–532). New York: Routledge.

Ignell, C., Davies, P., & Lundholm, C. (2017). Understanding "price" and the environment: exploring upper secondary students' conceptual development. *Journal of Social Science Education, 16*(1), 20–32. doi:10.2390/jsse-v16-i1-1556.

Jägerskog, A.-S. (2015). *Pictures and a Thousand Words: Learning Psychology through Visual Illustrations and Testing.* Licentiate thesis. Department of Psychology, Stockholm University.

Larsson, Å., & Halldén, O. (2010). A structural view on the emergence of a conception: Conceptual change as radical reconstruction of contexts. *Science Education, 94,* 640–664. doi:10.1002/sce.20377.

Lee, P. (2005). Putting principles into practice: Understanding history. In M. Donovan & J. Bransford (Eds.), *How students learn history, mathematics, and science* (pp. 31–78). Washington DC: The National Academic Press.

Lundholm, C. (2004). Learning about environmental issues in engineering programmes: A case study of first-year civil engineering students' contextualisations of an ecology course. *International Journal of Sustainability in Higher Education, 5*(3), 295–307.

Lundholm, C., & Davies, P. (2013). Conceptual change in the social sciences. In S. Vosniadou (Ed.), *International handbook of research on conceptual change* (2nd ed., pp. 288–304). New York: Routledge.

Lundholm, C., Hopwood, N. & Rickinson, M. (2013). Environmental learning: Insights from research into the student experience. In Brody, M., Dillon, J., Stevenson, R., & Wals, A. (Eds.), *International handbook of research on environmental education* (pp. 242–251). New York: Routledge.

Murstedt, L., Jansson, M., Wendt, Å., & Åse, C. (2014). Liberal liability: Students' understanding of a gender perspective in social science. *Journal of Social Science Education, 13*, 63–73. doi:10.2390/jsse-v14-i2-1237.

Philip, T. (2011). An "ideology in pieces": Approach to studying change in teacher sense-making about race, racism, and racial justice. *Cognition and Instruction, 29*(3), 297–329.

Piaget, J. (1936). *Origins of intelligence in the child*. London: Routledge & Kegan Paul.

Rehder, B. & Ross, B. H. (2001). Abstract coherent categories. *Journal of Experimental Psychology: Learning, Memory, and Cognition, 27*, 1261–1275. http://dx.doi.org/10.1037/0278-7393.27.5.1261.

Rottman, B. M., Gentner, D., & Goldwater, M. B. (2012). Causal systems categories: Differences in novice and expert categorization of causal phenomena. *Cognitive Science, 36*, 919–932. http://dx.doi.org/10.1111/j.1551-6709.2012.01253.x.

Sandahl, J. (2015). Preparing for citizenship: The value of second order thinking concepts in social science education. *Journal of Social Science Education, 14*(1), 18–29.

Shtulman, A., & Valcarcel, J. (2012). Scientific knowledge suppresses but does not supplant earlier intuitions. *Cognition, 124*, 209–215.

Sinatra, M. G., & Mason, L. (2013). Beyond knowledge: Learner characteristics influencing conceptual change. In S. Vosniadou (Ed.), *International handbook of conceptual change* (2nd ed., pp. 377–394). New York: Routledge.

Solomon, J. (1983). Learning about energy: how pupils think in two domains. *European Journal of Science Education, 5*, 49–59.

Tiberghien, A. (1994). Modelling as a basis for analysing teaching-learning situations. *Learning and Instruction, 4*, 71–88.

Torney-Purta, J. (1994). Dimensions of adolescents' reasoning about political and historical issues: Ontological switches, developmental processes and situated learning. In M. Carretero & J. F. Voss (Eds.), *Cognitive and instructional processes in history and the social sciences* (pp. 103–121). Hillside, NJ: Lawrence Erlbaum and Associates.

Vosniadou, S. (1994). Capturing and modelling the process of conceptual change. *Learning and Instruction, 4*, 45–69.

Vosniadou, S. (Ed.) (2008). *International handbook of research on conceptual change*. London: Routledge.

Wendt, M., & Åse, C. (2014). Learning dilemmas in undergraduate student independent essays. *Studies in Higher Education, 40*(5), 838–851.

Wheat, I. D. (2007). The feedback method of teaching macroeconomics: Is it effective? *System Dynamics Review, 23*(4), 391–413.

5

CONCEPTUAL CHANGE, RELATIONSHIPS, AND CULTURAL EPISTEMOLOGIES

Ananda Marin, Douglas Medin, and bethany ojalehto[1]

Introduction

In this chapter, we outline a systems-level perspective on concepts and conceptual change with respect to the natural world. We start from the position that concepts take their meanings from relations with other concepts within larger frameworks for organizing knowledge, from folk theories to epistemological orientations. On this view, conceptual change is a change in relations within such systems of meaning. Considerable research has already illuminated how cognitive development involves changes in conceptual relations within folk theories, or intuitive explanatory systems that structure learning within a content domain (e.g., folkpsychology, folkbiology, folkphysics) (Carey, 2009). Our research extends this perspective by placing those folk theories, and associated conceptual changes, in the context of broader epistemological orientations. Epistemological orientations are frameworks for understanding what is worthy of attention, observation, and explanation; they are thoroughly constituted by and constitutive of culture. For us, a focus has been on a particular cultural orientation known as relational epistemologies. Relational epistemologies are ways of knowing in which a central process of meaning making is both recognizing interconnections between all things and being in relations with others (Bang et al., 2013; Cajete, 2000). In this chapter, we argue that bringing relational epistemologies into contact with the theoretical literature on cognitive development could afford a new perspective on the nature of concepts and conceptual change.

Our research works through multiple cultural lenses to investigate how cognition interacts with epistemological orientations. Specifically, we investigate how cognition of the natural world is organized under distinct orientations associated with Western domain-specific epistemologies and Indigenous relational epistemologies. This line of investigation also leads us to ask how researchers' own cultural orientations frame the very questions that are posed about concepts and influence the tools that are used to study knowledge organization.

Concepts and conceptual change: two approaches

Much of the literature on conceptual development follows the view that concepts are "units of thought" that form the building blocks of domain-specific folk theories (e.g., Carey, 2009). On this account, conceptual change occurs within specific content domains and takes place either through gradual enrichment (i.e., learning) or fundamental conceptual change (Carey & Spelke, 1994). The latter form of change is considered especially important given that it involves restructuring the very cognitive frameworks that guide learning and acquisition of new knowledge. One classic example of proposed fundamental conceptual change is children's shift from a human-centered, heavily psychological biology to seeing humans as one animal among many and as a biological organism (Carey, 1985).

As an alternative approach, we treat concepts as embedded within epistemological orientations for organizing knowledge and behavior (Medin et al., 2013). Compared to domain-specific folk theories, these epistemological orientations are more encompassing and pervasive, as they arise from feedback loops among everyday practices, representations, and cultural values as well as (the more traditional cognitive units of) concepts and explanatory theories. We are broadly concerned with the sociocultural processes of learning and specifically with a relational epistemology perspective on conceptual change and knowledge organization. As one instance of such epistemological orientations, our analysis will focus on how viewing humans as part of nature (or apart from nature) influences conceptual organization and reasoning processes relative to the living world (Bang et al., 2007). For example, a view of humans as a part of nature may support the organization of activities and practices that attribute agency and intentionality to more than human kinds (Bang et al., 2015). The ontology of concepts and conceptual relations within such a system may systematically vary from a system where humans are viewed as apart from nature (Bang et al., 2015).

We believe that concepts and conceptual frameworks are culturally inflected. This leads to a systems-level view in which culture affects both the content and process of thought. Research on the cultural organization of folkbiological knowledge about fish illustrates this point (e.g., Medin et al., 2006). Native American Menominee and European-American fish experts were asked to categorize fish species and reason about fish–fish interactions. These two expert groups had comparable knowledge bases but there were substantial differences in how that knowledge was organized. European-Americans were more likely to favor a taxonomic organization (e.g., grouping fish based on species similarity) and Menominee more likely to favor an ecological organization (e.g., grouping fish based on habitat). These differences were evident both in spontaneous sorting of fish groups (i.e., the "content" of the category) as well as in sorting justifications (i.e., the "process" of causal reasoning underlying categorization). Thus, conceptual knowledge for a single domain can be formed around distinct explanatory principles, and this organization is critical for both conceptual content and process.

Terms like "concepts," "conceptual frameworks," and even "conceptual change" are somewhat imprecise in that they are not directly observed. Instead we observe conceptual behaviors in particular contexts and attempt to make inferences concerning what forms of knowledge or knowledge organization might support them. For the above example with fish experts, it is not clear whether both forms of organization were available to both samples of experts. In a follow-up study, Medin and colleagues asked both groups of experts to sort fish by habitat and found no cultural differences. This suggests that the main difference was in knowledge organization, not knowledge itself. Such findings indicate the importance of using multiple measures to assess concepts, as any single observation provides a partial lens on the underlying knowledge system.

Further evidence consistent with a cultural difference in the focus on taxonomic versus ecological relations comes from additional studies where ecological relations were directly probed. Pairs of fish (e.g., Northern, Muskie) were presented and experts were asked how each fish might affect the other. In what we call the speeded condition, all possible pairs of 21 fish species were presented, such that 420 relations were queried in about an hour. In a follow-up unspeeded condition given months later, 35 pairs were presented (70 relations), again in an hour. In the speeded condition, Menominee experts identified substantially more ecological relations, many of them reciprocal relations, than did the European-American fish experts. If these differences are differences in knowledge organization (presumably mediated by cultural values and practices) rather than knowledge per se they should disappear in the unspeeded condition. They did.

An epistemological approach also has direct implications for the methods and units of study that cognitive scientists work with to understand conceptual change. Elsewhere, we have argued that cultural epistemologies play a role in cognitive scientists' own paradigms (e.g., Medin & Bang, 2014a), making it important to consider how notions about concepts and domains affect both what research is done and how it is conducted. For example, more than 98 percent of the representations generated by Google images in response to the probe "ecosystems" do not include human beings, implicitly suggesting that humans are apart from nature. In contrast, a framework that views humans as a part of nature may expand our research lenses to include people in places and relations that include built human environments. In the former framework, "urban ecology" would be a misnomer but in the latter clearly worthy of attention (Bang & Marin, 2015). Toward this end, we have studied the microgenetic learning moments in everyday cultural practices that foreground human relationships with the natural world (e.g., berrypicking, fishing).

An epistemological perspective suggests that researchers should also consider how procedural tasks do or do not foreground human relations with other natural kinds.

In ongoing work (see Marin, 2013 for an overview and initial results), we have used parent–child learning on nature walks to study relational epistemologies. Veering away from indoor, seated research tasks, we asked parents and children to go on a series of walks in an urban forest preserve. Both the parent and child used a wearable camera to capture their interactions. Video data was subsequently synced in order to analyze how families were jointly attending and observing, and organized into clips of between-person and between-place interactions. These clips captured situated activity systems (Goodwin, 2003) where participants relied on various semiotic fields (e.g., verbal, visual, auditory, gestural, ambulatory) including the organization of walking to orient to each other and to the land. These ambulatory sequences (Marin, 2013) serve as a device for focusing on how learning emerges through the formations (Kendon, 2010) and arrangements (Stevens et al., 2008) that learners create with their bodies and in relation to land for the purpose of organizing sense making. This is one case where the research task design was motivated by Indigenous knowledge systems that foreground walking as a practice linked to knowing and understanding the natural world (Cajete, 1994). Such designs may provide a rich context for studying conceptual change as a process occurring over time and in vivo, where concepts take their meanings from relations with other concepts.

Humans in relation to non-human animals

One focal area of research on conceptual change has been children's conceptualization of humans in relation to non-human animals. Here there is somewhat of a paradox. First, children seem to have considerable difficulty with the notion that humans are also animals. At the same time, there is evidence that (urban) children generalize novel biological properties in a way that is consistent with the view that humans are the prototypical animal (Carey, 1985). A key question for theorists has been to explain the kind of conceptual change at stake in this developmental pattern.

One influential theory proposed a universal conceptual trajectory whereby children first reason about folkbiology from an anthropocentric standpoint, that is, they reason about non-human animals by analogy to humans (Carey, 1985). This notion is consistent with the claim that folkbiology is initially a part of folkpsychology and only emerges as a distinct domain with a qualitative shift in conceptual development. Support for this view came from studies showing that urban 5-year-old children in the U.S. tend to treat humans as the prototype for inductive reasoning about biological kinds. That is, they were more likely to think that a novel property attributed to humans extended to other animals than when this same novel property was attributed to dogs. They also generalized from humans to dogs much more than from dogs to humans. On Carey's view, children shift from a human-centered view, where all biological causes are seen as psychological ones (an immature psychological biology), to a new view that recognizes biological processes in addition to psychological ones. The conceptual change marks a shift in ontological categories available to the child.

A systems-level relational epistemology provides an alternative perspective on conceptual change. Specifically, developmental change may mark a shift in relational perspectives: as in the case of reasoning about human–animal categories, which marks a shift in the relationships that children draw between humans and other living creatures. These relationships, in turn, develop and are affected by cultural practices and artifacts like children's books and (Disney) movies. Instead of assuming that developmental trajectories are universal, we should at least consider the possibility that they are guided by such practices and artifacts.

There is mounting evidence that children's biological understanding is affected by cultural perspectives. First, subsequent studies using Carey's procedure with rural Indigenous (Menominee) and European-American children show that both culture and experience affect children's inductive reasoning about biological kinds (Medin et al., 2010; Waxman & Medin, 2007). The most striking evidence that anthropocentrism is a learned cultural model is that 3-year-old children do not show a human-centered perspective, but 4 and 5 year olds do (Herrmann et al., 2010). Further evidence that conceptual change depends upon the forms and contents provided by cultural practices comes from a comparative analysis of children's books that were or were not authored and illustrated by Native Americans (Bang et al., in press). Non-Native books are heavily anthropomorphic, largely showing animals playing human roles in human environments (e.g., wearing clothes, driving cars, etc.). In contrast, Native books show animals in natural habitats and illustrations commonly invite taking an animal's perspective.

Priming studies suggest that these cultural artifacts affect cognition. Waxman et al. (2014) hypothesized that urban children's anthropocentric model may be driven partly by images in children's media. To test this idea, they exposed young children to either anthropomorphic (Berenstain Bears) or naturalistic (Animal Encyclopedia) children's books prior to their completing standard category-based induction tasks. The results showed that inductive reasoning was reliably more biological and less anthropocentric in the Encyclopedia condition than in the Berenstain Bears condition. These priming studies suggest that there may be multiple conceptual models in play, and that children may take different perspectives on human–animal relations.

Prior accounts of conceptual development cited differences in human–animal category-based induction tasks as evidence for fundamental conceptual change. However, the research on cultural models and artifact priming allows for wider consideration of the ways in which conceptual change develops within cultural epistemologies. The evidence shows that children may negotiate multiple stances on human–animal relations, and cultural artifacts can support one or another perspective. Thus, one form of conceptual change may stem from the ability and propensity to shift between multiple perspectives on conceptual relations. The fact that urban 3 year olds do not show a human-centered biology suggests that anthropocentrism is a learned cultural model appearing later in development (in 5 year olds) and appearing not at all in other cultural communities. The relational perspective we have been employing as a lens on conceptual development calls attention to variations in cultural values and practices as central to understanding conceptual development and change.

Various theoretical approaches in the learning and developmental sciences have drawn a distinction between gradual learning versus radical conceptual change. The implication is that concepts can change in small ways until some threshold is reached that warrants the designation of fundamental change. Relational epistemologies can push back on this distinction in at least two ways. First, relational epistemologies encourage a process-oriented view of knowledge acquisition and organization as a participatory engagement between learners and environments. In many Indigenous communities, for instance, knowledge about nature is not simply acquired, but is a participatory activity with other life forms (Burkhart, 2004). The knowledge process need not have a decided outcome and may leave many things unknown. On this model, conceptual change may be a continual process rather than a well-defined shift between "old" and "new" forms.

Second, relational epistemologies emphasize the role of the researcher in determining which kinds of difference are considered fundamental. For example, seeing humans as animals versus seeing humans as part of nature might be considered more or less fundamental to different observers. Certainly it is the case that developmental literature focuses heavily on the former and virtually not at all on the latter. But arguably, coming to appreciate one's place and role within the natural world may be the far more critical conceptual task—for individual development as well as society more broadly (Medin & Bang, 2014b). As another example, consider that cognitive scientists' domain-specificity theories have led them to frame questions of conceptual change in terms of those categories (e.g., biology versus psychology). This has led researchers, including ourselves, to rely on stimuli that include natural kinds considered alive on Western ontologies while excluding other natural kinds such as stones, soil, water, and air. From a relational epistemology perspective, this misses a huge part of the conceptual landscape and ignores critical developmental questions concerning the relationships between and among organisms and ecologies. In short, the distinction between gradual versus fundamental conceptual change may be largely contingent on the goals of the researcher and their valued methods and questions.

Conclusion

Our findings highlight the importance of context and relationality at every step, from the social and ecological processes of child–parent engagement with their environments, to the cultural practices that structure conceptual change and afford shifting perspectives, to the scientific practices that allow us to investigate these very questions.

Two key considerations about conceptual change have emerged. First, acquiring conceptual knowledge or knowledge representation (in terms of individual concepts) is only part of the story. What also matters is how these concepts are taken up in multiple perspectives for different uses. Many of the comparative differences in cognition across ages or cultures may arise in large part from such shifts in relational perspectives implicit in cultural artifacts and practices. Just as cultural differences in biological knowledge among fish experts reflect multiple ways of organizing relationships between concepts (taxonomic versus ecological), so too may developmental differences in anthropocentric or biological reasoning reflect different perspectives on human–animal categories. Second, the developmental and cultural evidence suggests that people hold multiple conceptual perspectives. This complicates the interpretation of findings where developmental change may be due to a change in concepts or the shifting accessibility of concepts—or both, if concepts are seen as relational perspectives, where either aspect is implicated in the other. Investigating what is at stake in conceptual change may demand different methodologies than have typically been employed, including priming studies (Oyserman & Lee, 2008) and sociocultural analyses of learning in context. It is difficult to imagine understanding conceptual change without attending to sociocultural contexts.

Note

1 Authors listed in alphabetical order.

References

Bang, M., Alfonso, J., Faber, L., Marin, A., Marin, M., Waxman, S.,... & Medin, D. (in press). Perspective taking and psychological distance in children's picture books: Differences between Native and non-Native authored nooks. *Early Childhood Research Quarterly*.

Bang, M., & Marin, A. (2015). Nature–culture constructs in science learning: Human/non-human agency and intentionality. *Journal of Research in Science Teaching, 52*(4), 530–544.

Bang, M., Marin, A., Medin, D., & Washinawatok, K. (2015). Learning by observing, pitching in, and being in relations in the natural world. *Advances in Child Development and Behavior, 49*, 303–313.

Bang, M., Medin, D., & Atran, S. (2007). Cultural mosaics and mental models of nature. *Proceedings of the National Academy of Sciences, 104*, 13868–13874.

Bang, M., Warren, B., Rosebery, A. S., & Medin, D. (2013). Desettling expectations in science education. *Human Development, 55*(5–6), 302–318.

Burkhart, B. Y. (2004). What Coyote and Thales can teach us: An outline of American Indian epistemology. In A. Waters (Ed.), *American Indian thought: Philosophical essays* (pp. 15–26). Malden, MA: Blackwell.

Cajete, G. (1994). *Look to the mountain: An ecology of indigenous education.* Durango, CO: Kivaki Press.

Cajete, G. (2000). *Native science: Natural laws of interdependence.* Santa Fe, NM: Clear Light Publishers.

Carey, S. (1985). *Conceptual change in childhood.* Cambridge, MA: Bradford Books, MIT Press.

Carey, S. (2009). *The origin of concepts.* New York: Oxford University Press.

Carey, S., & Spelke, E. (1994). Domain-specific knowledge and conceptual change. In L. A. Hirschfeld & S. A. Gelman (Eds.), *Mapping the mind: Domain specificity in cognition and culture* (pp. 169–200). Cambridge: Cambridge University Press.

Goodwin, C. (2003). Pointing as situated practice. In S. Kita (Ed.), *Pointing: Where language, culture and cognition meet* (pp. 217–241). Mahwah, NJ: Lawrence Erlbaum.

Herrmann, P., Waxman, S. R., & Medin, D. L. (2010). Anthropocentrism is not the first step in children's reasoning about the natural world. *Proceedings of the National Academy of Sciences, 107*(22), 9979–9984.

Kendon, A. (2010). Spacing and orientation in co-present interaction. In A. Esposito, N. Campbell, C. Vogel, A. Hussain, & A. Nijholt (Eds.), *Development of multimodal interfaces: Active listening and synchrony* (pp. 1–15). Berlin: Springer.

Marin, A. M. (2013). *Learning to attend and observe: Parent-child Meaning making in the natural world.* Unpublished Doctoral Dissertation. ProQuest LLC.

Medin, D. L., & Bang, M. (2014a). *Who's asking? Native science, western science, and science education.* Cambridge, MA: MIT Press.

Medin, D. L., & Bang, M. (2014b). The cultural side of science communication. *Proceedings of the National Academy of Sciences,* www.pnas.org/cgi/doi/10.1073/pnas.1317510111.

Medin, D., Ojalehto, B., Marin, A., & Bang, M. (2013). Culture and epistemologies: Putting culture back into the ecosystem. In M. Gelfand, C. Y. Chiu, & Y. -Y. Hong (Eds.), *Advances in culture and psychology series* (pp. 177–217). Oxford: Oxford University Press.

Medin, D. L., Ross, N. O., Atran, S., Cox, D., Coley, J., Proffitt, J. B., & Blok, S. (2006). Folkbiology of freshwater fish. *Cognition, 99*(3), 237–273.

Medin, D., Waxman, S., Woodring, J., & Washinawatok, K. (2010). Human-centeredness is not a universal feature of young children's reasoning: Culture and experience matter when reasoning about biological entities. *Cognitive Development, 25*(3), 197–207.

Oyserman, D., & Lee, S. W. (2008). Does culture influence what and how we think? Effects of priming individualism and collectivism. *Psychological Bulletin,* 134(2), 311.

Stevens, R., Satwicz, T., & McCarthy, L. (2008). In-game, in-room, in-world: Reconnecting video game play to the rest of kids' lives. In K. Salen (Ed.), *The ecology of games: Connecting youth, games and learning* (pp. 41–66). Cambridge, MA: MIT Press.

Waxman, S. R., Herrmann, P., Woodring, J., & Medin, D. (2014). Humans (really) are animals: Picture-book reading influences five-year-old urban children's construal of the relation between humans and non-human animals. *Frontiers in Psychology, 5,* 1.

Waxman, S., & Medin, D. (2007). Experience and cultural models matter: Placing firm limits on anthropocentrism. *Human Development, 50,* 23–30.

6

CONCEPTUAL CHANGE

A cultural-historical and cognitive-developmental framework

Geoffrey B. Saxe

In this chapter, I describe my approach to understanding concepts and conceptual change. I illustrate the approach's utility through the sketch of a published study on number conducted in remote and rapidly changing Oksapmin communities in Papua New Guinea, where I completed fieldwork in 1978, 1980, 2001, and 2014.

One area of marked change in Oksapmin communities is conceptual thinking related to number. Traditionally, people used a 27-body-part counting system as depicted in Figure 6.1. Arithmetical problem-solving did not emerge in traditional practices, but with the emergence of a Western currency-based economy in the 1960s, some people began to conceptualize and find solutions to arithmetical problems. In this chapter, I use the Oksapmin case to ask how conceptual changes occur in communities, like the emergence of a 27-body-part arithmetic in Oksapmin. Such a question goes to the heart of questions like, what constitutes conceptual activity and conceptual change, both for individuals as well as in the talk and action of collective life?

A foundational assumption in my work is that concepts should be treated as processes occurring in time, rather than mental objects, a view that shares affinities with other treatments of conceptual change (e.g., diSessa, 1988; Sfard, 2008). Moreover, concepts as well as conceptual change should be understood as occurring in multiple strands that occur on multiple time scales (Saxe, 2014): over short durations, as individuals cognize and structure solutions to problems during "in-the-moment" activities (microgenesis); over extended periods of individual development, as individuals create new ways of thinking (ontogenesis); and, over durations in community life, as the common ground of talk and action is (often unwittingly) reproduced and altered in networks of interlocutors (sociogenesis). At its crux, my approach is about the interplay between micro-, socio-, and ontogenetic processes through time. To illustrate the approach, I focus on *representational forms* used in communities, like the Oksapmin 27-body-part counting system, and the *cognitive functions* like arithmetic that these forms serve in processes of micro-, socio-, and ontogenesis.

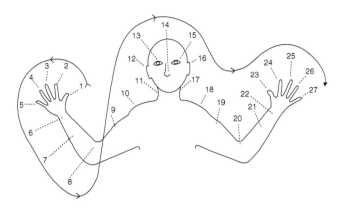

FIGURE 6.1 Body part positions in the Oksapmin 27-body part counting system.

An illustrative case of micro-, socio-, and ontogenetic developments through participation in collective practices of economic exchange

In June, 2001, en route to Oksapmin communities, I spent several days in a mining town in the highlands of Papua New Guinea, along with two of my doctoral students and my 19-year-old son. Shortly after arriving, I encountered some Oksapmin people who had relocated to the town. During the unexpected reunion, the seeds of a study emerged. I thought that I heard a word form that sounded like "*fu*" used in conjunction with a body part name. I questioned people about its meaning. My interlocutors indicated that uttering *fu* after a body part meant to double the body part's value. For me, this was a remarkable moment. In my 1978 and 1980 visits, I had documented that arithmetic using the body system was alien to Oksapmin elders. Indeed, the functions of the body system were largely about counting valuables, indicating relative spatial positions (of places on a path), or producing measurements of string bags, a common cultural artifact (see Saxe, 2014).

There was another issue about *fu* that sparked my curiosity. The word form, "*fu*," had a resonance with my earlier visits in 1978 and 1980. As captured in the woman's display in Figure 6.2a, people exclaimed "*fu!*" with fisted hands erupting upon completing an enumeration of all 27 body parts. So, I wondered, was the doubling "*fu*" the same word form as the fisted *fu*? A different word entirely? If the same word, was the new use of *fu* an unrelated development to fisted *fu*? Further, if there were continuity between the *fu*'s, then a number of questions followed. First, in processes of sociogenesis how could *fu* come to carry a doubling function in the common ground of talk between interlocutors, one seeded by a fisted *fu*? Further, what might be the cognitive processes involved in in-the-moment cognitive work

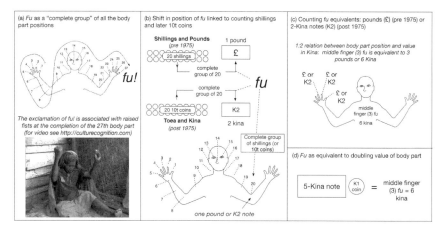

FIGURE 6.2 The working hypothesis: *Fu* as shifting from (a) 27th position, to (b) the 20th position, to (c) the K2 note (post 1975), to (d) the double of a body part value (in Kina).

such that *fu* becomes a means to serve the communicative function of double? But these questions are getting ahead of the sequence of events that occurred in 2001, which led to a series of empirical studies.

Entering the Oksapmin world

After the brief stay in the mining town, we flew to a dirt landing strip in one of the Oksapmin valleys and hiked to the area where we would reside. Not long after settling, I queried old Oksapmin friends and new acquaintances about *fu* and the origins of its doubling meaning. The direct questions revealed little. What I did learn from some older people was that *fu* in talk meant something like "a full group of plenty of things." I took this to be a fact of interest but was unclear of its import for a sociogenetic analysis that might link the fisted and doubling *fu*'s. Then, one day, rooted in a hunch linked to my earlier visits to the Oksapmin, I organized informal conversations with several people in which I took a less direct but ultimately more productive investigative tack.

The hunch

My hunch was related to the history of currency and economic exchange in the Oksapmin area and the use of the body system to count currency units. I knew that the first Western currency to circulate in Oksapmin was the Australian pound and shilling, with 20 shillings the equivalent to one pound. Further, during my early visits, I learned that some people used body parts only up to the elbow (20th body part position) not pinky (27th body part position) when dealing with currency. I wondered, might this 20:1 shilling-pound relation and then attenuation of the body system at elbow (20) have something to do with the emergent doubling meaning of *fu*? Further, I also knew that in contemporary practices, people referred to the 2-Kina note as a "faun" (pound) and the 10-toea coin as a "siling" (shilling). The continuity in language between pounds-shillings and Kina-toea preserved the 20:1 relation. Might the 20:1 relation be implicated in a shift from the fisted *fu* to the doubling-body-part-value *fu*? I was puzzled and curious.

The hunch crystallized into a working hypothesis when I had the occasion to visit with three adults—an elder, an older adult, and a middle-aged adult. I thought to pose my inquiry about *fu* in a different manner than my earlier more direct questioning that solicited people's reflections about the past. Now, I asked people of different generations about the present—with what position in the body count system was *fu* associated? The answers were provocative. I found that the elder insisted that the position for *fu* was the little finger (27); the middle-aged adult insisted that *fu* was at the elbow (20); the older adult said that it was either the elbow (20) or the little finger (27). Upon reflection and if corroborated by others, I thought that I had stumbled upon a working explanatory hypothesis that could account for the fisted *fu* seeding a doubling *fu*.

The working hypothesis

My working hypothesis, which was refined over the course of several empirical studies, is illustrated in Figure 6.2 (for an elaboration, see Saxe, 2014; Saxe & Esmonde, 2005). It took the following form. If one of *fu*'s very early meanings was a "complete group of plenty," then the early use of *fu* to mark the 27th body part would seem a meaningful trope. Indeed, *fu!* could be used to refer to a complete enumeration of all of the 27 body part positions (see Figure 6.2a). Subsequently, in the 1960s, with the emergence of the money economy and exchanges of currency, the shift for *fu* from pinky (27) to elbow (20) could be related to the fact that 20 shillings was equivalent to a pound; thus, 20 shillings would constitute a complete group of shillings, as depicted in Figure 6.2b, leading to *fu* to be a completion of a count of 20 shillings at the elbow (20) or a pound, the complete group. Still later, when currency shifted to Kina and toea, a pound (or *fu*) became the equivalent of a 2-Kina note (and shillings the equivalent of 10 toea coins). Thus, individuals could refer to three 2-Kina notes (K2) notes as middle finger (3) *fu*, the equivalent of six Kina (Figure 6.2c). Finally, the use of *fu* to express Kina with body parts in communicative interactions may have generalized for some to a doubling function of *fu* independent of the reference to counts of K2 notes. This possibility is illustrated in Figure 6.2d, in which a 5-Kina note and a 1-Kina coin are treated as middle finger (3) *fu* or six Kina (and no longer is the reference to K2 notes a necessary intermediary in the use of *fu* to serve a doubling.). Of course, this story is replete with speculation. But with such a working hypothesis as a guide, I could design studies that would either provide corroboration, nuance, or refutation of the contours of the sociogenetic trajectory.

The empirical approach

My research approach was to sample multiple individuals from four cohorts (15–20 people in each cohort) that would provide a needed historical perspective. The first cohort would be steeped in traditional practices (elders), and the fourth cohort would be engaged with contemporary practices (schooled adolescents). The second and third cohorts would occupy intermediate positions on the traditional to contemporary continuum (unschooled adults, schooled adults). In my interviews with individuals from each cohort, I would focus their thinking on several questions, each of which would bear on the working hypothesis.

Question #1: What is the meaning (communicative function) of fu in everyday talk?

To explore the everyday meanings of *fu*, we asked interviewees whether they had ever heard *fu* in talk, and if so, what it meant. As I expected, many people cited the meaning of "complete group of plenty," expressing the idea in varied ways. But also as expected, knowledge and use of *fu* differed over cohort. As shown in Figure 6.3, among the elders, people who were adults when the first missionaries

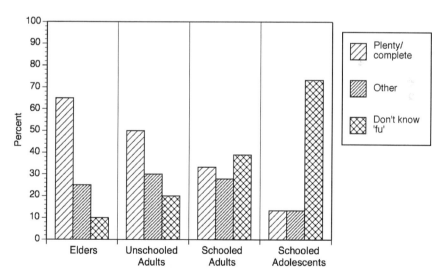

FIGURE 6.3 Percentage distribution of plenty/complete/group meaning for *fu* as a function of cohort.

Source: Reproduction of Figure 74 from Saxe, G. B. (2012). *Cultural development of mathematical ideas*. Cambridge: Cambridge University Press. All rights reserved. Reprinted with permission from Cambridge University Press.

arrived in the early 1960s, a majority identified *fu* as something akin to a complete group of plenty. In contrast, in the younger populations, this knowledge of *fu* was less common. Only about one half of the unschooled adults identified *fu* as something akin to "a complete group of plenty of things"; among the schooled adults and schooled adolescents, the percentage identifying *fu* with this meaning dipped to about 35 percent and 10 percent, respectively. Such findings suggest that there was a time in the not too distant past when the intensive quantifier, "*fu*," had a meaning that was represented in a large segment of the population, "complete group of plenty of things." But, in life today, it is diminishing, especially among the younger generations.

Question #2: Where is the location of fu on the body?

Building directly upon the generational differences about positions of *fu* on the body captured in my serendipitous discussions with the three Oksapmin men noted earlier, I asked people from the four cohorts the positional location of *fu* on the body. As shown in Figure 6.4, I found that among the elders, many indicated that *fu* was located at the 27th body part; however, a small minority of the elders indicated that *fu* was located at the 20th and still others indicated a different body part, with only one elder indicating that they did not know the position of *fu* on the body. In contrast for schooled and unschooled adults, the modal response is that *fu* is located at the 20th position, and for the schooled adolescents the large majority indicate that they did

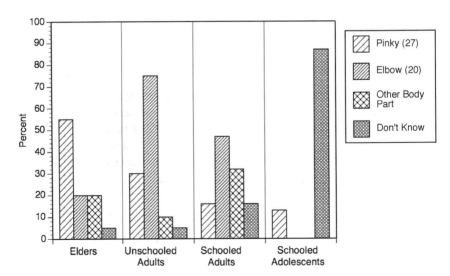

FIGURE 6.4   Percentage distribution of references to *fu* on body prior to probe questions as a function of cohort.

not know the position of *fu*. These findings were consistent with my initial informal intergenerational interviews with the three adults; they corroborate the working hypothesis that there was a historical shift in the function of *fu* from completion of 27 body parts to the completion of 20 body parts (see Figure 6.2b), a process linked to the use of Western currencies in economic exchanges.

Question #3: What is the value of fu in the selection of currency tokens?

If the 20:1 relation between shillings and pounds led to the association of *fu* with a pound and then the K2 note, then one would expect the identification of the two-Kina note as *fu*. To explore this conjecture, I asked individuals in different cohorts to select from an array of currency tokens that indicated *fu*. Elders and unschooled adults commonly associate *fu* with the two-Kina note. In contrast, this association declined for the schooled adults and adolescents, again pointing to the connection between *fu* and the pound, and *fu* and the two-Kina note.

Question #4: How is fu used in quantification practices?

As a final effort to establish corroborative support for the initial hunch, I presented people with various currency and non-currency tokens to quantify. I made use of different arrays of tokens based upon the following root values: 4, 6, 11, 21, and 29. These values were presented in the form of stones, currency of lesser value (40 toea, 60 toea, K1.10, K2.10, and K2.90) and currency of greater value (K4, K6, K11, K21, and K29), and people were asked to determine their value in the Oksapmin language (for the array of tokens constituting each value, see Saxe, 2014). We coded every time *fu* occurred in people's quantifications. Figure 6.5 shows that *fu* was used across the three cohorts studied—elders, unschooled adults, and schooled adults, but frequency of use varied across conditions. As revealed in Figure 6.5, *fu* is rarely used to quantify stones. However, *fu* is used to quantify currency of greater value, most typically K21 and K29 (and sometimes K11). Another feature of the findings is that the use of *fu* is not restricted to use for only collections of K2 notes. Consistent with the working hypothesis illustrated in Figure 6.2d, those who incorporated *fu* into their representations used *fu* as double the value of currency rather than an enumeration of K2 notes.

Figure 6.6 provides a representation of the shifting relations between the word and gestural form of *fu* and the functions that it serves over recent cultural history in the Oksapmin world. The staggered horizontal lines depict the varied functions of *fu*; the lines indicate duration of use and the bold sections of the line segments indicate an informed speculation about the period during which a particular function was more commonly used. The figure is intended to capture shifting form–function relations (horizontal lines) in the sociogenesis of *fu* in Oksapmin communities. But it does not capture well the developmental mechanisms that led to the sociogenesis.

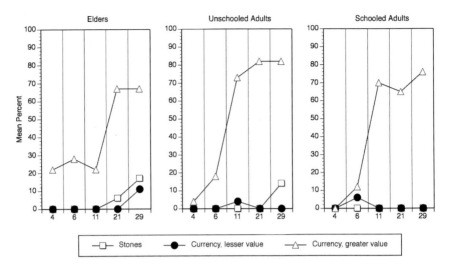

FIGURE 6.5 Percentage use of *fu* by cohort, cognate value, and task condition.

Source: Reproduction of Figure 79 from Saxe, G. B. (2012). *Cultural development of mathematical ideas*. Cambridge: Cambridge University Press. All rights reserved. Reprinted with permission from Cambridge University Press.

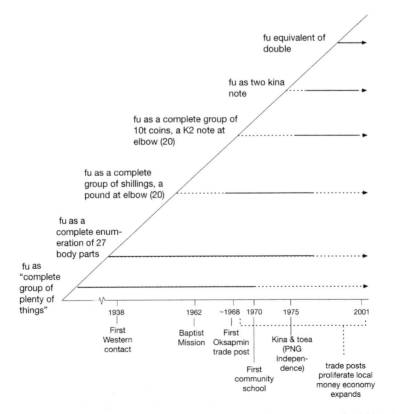

FIGURE 6.6 Shifting form–function relations related to *fu* over recent cultural history (not to scale).

A cultural-developmental, cultural-historical framework

How might the shifting relations between cultural forms and functions shift through time in processes of micro-, onto-, and sociogenesis? Figure 6.7 contains a general framework that I make use of in a model of the interplay between these developmental processes rooted in human activity (see Saxe, 2014).

For illustrative purposes the schematic in Figure 6.7 focuses on three individuals (I_1, I_2, I_3), in past, present, and future activities (note, to adequately reflect the Oksapmin world, the figure would be constituted by thousands of individuals in overlapping networks). At the figure's center, in the present, an individual is engaged in a microgenesis of a representation such as the use of *fu* (I_{2b}); the microgenesis is a conceptual act in which the individual coordinates varied cognitive and material resources to serve problem-solving and communicative functions sometimes in the back and forth interactions with others, like individuals $I_{1(b)}$ and $I_{3(b)}$. In this process, the very same microgenetic constructions also are moments in sociogenetic processes. Indeed, from a sociogenetic perspective, as interlocutors work to make their communicative intents understood to one another in microgenetic acts, they unwittingly reproduce and alter cultural forms of representation to make their communicative intents understood. The figure

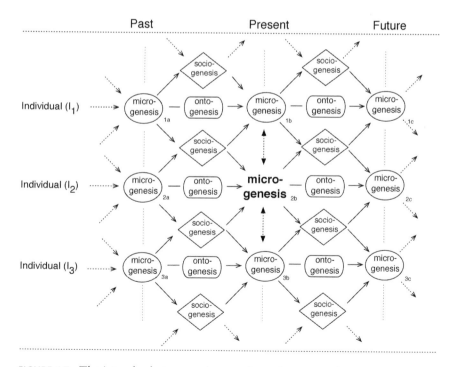

FIGURE 6.7 The interplay between micro, socio, and ontogenetic processes.

Source: Reproduction of Figure 4 from Saxe, G. B. (2012). *Cultural development of mathematical ideas*. Cambridge: Cambridge University Press. All rights reserved. Reprinted with permission from Cambridge University Press.

also reflects that the microgenetic constructions are moments in individuals' own ontogenetic trajectories in their elaboration of form–function relations, whether Individual $1_{(1a,1b,1c)}$, Individual $2_{(2a,2b,2c)}$, or Individual $3_{(3a,3b,3c)}$.

In the Oksapmin work described in this chapter, I privileged a specific form of representation, the word form *fu* and its varied functions within and across the activities of individuals over immediate and longer stretches of time. I have found this heuristic framework useful in illuminating developmental processes across a wide range of collective practices, in and out of Oksapmin communities, related to understanding processes of conceptual change. Examples include analyses of candy sellers plying their trade in urban Northeastern Brazil (Saxe, 1991); young children engaged with numerical play in working and middle class home settings in Brooklyn, New York (Saxe, Guberman, & Gearhart, 1987); elementary school children engaged with play of educational games (Saxe & Guberman, 1998; Saxe et al., 2010); straw weavers in rural Northeastern Brazil (Saxe & Gearhart, 1990); as well as upper elementary children engaged with mathematics lessons in classroom communities (Saxe, de Kirby, Kang, Le, & Schneider, 2015). Across these analyses, I have worked with my students and colleagues to illuminate how the individual and the collective are part and parcel of an understanding of the microgenetic, ontogenetic, and sociogenetic processes intrinsic to conceptual activity and conceptual change.

References

diSessa, A. (1988). Knowledge in pieces. In G. Forman & P. Pufall (Eds.), *Constructivism in the computer age* (pp. 49–70). Hillsdale, NJ: Erlbaum.

Saxe, G. B. (1991). *Culture and cognitive development: Studies in mathematical understanding.* Hillsdale, NJ: Lawrence Erlbaum Associates, Inc.

Saxe, G. B. (2012/2014). *Cultural development of mathematical ideas: Papua New Guinea studies.* Cambridge: Cambridge University Press.

Saxe, G. B., de Kirby, K., Kang, B., Le, M., & Schneider, A. (2015). Studying cognition through time in a classroom community: The interplay between "everyday" and "scientific" concepts. *Human Development, 58,* 5–44. doi:10.1159/000371560.

Saxe, G. B., Earnest, D., Sitabkhan, Y., Haldar, L. C., Lewis, K. E., & Zheng, Y. (2010). Supporting generative thinking about the integer number line in elementary mathematics. *Cognition & Instruction, 28*(4), 433–474.

Saxe, G. B., & Esmonde, I. (2005). Studying cognition in flux: A historical treatment of fu in the shifting structure of Oksapmin mathematics. *Mind, Culture, and Activity Special Issue: Combining Longitudinal, Cross-Historical, and Cross-Cultural Methods to Study Culture and Cognition, 12*(3–4), 171–225.

Saxe, G. B., & Gearhart, M. (1990). A developmental analysis of everyday topology in unschooled straw weavers. *British Journal of Developmental Psychology, 8,* 251–258.

Saxe, G. B., & Guberman, S. R. (1998). Emergent arithmetical environments in the context of distributed problem solving: Analyses of children playing an educational game. In J. Greeno & S. Goldman (Eds.), *Thinking practices* (pp. 237–256). Hillsdale, NJ: Erlbaum.

Saxe, G. B., Guberman, S. R., & Gearhart, M. (1987). Social processes in early number development. *Monographs of the Society for Research in Child Development, 52, Serial No. 162.*

Sfard, A. (2008). *Thinking as communicating.* Cambridge: Cambridge University Press.

Elements, ensembles, and dynamic constructions

Bruce Sherin

Introduction

I have been asked to write the synthesis for Part I of this volume, which focuses on *the nature of concepts and conceptual change*. Each chapter in this part was written by an author or team representing one of the luminaries in the field of conceptual change research. Not every important point of view is represented. But enough are represented to give a sense of the space of the diverse viewpoints and approaches in the wider field.

The larger goal of this book is to look for "convergence and complementarity" in the diverse viewpoints that exist in conceptual change research. That means that my task in this synthesis is to look for consensus across the chapters in this part, and to provide the start of a synthesis. Given the foundational nature of this part of the larger volume, this task is particularly important; it is unclear what it would mean to find points of convergence in the later parts if we cannot find much in the way of agreement about the nature of concepts and conceptual change.

I am going to assume that the stage has been set by the preceding chapters, and that the reader has some familiarity with the field of conceptual change research. This will allow me immediately to jump in with the task of creating a synthesis. I will do so in two steps. In the first step, I will describe what I believe are the main impediments to finding consensus. Then, in the second step, I will attempt to chart a way forward in creating a synthesis of the disparate work in this part.

The challenges are substantial. There are, of course, disagreements among the authors represented in this volume. But the real difficulties arise from misalignments between research programs that go beyond straightforward disagreements. For example, one type of misalignment arises from the fact that the authors are, in some cases, addressing different target phenomena; in other words, when they talk about "conceptual change," they are not even talking about the same thing. This presents us with a choice: Should we try to find consensus among these different voices? Or should we divide into separate fields, focused on the different target phenomena?

Even more challenging is the problem of theoretical incommensurabilities (Kuhn, 1962). Where these researchers *are* looking at the same phenomenon, they do so using very different lenses, and different language. This presents us with a similar choice. Should we attempt to create one master theory? Or should we accept that there are multiple valid lenses for looking at the phenomena of conceptual change?

Finally, there are challenges that might be called *empirical*. In some places, researchers have obtained empirical results that seem to be contradictory. It is in discussing these challenges that I tackle the infamous "coherence" debate (e.g. diSessa, Gillespie, & Esterly, 2004; Vosniadou, 2002). However, the reader will see that this debate has a relatively small role in my narrative. I believe that these empirical difficulties are much easier to address than the other two types of challenges.

I don't want to give too much away at this point, but I should probably give the reader some sense of where I am heading with my proposed synthesis. First, I am *not* going to argue that we should divide ourselves into separate fields, focused on different phenomena. Even when talking about distinct phenomena, I will argue there are several ways in which our work is mutually relevant. Furthermore, in one sense, we *should* be working on different target phenomena; we should recognize that we each can only work on one part of the larger range of phenomena associated with conceptual change.

With respect to a theoretical synthesis, I will argue that there is already a sort of proto-consensus emerging; namely, it has been argued, that we can move toward consensus by recognizing that some authors are talking about *elements*, while others are talking about *ensembles* of those elements, and most seem to view conceptual change as some kind of reorganization of multiple elements (Amin, Smith, & Wiser, 2014). I believe we can make progress by agreeing on some language roughly along these lines.

In my proposal for a theoretical synthesis, I will also argue that the field, as a whole, suffers from a sort of *ontological slippage*. Our theoretical entities—such as the notion of "concept"—should gain precision from the way they are situated in our larger theories. But when we use terms such as "concept," we often do so, tacitly, against a backdrop of shifting theoretical frameworks. This leads to slippage in the ontology of our theoretical constructs.

Finally, I will suggest that a particular type of empirical work is necessary to push us toward a consensus view of conceptual change. Most fundamental empirical disagreements do not revolve around the question of coherence, at least as it has usually been conceived. Instead, it relates to the sensitivity of people to properties of scientific explanations, such as their consistency and adequacy, a theme which is addressed in some detail elsewhere in this volume (see Part III & Chinn, Synthesis III; Part IV & Smith, Synthesis IV). I will make the case that we need to be more aware that our empirical results are specific to the particular subject matter and contexts that we study.

Impediments to consensus

The problem of different target phenomena

If we are going to attempt to synthesize the different voices in this part, then we are tacitly assuming that they are talking about the same things—that is, in their studies of "conceptual change" they are talking about the same target phenomenon. Of course, the simple fact that two authors are using the same phrase (i.e. "conceptual change") does not guarantee that the target phenomena they address are the same. Consider two groups of scientists who are studying "worms." One group might be studying bugs that live in the ground. Others might be studying bugs that live in computer software. There are many metaphors that connect the two target phenomena (hence, the common language.) But attempts to synthesize the research of these two groups would, of course, be quite misguided.

I will argue below that the authors of the chapters in this part—and researchers in the field of conceptual change more broadly—are indeed working on different target phenomena. In some respects, this is the biggest impediment we face in attempting to forge a consensus. If the target phenomena are too disparate, then perhaps different groups of conceptual change researchers should go their separate ways. However, in other respects, these impediments are easier to address than those I discuss under the heading of theoretical incommensurabilities. The problem of different targets is important but, for the most part, it is not difficult to understand. In what follows, I provide a brief map of the different target phenomena addressed in the literature on conceptual change, as reflected in the chapters in this part.

Knowledge change during formal STEM instruction

One type of research that uses the phrase "conceptual change" adopts, as its target phenomenon, *knowledge change during formal STEM instruction*. (I'll call this "instruction-driven change" for short.) There is a relatively straightforward narrative that is often told about the history of this work. In the 1970s, researchers began to pay attention to the "prior conceptions" that students bring to the learning of science (Driver & Easley, 1978). A sprawling field of research began to develop, in which researchers mapped these prior conceptions across a wide range of domains (Smith, diSessa, & Roschelle, 1993). This, in turn, led to research on what happens to these prior conceptions when students come into contact with formal instruction in the related discipline (Posner, Strike, Hewson, & Gertzog, 1982).

This is the phenomenon of interest in this flavor of conceptual change research: A student, usually a child, possesses knowledge gained prior to some formal instruction in a discipline. This prior knowledge might come from direct experience of the physical world, informal discussions with adults or other children, or prior formal instruction. The focus is on the change to the child's knowledge that occurs as a result of formal STEM instruction.

Note that this is a class of change phenomena that occurs at a particular timescale—what might be termed an *instructional* timescale. These changes may occur over days, weeks, or even months. But, typically, the focus is somewhere in the middle, on the changes to knowledge that occur over weeks of formal instruction.

There are some other ways in which the target phenomenon is usually narrowed in conceptual change research that looks at instruction-driven change (though there are exceptions to all of these generalities):

- The focus is on areas of subject matter that seem to pose persistent difficulty—disciplines in which many students initially possess conceptions that are at odds with formal scientific ideas, and in which it is difficult to move students from these initial conceptions to the formal scientific ideas. For example, seminal work by Posner and colleagues focused on the learning of Special Relativity (Posner et al., 1982). More recent work has looked at learning about properties of complex systems (e.g. Chi, 2005). In this way, the study of conceptual change is contrasted with the study of more routine learning. In short, the focus of instruction-based conceptual change research is on subject matter that is difficult to learn. The contrast between conceptual change and less dramatic varieties of learning has also been made elsewhere in this book (e.g. Amin, Synthesis II).
- Instruction-driven conceptual change research has generally looked at Western students learning Western science. I do not intend for this to be read as a critique. There are many (millions) of Western students learning Western science. If we can better understand so as to improve the learning that occurs in just this context, that would be a worthwhile achievement. However, we must, of course, expect to discover important differences if we cast our net more widely (e.g. Samarapungavan, Vosniadou, & Brewer, 1996).
- The focus has tended to be on certain narrow areas of subject matter. The great majority of this research is on science learning. Within science, a lot of effort has been directed to a few areas of subject matter, such as heat and temperature (Wiser, 1988) and mechanics (diSessa, 1993).

The majority of the chapters in this part adopt this instruction-driven knowledge change as the primary target of their research. For example, Stella Vosniadou states that her research "showed that young children form initial conceptions based on phenomenal experience, while older children, who have been exposed to science instruction, provide synthetic or fragmented conceptions that are in between the phenomenal and the scientific" (Vosniadou, Chapter 2, this volume, p. 18). This is also the primary target of Lundholm (Chapter 4, this volume) and diSessa (Chapter 1, this volume), as well as Henderson, Langbeheim and Chi (Chapter 3, this volume). The work of Lundholm stands out, however, in that she focuses on the study of conceptual change in subject matter areas that have not been the traditional focus, notably domains in social science such as economics.

Development

Next, there is conceptual change research that examines what might be termed *developmental* phenomena. This research is not focused on changes that occur over the course of weeks of dedicated instruction in a subject matter area. Instead it is focused on change that happens over developmental time—the months or years during which a child matures.

Although development-focused conceptual change research is focused on a different target phenomenon, it nonetheless looms large in research focused on instruction-driven change. The developmental work is frequently cited and treated as foundational by researchers who study instruction-driven change. And the boundaries are often blurred.

Exposure to formal instruction can still be part of the story when developmental phenomena are the object of conceptual change research, but its role is understood somewhat differently. In prototypical instruction-based conceptual change research, prior conceptions provide a baseline of knowledge, and the study is of changes to this baseline that occur as a result of focused instruction in a subject matter area. In contrast, in studies of development-based conceptual change, changes that occur over a larger period of time are the target of study. Formal instruction can be part of what drives this change, but it is just one among a variety of relevant experiences.

Susan Carey's landmark study, described in her book *Conceptual change in childhood,* is a prototypical example of conceptual change research that looks at developmental phenomena (Carey, 1985). Carey's focus was on how children understand the biological world. Her core argument was that there is a dramatic reorganization of knowledge about the biological world with development, which is driven by a gradual accrual of biological knowledge, knowledge that is accrued in a variety of contexts, both formal and informal. More recently, researchers in Science Education have worked on the development of *Learning Progressions,* which draw together insights about learning in formal and informal settings (e.g. Wiser, Smith, & Doubler, 2012). Chapter 5 in this part by Marin, Medin, and ojalehto can perhaps be seen as coming out of this tradition, though, as we will see, it represents a theoretical stance that is far from typical of the development-based conceptual change tradition. For example, it is not clear that changes to *individual knowledge* are their object of focus. I will say more about this below.

Sociogenesis

When developmental change is the target of conceptual change research, the focus is on phenomena of ontogenesis—how an individual changes over developmental time. A third type of research that uses the phrase "conceptual change" looks at phenomena of *sociogenesis*, how the "concepts" of groups of individuals change over time.

In instruction-based conceptual change, change was seen as being driven by focused instruction in a topic area. In development-based conceptual change, change was seen as occurring as the result of a variety of experiences of an individual, including formal instruction, as well as informal interaction with other individuals. When sociogenesis is the phenomenon of interest, change may again be driven by a variety of forces—forces that sometimes include external influences on a community. Furthermore, when sociogenesis is the target phenomenon, the timescale is longer than that of developmental conceptual change phenomena; it is on the order of lifespans, and even generations.

This type of sociogenesis is part (but *only* part) of the focus of the chapter by Saxe. In Chapter 6, Saxe looks at the changing meaning of a word, "fu," used by the Oksapmin of Papua, New Guinea. As described by Saxe, *fu* played a changing role in the counting activities of the the Oksapmin. At an earlier time, *fu* meant something akin to "a complete group of plenty." Later, it came to be associated with a meaning of doubling. In between, it had a number of related meanings, including the number of shillings (20) that could be traded for a pound. Saxe ascribes these changes, at least in part, to one type of external influence on the Oksapmin, namely changes in economic practices that occurred as a result of external influences on the Oksapmin community. The timescale of the phenomena he studies are clearly on the order of generations; he does his work by comparing the use of the word *fu* across generations, and across his two visits to New Guinea, which occurred over 20 years apart.

As we will see, it is a bit of a simplification to describe Saxe's work as solely focused on sociogenesis. Saxe is very explicit that he understands conceptual change to be a fundamentally multi-level phenomenon. But sociogenesis is certainly a *part* of his focus, and the study of these long timescale processes are a feature of his work that clearly distinguishes the target of his investigations from those of the other researchers represented in this part of the book.

Finally, in talking about sociogenesis, we might also want to include some research not represented in this part's chapters. Some researchers concerned with historical change in the disciplines—especially in science—have also used the phrase "conceptual change" (e.g. Nersessian, 1992, 2002). In that case, they are talking about changes, over time, in scientific concepts, as they are used by scientists. Researchers have also drawn from examples in the history of mathematics (Núñez, 2005).

Theoretical incommensurabilities

Clearly, the problem of different targets poses a significant impediment to synthesizing research that describes itself as about "conceptual change." If researchers are working on different problems—if they are trying to explain distinct phenomena—then it simply might not make sense to find points of consensus and synthesize their work.

But there are other significant impediments with which to contend. Even when researchers are targeting the same phenomena, they may do so using the lenses provided by different theoretical frameworks. Of course, in some cases it might not be too difficult to reconcile theoretical frameworks. For example, suppose Research Team #1 uses Category A in their theoretical framework, but Research Team #2 divides Category A into two categories, B and C. In that case, it should not be difficult to reconcile the work of the two teams. However, if the two research teams use categories that divide up the space in ways that are fundamentally different, then reconciling their work might simply not be possible. In that case, the frameworks might be said to be *incommensurable* (Kuhn, 1962), and it might not be possible to put the frameworks into alignment.

There is good reason to worry that this might be the case for research on conceptual change. We can begin by simply noting that there are quite a few theoretical entities named by the authors of the chapters in this part, and a greater number across the wider literature on conceptual change. There are *concepts, p-prims, ontologies, coordination classes, mental models, domain-specific folk theories, cultural framework theories, epistemological orientations*, etc. This is not the fault of any one of us. But it is a problem for us all.

In some cases, researchers might be using different words to describe the same theoretical construct. When that is the case, the task of synthesis will be relatively easy; we simply have to provide the mapping that aligns one set of terms to another. Alternatively, the theoretical terms might name different pieces of a larger theoretical puzzle. When that is the case, then our job as synthesizers is to explain how the pieces fit together. Finally, where the frameworks are truly incommensurable, then synthesis will not be possible, but we can work to understand the conditions under which each of the lenses provides the most insight.

Elements, ensembles, and other stuff

One thing seems clear to me, and to several of the authors in Part I: There is a distinction between constructs that describe small, constituent elements of some type of system, and constructs that describe ensembles of those elements. At the level of constituent elements, diSessa's (1993) *p-prims* are the prime example, both in the chapters here, and the literature more broadly. Although diSessa states that p-prims are likely just one among many types of sub-conceptual elements, they have nonetheless become the stand in—or at least, the exemplar—of sub-conceptual elements that potentially make up ensembles. In the wider literature, other candidates for sub-conceptual elements include *facets* (Minstrell, 1989), *core intuitions* (Brown, 1993; and Chapter 10, this volume), and *image schemas* (Lakoff, 1990). More generically, terms such as *concept* and *conceptual element* sometimes seem to be used to refer to smaller elements.

At the level of ensembles, there is much more theoretical diversity, and sorting through the terminology is tricky enough that it is not possible to do so here. Some of the ensemble-related terminology clearly is intended to name *types* of collections of elements. But other terminology might be more properly understood to name *characteristics* of ensembles, or constraints on the assembly of elements into ensembles.

There are many examples just within the chapters included in this part. DiSessa, himself, names *coordination classes* as one type of ensemble—an ensemble that is partly constituted by p-prims. Vosniadou, for example, has *framework theories*; Marin, Medin, and ojalehto have *epistemological orientations* and *cultural framework theories* (which they contrast with *domain-specific framework theories*).

The use of diverse terminology does present challenges when seeking to forge a consensus. But the simple recognition that some authors are talking at the level of elements, while others at the level of ensembles, might help to alleviate some of the confusion, and perhaps even dissolve some of the ongoing debates in the field. In fact, some authors have argued that the field already seems to be drifting into a synthesis along these lines (Amin et al., 2014). Others have self-consciously proposed similar syntheses (Brown & Hammer, 2008).

I will say more about that possibility in the latter half of this synthesis. Here I will simply note that some of the authors in this part have themselves pointed to this possibility. For example, Vosniadou, in her discussion of *framework theories*, is focusing her attention at the level of ensembles of knowledge. But she states (Chapter 2, this volume, p. 22): "we do not in principle exclude the possibility that knowledge elements such as p-prims might be present in our (sub)conceptual knowledge system." Similarly, Henderson, Langbeheim, and Chi state (Chapter 3, this volume, p. 30) "Our theory does not frame students' knowledge as rigid or static, nor does it contradict the framework that describes knowledge as a dynamic web of ideas that are based on experiential encounters and intuitions."

There are some other theoretical issues to sort out. The above paragraphs paint a picture of a relatively homogeneous system—a conceptual ecology—composed of elements and some sort of generic ensembles. But there is a question of how *heterogeneous* this ecology might be, and how much this heterogeneity might matter for understanding conceptual change. Are there many types of elements? Is there more than one kind of ensemble?

There are several important questions that pertain to possible heterogeneity in our theoretical constructs. Note that much of the discussion above was about STEM content knowledge, narrowly construed—knowledge about what diSessa calls, in his chapter, "situations that might also be construed from the viewpoint of professional science." (Chapter 1, this volume, p. 9) But the authors in this part propose theoretical constructs that do not seem to be narrowly about content. For example, Marin, Medin, and ojalehto discuss *epistemological orientations* which are "more encompassing and pervasive" than "domain-specific folk theories" (Chapter 5, this volume, p. 44). Ludholm (Chapter 4, this volume) has constructs that depart even more significantly from a narrow focus on science content; for example, she argues that *values* and *sense-of-self* are particularly important to learning in the social sciences.

Similarly, Henderson et al. argue for the importance of a focus on the *ontologies* possessed by individual learners. Quoting Keil (1979), they define an intuitive ontology as "one's conception of the basic categories of existence, of what sorts of things there are" (Henderson et al., Chapter 3, this volume, p. 26). Henderson and colleagues talk about "schemas" associated with various ontologies, such as a *sequential* schema and an *emergent* schema. Does this mean we should treat them as a distinct type of element in the conceptual ecology, or some type of abstraction over elements?

More generally, we will have to consider how to integrate these constructs, which seem to be less narrowly focused on content, into our larger story. It could be, for example, that constructs like epistemological orientations are emergent properties of a content-focused knowledge system, and constructs, such as framework theories, might be more properly understood as constraints on how to assemble knowledge elements. Alternatively, they might be elements or even distinct ensembles in their own right. The question of how to integrate these other constructs is a central theme in the syntheses of Parts III (Chinn) and IV (Smith) in this volume.

Ontological slippage in our own theories

In the preceding section, I discussed the variety of theoretical constructs employed by the authors in this part, and how those constructs might be brought together into a grand synthesis. But forging such a synthesis requires that there are not any profound incommensurabilities among our theoretical frameworks. If there are, this would be a serious impediment to creating a synthesis.

In this section, I want to draw attention to some more profound incommensurabilities, namely problems of *ontological* incompatibility (Keil, 1979). To be clear, I am not talking about the ontologies of learners. Rather, I am talking about the ontological kinds of theoretical entities in our own theories of conceptual change.

Some of my points in the preceding section could be understood as contrasting ontologies. For example, I contrasted theoretical entities that were treated as elements, with theoretical entities that were emergent properties of systems of elements. Ontological divides of this sort are very important to understand as we seek to forge consensus. But there are even more fundamental ontological divides than was suggested by the discussion in the preceding section. So I want to back up and consider the ontologies of our theories more carefully.

To begin, I note that theoretical terms take their meaning—and ontological kind—from the larger theories in which they participate. I'll explain this first with an example from physics—*force*. In Newtonian physics, *force* is best understood as defined by the roles that it plays within that theory, notably its role in the equation $F = ma$. Its ontological kind in that theory is a bit tricky to pin down, but it might be best understood to be a particular kind of event. In contrast, in the pre-Newtonian Impetus theory, force is more like a kind of "stuff" that can be imbued in objects. In addition to these theory-based meanings of the word *force*, it also has, of course, a number of everyday meanings.

For our use of "force" to have scientific precision, then we must be using it with one theoretical context in mind, at least tacitly. If this tacit theoretical context shifts, the meaning of the word force will shift; even its ontological kind may change. If we slip into everyday usage of the word force, then it loses scientific precision, and the ontological kind might not be well-defined.

In the literature on concepts and conceptual change, I believe we are guilty of just these sorts of shifts. In one class of accounts of conceptual change, our theories are cognitive models, and the entities in our theories are mental representations. In cognitive models, cognitive processes act on mental representations to produce behavior. In these theories, the representations and processes are mutually defining, just as force and mass are mutually defining; one is not meaningful without the other. Mental representations thus get their meaning from how they participate in cognitive processes. Another way to say this is that mental representations get their meaning from the *causal* role they play in models of cognition. So, for example, if we have a mental representation corresponding to that of the "concept" of "mammal," this concept would be defined by the causal role the mental representation plays in our models of cognition.

Another class of accounts might be called distributed or socio-cognitive. In that type of account, in addition to mental representations, our models might include physical entities, including spoken and written words. In that case, the concept of mammal might be (at least partly) associated with the spoken word "mammal." It would still be defined by the role it plays in the larger models, which now include mental representations, as well as material and symbolic artifacts.

There are other possibilities that depart more dramatically from either of these cognitive models. Rather than treating the concept of mammal as an element in one of these models, we might treat the concept of mammal as something like the idea, as it is appears in a textbook. This might be said to be the concept of mammal, "in the abstract." It is the idealized version of the concept that, for example, might appear in learning objectives. Unlike a mental representation, a textbook concept of mammal does not get its meaning from its causal role in a cognitive model; rather, it gets its meaning from the network of statements of laws in which it appears. Finally, we sometimes use the word "concept" more informally. In this case, it would take its meaning from its usage in everyday language, rather than a theoretical context.

Theories based on these varied ontologies look very different. For example, suppose we are building a theory of conceptual change that is based on textbook concepts. In that case, we might state that a learner began with an understanding of physics consistent with $F = mv$ (i.e. forces cause velocities), and ultimately acquired an understanding consistent with Newton's second law, $F = ma$ (i.e. forces are associated with accelerations). In terms of textbook concepts, the starting and ending state are thus specifiable in this relatively compact form, and mass is defined by its role in these laws.

Contrast this type of theory with one that seeks to describe the mental representations of the learner at the starting and ending state. If someone has an understanding consistent with Newton's second law, this certainly requires a complex and extensive set of mental representations. It requires, for example, knowledge of how to apply the laws in particular circumstances, and it likely requires this knowledge to be hooked up with physical intuition. In this type of theory, mental representations associated with an understanding of mass get their meaning from how they participate in the cognitive models that produce the relevant reasoning.

Hopefully it is clear to the reader that these two types of theorizing about conceptual change are built upon radically different ontologies. They are fundamentally and dramatically different and, if we were to confuse them, we would be making a big mistake. Nonetheless, I think it is a mistake that we make with great regularity. I am not going to list examples and name names, in part because I would have to list just about everyone's name (including my own).

Really, there are two types of impediments posed by these ontological issues. The first is the problem that frameworks that make use of one ontology cannot be straightforwardly synthesized with frameworks that make use of another. The second problem is the more pernicious problem of ontological slippage: our slippage from one ontology to another muddies the waters in a way that makes it extremely difficult to construct a meaningful synthesis.

Awareness, language, and other theoretical complexities

Finally, there are some places where the authors of Part I traipse over theoretical ground that is notoriously difficult. This is theoretical ground that is more than tricky; it is epically tricky. Because the issues are so difficult, it is hard to know how we are going to sort out any contradictions among authors.

First, there are issues of awareness and consciousness. In some early writings on conceptual change, it was posited that conceptual change is a highly rational process, in which the learner explicitly considers alternative frameworks, and chooses among them based on their merits. The 1982 paper by Posner et al. is the oft-cited reference in this vein (Posner et al., 1982).

More recent theorizing, including by the same authors (Strike & Posner, 1992), has definitively moved away from any claims that conceptual change is a rational process requiring a high level of learner awareness. But awareness, as a construct, has not disappeared from discussions of conceptual change. And, in some cases, important claims seem to hinge on issues of awareness. For example, Henderson et al. (Chapter 3, this volume) argue that scientists can shift among ontologies with awareness. DiSessa (Chapter 1, this volume) argues that p-prims cannot be "considered" by learners. The contrast between implicit and explicit processing is also an important topic in Smith's synthesis of Part IV (this volume).

In some cases, these issues might not be too terribly subtle, and an informal notion of "awareness" might suffice. However, often, I believe, the issues require deeper theoretical treatment of awareness. The problem here is simply that awareness is a slippery construct. There is certainly no clear consensus about how to integrate awareness and consciousness into a cognitive perspective. Thus, if sorting out differences among authors requires us to address issues of learner awareness, that is going to pose a significant difficulty. I suspect we can do so without completely solving the problem of the nature of consciousness. But there is work to do here.

The final set of issues has to do with language and conceptual change. (These issues are probably related to issues of awareness, but, since we don't understand awareness, it is hard to know.) Issues of language show up here and there in these chapters. For example, Saxe's work is focused on tracking evolution of the use of a particular linguistic form, and diSessa (Chapter 1, this volume, p. 12) tells us "there are no common words for p-prims."

At a high level, the problem here is the same as that posed by issues of awareness. There is no clear consensus about how to think about the relationship between language and cognition. (Note: Part II of this book is devoted to considering the relationship between language, along with other representations, and conceptual change. So we can hope that some of the difficulties are addressed there.)

Empirical differences

The last category of impediment I will discuss consists of *empirical disagreements*, places in the literature where researchers have obtained experimental results that seem, at least, to be contradictory. It is actually quite difficult to find clear experimental disagreements, in these chapters or the literature more broadly. But of those that do exist, many relate to the infamous "coherence" debate (diSessa, 2013; Vosniadou & Skopeliti, 2014).

The coherence debate relates to questions concerning the character of the *ensembles* discussed in the preceding question. One version of the core question asks whether, in advance of instruction, the ensembles can be considered to be, in some manner, theory-like. If they are indeed theory-like, then this leads to an empirical prediction; namely, learners should give answers that are consistent across the range of contexts to which the theory-like ensemble applies.

One of the authors in Part I, Stella Vosniadou, has been a central figure in the coherence debate. In early seminal research, she presented evidence that children, of a range of ages, exhibited consistent mental models of the shape of the Earth (Vosniadou & Brewer, 1992). Over the decades that followed, experiments conducted by other researchers produced results that were said to contradict those of Vosniadou's earlier research (Nobes et al., 2003; Schoultz, Säljö, & Wyndhamn, 2001; Siegal, Butterworth, & Newcombe, 2004). These later experiments, however, employed different methods than Vosniadou.

More recently, diSessa, Gillespie, and Esterly (diSessa et al., 2004) published what they described as a replication study, which attempted to replicate published results by Ioannides and Vosniadou (2002) concerning how students understand force. They reported that they were not able to find the coherence obtained by Vosniadou. However, Vosniadou, in her chapter here, argues that the experiment of diSessa and colleagues was a flawed replication.

Even with these disputes, I believe it is becoming increasingly clear that the two sides in the coherence debate are closer to agreement, at least on the empirical facts, than has historically been suggested. To support this claim, I will start by saying that we should all first admit that we know the answer to the question of coherence. Because this point is important, I will set it off here and write it centered in italics:

> *When asked science-related questions, sometimes people are consistent, and sometimes they are not. It depends upon the person and the topic.*

If you were, for example, to ask me, Bruce Sherin, about the shape of the Earth, I would, with great consistency answer questions in a manner consistent with the Earth being (at least roughly) a sphere. In contrast, when I asked my daughter about the shape of the Earth, when she was four years old, she gave a lengthy monologue, clearly composed on the spot, that ranged over a great deal of territory, but focused most centrally on the friendly space-hyenas that apparently live on the planet Earth.

So, sometimes people are consistent, and sometimes they are not. Furthermore, researchers associated with the coherence side of the debate have been at pains to explain that they have been somewhat misunderstood, and that their perspectives do not imply quite the degree of consistency and coherence that has often been assumed. This, in fact, is perhaps the central point of Vosniadou's chapter here. Thus, to the extent there are empirical disagreements, they are disagreements about the *degree* of coherence that exists within specific domains, and for specific populations.

If we agree with my claim above, are there any domain-spanning, *empirical* differences that remain? Vosniadou, in her chapter, argues that the core difference is that she believes "students are sensitive to issues of internal consistency and explanatory adequacy." (Chapter 2, this volume, p. 23). DiSessa, in contrast, believes that this type of sensitivity varies significantly across individuals. This may be where there are real empirical differences that will perhaps be amenable to further research. I will say more about this later.

Toward a synthesis

Should we go our separate ways?

In the first section of this contribution, I laid out what I see as the main impediments for finding consensus across researchers in how we study and describe "The nature of concepts and conceptual change." Now, in this second section, I begin the task of laying some of the groundwork for a synthesis.

The first question to settle is whether it even makes sense to create a synthesis that spans the full set of chapters in this part, and the larger space of research on conceptual change. I argued above that studies of conceptual change address target phenomena that are, in some cases, profoundly different. I also argued that the theoretical lenses employed might, at times, be incommensurable. Do these observations mean that any attempt to forge a synthesis is misguided?

I believe it is productive (and appropriate) to adopt the attitude that, while not always overlapping, the work we are conducting is at least complementary; we have been working to divide and conquer the larger problem of understanding conceptual change. From this point of view, forging a synthesis simply means, in some cases, recognizing that we are each working on relatively distinct sub-parts of the same larger endeavor. For example, the more culturally-sensitive perspective adopted by Marin, Medin, and ojalehto suggests that studies of how Western students learn Western science only illuminate one small part of the larger set of phenomena that should be addressed in research on conceptual change.

In some cases, varieties of research on conceptual change might be relatively distinct, while still constraining each other around the edges. For example, work on developmental phenomena might constrain our models of sociogenesis, and vice versa.

Finally, it is true that the field has made use of quite divergent theoretical lenses. But this does not mean we must see these theoretical lenses as strict alternatives, in which only one lens can be the correct lens. Rather, we can see each lens as making idealizations, which might be appropriate for particular purposes. For example, we could accept that, in some deep way, conceptual change is not an individual-level phenomenon, while, in some circumstances, we can take as our object of study changes to individuals against a presumed-to-be-unchanging background.

Common theoretical language

The above section concludes that we should not separate into distinct fields, and that we can at least see our work as complementary. Now we want to see if we can go farther. One question is whether, as part of forging a synthesis, we can converge on some common theoretical language, even if that language might have different meanings in different research contexts. If we abstract up a level, it is possible to find commonalities across the chapters, which suggest such a synthesis might be possible:

- There is a system of elements, described at multiple levels.
- This system exhibits at least some variability in behavior depending on context.
- Changes to the system are often driven by some sort of external influence.
- Change can be slow and incremental.
- The changes might result in the construction of "hybrids."

Viewed at this high level of abstraction, it seems possible that we might be able to employ a common theoretical language. However, there are really two types of cases: (1) cases in which we really mean the same thing when we use common terms, and (2) cases in which our use of the same terms is more properly understood to be metaphorical.

Let's try to clarify this situation a bit. To start, a first step is to deal with the sort of ontological slippage I discussed earlier. Here, I want to put one of my own stakes in the ground: I think we should proceed with the assumption that what we are doing is building *models*. This means that any constructs that we include in our theoretical discussions should be understood to get their import from the causal role that they play in larger models. As much as possible, our theoretical entities should be strictly defined by their role within a model. Note that it requires us to do more than to be clear that we are building models. Ontological clarity also requires us to be clear about the types of things we are building models *of*. This directive sets a high bar, since it requires we have models. But this need only be the ideal toward which we strive.

Next, as I said earlier, there is one type of loose theoretical consensus that already seems to be emerging in the field (Amin et al., 2014; Brown & Hammer, 2008). Namely, the consensus that some of the apparent problems in the field might be ameliorated if we recognize that some claims in the literature constitute theorizing about elements, whereas others constitute theorizing about ensembles of elements. I see no reason that we cannot, as a field, go ahead with that as an assumption. As terminology, I like the terms "element" and "ensemble." Note that I prefer the term "element" to "p-prim," because it is clearly more generic. (DiSessa has always intended "p-prim" to have a more narrow meaning.)

To this pair of theoretical terms, I want to add a third. In past work I have discussed what I called *dynamic mental constructs* or just DMCs (Sherin, Krakowski, & Lee, 2012). The observation is that as researchers we often name entities that, in some manner, are constructed in the moment, and not stored. A good example of such a dynamically constructed entity is the term "mental model," as it is used by Vosniadou and Brewer (Vosniadou & Brewer, 1992) as well as across much of the literature in which the term is employed.

This theoretical language is very generic. For example, using the term "element" potentially gives a single name to what might be diverse entities. It is hard to know how far we can get with such a simplification. To draw an analogy: in statistical mechanics, the properties of gases are understood by treating all gases as the same, as composed of molecules that are bouncing around. For many conclusions about the behavior of gases, the exact constitution of these molecules doesn't matter; we can make a lot of progress in understanding gases by treating them all the same, as made up of generic molecules. The same sort of simplification might hold for conceptual change. Perhaps we can make substantial progress by treating all elements as just elements. However, my hunch is that, unlike the case of molecules, true progress will require us to distinguish among types of elements.

Even more work, I believe, is needed at the level of ensembles. As I pointed out earlier, there is quite a bit of theoretical diversity in the sorts of ensembles that are described; in these chapters alone, there are *coordination classes, framework theories, orientations*, etc. Furthermore, these ensemble-level constructs are slippery, and are often the subject of misunderstandings, as evidenced by the need for the authors here to tell readers that their ensemble-level constructs have been misunderstood.

My intent here is not to be critical of authors who have attempted to talk about ensemble-level constructs. These constructs are just more difficult to talk about. But I believe that we will be on more solid ground if we strive toward the construction of models, even simple ones, that consist of elements. I also think that clearly separating out dynamic constructions from ensembles will help.

Finally, some of the chapters in this part give me reasons to believe that we will need more specific terms than "element" and "ensemble." For example, Lundholm draws our attention to important differences across scientific domains, in particular how they treat causality. We also need to figure out how we are going to incorporate "meta" elements, such as ontological kinds and epistemological beliefs. They might be incorporated as other types of elements. Or they might, in some manner, be treated as properties of ensembles. Finally, if we wish to keep "awareness" as part of our theoretical vocabulary, that too must be incorporated.

Empirical directions

In the above section, I presented steps toward a theoretical synthesis. In this final section, I discuss how I believe we can move beyond empirical differences. To begin, I hope it has been clear from my preceding discussion that empirical differences are not the primary impediment to forging a consensus. The main difficulties are rooted in the interpretation of the results and perhaps in what types of studies are most important to conduct.

The above musings have led me to conclude that the best way to move forward is to adopt an empirical approach that is self-conscious in looking across subject-matter areas and contexts. If we accept that properties of concepts and conceptual change may, in some manner, be specific to subject-matter domains and individuals, then we need an empirical program that is systematic in looking across domains and populations.

Furthermore, I believe that the above discussion implies that we need to study whether and how individuals are sensitive to issues of consistency and explanatory power, in a way that transcends domains. Some of the most fundamental empirical disagreements seem to rest on this question. Some elements of the extensive research on things such as students' epistemological beliefs about science and mathematics might be relevant here (Elby & Hammer, 2001; Schoenfeld, 1985; Schommer & Walker, 1995). But my hunch is that we can study this sensitivity in a way that is more narrow (and tractable) than the broader literature on naïve epistemology.

Related to this are issues of consciousness and awareness. Again, some disputes seem to hinge around whether learners and experts are aware, for example, of shifts between multiple perspectives. This seems like another important (and tractable) target for empirical investigation, even if we don't fully understand what awareness is.

Finally, some of the biggest questions that remain are, in a sense, empirical, but they are empirical in a way that will make them difficult to resolve. Take, for example, the question of whether conceptual change can be treated as an individual-level phenomenon. This is not a question that can be answered by a small number of studies. Instead, we must simply pursue a program, and see when it fails, or proves to be productive. The possibility of treating "elements" and "ensembles" generically, similarly, can only be determined through the broader success of a research program.

Acknowledgments

I am grateful to the authors of the chapters in this part, for stimulating reading, as well as for substantial comments on drafts of this synthesis. I also thank Tamer Amin and Olivia Levrini for their extensive guidance and suggestions.

References

Amin, T. G., Smith, C. L., & Wiser, M. (2014). Student conceptions and conceptual change: Three overlapping phases of research. In N. Lederman & S. Abell (Eds.), *Handbook of research on science education* (vol. 2, pp. 57–81). London: Routledge.

Brown, D. E. (1993). Refocusing core intuitions: A concretizing role for analogy in conceptual change. *Journal of Research in Science Teaching, 30*(10), 1273–1290.

Brown, D. E., & Hammer, D. (2008). Conceptual change in physics. In S. Vosniadou (Ed.), *International handbook of research on conceptual change* (pp. 127–154). London: Routledge.

Carey, S. (1985). *Conceptual change in childhood.* Cambridge, MA: MIT Press.

Chi, M. T. H. (2005). Commonsense conceptions of emergent processes: Why some misconceptions are robust. *Journal of the Learning Sciences, 14,* 161–199. https://doi.org/10.1207/s15327809jls1402.

diSessa, A. A. (1993). Toward an epistemology of physics. *Cognition and Instruction, 10*(2 & 3), 105–225.

diSessa, A. A. (2013). A bird's-eye view of the "pieces" vs "coherence" controversy (from the" pieces" side of the fence"). In S. Vosniadou (Ed.), *International handbook of research on conceptual change* (pp. 31–48). London: Routledge.

diSessa, A. A., Gillespie, N. M., & Esterly, J. B. (2004). Coherence versus fragmentation in the development of the concept of force. *Cognitive Science, 28,* 58.

Driver, R., & Easley, J. (1978). Pupils and paradigms: A review of literature related to concept development in adolescent science students. *Studies in Science Education, 5,* 61–84.

Elby, A., & Hammer, D. (2001). On the substance of a sophisticated epistemology. *Science Education, 85,* 554–67.

Ioannides, C. & Vosniadou, S. (2002). The changing meanings of force. *Cognitive Science Quarterly, 2*(1), 5–62.

Keil, F. (1979). *Semantic and conceptual development.* Cambridge, MA: Harvard University Press.

Kuhn, T. S. (1962). *The structure of scientific revolutions.* Chicago, IL: University of Chicago Press.

Lakoff, G. (1990). *Women, fire, and dangerous things: What categories reveal about the mind.* Cambridge: Cambridge University Press.

Minstrell, J. (1989). Teaching science for understanding. In L. B. Resnick & L. E. Klopfer (Eds.), *Toward the thinking curriculum: Current cognitive research* (pp. 129–149). Alexandria, VA: Association for Supervision and Curriculum Development.

Nersessian, N. J. (1992). How do scientists think? Capturing the dynamics of conceptual change in science. In R. N. Giere (Ed.), *Cognitive models of science* (pp. 5–22). Minneapolis, MN: University of Minnesota Press.

Nersessian, N. J. (2002). Maxwell and the "method of physical analogy": Model-based reasoning, generic abstraction, and conceptual change. In D. Malament (Ed.), *Reading natural philosophy: Essays in the history and philosophy of science and mathematics* (pp. 129–166). Lasalle, IL: Open Court.

Nobes, G., Moore, D. G., Martin, A. E., Clifford, B. R., Butterworth, G., Panagiotaki, G., & Siegal, M. (2003). Children's understanding of the earth in a multicultural community: Mental models or fragments of knowledge? *Developmental Science, 6*, 72–85.

Núñez, R. E. (2005). Creating mathematical infinities: Metaphor, blending, and the beauty of transfinite cardinals. *Journal of Pragmatics, 37*(10), 1717–1741.

Posner, G. J., Strike, K. A., Hewson, P. W., & Gertzog, W. A. (1982). Accommodation of a scientific conception: Toward a theory of conceptual change. *Science Education, 66*, 211–227.

Samarapungavan, A., Vosniadou, S., & Brewer, W. F. (1996). Mental models of the earth, sun, and moon: Indian children's cosmologies. *Cognitive Development, 11*(4), 491–521.

Schoenfeld, A. H. (1985). Metacognitive and epistemological issues in mathematical understanding. In E. A. Silver (Ed.), *Learning and teaching mathematical problem solving: Multiple research perspectives* (pp. 361–379). Hillsdale, NJ: Lawrence Erlbaum.

Schommer, M., & Walker, K. (1995). Are epistemological beliefs similar across domains? *Journal of Educational Psychology, 87*, 424–32.

Schoultz, J., Säljö, R., & Wyndhamn, J. (2001). Heavenly talk: Discourse, artifacts, and children's understanding of elementary astronomy. *Human Development, 44*, 103–118.

Sherin, B. L., Krakowski, M., & Lee, V. R. (2012). Some assembly required: How scientific explanations are constructed during clinical interviews. *Journal of Research in Science Teaching, 49*(2), 166–198.

Siegal, M., Butterworth, G., & Newcombe, P. A. (2004). Culture and children's cosmology. *Developmental Science, 7*, 308–324.

Smith, J. P., diSessa, A. A., & Roschelle, J. (1993). Misconceptions reconceived: A constructivist analysis of knowledge in transition. *Journal of the Learning Sciences, 3*, 115–163.

Strike, K. A., & Posner, G. J. (1992). A revisionist theory of conceptual change. In R. A. Duschl & R. J. Hamilton (Eds.), *Philosophy of science, cognitive psychology, and educational theory and practice* (pp. 147–176). New York: State University of New York Press.

Vosniadou, S. (2002). On the nature of naïve physics. In M. Limón & L. Mason (Eds.), *Reconsidering conceptual change: Issues in theory and practice* (pp. 61–76). Dordrecht: Kluwer Academic Publishers.

Vosniadou, S., & Brewer, W. (1992). Mental models of the Earth: A study of conceptual change in childhood. *Cognitive Psychology, 24*, 535–585.

Vosniadou, S. & Skopeliti, I. (2014). Conceptual change from the framework theory side of the fence. *Science & Education, 23*(7), 1427–1445.

Wiser, M. (1988). The differentiation of heat and temperature: History of science and novice-expert shift. In S. Strauss (Ed.), *Ontogeny, phylogeny, and historical development* (pp. 28–48). Norwood, NJ: Ablex.

Wiser, M., Smith, C. L., & Doubler, S. (2012). Learning progressions as tools for curriculum development. In A. C. Alonzo & A. W. Gotwals (Eds.), *Learning progressions in science* (pp. 359–403). The Netherlands, Sense Publishers.

PART II

Representation, language, and discourse in conceptual change

Editor: Tamer G. Amin

Orientation

This part of the book examines the broad theme of representation and conceptual change. In this part, we learn that when studying conceptual change it is important to consider how conceptual knowledge is represented and the roles that representations of various kinds play in the process of change. Both internal (mental) and a wide range of external representations are considered.

In the first contribution, Bruce Sherin looks at the relationship between the use of equations and conceptual change in the context of learning physics. He begins by reflecting deeply on what it means to consider the function of a representation in conceptual change. He goes on to suggest two functions in the case of equations: first, they can be seen as tools that affect the way that learners make productive use of elements within their intuitive sense of mechanism; second, equations are also a "world" of their own that learners experience about which they develop new kinds of intuitions. Susan Gelman and Jasmine DeJesus focus on language. They show that learning a category label encourages both children and adults to adopt an essentialist assumption with respect to that category, both supporting and hindering subsequent conceptual change. Miriam Novack, Eliza Congdon, Elizabeth Wakefield, and Susan Goldin-Meadow study the connection between gestures and conceptual change. They show that the analysis of gestures used by learners while solving mathematical problems can reveal aspects of their understanding not revealed in speech and can help identify transitional knowledge-states. Moreover, they provide evidence suggesting that the use of gestures can, in fact, play a causal role in conceptual change. In his contribution, David Brown offers a perspective on conceptual change in which a variety of different types of knowledge elements play an important role. In his systemic account, Brown shows that productive conceptual change involves the successful integration of both implicit and explicit knowledge types. Roger Säljö cautions against what he sees as too sharp a distinction between internal (mental) and external representations. Using the case of students learning to use a Carbon Footprint Calculator, he argues that, in some important sense, concepts may not be in the head as we typically assume. Finally, David Treagust, Mihye Won, and Felicity McLure show that the use of a wide range of representations—such as diagrams, physical models, analogies—are important tools that can be used to teach for conceptual change. They discuss a program of research showing the kinds of meaningful conceptual understanding that learners can achieve, especially if instruction integrates the use of multiple representations at multiple levels of analysis.

The contributions in this part of the book are diverse in their attention to different age groups, the interest in concepts from different domains, the focus on development and learning in either informal or formal settings, and the use of a range of quantitative and qualitative methods. But as the reader will see, and as explored in the synthesis chapter by Amin, the chapters both converge and complement each other in interesting ways. For example, they converge in a commitment to understanding the role that different representations play in conceptual change and how these representations interact. They complement each other in the extent to which they focus on either iconic (analogical) or propositional (language-like) representations or interactions between both types; in how they contribute to our understanding of different kinds of knowledge change; and the mechanisms that realize them.

7

CONCEPTUAL CHANGE AND SYMBOL USE IN PHYSICS

Bruce Sherin

Introduction

My task here is to consider the roles that equations play in any conceptual change associated with the learning of physics. There is good reason to think that this might be quite interesting ground within which to examine the roles of external representations in learning. Certainly, the experience of the introductory physics student is that the physics class involves the writing and manipulation of many equations, such as $F = ma$ and $x = x_o + v_o t + \frac{1}{2} at^2$. But it is not just new physics students who feel that equations play a uniquely central role in physics learning. The well-known physicist Richard Feynman (1965) wrote:

> it is impossible to explain honestly the beauties of the laws of nature in a way that people can feel, without their having some deep understanding in mathematics. I am sorry, but this seems to be the case.
>
> *(p. 39)*

Feynman seems to believe that physics equations are much more than tools for computation, they play a deep role in how physics is understood. If this is the case, it seems certain that equations must play central and important roles in physics understanding and conceptual change. Understanding these deep and important roles is the charge of this chapter.

On functions

However, like any good academic, I must begin by protesting that the analytic task I have been assigned is more difficult than it might seem. The problem has to do with the word "role" above. What do we mean when we ask about the role of equations in conceptual change? I believe that we are, in essence, asking about the *functions* of equations.

Philosophers of science have long argued over how to construct a definition of function that has the right properties. Despite space limitations, I will try to provide the reader with a sense for the seriousness of the difficulties. A good place to begin is an early seminal article by Larry Wright (1973).

Following Wright, let us consider the functions of the human nose. We all would probably agree that one function of the nose is to provide a passageway for air, and another is perhaps to provide the locus for our sense of smell. But there are many other candidate functions about which it might be harder to find consensus. For example, the nose probably provides some structural support for the face. Also, it might be said to have aesthetic functions; if we did not have noses, we would probably be judged to be unattractive. And, for some of us, our noses perform the very important function of holding up our eyeglasses. We can similarly wonder, for example, how we can definitively state that the function of the heart is to pump blood, rather than to make heart-pumping noises.

Philosophers of science see these problems as having important implications, particularly for biology and psychology. Thus, many have proposed solutions. Wright, for example, attempts to distinguish the *true* function of an entity like the heart from *accidental* functions. For Wright, the key feature of a true function is that it plays a role in an explanation of why the entity exists. For a designed artifact, this true function will generally align with the designer's intent. For a biological organ such as the heart, the function will play a role in an evolutionary explanation for the existence of that organ.

Wright's approach is unlikely to be the correct one when considering external representations, perhaps the most complexly multifunctional artifacts of human creation. Consider, for example, the numerous functions that have been proposed for natural language. It has been proposed that:

1 Language plays a communicative function, allowing one person to convey thoughts to another person (e.g. Carruthers, 2002).
2 Language acts as a "tool" (Clark, 1997) or "cognitive scaffold" (Carruthers, 2002), simplifying certain types of reasoning tasks.
3 Language provides the very medium of thought. From this point of view, there is no human reasoning without language (e.g. Clark, 1997).
4 Language plays a role in "sculpting" knowledge and cognition (e.g. Carey, 2009; Carruthers, 2002).

Natural language is probably an extreme case, even among external representations, in terms of its degree of multifunctionality. Nonetheless, it is not hard to imagine analogs, in the case of physics equations, for most of these functions.

We could attempt to construct a definition that clearly selects one of these possibilities as *the* function of natural language or physics equations. But, even if we could, I doubt that it would produce the analysis that we want. External representations seem, to me, to have many "true" functions. A better alternative, I believe, is to think of the identification of the function of an entity as a type of analysis, with the functions identified being relevant to a set of choices made by the analyst. Cummins (1975) describes an approach of just this sort. In Cummins' framework, if we wish to identify the function of an *entity x*, then we must identify a *system S*, of which *x* is a part, and finally we must identify a *capacity* of *S* that we wish to explain. Using an approach of this sort, an analyst can produce multiple, distinct analyses of the function of an entity such as a nose, heart, or equation.

Functions of equations in conceptual change

The data

I now turn, in earnest, to consider the case of equations and conceptual change in physics. Some data will help to ground the discussion that follows.

In my work on symbol use in physics, I have drawn on a corpus of interviews with five pairs of moderately advanced (third semester) physics students at a university in the United States (Sherin, 1996, 2001, 2006). In these interviews, pairs of students were recorded as they stood at a whiteboard, and solved a sequence of problems. To illustrate my points in this chapter, I will draw primarily on the work of one pair of students, Alan and Bob, as they solved a problem I called the *Shoved Block* problem. In this problem, a heavier and a lighter block are both at rest on a surface. Both blocks are then shoved, so that they start moving across the table with the same velocity. Eventually, because of friction, both blocks come to rest. The question the students have to answer is: Which block travels farther?

In response to this question, students stated one or both of two intuitions. They sometimes said that the larger block would experience a greater frictional force, and thus would travel a shorter distance. Other times they said that the larger block is heavier and thus harder to stop. Alan and Bob began by stating both of these intuitions.

ALAN: And then if the block was heavier, it'd just mean that our friction was greater, and it would slow down quicker.

★ ★ ★

ALAN: Something seems strange about that because if you had like a block coming at you, a big heavy block, and a small lighter block. Two different instances. And you have this big heavier block coming toward you and you want it to slow down, it certainly takes much more force for you to slow down the bigger heavier block than the lighter one.

BOB: Oh wait, that's true!

$$F_f = \mu mg$$

$$mg\mu = mg$$

$$a = g\mu$$

FIGURE 7.1 A reproduction of Alan and Bob's work on the Shoved Block problem.

Thus, Alan and Bob were faced with two intuitions that made conflicting predictions. To resolve this conflict, they began writing equations on the white board. They wrote an expression for the force on the block—the force of friction—then plugged this expression into $F = ma$. What they discovered was that the masses dropped out of the resulting equation (see Figure 7.1). The implication of this, as Alan and Bob correctly ascertained, is that the motion is independent of the mass of the blocks, and thus both blocks travel the same distance. They commented:

BOB: So, I mean the masses drop out.
ALAN: Right, so, actually, they should both take the same.
BOB: Wait a minute. Oh, they both take the same! [surprised tone]. ... So, no matter what the mass is, you're gonna get the same acceleration.

All of the students I interviewed applied the intuition that the heavier block would travel a shorter distance. But the intuition that a heavier block would be hard to stop was more rare, often requiring follow-up questions to nudge students toward this perspective on the situation.

Applying the Cummins framework

I will now attempt to apply Cummins' framework to the case of physics equations. This requires us to identify the element x, the larger system S, and the capacity we are trying to explain. While this might seem straightforward, we will quickly see that all three components pose substantial difficulty.

First, consider the element x, whose functions we are trying to identify. I have been saying that we want to know the functions of "equations." However, that hides quite a bit of ambiguity. For example, we could ask about the function of the equation $F_f = \mu mg$ in Figure 7.1. But what do we mean by this? Do we mean the specific realization of this equation on the medium of the whiteboard? Do we mean the equation as represented in the minds of Alan and Bob? Or do we mean the equation, somehow understood in the abstract?

The next element in Cummins' analysis is the system S. It is clear that the physics equations written by Alan and Bob participate in a complex system, one that includes other representational forms, such as gestures and natural language. It also includes many other types of elements, such as internal representations in the minds of Alan and Bob. Furthermore, there are many different perspectives we could adopt, each leading us to understand this system differently. Thus, to make any sort of progress on a functional analysis, it is clear we are going to have to adopt one perspective, and drastically limit the elements of the system to which we attend.

Here I adopt a straightforward cognitive view, and I will consider a simplified partial system that includes an individual's knowledge—mental representations—and the equations they are using. To further simplify this project, I will focus on only a subset of this knowledge: a knowledge subsystem that exists prior to formal instruction that diSessa calls the sense-of-mechanism (diSessa, 1993) and knowledge that I have called *symbolic forms* (Sherin, 2001). I now briefly discuss each of these in turn.

The sense-of-mechanism consists of elements that diSessa calls phenomeno-logical primitives or just p-prims, for short. These elements are described as *phenomenological* because they are presumed to be abstracted from experiences of interacting in the natural world. They are described as *primitive* because they cannot be broken into smaller components and they constitute the base level of our explanations of physical phenomena. Examples of p-prims include elements that diSessa calls *balancing*, *blocking*, and *force-as-mover*. So, for example, a person might say that an object didn't move because it was *blocked* by a wall.

We can understand Alan and Bob's conflicting intuitions in terms of p-prims. The first prediction, that the heavier block travels a shorter distance, can be seen as a somewhat refined application of diSessa's *force-as-mover* p-prim. The second, that a heavier block is harder to stop, can be considered an application of his *spontaneous resistance* p-prim.

The sense-of-mechanism consists of dozens, perhaps more, of these simple elements. Furthermore, the system is only weakly structured. diSessa describes relationships in the system in terms of weighted *priorities*. These priorities capture how likely an element is to be activated, given a context that includes other active elements. It also captures how likely an element is to remain activated.

In my own work, I have argued that when students use equations, they develop new intuitions about this symbolic "world." For example, Alan and Bob saw a case in which the canceling of the mass from an equation was critical. In the physical world, we can have experiences of the balancing or canceling of influences. But something similar is true with symbol use in physics; we can have an understanding of a sort of canceling that is rooted in experiences with symbols.

In prior work (see details in Sherin, 1996, 2001), I argued that, as a result of activities involving symbol use, students develop a new type of knowledge I call *symbolic forms*. Each symbolic form consists of two elements, a symbol template and a conceptual schema. For example, a symbol template of the form $\square = \square$, in which two expressions are set equal, is associated with the conceptual schema of *balancing*. And a template of the form $\square + \square$ is associated with the conceptual schema *parts-of-a-whole*. Furthermore, I argued that the system of symbolic forms has many of the same properties as the sense-of-mechanism; it consists of a large number of primitive elements in a system that is only weakly structured.

The last component of Cummins' analytic framework is the *capacity* of the system *S* to be explained. Clearly, equations contribute to many capacities, such as the ability to solve problems, make predictions, and derive new relationships. However, what we care about here is how equations contribute to conceptual change; how equations contribute to the ability of the larger system *S* to alter itself. This is a strange sort of capacity; likely it departs somewhat from the sort of capacity that Cummins and other philosophers have generally had in mind.

Identifying the functions

We now have a sketch of one analytic framework in the style of Cummins: We are going to look at the function of physics equations, within a larger system that includes p-prims and symbolic forms, and with a focus on the capacity of the system to experience conceptual change. The purpose of explicitly articulating an analytic framework was to bring some clarity to our discussion, but also to raise some caveats: that we were not clear what we mean by "equation"; we can only focus on small parts of the larger system; and the "capacity" is a strange one, and perhaps stretches Cummins' framework beyond the range for which it was intended.

Equations and changes to the sense-of-mechanism

We are interested in how equations can function to change the subsystems consisting of p-prims and symbolic forms. We start with p-prims: Looking to the work of Alan and Bob for inspiration, what can we say about how the use of equations must have led to changes to p-prims?

One question we can ask is whether there are residual effects on the system of p-prims that would persist, in the absence of symbols. We can only speculate, of course, but there are a number of interesting possibilities. As noted, it was rare for students to draw on the intuition that a heavier block is harder to stop. This suggests that, prior to physics instructions, the *spontaneous resistance* p-prim might have a comparatively low priority for students. Thus, one possibility is that experiences of symbol use, such as the one described above, could increase the priority of *spontaneous resistance*, leading it to be used more frequently in the absence of equations. This is a nice result, since a core and somewhat unintuitive feature of Newton's laws is that they require us to see an object's mass as a kind of intrinsic resistance to changes in motion.

More generally, it seems possible that the priorities of elements in the sense-of-mechanism might be tuned, in many ways, by the use of equations. In cases such as the one above, this could be caused by episodes in which a conflict is resolved. In other cases, it could occur because equation use tends to draw on some intuitive elements and not others. For example, as I have argued elsewhere, elements related to balancing might be employed frequently, while elements related to constraints, such as blocking, will be used only rarely (Sherin, 2006).

Generally speaking, these changes are in the direction that a physics teacher would appreciate, producing more Newtonian predictions and explanations, even in the absence of equations. But we have to be careful in how far we push this line of reasoning. The learning of physics doesn't only or primarily mean learning to reason correctly in the absence of equations; it means learning to reason *with* equations. Note, for example, that by using equations Alan and Bob were able to draw a correct conclusion, even though their system of intuitive reasoning produced inconclusive results.

The point is that it is perhaps not correct to see the system of p-prims as tuned by the use of equations, so that it increasingly approximates Newton's laws. Rather, the sense-of-mechanism only needs to be tuned so that it can do the work that is required of it during activities of symbol use. This is a subtle and important point, with profound implications for how we understand the functions of physics equations in conceptual change. It means that adjustments in the sense-of-mechanism might, in principle, be quite idiosyncratic; the resulting knowledge system might retain the unique fingerprint of equations and their uses.

New knowledge developed: symbolic forms

Finally, we look at the functions of equations in relationship to changes to the system of symbolic forms. Of course, the system of symbolic forms will, like the system of p-prims, be tuned by and for the use of equations. But, more importantly, I argued that symbolic forms are brought into existence by work with equations. Rather than thinking of equations as tools that a person uses, we can think of them as a new world with which a person interacts. This world has its own character and, through symbol use, a physics student can develop intuitions about this world.

If this viewpoint is correct, it has important implications for how we can think about the functions of symbol use in conceptual change. Symbol use doesn't only have to be seen as tuning existing knowledge. It even goes beyond the adding of new elements to existing systems. We can see it as adding an entirely new wing of intuitive knowledge on which physical reasoning can be based.

Conclusions

I propose two simple slogans to capture the functions of equations in conceptual change in physics. The first is *Intuitive knowledge is adapted by and for symbol use.* When I say that intuitive knowledge is tuned *by* symbol use, I mean that the back and forth of work with equations tends to draw on some parts of intuitive knowledge more than others, and thus drives changes to the priorities of those elements. When I say knowledge is tuned *for* symbol use, I mean to emphasize my observation that intuitive knowledge systems will be tuned for the very specific roles that they must play in symbol use. This tuning might be idiosyncratic.

My second slogan is *Physics equations provide a new domain of experience.* The idea is that symbols and their manipulations become a new world about which students can develop intuition. If this is correct, it is a profoundly important function of equations in conceptual change in physics. It is a function that perhaps lies at the root of Feynman's (1965, p. 39) statement that "it is impossible to explain honestly the beauties of the laws of nature in a way that people can feel, without their having some deep understanding in mathematics."

References

Carey, S. (2009). *The origin of concepts.* Oxford: Oxford University Press.

Carruthers, P. (2002). The cognitive functions of language. *Behavioral and Brain Sciences, 25*(6), 657–674. http://doi.org/10.1017/S0140525X02000122.

Clark, A. (1997). *Being there: Putting brain, body, and world together again.* Cambridge, MA: MIT press.

Cummins, R. (1975). Functional analysis. *Journal of Philosophy, 72,* 741–765.

diSessa, A. (1993). Toward an epistemology of physics. *Cognition and Instruction, 10*(2 & 3), 105–225.

Feynman, R. (1965). *The character of physical law.* Cambridge, MA: MIT Press.

Sherin, B. L. (1996). *The symbolic basis of physical intuition: A study of two symbol systems in physics instruction.* Unpublished Doctoral Dissertation. University of California, Berkeley.

Sherin, B. L. (2001). How students understand physics equations. *Cognition and Instruction, 19*(4), 479–541.

Sherin, B. L. (2006). Common sense clarified: The role of intuitive knowledge in physics problem solving. *Journal of Research in Science Teaching, 43*(6), 535–555.

Wright, L. (1973). Functions. *The Philosophical Review, 82*(2), 139–168.

8

THE LANGUAGE PARADOX

Words invite and impede conceptual change

Susan A. Gelman and Jasmine M. DeJesus

Human language is a powerful mechanism for transmitting knowledge across generations. Learning that whales are not fish or that birds have hollow bones requires a conventional language system to express culturally relevant concepts (e.g., "whales," "birds"). In this chapter, we suggest that category labels not only permit us to efficiently communicate concepts to one another, but also reflect assumptions that both *invite* and *impede* conceptual change. Category labels invite conceptual change by referring to concepts that are assumed to link to deeper explanatory content to which experts have access. That is, words refer to placeholder concepts that do not have fixed content and thus can be modified. At the same time, labels impede conceptual change by reifying categories, thereby leading children and adults to underestimate within-category variability, overestimate the barriers between categories, and treat categories as unchanging. We also argue that the power of language to both invite and impede conceptual change has important consequences for science instruction and social cognition.

Our organizing framework is "Psychological Essentialism" (henceforth "essentialism," which is a claim about human representations, not a metaphysical claim about reality). Essentialism is an implicit belief that certain categories comprise not just known features but also indefinitely many less obvious features; that categories are immutable; that category boundaries are absolute; and that there is an inherent "essence" that causes the known and unknown features of the category (Gelman, 2003; Medin, 1989). For example, gender essentialism implies that everyone is either male or female, that gender differences are inborn and immutable, and that gender differences in behavior and abilities largely result from genetic differences between men and women. Different cultures essentialize different categories, but every culture thus far studied essentializes natural kinds (basic-level categories of animals, plants, and natural substances) and at least a subset of social categories (e.g., gender, language) (Moya, Boyd, & Henrich, 2015), and fails to essentialize simple artifact categories (e.g., cups, shoes) (Keil, 1989). Psychological essentialism is a realist position—categories are discovered rather than invented. Importantly, the words of ordinary language (bird, woman, gold) are often assumed to reflect this reality, and thus to "carve up nature at its joints."

As discussed below, we assume a "theory theory" view of conceptual development, in which concepts are part of a network of broader ontologies and explanatory systems. Because conceptual change entails changes in the ontologies and categories that comprise a theory (Carey, 2009), essentialist assumptions about language have direct implications for how children revise their concepts. Although essentialism is theorized to emerge from domain-general principles of cognitive development (Gelman, 2003), not all categories are essentialized (e.g., natural kinds and some social kinds, but not artifacts). Thus, the scope of the current framework is domain-specific.

Words invite conceptual change

At first blush, words may appear to be simply a shorthand for a set of known properties: the word "bird," for example, is equivalent to "animal with wings and feathers that lays eggs and can fly." On such a view, conceptual change takes place by adding or modifying features (e.g., birds have hollow bones; not all birds fly), but the word "bird" itself does not play a role in this process, other than as a tag for a collection of features. Importantly, however, experiments with adults *and* young children reveal that words do not simply summarize known properties. Instead, when hearing a word, people expect it to capture a wealth of properties, both known and unknown. In this sense, a word is a "placeholder" that people expect to be filled in with content supplied by experts—in short, an invitation for conceptual change.

As evidence for this placeholder notion, when children learn a new fact about one instance of a category, they generalize that fact to other instances of the category, even when the items are perceptually dissimilar (Gelman & Markman, 1986). Thus, for example, when children learn that a blackbird feeds its baby mashed-up food and a bat feeds its baby milk, they infer that a flamingo will feed its baby mashed-up food because both the blackbird and the flamingo receive the same label ("bird") and thus are members of the same essentialized category. This result has been replicated with a range of familiar and novel categories with children as young as 15 months of age (Graham, Keates, Vukatana, & Khu, 2012). The important point here is that labels carry an expectation that known features are preliminary and incomplete, and will change as one acquires more facts, either from observation or interactions with experts.

Children view labels not only as inviting additional features, but also as permitting revisions to existing features. They defer to expert labelers to revise their categorization of atypical instances and are open to the idea that what an item *looks like* does not necessarily indicate what it *is*. Thus, for example, when encountering a legless lizard, preschoolers accept an adult's surprising label ("This is a lizard"), and infer that the animal will share properties with other lizards, even though it looks like a snake (Gelman & Markman, 1986; Lane, Harris, Gelman, & Wellman, 2014).

Although language directs children's reasoning on these tasks, children selectively use labels and do not passively take in what they are told. They make use of a label's content, form, and context to judge its relevance for inductive inferences (Booth, 2014; Gelman & Davidson, 2013; Graham & Diesendruck, 2010; Walker, Lombrozo, Legare, & Gopnik, 2014). Categories need not even be labeled in order for children to make rich inferences about category members. For example, children rely on a speaker's language or accent to make a range of social judgments (Kinzler & DeJesus, 2013; Kinzler, Shutts, DeJesus, & Spelke, 2009).

An important corollary to the essentialist framework is that children expect to learn from others (Csibra & Gergely, 2009; Gelman, 2009; Harris & Koenig, 2006), and expect that others will supply critical information to modify their existing concepts (see also Keil, 2012, on the division of cognitive labor). Children actively solicit, evaluate, and incorporate others' testimony with remarkable skill and flexibility, and are sensitive to the speaker's reliability, certainty, intelligence, cultural background, and personality (e.g., Kinzler, Corriveau, & Harris, 2011).

Words impede conceptual change

The very evidence that labels invite conceptual change also illustrates that labels can be barriers to further revision. Recall that essentialism is the foundation for children's inference that labels link to, as yet unknown, properties and that appearances may be deceiving. This essentialist structure also leads people to assume that categories are fixed and unchanging, to underestimate within-category variability, and to overestimate the barriers between categories (Gelman, 2003). Because these assumptions conflict with more scientifically accurate representations of categories (Leslie, 2013), they can undermine learning scientific concepts.

Labels may reify categories, thereby encouraging children and adults to treat categories as immutable, rather than open to revision. For instance, children (appropriately) reject the possibility that a raccoon could become a skunk, even if the raccoon were physically transformed by dying its fur or installing a smelly sac (Keil, 1989). However, they also (inappropriately) reject the possibility that a girl could develop expertise in "boy" activities if provided with sufficient environmental experience (Taylor, Rhodes, & Gelman, 2009). Labels also lead children to treat boundaries between categories as objectively correct and reject alternative proposals to classify items (Diesendruck, Goldfein-Elbaz, Rhodes, Gelman, & Neumark, 2013). For example, children report that it is wrong for a community to consider a dog and a cat the same kind of animal, or a boy and a girl the same kind of person. Children also have difficulty appreciating within-category variability, focusing instead on within-category similarities (Rhodes, Brickman, & Gelman, 2008). Thus, unless primed to consider within-category variability, children do not appreciate that a more diverse sample of instances of a category (e.g., a robin and a penguin) provides stronger evidence for making inferences about another category member than a more homogeneous sample (e.g., two robins).

Not all linguistic constructions trigger essentialism. The expectation that categories will have fixed features is specifically linked to the use of common noun labels, applying even to novel categories. For instance, in one study, 5- to 7-year-olds heard about individuals who were described either with a noun label (e.g., "carrot-eater") or a verbal predicate (e.g., a person who "eats carrots whenever she can"; Gelman & Heyman, 1999). Despite the subtlety of the linguistic distinction, children viewed behaviors framed with a noun label as more stable over time and across situations (e.g., even when the individual's family opposed that behavior) compared to behaviors framed with a verbal predicate.

A further way that essentialist assumptions may impede conceptual change is via generics, such as "Birds lay eggs." Generics are generally true, yet ignore important exceptions; for example, "birds lay eggs" is considered true even though most birds actually cannot lay eggs (e.g., male birds and baby birds). Generics are frequent in child-directed speech, acquired early in childhood, and appear to be a default mode of generalizing (Leslie & Gelman, 2012). When children hear generics about a novel category, they are more likely to treat that category in essentialist ways (Gelman, Ware, & Kleinberg, 2010; Rhodes, Leslie, & Tworek, 2012). These observations suggest another way that language encourages children to treat categories as relatively unvarying and thus overlook relevant counterevidence to induce conceptual change.

Implications for conceptual change in science and social reasoning

The proposal that labels invite and impede conceptual change has important implications for children's learning of science and reasoning about the social world. In this section, we briefly sketch out some of these implications.

In one key respect, psychological essentialism mirrors the scientific enterprise—both are guided by the assumption that the world has an underlying structure that will be further specified through the process of discovery. Just as children have the intuition that some unknown properties make a raccoon a raccoon and not a skunk, the nature of scientific inquiry assumes that there are unknown truths in the world that are the job of scientists to discover. If words are considered placeholders that can be filled in with expert knowledge, then category labels may invite conceptual change in scientific domains by highlighting critical gaps in knowledge that are ripe for new discoveries. Even a preschooler can appreciate that raccoons may share internal commonalities, and this appreciation may both motivate deeper investigations and permit children to learn from scientific instruction (Gelman, 2003).

However, essentialist commitments may also present unique obstacles for understanding and accepting scientific evidence (Gelman & Rhodes, 2012). This is perhaps most evident when considering evolutionary theory, a framework that requires conceptual change from children's initial creationist assumptions (Evans, 2008). Evolutionary theory entails moving from a view of species as immutable, relatively unvarying, and with sharp taxonomic boundaries (consistent with essentialism) to a view of species as evolving over time, importantly variable, and having probabilistic, permeable boundaries (none of which correspond to essentialism). In other words, though the intuition that category members share key properties promotes early learning about individual categories, this belief also serves as a barrier to understanding Darwinian evolution (Emmons & Kelemen, 2015). Moreover, such obstacles are broader than those blocking conceptual change in the species concept. Conceptual change in science typically requires ontological change (Carey, 2009): reconceptualizing concepts such as force or electricity as emergent processes rather than material substances (Chi, 2005); replacing deterministic explanations with more probabilistic explanations (Strevens, 2000); and replacing single inherent causes with structural or systemic causes (Cimpian & Salomon, 2014). In these respects, labels may restrict learning, given the ontological assumptions that they entail: that labels refer to "things" rather than processes, that categories have discrete boundaries rather than probabilistic distributions; and that causes are inherent in the objects of inquiry rather than the outcome of lawlike interactions.

In addition to its implications for scientific reasoning, essentialism has important consequences for social reasoning. Thinking about categories as fixed may contribute to the persistence of stereotypes. If children and adults believe that categories are unchanging and that category members are inherently alike, then labeling an individual as a member of a social group can promote stereotypic inferences (Waxman, 2010). As noted earlier, labeling an individual as male or female can lead to a variety of assumptions about that person's beliefs and abilities, regardless of that person's actual beliefs or abilities, or whether that person even identifies with that label.

Essentialist reasoning can also shape self-concepts. People with a fixed mindset about their abilities ("entity" theorists) tend to believe that their abilities cannot change and consequently are less likely to persist after a setback, as compared to people with an "incremental" mindset who believe that their abilities can improve with effort (Dweck, 2006). Language plays a critical role in shaping these beliefs. Children who heard more praise labeling their abilities ("you're so smart") at age 14–38 months were more likely to hold a fixed mindset at age 7–8 compared to children praised for their effort ("you must have tried hard") (Gunderson, Gripshover, Romero, Dweck, Goldin-Meadow, & Levine, 2013). Similarly, children were less likely to persist in a drawing task after a setback if they had previously received feedback labeling them as "a good drawer" rather than feedback emphasizing their effort ("you did a good job drawing") (Cimpian, Arce, Markman, & Dweck, 2007). These findings highlight the power of labels to guide self-relevant beliefs and motivations.

Conclusions

We have proposed that category labels both invite and impede conceptual change, and that these effects stem from essentialist assumptions. On the one hand, essentialism is a placeholder notion, in which members of a category share non-obvious features and a causal "essence." This perspective motivates the discovery of new and unexpected aspects of categories. On the other hand, essentialism promotes viewing categories as immutable and having sharp boundaries. This perspective may stand in the way of considering competing views, and impede conceptual changes that require alternative ontological frameworks (e.g., evolutionary models of species; causes that are systemic rather than inherent in an individual). An important question for future research is how programs may build on these observations to engage children in conceptual change. If labels have the power to undermine conceptual change, understanding the contexts in which that undermining occurs is critical when developing education programs and interventions.

References

Booth, A. E. (2014). Conceptually coherent categories support label-based inductive generalization in preschoolers. *Journal of Experimental Child Psychology*, *123*, 1–14.

Carey, S. (2009). *The origin of concepts*. New York: Oxford University Press.

Chi, M. T. H. (2005). Commonsense conceptions of emergent processes: Why some misconceptions are robust. *Journal of the Learning Sciences, 14*, 161–199.

Cimpian, A., & Salomon, E. (2014). The inherence heuristic: An intuitive means of making sense of the world, and a potential precursor to psychological essentialism. *Behavioral and Brain Sciences*, *37*(5), 461–480.

Cimpian, A., Arce, H. M. C., Markman, E. M., & Dweck, C. S. (2007). Subtle linguistic cues affect children's motivation. *Psychological Science*, *18*(4), 314–316.

Csibra, G., & Gergely, G. (2009). Natural pedagogy. *Trends in Cognitive Sciences*, *13*(4), 148–153.

Diesendruck, G., Goldfein-Elbaz, R., Rhodes, M., Gelman, S., & Neumark, N. (2013). Cross-cultural differences in children's beliefs about the objectivity of social categories. *Child Development, 84*(6), 1906–1917.

Dweck, C. S. (2006). *Mindset: The new psychology of success*. New York: Random House.

Emmons, N. A., & Kelemen, D. A. (2015). Young children's acceptance of within-species variation: Implications for essentialism and teaching evolution. *Journal of Experimental Child Psychology, 139*, 148–160.

Evans, E. M. (2008). Conceptual change and evolutionary biology: A developmental analysis. *International handbook of research on conceptual change* (pp. 263–294). London: Routledge.

Gelman, S. A. (2003). *The essential child: Origins of essentialism in everyday thought.* New York: Oxford University Press.

Gelman, S. A. (2009). Learning from others: Children's construction of concepts. *Annual Review of Psychology, 60,* 115–140.

Gelman, S. A., & Davidson, N. S. (2013). Conceptual influences on category-based induction. *Cognitive Psychology, 66,* 327–353.

Gelman, S. A., & Heyman, G. D. (1999). Carrot-eaters and creature-believers: The effects of lexicalization on children's inferences about social categories. *Psychological Science, 10*(6), 489–493.

Gelman, S. A., & Markman, E. M. (1986). Categories and induction in young children. *Cognition, 23*(3), 183–209.

Gelman, S. A., & Rhodes, M. (2012). 'Two-thousand years of stasis': How psychological essentialism impedes evolutionary understanding. In K. S. Rosengren, S. Brem, E. M. Evans, & G. Sinatra (Eds.), *Evolution challenges: Integrating research and practice in teaching and learning about evolution* (pp. 3–21). New York: Oxford University Press.

Gelman, S. A., Ware, E. A., & Kleinberg, F. (2010). Effects of generic language on category content and structure. *Cognitive Psychology, 61*(3), 273–301.

Graham, S. A., & Diesendruck, G. (2010). Fifteen-month-old infants attend to shape over other perceptual properties in an induction task. *Cognitive Development, 25*(2), 111–123.

Graham, S. A., Keates, J., Vukatana, E., & Khu, M. (2012). Distinct labels attenuate 15-month-olds? Attention to shape in an inductive inference task. *Frontiers in Psychology, 3*(586), 1–8.

Gunderson, E. A., Gripshover, S. J., Romero, C., Dweck, C. S., Goldin-Meadow, S., & Levine, S. C. (2013). Parent praise to 1-to 3-year-olds predicts children's motivational frameworks 5 years later. *Child Development, 84*(5), 1526–1541.

Harris, P. L., & Koenig, M. A. (2006). Trust in testimony: How children learn about science and religion. *Child Development, 77*(3), 505–524.

Keil, F. C. (1989). *Concepts, kinds, and cognitive development.* Cambridge, MA: MIT Press.

Keil, F. C. (2012). Running on empty? How folk science gets by with less. *Current Directions in Psychological Science, 21*(5), 329–334.

Kinzler, K. D., Corriveau, K. H., & Harris, P. L. (2011). Children's selective trust in native-accented speakers. *Developmental Science, 14*(1), 106–111.

Kinzler, K. D., & DeJesus, J. M. (2013). Children's sociolinguistic evaluations of nice foreigners and mean Americans. *Developmental Psychology, 49*(4), 655–664.

Kinzler, K. D., Shutts, K., DeJesus, J., & Spelke, E. S. (2009). Accent trumps race in guiding children's social preferences. *Social Cognition, 27*(4), 623–634.

Lane, J. D., Harris, P. L., Gelman, S. A., & Wellman, H. M. (2014). More than meets the eye: Young children's trust in claims that defy their perceptions. *Developmental Psychology, 50*(3), 865–871.

Leslie, S. (2013). Essence and natural kinds: When science meets preschooler intuition. *Oxford Studies in Epistemology, 4,* 108–165.

Leslie, S., & Gelman, S. A. (2012). Quantified statements are recalled as generics: Evidence from preschool children and adults. *Cognitive Psychology, 64*(3), 186–214.

Medin, D. L. (1989). Concepts and conceptual structure. *American Psychologist, 44*(12), 1469.

Moya, C., Boyd, R., & Henrich, J. (2015). Reasoning about cultural and genetic transmission: Developmental and cross-cultural evidence from Peru, Fiji, and the United States on how people make inferences about trait transmission. *Topics in Cognitive Science, 7*(4), 595–610.

Rhodes, M., Brickman, D., & Gelman, S. A. (2008). Sample diversity and premise typicality in inductive reasoning: Evidence for developmental change. *Cognition, 108*(2), 543–556.

Rhodes, M., Leslie, S., & Tworek, C. M. (2012). Cultural transmission of social essentialism. *Proceedings of the National Academy of Sciences, 109*(34), 13526–13531.

Strevens, M. (2000). The essentialist aspect of naïve theories. *Cognition, 74,* 149–175.

Taylor, M. G., Rhodes, M., & Gelman, S. A. (2009). Boys will be boys; cows will be cows: Children's essentialist reasoning about gender categories and animal species. *Child Development, 80*(2), 461–481.

Walker, C. M., Lombrozo, T., Legare, C. H., & Gopnik, A. (2014). Explaining prompts children to privilege inductively rich properties. *Cognition, 133*(2), 343–357.

Waxman, S. R. (2010). Names will never hurt me? Naming and the development of racial and gender categories in preschool-aged children. *European Journal of Social Psychology, 40*(4), 593–610.

9

GESTURE'S ROLE IN REFLECTING AND FOSTERING CONCEPTUAL CHANGE

Miriam A. Novack, Eliza L. Congdon, Elizabeth M. Wakefield, and Susan Goldin-Meadow

Conceptual change is a powerful process by which people make a qualitative shift in the way they understand a concept. Often researchers consider a child's verbal descriptions when trying to understand the process of conceptual change. In this chapter, we step back from explicit verbal language to argue that another representational format—the spontaneous gestures we produce when we talk—can offer a unique perspective on the *process* of conceptual change. We first describe how gesture[1] can be an indicator of when a child will undergo a shift in conceptual understanding. We then describe how the act of producing gesture, or even seeing gesture, can play a direct role in enhancing and expediting conceptual change by helping the learner to integrate new ideas into their pre-existing conceptual knowledge. We end by briefly discussing some of the mechanisms through which gesture may have its effects, arguing that gesture's influence resides not in a single one of its properties, but in the unique combination of its intrinsic, defining features.

Gesture indexes moments of conceptual change

One of the unique features of gesture is that it happens with the hands, allowing individuals to simultaneously express one idea in their speech and a separate idea in their gesture, so called "gesture–speech mismatches" (Goldin-Meadow, 2003). A mismatch occurs when gesture conveys information that is different from, but has the potential to be integrated with, the information conveyed in the speech it accompanies (e.g., twirling one's hands upward while saying, "he walked up the stairs" to represent a *spiral* staircase). Note that cases where the information in gesture and speech cannot be integrated are considered errors, not mismatches (e.g., saying "left" while pointing to the right). In most cases, when a novice has produced a mismatch, the speaker will not have actually integrated the information in gesture with the information in speech, although the potential to do so is there. Indeed, that potential may be part of the impetus for change. Research shows that when a speaker produces gesture–speech mismatches on a task, the learner is on the verge of conceptual change with respect to that task (Church & Goldin-Meadow, 1986). In other words, mismatches between speech and gesture precede and predict a learner's moment of insight (Goldin-Meadow, 2011).

One example of how gesture predicts children's developing understanding can be found in the classic Piagetian liquid conservation task. If a child who does not yet understand the principle of conservation is asked *why* he believes that the water poured from a tall thin container into a short narrow container is now a different amount, the child may respond with the explanation, "Because this one [the taller container] is bigger than this one [the shorter container]," showing that he is focused on only one dimension—the height of the containers. But examining the child's gesture often reveals that the child knows more than he can say. In a seminal study, Church and Goldin-Meadow (1986) coded the meaning expressed in these gestures, and found that some children produced speech-gesture mismatches. For example, one child used a C-handshape to illustrate the *widths* of the tall and short containers while talking exclusively about the *heights* of the containers. Although this child expressed misunderstanding about the concept of conservation in his speech, his mismatching gesture and speech indicated that he was ready to learn conservation and, indeed, did learn when provided with instruction. In general, children who produce gesture–speech mismatches while explaining a task are particularly likely to benefit from instruction on that task, suggesting that they were ready to learn. In this case, gesture serves as a nonverbal marker for identifying children who are on the brink of understanding this fundamental physical concept.

Gesture also has been found to serve as a marker of change in the domain of mathematical equivalence, where children must understand that two sides of a mathematical equation are equal to each other. Perry, Church, and Goldin-Meadow (1988) found that children would give incorrect strategies in speech, but correct strategies in gesture, while explaining their reasoning to problems such as $3 + 4 + 5 = \_\_ + 5$. For example, a child gave 12 as the answer to the previous problem and said, "I added the 3, 4, and 5, and got 12"— a solution that reveals the misconception that an equals sign means *add up the numbers to the left of the equals sign*. However, while explaining this incorrect strategy in speech, that same child pointed to the 3 and the 4, indicating a different, correct strategy for solving the problem, one that would allow her to *group* the first two addends to arrive at the correct solution (because the remaining numbers on each side of the problem are equal addends).[2] Children producing gesture–speech mismatches were again more likely to profit from instruction than children producing gesture–speech matches, suggesting that their gestures served as an indicator that these children were on the brink of conceptual change.

Gesture promotes conceptual change

The work reviewed thus far suggests that spontaneous gesture can serve as an index of a child's readiness to learn a new idea or concept. Yet gesture does more than just index that a child is on the verge of conceptual change—the act of producing gesture is causally linked to the process of conceptual change itself.

Studies in which gesture is explicitly encouraged, rather than fortuitously observed, offer some evidence for this claim. For example, Broaders, Cook, Mitchell, and Goldin-Meadow (2007) manipulated the rate of children's gesture production in a math problem-solving paradigm. At the beginning of the experimental procedure, all children were asked to solve and explain their answers to six mathematical equivalence problems (e.g., $6 + 3 + 8 = \_\_ + 8$) to establish a baseline rate of spontaneous gesture production. Then, children were asked to solve and explain six more problems, but, this time, one group of children was told to keep their hands still, one group was told to gesture, and the final group was not told anything specific about hand movements. Although participants in all three groups produced the same number of different problem-solving strategies in speech after the manipulations, children in the "told to gesture" group produced significantly more problem-solving strategies in gesture than the other two groups—strategies that they had not produced during baseline and that, for the most part, were correct. Moreover, the children who had begun producing new ideas in gesture when told to move their hands were more likely to learn when subsequently given equivalence instruction. These effects suggest that being told to gesture can lead to increased rates of gesture–speech mismatches, which, in turn, lead to learning.

In other work, researchers have facilitated conceptual change by asking children to produce *specific* mismatching gestures. For example, in one study, children were taught to produce a grouping gesture (a *v-point* to the first two addends on the left-hand side of the equation, followed by a *one-finger point* to the blank) while saying the equalizer strategy aloud ("I want to make one side equal to the other side") (Goldin-Meadow, Cook, & Mitchell, 2009). In the equation, $4 + 2 + 7 = \_\_ + 7$, the children would make a *v-point* gesture to the 4 and the 2, then a single point to the blank. A second group was taught the same mismatching speech and gesture, but were taught to produce the grouping gesture under the incorrect grouping addends (2 and 7 in this example). A third group was taught only to reproduce the spoken equalizer strategy. Children who produced the correct gesture and mismatching speech learned significantly more from a math lesson than children who did not produce any gesture. This result makes it clear that being instructed to produce mismatching gesture and speech promotes conceptual change. Surprisingly, children who produced the *grouping* gesture but pointed it at two incorrect numbers also learned more from the math lesson than children in the speech alone condition, although they learned less than children in the fully correct gesture condition. This pattern suggests that gesture did more than just draw the learner's attention to particular numbers since, in this condition, the learner's attention was drawn to the wrong two numbers. The children also gleaned the idea of grouping two numbers from the gestures they produced, as evidenced by the fact that they (and the children in the fully correct gesture group) incorporated the grouping strategy into their spoken explanations after training. The children had learned and internalized a new problem-solving strategy that they had only ever produced in gesture.

Gestures are not the only type of movement commonly produced in instructional settings. Actions on representational objects, such as mathematical manipulatives, are often used to help children gain insight into difficult problems. Yet recent work has demonstrated that children who learned mismatching strategies through speech and gesture learn more flexibly than children who learned mismatching strategies through speech and actions-on-objects. In this study, Novack, Congdon, Hemani-Lopez, and Goldin-Meadow (2014) taught children to produce either a grouping gesture (*v-point to the first two addends followed by a point to the blank*) or a grouping action (*picking up number tiles from the first two addends and holding them in the blank*). Children in both groups initially learned how to solve problems, but only children in the gesture group were able to flexibly transfer that understanding to novel problem contexts and solve problems of a different format than they had seen in training. Thus, in this case, learning through mismatching speech and actions-on-objects led to shallow understanding, whereas learning through mismatching speech and gesture supported deep conceptual change that could be flexibly applied and generalized.

Mechanisms of gesture

We have shown that gesture can reflect the process of conceptual change. We also reviewed evidence suggesting that gesture can play a causal role in bringing conceptual change about—giving learners new ideas. How does gesture play a role in conceptual change? We argue that gesture promotes conceptual change, not through a single property or mechanistic pathway, but rather through a combination of properties that it naturally brings together. To conclude this chapter, we briefly discuss three of these properties: gesture's relation to spoken language, its reliance on the manual modality (and thus engagement of the manual motor system), and its status as a representational symbol. Although this list of gesture's properties is not all-inclusive, it does emphasize how gesture's different facets can combine to promote conceptual change.

First, because gesture and speech occur in two different modalities, gesturing allows for the *simultaneous* expression of two ideas (i.e., mismatches). Asking children to conceptually activate two pieces of information at the same time, in this case, through speech and gesture, has been found to have positive effects on learning (Alibali & Goldin-Meadow, 1993). This effect may occur, in part, by helping learners activate and integrate multiple hypotheses while in a state of conceptual uncertainty. Indeed, children learn more from instruction that contains two different strategies, one in speech and the other in gesture, than from instruction containing the same two strategies in speech (Singer & Goldin-Meadow, 2005). Critically, the timing of the bimodal information is important—children learn best when the two different strategies are presented simultaneously (one in speech *at the same as* the other in gesture), and not when the two strategies are presented sequentially (one in speech *followed by* the other in gesture, Congdon et al., 2017).

Another important property of gesture may be its specific reliance on the manual modality. Although it is possible to simultaneously express multiple ideas through other modalities (e.g., visual/pictorial information can be combined with auditory/verbal information, see Mayer, 2005), these non–body-based modalities may fall short, relative to gesture. Indeed, we know that gesture enhances learning even if it offers no new information beyond speech, but presents the same information in a different format. For example, children taught to produce the same strategy in gesture and speech during math instruction retained what they learned longer than children taught to produce the strategy only in speech (Cook, Mitchell, & Goldin-Meadow, 2008). As another example, children taught to produce the same information in gesture and speech learned more about a language concept than children taught to produce the information only in speech (Wakefield & James, 2015). Even gestures produced without any speech at all can have positive effects on thinking and learning (e.g., Brooks & Goldin-Meadow, 2016; Cook et al., 2008). Taken together, these findings suggest a second mechanism through which gesture may be able to support learning and conceptual change—its capacity to engage the manual motor system. Neural evidence from previous work in the action learning literature suggests a long-lasting benefit of learning through engaging the manual motor system (James & Swain, 2011), and recent work shows a similar effect after information has been learned through gesture (Wakefield, Congdon, Novack, Goldin-Meadow, & James, under review).

Finally, although engaging the manual motor system clearly is important, not *all* manual motor activity is useful for learning. For example, meaningful gesture facilitates learning better than meaningless gesture-like hand movements (Brooks & Goldin-Meadow, 2016), and supports transfer better than hand actions on objects (Novack et al., 2014). Thus, a third important feature of gesture, its status as a *representational* action, is likely to be critical in gesture's success as a tool for conceptual change (Novack & Goldin-Meadow, 2017). As representational action, gesture differs from other types of actions (such as object-directed actions) in that it occurs in the air, *off* objects, and therefore transiently represents or references ideas, rather than creating change in the physical world. Object-directed actions can cause learners to focus on irrelevant physical features of objects or to be distracted by the alternative functions of the objects (Uttal, O'Doherty, Newland, Hand, & DeLoache, 2009). Gestures, by contrast, are not beholden to the affordances of any single object or set of objects, but instead provide an abstract representation that highlights selected features of a concept or idea. This physical and metaphorical "distance" from physical objects and real-world actions might allow learners to form a flexible representation of a new idea that is broadly applicable to novel contexts and situations. As gestures are abstracted representations, they may even evoke schematic knowledge structures, similar to Jean Mandler's (2004) *image schemas*, schematic conceptualizations that exist at a level between sensorimotor functions and language, and that help individuals organize perceptual information into abstract concepts.

Conclusion

We have shown that gesture is a powerful non-verbal cue that promotes and reflects conceptual change. Like language itself, gesture provides a window into a learner's thinking and provides an avenue through which new information can infiltrate the learner's cognitive system. But despite its power to affect thinking and learning, gesture is comparatively understudied and its influence is often ignored in instructional settings. Here we emphasize the importance of taking gesture and its relation to spoken language into account when researching conceptual change and when developing learning interventions or instructional techniques. We have proposed mechanisms that may help explain *why* gesture is such a powerful learning tool, paving the way for a better understanding of when and how to harness it for learning. We suggest that gesture may be most useful in promoting conceptual change not because of any single feature it possesses, but because it brings together a number of powerful mechanisms within a single process. In other words, although it is possible for other cues to engage the manual motor system, to occur at the same time as speech, or to serve as representational symbols, no single tool performs *all* of these functions and at the same time. Gesture's power may stem from a unique combination of properties that collaborate to form a useful tool for conceptual change.

Acknowledgment

This work was supported by the National Institutes of Health Grant R01-HD047450 and by the National Science Foundation Grant BCS-0925595 to S. Goldin-Meadow; the National Science Foundation Grant SBE-0541957 (Spatial Intelligence and Learning Center, S. Goldin-Meadow is a co-principal investigator); a grant from the Institute of Education Sciences, U.S. Department of Education (R305 B090025) to the University of Chicago in support of E. Congdon and M. Novack; and National Science Foundation grant BCS-1422224 to Goldin-Meadow in support of Wakefield.

Notes

1 Here, 'gesture' refers to iconic, metaphoric and deictic gestures as defined by McNeill (1992).
2 The add-to-equal-sign strategy expressed in speech seems, on the surface, to be incompatible with the grouping strategy expressed in gesture. However, the strategy in

speech reveals that the child has, at some level, recognized that the equal sign divides the problem into two parts, an insight that has the potential to be integrated with the grouping strategy expressed in speech.

References

Alibali, M. W., & Goldin-Meadow, S. (1993). Gesture-speech mismatch and mechanisms of learning: What the hands reveal about a child's state of mind. *Cognitive Psychology, 25*, 468–523.

Broaders, S. C., Cook, S. W., Mitchell, Z., & Goldin-Meadow, S. (2007). Making children gesture brings out implicit knowledge and leads to learning. *Journal of Experimental Psychology, 136*, 539–550. doi:10.1037/0096-3445.136.4.539.

Brooks, N., & Goldin-Meadow, S. (2016). Moving to learn: How guiding the hands can set the stage for learning. *Cognitive Science, 40*(7), 1831–1849. doi:10.1111/cogs.12292.

Church, R. B., & Goldin-Meadow, S. (1986). The mismatch between gesture and speech as an index on transitional knowledge. *Cognition, 23*, 43–71. doi: 10.1016/0010-0277(86)90053-3.

Congdon, E. L., Novack, M. A., Brooks, N. B., Hemani-Lopez, N., O'Keefe, L., & Goldin-Meadow, S. (2017). Better together: Simultaneous presentation of speech and gesture in math instruction supports generalization and retention. *Learning and Instruction 50*, 65–74. http://dx.doi.org/10.1016/j.learninstruc.2017.03.005.

Cook, S. W., Mitchell, Z., & Goldin-Meadow, S. (2008). Gesturing makes learning last. *Cognition, 106*, 1047–1058. doi:10.1016/j.cognition.2007.04.010.

Goldin-Meadow, S. (2003). *Hearing gesture: How our hands help us think*. Cambridge, MA: Belknap Press of Harvard University Press.

Goldin-Meadow, S. (2011). Learning through gesture. *WIREs: Cognitive Science, 2*, 595–607. doi:10.1002/wcs.132.

Goldin-Meadow, S., Cook, S. W., & Mitchell, Z. A. (2009) Gesturing gives children new ideas about math. *Psychological Science, 20*, 267–272. doi:10.1111/j.1467-9280.2009.02297.x.

James, K. H., & Swain, S. N. (2011). Only self-generated actions create sensory-motor systems in the developing brain. *Developmental Science, 14*, 673–687. doi:10.1111/j.1467-7687.2010.01011.x.

Mandler, J. M. (2004). *The Foundations of the mind: Origins of conceptual thought*. New York: Oxford University Press.

Mayer, R. E. (2005). Cognitive theory of multimedia learning. In R. E. Mayer (Ed.), *The Cambridge handbook of multimedia learning* (pp. 40–72). New York: Cambridge University Press.

McNeill, D. (1992). *Hand and mind: What gestures reveal about thought*. Chicago, IL: The University of Chicago Press.

Novack, M. A., Congdon, E. L., Hemani-Lopez, N., & Goldin-Meadow, S. (2014). From action to abstraction: Using the hands to learn math. *Psychological Science, 25*, 903–910. doi:10.1177/0956797613518351.

Novack, M. A., & Goldin-Meadow, S. (2017). Gesture as Representational Action: A paper about function. *Psychonomic Bulletin and Review, 24*(3), 652–665. doi:10.3758/s13423-016-1145-z.

Perry, M., Church, R. B., & Goldin-Meadow, S. (1988). Transitional knowledge in the acquisition of concepts. *Cognitive Development, 3*, 359–400. doi:10.1016/0885–2014(88)90021-4.

Singer, M. A., & Goldin-Meadow, S. (2005). Children learn when their teacher's gestures and speech differ. *Psychological Science, 16*, 85–89.

Uttal, D. H., O'Doherty, K., Newland, R., Hand, L. L., & DeLoache, J. (2009). Dual representation and the linking of concrete and symbolic representations. *Child Development Perspectives, 3*(3), 156–159. doi:10.1111/j.1750–8606.2009.00097.x.

Wakefield, E. M., Congdon, E., Novack, M., Goldin-Meadow, S., & James, K. H. (under review). Learning math through your hands: The neural effects of gesture-based instruction in 8-year-old children.

Wakefield, E. M., & James, K. H. (2015). Effects of learning with gesture on children's understanding of a new language concept. *Developmental Psychology, 5,* 1105–1114. doi: 10.1037/a0039471.

10

IMPLICIT CONCEPTUAL DYNAMICS AND STUDENTS' EXPLANATORY MODEL DEVELOPMENT IN SCIENCE

David E. Brown

The work I discuss here is complementary to work done focusing on conceptual metaphor and learning in science (e.g., Amin, 2009, 2015; Dreyfus, Gupta, & Redish, 2015; Jeppsson, Haglund, & Amin, 2015). Both explore unconscious, implicit image schemas and how they influence conscious thinking and reasoning. Researchers focusing on conceptual metaphor look at the interaction of these implicit image schemas with conscious, linguistically articulated ideas. In my work I focus attention more on conscious *imagistic* reasoning, with a recognition of the importance of linguistic resources (Cheng & Brown, 2010). Amin (2009, 2015) has used the term "construal" to indicate the interplay of conscious language-based resources with implicit conceptual metaphors in interpreting the meaning of linguistic expressions of both students and experts. To consideration of these "linguistic construals" I would like to add consideration of "imagistic construals" as students make meaning of conscious images of phenomena or models through connection with implicit image schemas.

Recently I have written about the need to consider students' conceptions as dynamically emergent structures rather than as more static, mechanistic structures. This general dynamic view has a number of advantages over the intuitively seductive and linguistically supported mechanistic view of students' conceptions (Brown, 2014; Brown & Hammer, 2013), but it remains a view of the general nature of students' ideas rather than an exploration of specific student ideas. Here I will discuss an interpretive stance on students' specific conceptions, which focuses on conscious ideas, implicit ideas, and their interplay.

Exploring conscious and implicit ideas

In the early 1990s, I conducted some interviews with high school students, exploring their ideas of electricity and simple circuits. Much prior work had been conducted on students' conceptions concerning electrical circuits (e.g., Closset, 1983; Duit, 1985; Shipstone, 1988). In virtually all of this work, an assumption was made that students brought with them to instruction some version of a model involving the movement of an invisible substance through the wires, light bulbs, or other circuit components. I viewed my interviews as an attempt to explore these models. However, one of the students, "Tanya," expressed ideas that were very difficult to categorize under one of these models. I saw the need for a framework for interpreting students' conceptions that focused attention on multiple dimensions of students' ideas, such as verbal-symbolic or imagistic; conscious or intuitive; and domain specific or domain general (Brown, 1993). In this section I will articulate this framework and discuss how it has been used in cases of interpreting students' conceptions.

Tanya had the following response to a question about whether a bulb would light in a simple circuit (Figure 10.1a):

INTERVIEWER (I): What then happens at the bulb?

TANYA (T): Certain, like maybe the charges certain things happen to different wires and then they, the charges that they make up or, or you know when you put them together and it does a certain thing and it makes the light bulb turn on.

I: Ok.

T: Kinda.

I: Ok, so you're still saying that the light bulb turns on. Could you say a little bit more about why the light bulb lights?

T: Cause of the currencies that are coming through the wire and the charges that they produce and make that causes the light bulb to turn on.

I had introduced the term "current," but Tanya often changed this to the term "currency." The final student quote above seems most appropriately paraphrased as follows (changes or additions italicized): "Cause of the *influences* that are coming through the wire and the *energy (agency) that creates* that causes the light bulb to turn on." For Tanya, there seems to be an agent (the battery), a patient (the bulb),

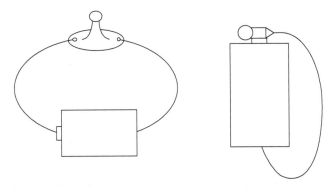

FIGURE 10.1 Simple circuits: (a) Bulb in bulb holder (b) Bulb alone.

an instrument (wires), and the agent influences the patient using the instrument. Attempts at getting her to articulate a more coherent model failed rather strikingly. For example, consider the following transcript segment asking whether the bulb would light in the configuration shown in Figure 10.1b:

T: I'd say it wouldn't turn on … because the tip would have to be against it somehow in order for it to, cause the tip still, although maybe it doesn't have as much energy down in the tip it still puts enough out that you'd have to use it and it's not enough maybe with this, with just this side of the light bulb.

   [We try it and the bulb lights. She is visibly surprised and impressed by the result. I include a time stamp below to show the passage of time.]

00:00 T: Oh no, it did turn on. Wrong again … I'm thinking that no matter what position the bulb is in and as long as the side of the bulb is touching the battery it's gonna come on if your wires are in the same place; except unless its upside down or something.

★ ★ ★

00:41 T: [spontaneously mentions configuration as lighting]

★ ★ ★

01:54 T: [About this configuration] No, that was what we were gonna try … I would say that it wouldn't turn on because the tip's not touching the battery.

Her teacher described her as a student with a particularly good memory. My interpretation of her striking inability to remember these surprising and salient experiences even minutes later is that, lacking the ability to relate the experiences to a conscious model, she was at the mercy of her intuitive ideas (implicit models and core intuitions) which dynamically reorganized (Brown, 2014) and eroded her memory of the experiences.

Interpretive framework

Motivated by my experiences with Tanya and other students, I have developed an interpretive framework that attempts to make explicit multiple dimensions of students' conceptual resources (Hammer, 2000). In addition to focusing the analyst on these multiple dimensions, the framework also enables articulation of interactions among the multiple dimensions.

Conscious resources

In analyzing interviews or other interactions with students, an assumption of the framework is that they are always consciously thinking about something. For example, if they were asked what they think "electricity" means, we can assume they are thinking about their interpretation of this term, especially if they use this term and relate it to other terms. In this case, they are drawing on their *verbal-symbolic knowledge* such as learned generalizations, definitions, technical vocabulary, equations, or other formalisms (Nathan, 2012). Alternatively, if they are asked whether they think a bulb would light when shown a configuration of batteries, bulbs, and wires, we can assume a *conscious image of a specific situation*. In some cases (Tanya was not one of these) the student will give evidence of thinking about unseen elements interacting to give rise to observable phenomena, such as charges or current moving in the wires—this is evidence that the student is drawing on a *conscious explanatory model*. Of course the student's thinking may involve two of these or even all three-verbal-symbolic knowledge, a conscious model of a specific situation, and a conscious explanatory model.

Intuitive resources

Another assumption of the framework is that the student will be drawing on unconscious, intuitive resources. These might be domain specific assumptions or domain general causal intuitions. As an example of domain specific assumptions, what I call *implicit models*, the student may implicitly think of the unseen stuff flowing through wires as similar to water flowing in a gutter (as opposed to water moving under pressure in a garden hose), and therefore able to "back up" and "collect." Domain general *core intuitions* are the students' unconscious assignment of various types of agency to actors in the situation. For example, the battery might be seen by the student as having its own agency and so would be considered an *initiating agent*. The student might consider the charge squirted into the wires by the battery as having agency given to it by the battery and so would be considered an *initiated agent*. Since the bulb is affected by the charge, it might be considered an *affected responder*.

Since these core intuitions are considered to be unconsciously imagistic, I have found it helpful to use icons to represent them rather than words (see Figure 10.2).

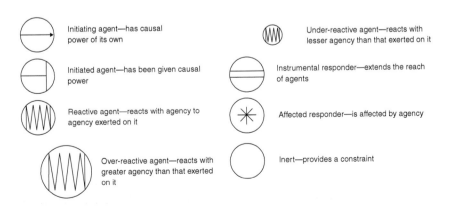

FIGURE 10.2 Attributive cluster elements.

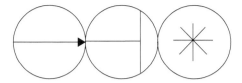

FIGURE 10.3 Attributive cluster showing the battery as initiating agent, charge as the initiated agent, and the bulb as the affected responder.

This iconic representation allows for the "chaining" of intuitive causal attributions into *attributive clusters* that represent an interpretation of the student's intuitive causal take on a situation. For example, if the analyst has evidence that the student is thinking of the battery as an *initiating agent* sending charge as an *initiated agent* to the bulb, which is *affected* by the charge, this attributive cluster could be drawn as in Figure 10.3.

Interactions of conceptual resources

I have found it useful to use framework diagrams to capture "interpretive snapshots" of imagistic and verbal-symbolic conceptual resources and their interactions at points throughout an interview. To illustrate this, I will discuss two diagrams: one an interpretive snapshot of Tanya's ideas and one an interpretive snapshot of the ideas of another student, "Brian," who seemed to discuss explanatory models in connection with intuitive ideas.

Figure 10.4a shows an interpretive snapshot of Tanya's ideas at the point in the interview discussed above, indicating the implicit models of the battery as a signal sender and the bulb as responding to this signal. For this reason, the bulb seemed to be considered as a reactive agent. The symbol for reactive agent is drawn larger than that for initiating agent to indicate that the bulb is an over-reactive agent, supplying more agency than that impressed on it to "awaken" it (as, for example, in pulling a trigger).

I show no explanatory models as there was no evidence that she was thinking about the circuit as involving unseen elements such as charge or current ("currency" seemed to be the direct influence of the battery on the bulb). I also show no verbal-symbolic knowledge as she did not express any learned technical vocabulary or generalizations.

By contrast, consider the case of Brian (shown in Figure 10.4b), who was quite clearly considering explanatory models. The following response came after some tutoring sessions in which the idea of the battery as a pressure source was discussed (Brown & Steinberg, 1993):

I: Where do the charges come from?
B: I'd say from the battery, but just like we were talking last time you were saying that was a source of pressure more than a source of charge, but, hmm,

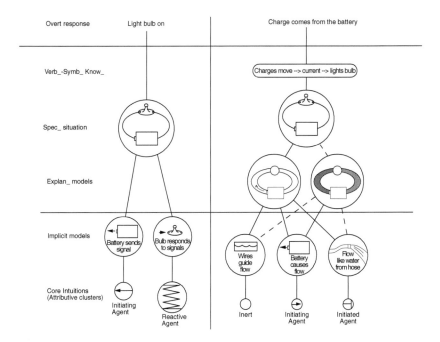

FIGURE 10.4 Framework diagrams: (a) Tanya (b) Brian.

> I'd say the battery's still, unless the charge is always in the wires and the battery just causes it to be drawn through ... I'll say the battery ... when this is connected up, these two ends are connected, then the, this is drawn to the negative end so it just basically moves from here [positive end] to the negative end.

In this case, unlike Tanya, Brian was able to compare and contrast two competing explanatory models. In his preferred model on the left, the battery squirts charge into initially empty wires. This charge then moves to the bulb and lights the bulb. This explanatory model seems to be connected to three implicit models which exert a subliminal influence on his thinking: (1) wires guide flow, much like a river channel guides the flow of a river; (2) batteries are the cause of the flow; and (3) flow is like water from a hose (i.e., unconstrained, therefore what happens downstream does not cause back pressure affecting what happens upstream). These implicit models seem connected to the domain independent core intuitions of inertness, initiating agency, and initiated agency, respectively.

Influencing imagistic construals

Can conscious consideration of imagistic resources such as explanatory models help students bring their implicit conceptual resources into greater alignment with canonical models? Brown and Clement (1989) talk about explanatory models as enriching students' ideas of target phenomena with new elements. Brown (1993) discusses this enrichment as providing opportunities for students to attribute agency in ways that are different from their initial intuitive causal take on the situation. Cheng and Brown (2015) explored supporting such explanatory model construction in the context of magnetism through scaffolding the use of the modeling criteria of visualization (explicitly visualizing unseen elements that could explain observable phenomena) and explanatory power (employing the same model across multiple phenomena). The students so scaffolded had strikingly more sophisticated, coherent, and canonical explanatory models than students scaffolded to consider and critique explanatory ideas but not explicitly scaffolded in these modeling criteria.

Discussion

Both this work exploring imagistic construals and the work of those exploring linguistic construals consider a world of hidden conceptual dynamics that underlie and provide grounding for consciously maintained and overtly expressed linguistic and imagistic resources. The framework discussed here has been designed with manipulation of imagistic resources as the focus, such as the construction of explanatory models, rather than the linguistic resources that are the focus of those interested in conceptual metaphor. But both perspectives emphasize the need to not only listen to what students say and explicitly express imagistically, but the need to also read between the lines of what they articulate to interpretively conjecture about their implicit image schemas that provide intuitive grounding for their more conscious ideas.

Those exploring conceptual metaphor and linguistic construals in science learning ask essentially how linguistic resources can be used to help refocus image schemas to support more canonical linguistic construals. My closely related question is "how can the conscious manipulation of imagistic resources be used to help refocus image schemas to support more canonical imagistic construals?" Both take the position that students have conscious control over certain cognitive actions that are linked to unconscious image schemas. Both ask the questions in related but complementary ways: "How can we help students manipulate conscious conceptual resources to better marshal their unconscious and dynamic image schemas into understandings closer to those of scientists?" Exploring this question further is likely to have significant educational payoff.

References

Amin, T. G. (2009). Conceptual metaphor meets conceptual change. *Human Development, 52*(3), 165–197.

Amin, T. G. (2015). Conceptual metaphor and the study of conceptual change: Research synthesis and future directions. *International Journal of Science Education, 37*(5–6), 966–991.

Brown, D. E. (1993). Refocusing core intuitions: A concretizing role for analogy in conceptual change. *Journal of Research in Science Teaching, 30*(10), 1273–1290.

Brown, D. E. (2014). Students' conceptions as dynamically emergent structures. *Science & Education, 23*(7), 1463–1483.

Brown, D. E., & Clement, J. (1989). Overcoming misconceptions via analogical reasoning: Abstract transfer versus explanatory model construction. *Instructional Science, 18*(4), 237–261.

Brown, D. E., & Hammer, D. (2013). Conceptual change in physics. In S. Vosniadou (Ed.), *International handbook of research on conceptual change* (2nd ed., pp. 121–137). New York: Routledge.

Brown, D. E., & Steinberg, M. S. (1993). *Analogical models-boon or bane in science instruction?* Paper Presented at the Third International Seminar on Misconceptions and Educational Strategies in Science and Mathematics, Ithaca, NY.

Cheng, M. F., & Brown, D. E. (2010). Conceptual resources in self-developed explanatory models: The importance of integrating conscious and intuitive knowledge. *International Journal of Science Education, 32*(17), 2367–2392.

Cheng, M. F., & Brown, D. E. (2015). The role of scientific modeling criteria in advancing students' explanatory ideas of magnetism. *Journal of Research in Science Teaching, 52*(8), 1053–1081.

Closset, J. L. (1983). *Sequential reasoning in electricity.* Research on Physics Education. Proceedings of the First International Workshop. La Londe les Maures, 313–319.

Dreyfus, B. W., Gupta, A., & Redish, E. F. (2015). Applying conceptual blending to model coordinated use of multiple ontological metaphors. *International Journal of Science Education, 37*(5–6), 812–838.

Duit, R. (1985). Students' representations of the topological structure of the simple electric circuit. In R. Duit, W. Jung, & C. von Rhoeneck (Ed.), *Aspects of understanding electricity* (pp. 83–93). Kiel: Schmidt & Klaunig.

Hammer, D. (2000). Student resources for learning introductory physics. *American Journal of Physics, 68*, S52–S59.

Jeppsson, F., Haglund, J., & Amin, T. G. (2015). Varying use of conceptual metaphors across levels of expertise in thermodynamics. *International Journal of Science Education, 37*(5–6), 780–805.

Nathan, M. J. (2012). Rethinking formalisms in formal education. *Educational Psychologist, 47*(2), 125–148.

Shipstone, D. M. (1988). Pupils' understanding of simple electrical circuits: Some implications for instruction. *Physics Education, 23*, 92–96.

11

CONCEPTUAL CHANGE, MATERIALITY AND HYBRID MINDS

Roger Säljö

Introduction

Studies of conceptual change, and conceptual thinking more generally, are mostly grounded in a Cartesian world view, where there is a sharp line of division between an inner, cognitive world of mental entities and an outside world of physical objects and activities. According to this dualist world view, which has an amazing ability to reproduce itself, thinking takes place by means of representations that are somehow mental copies, or models, of 'real', external objects and events. To think is to be able to manipulate representations, and to develop/learn is to change representations (concepts, schemata), thus replacing earlier versions with more advanced ones, usually better approximating those relevant in contexts of scientific reasoning. Variants of this approach underpin most research on learning, development and conceptual change in cognitive science, psychology and educationally orientated research on concept acquisition (cf. Vosniadou, 2008).

In this chapter, the basic argument is that concepts and conceptual change are as much features of artefacts and the external world as they are of thinking. A ruler, a compass and an app for gaming or navigation all embody conceptual distinctions that the user engages with when using the artefact. There is no easily distinguishable line of division between the artefact and human reasoning in situated practices; the mind and the artefact are part of a cognitive ecology where understanding emerges and social action follows. In Vygotskian (1978) language, the artefact and its semiotic resources (concepts, numbers, etc.) mediate the activity of measuring, of navigating and of playing a game. Acts of thinking in this sense are 'instrumental acts' (Vygotsky, 1981), where human mental functioning is structured, and sometimes reorganized, by means of integration of external artefacts – or cultural tools (Wertsch, 1998) – into reasoning. Paper and pencil, as tools for remembering or doing arithmetic, are examples of arte-facts that dramatically reorganized the cognitive activities that go into recalling information and calculating. Taking a historical perspective, human thinking (and communication) to an increasing extent takes place in co-ordination with a world of specialized and sophisticated cultural tools or, to use Donald's (2010) expression, with 'symbolic technologies'. As innovations in symbolic technolo-gies make their way into our daily practices, the cognitive ecology of which we are a part changes.

Symbolic technologies and reasoning

The dependence of cognitive activities on external artefacts is seldom acknowl-edged in psychological, and even less in neuroscience, research. On the contrary, experiments, research interviews or psychological tests are often organized in such a fashion that people are separated from the symbolic technologies they normally rely on. This is an unfortunate premise for research if we are to the-orize conceptual change in a world where cognition, to borrow Lave's (1988, p. 1) formulation, is 'stretched over, not divided among – mind, body, activ-ity and culturally organized settings' where people and symbolic technologies inter-act.

The alternative to such mainstream approaches to cognition offered here is that what is unique about humans is not that we 'have' concepts and internal representations, or even that we have powerful brains, but rather that our mind is best conceived of as a hybrid mind that operates through 'mergers and coa-litions' (Clark, 2003, p. 3) with artefacts in the surrounding world. It is not a stand-alone device that is bounded by the skull of the individual, but, rather, to continue using Clark's metaphors, it is 'leaky'. Information, numbers, procedures and so on move between the cognizing individual and the outside world and its artificial memory systems such as texts, databases, calculators and an increasingly diverse range of symbolic technologies. Thus, for hybrid minds – unlike individ-ual brains – thinking and remembering take place through co-ordination with symbolic technologies (and with other people) to which we have outsourced elements of what used to be internal cognitive activities. These tools, by reorgan-izing instrumental acts, furthermore serve as 'cognitive amplifiers' (Nickerson, 2005) that take our capacities way beyond what nature has equipped us with.

And it is also through constant interaction with such external resources that we socialize ourselves as cognitive agents in a designed world. We learn to think and act by using the symbolic technologies that we have access to. And, as Boivin (2008, p. 223) argues, this vital role of adaptation to cultural environments seems to apply even in an evolutionary perspective: 'We are, indeed, the 'the self-made species', with everything from our distinctive morphology to our unique brains having been shaped in some measure by our own activities and by the increas-ingly complex material and cultural environment we have generated' over tens of thousands of years (cf. Donald, 2010). To leave the impressive fruits of this accumulation of symbolic technologies outside our inquiries into conceptual change is like studying contemporary human communication and networking without considering the role and affordances of smartphones and digital media in our daily lives.

Conceptual change in a world of symbolic technologies

To understand conceptual change in the context of hybrid minds thus involves understanding how individuals learn to co-ordinate with symbolic tools in order to avail themselves of the intellectual powers that are partially outsourced. Following such a line of thinking, one would not assume that children learn about time by developing a general concept of time that they project onto the world. Rather, they gradually appropriate the idea of time, and units of time, by seeing watches and clocks in various situations, asking questions about their function and design (why are there two, or even three, hands? what are the numbers for?), and eventually realizing that our concepts of time – hours, minutes, seconds – are organized in specific manners and built into the artefact. Thus, it is the prolonged interaction with clocks and watches under adult guidance that produces something we can refer to as a conceptual understanding of time. Or, in other words, the concepts emerge through engagement with an object that nowadays is rather prominent in the world and that triggers curiosity and calls for explanations. In our time, we may take such experiences as prototypical for much of the conceptual development that we experience and that we study in developmental research.

The idea that much conceptual change emerges from engagement with symbolic technologies points to the necessity of analysing learning trajectories in terms of how concepts and uses of artefacts co-evolve, that is, our 'unit of analysis' (Säljö, 2009) has to take this interdependence between people and tools into account. The perspective outlined in this chapter should not be read as denying that conceptual change may emerge from internal reflective thinking where no *external* tools are part of a cognitive process or an insight. This may indeed happen, for instance, when imagining how to solve a problem, when counting or when thinking about how to plan a trip. On the other hand, the perspective implies that our ways of engaging in such, seemingly mental, tasks emerge from previous experiences with symbolic technologies that we may no longer need *in situ* to perform a task. Any study of how two and three year olds learn to operate with letters, symbols and apps in contexts of gaming on the touch-screen of a tablet or smartphone would most likely reveal how mastery of some central symbolic universes have moved down in ages in a rather dramatic manner. However, in this context I would like to exemplify my argumentation by using an illustration of how students encounter a symbolic technology that is currently making its way into society, and that is gaining increasing attention as a significant conceptual resource for understanding what we do, and the consequences for the future of what we do.

Conceptualizing the idea of a carbon footprint

Almost every day we hear about how our lifestyles are not viable in a long-term perspective owing to the negative impact they have on the environment (Rockström et al., 2009). A central element of this debate across the world about the consequences of human induced environmental change is the concept of CO_2 (carbon dioxide) emissions. The debate concerns emissions that are generated by human activities and in particular through the combustion of fossil fuels. Scholars, experts in international agencies and politicians are grappling with the problems of how to agree on targets for policies and how to introduce and enforce policies that will reduce emissions.

At the conceptual level, the models for studying the effects of emissions are very complex, to put it mildly. Given the number of factors that have to be taken into account, and the many disciplinary types of knowledge that are relevant to consider, the complexity of the modelling is not surprising. The matter is also contested. Still there are people, even those aspiring to reach important political offices in the world, who are sceptical about, or even deny, the claim that human induced emissions pose unacceptable threats to the environment. But, clearly, understanding the relationship between human behaviours and their impact on the environment is, and will increasingly be, a critical element of politics and of learning for citizenship.

Over the past few years, we have seen the emergence of a symbolic technology that makes it possible to conceptualize and discuss emissions in new manners: carbon footprint calculators (CFC) (cf. Fauville, Andersson-Lantz, Mäkitalo, Dupont, & Säljö, 2016). CFCs have been designed by researchers, international organizations in the environmental area, museums and other agencies. There are dozens of CFCs to be downloaded and many are available as apps. The basic principle of a CFC as a symbolic technology is that it allows the user to measure the CO_2 emissions in weight units (kilogrammes, tons). By entering values that give information about a person's lifestyle, such as travelling by car or plane, food habits, heating of houses and so on, the calculator converts a range of behaviours to a measurable output indicating the footprint (see Figure 11.1).

Depending on the design of the CFC, the user can make a number of comparisons and analyses. Country averages may be compared, and the user's footprint may be compared to the average of the citizens of her/his country or of the world. The CFC can be used to project the environmental impact of a car or a house to be bought. The area of usage is expanding rapidly. Nowadays, the seller/producer of a product may analyse the environmental impact of the item they are to launch, perhaps even comparing it to what is already on the market.

CFCs are of course important for teaching in the area of environmental education as well, and that is where we have studied them. Focusing specifically on issues of conceptual change, several observations are interesting when students (16 years of age) engage with such an artefact. First, it is obvious that an interface of this kind is familiar to students. Prior exposure to similar interfaces seems to

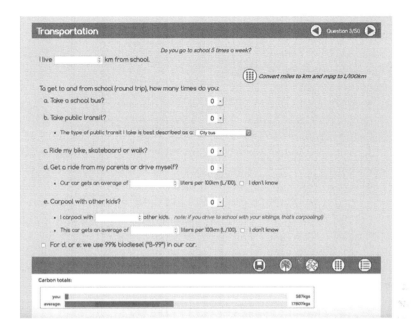

FIGURE 11.1 Interface of Carbon Footprint Calculator.
Reproduced with permission from Géraldine Fauville.

have prepared them for this kind of digital literacy practice of reading a text, entering values and coming out with a result. Thus, the students are digitally literate in this sense. Second, the threshold for entering information and utilizing the output measures in meaningful discussions is quite low. After a limited exposure to the tool, students are able to argue about matters such as what the petrol prices in different parts of the world imply for the extent to which people use cars. They are also able to analyse their own behaviours in quite sophisticated manners. In the following (abbreviated) quote (cf. Edstrand, 2015, p. 14), the students, while attending to the outcomes of the footprint calculator exercise, discuss driving between two cities as part of a longer deliberation in class about travelling and environmental impact.

01. PETER: I drove-drove from Strömsta this weekend (.) Strömsta to Gothenburg (.) it's almost-it has to be like eighteen miles [Swedish miles, 180 kms] or something that we drove
02. TOM: m m m m
03. PETER: that's quite lots of carbon dioxide (.) we were three persons in the car
04. TOM: m:
05. PETER: although a Volvo V70 diesel I think it runs forty-eight something per mile ((Albin and Jim look at each other and laugh))
06. PETER: so it's kind of less than if it would've been a gasoline car (.) older design this is then a newer Volvo V70

07. TOM: m m m
08. PETER: best would have been biogas
09. TOM: m m m[four turns left out]
14. PETER: but diesel it uses less and it's sti:ll (.) it's not renewable (.)but it's(.) fossil fuel

In this short excerpt, we see how Peter introduces his own activity (of learning to drive) as an illustration of environmental impact. He was driving 180 kms, which, he claims, produces lots of emissions (03). At the same time, he makes several arguments that are relevant to consider when discussing footprints. He points out that they were three people in the car (03) (which is better than one); he points out that he was driving a modern diesel car with a low fuel consumption and therefore a low impact in comparison to an older model using petrol (05); he says that biogas would have been best, since it is renewable energy (08, 14). Even though a modern diesel car is environmentally preferable to an older petrol car, it is still fossil fuel. In many respects, this is quite a sophisticated and concrete analysis of his own personal behaviours, and he also connects them to broader issues of environmental impact in the transport sector.

Peter thus invokes and relies on a number of concepts as he argues, and his reasoning is contingent on his use of the CFC as a tool for concretizing and quantifying the concept of carbon footprints. Thus, his reasoning unfolds at the intersection between his own experiences, insights and an artefact that serves as an instrument for thinking and for making claims. Of course, we do not know to what extent he would have been able to produce a similar analysis without this tool, but this is not so very interesting, since the whole discussion is grounded in the collaboration with the artefact.

Another short excerpt (this time from a questionnaire, cf. Fauville et al., 2016, p. 189) illustrates how the information provided by such a tool is integrated into reasoning about the environment. Here a student from Croatia expresses her reactions to seeing her own footprint:

> I always think that I am the average person as many in my country. But when I took my footprint, I was really shocked and surprised, because it was much higher!!

The reaction is triggered by an analytical exercise in which her behaviours have been converted into a measurable output that lends itself to analysis and comparison. Again, the activity involves a division of labour between an artefact and a hybrid mind, and the outcome is a conceptually mediated insight.

Conceptual change and the hybrid mind

The 'leaky' nature of a hybrid mind implies that it is best studied not as an independent universe of cognitive structures or conceptual resources but rather in relational terms and as relying on symbolic technologies. As new such technologies are integrated into our daily practices, our manners of thinking and communicating are transformed, and there will be a new division of labour between minds and artefacts when remembering, solving problems or searching for information (Mäkitalo, Linell, & Säljö, 2016). From an educational point of view, we also have to realize that much of our conceptual learning today takes place through collaboration with such tools. In this sense, and through the omnipresence of symbolic technologies, schools have rapidly lost control over how children learn and appropriate concepts in many areas. It is also interesting how people, by relying on such often highly 'blackboxed' tools (Latour, 1999), are able to handle complex information without fully understanding the functionality of the tool or the scientific concepts involved. This is illustrated in the excerpt above when the students relatively freely make calculations and draw conclusions without being familiar with all the distinctions and concepts from a range of sciences that the tool embodies. They understand as part of a specific, situated practice rather than as part of the types of hierarchically organized knowledge that schools traditionally build on.

Of course, education does not become educational by just introducing digital tools, this is not my point. But in teaching and learning we have to consider the significant role for conceptual change and conceptual knowledge that the collaboration with such tools represents. Accepting the materiality of concepts also forces us to realize that concepts are enactive, they are tools for social action, and not merely passive representations (Malafouris, 2013). Through conceptual knowledge embedded in symbolic technologies, we are able to structure and model the world, and we can dialogue with it by testing assumptions and hypotheses in manners that we have never been able to do before, we can even change it. The friction between symbolic technologies and a hybrid mind in situated action is an important source of conceptual change in a world of increasingly sophisticated cultural tools.

References

Boivin, N. (2008). *Material cultures, material minds. The impact of things on human thought, society and evolution.* New York: Cambridge University Press.

Clark, A. (2003). *Natural-born cyborgs: Minds, technologies, and the future of human intelligence.* New York: Oxford University Press.

Donald, M. (2010). The exographic revolution: Neuropsychological sequelae. In L. Malafouris & C. Renfrew (Eds.), *The cognitive life of things. Recasting the boundaries of mind* (pp. 71–80). Cambridge: The McDonald Institute for Archaelogical Research, University of Cambridge.

Edstrand, E. (2015). Making the invisible visible: How students make use of carbon footprint calculator in environmental education. *Learning, Media and Technology, 41*(2), 416–436. doi:10.1080/17439884.2015.1032976.

Fauville, G., Andersson-Lantz, A., Mäkitalo, Å., Dupont, S., & Säljö, R. (2016). The carbon footprint as a mediating tool in students' online reasoning about climate change. In O. Erstad, K. Kumpulainen, Å. Mäkitalo, K. Schrøder, P. Pruulman-Vengerfeldt, &

T. Jóhannsdøttir (Eds.), *Learning across contexts in the knowledge society* (pp. 179–202). London: Sense.

Latour, B. (1999). *Pandora's hope. An essay on the reality of science studies.* Cambridge, MA: Harvard University Press.

Lave, J. (1988). *Cognition in practice.* Cambridge, MA: Cambridge University Press.

Mäkitalo, Å., Linell, P., & Säljö, R. (Eds.). (2016). *Memory practices and learning: Interactional, institutional and sociocultural perspectives.* Charlotte, NC: Information Age Publishing.

Malafouris, L. (2013). *How things shape the mind. A theory of material engagement.* Cambridge, MA: MIT Press.

Nickerson, R. S. (2005). Technology and cognition amplification. In R. Sternberg & D. Preiss (Eds.), *Intelligence and technology. The impact of tools on the nature and development of human abilities.* (pp. 3–27). Mahwah, NJ: Erlbaum.

Rockström, J., Steffen, W., Noone, K., Persson, Å., Chapin, F. S., Lambin, E. R. Lenton, T. M., Scheffer, M. Folke, C., & Schnellhuber, H. J. (2009). A safe operating space for humanity. *Nature, 461*(7263), 472–475.

Säljö, R. (2009). Learning, theories of learning and units of analysis in research. *Educational Psychologist, 44*(3), 202–208.

Vosniadou, S. (Ed.). (2008). *International handbook of research on conceptual change.* Abingdon, Oxon: Routledge.

Vygotsky, L. S. (1978). *Mind in society: The development of higher psychological processes.* Cambridge, MA: Harvard University Press.

Vygotsky, L. S. (1981). The instrumental method in psychology. In J. V. Wertsch (Ed.), *The concept of activity in Soviet psychology* (pp. 134–143). Armonk, NY: Sharpe.

Wertsch, J. V. (1998). *Mind as action.* New York: Oxford University Press.

12

MULTIPLE REPRESENTATIONS AND STUDENTS' CONCEPTUAL CHANGE IN SCIENCE

David F. Treagust, Mihye Won, and Felicity McLure

Conducting research in science classrooms from the vantage point of conceptual change and the varied uses of multiple representations can provide a powerful theoretical framework for developing a better understanding of teaching and learning in science. While there are a few exceptions, research on the use of multiple representations in learning science usually does not link overtly to conceptual change but rather to students' science achievement. Consequently, there is a need to make a clear and persuasive link between the two literatures (multiple representations and conceptual change) that have not been sufficiently linked before. This chapter examines a theoretical framework based on conceptual change studies involving epistemological, ontological, and social/affective dimensions, and reviews some research studies on the use of multiple representations in teaching and learning science to examine how analogies and analogical models, diagrams, multi-level representations can contribute to conceptual change. While most reviewed studies do not consider all three aspects of conceptual change at the same time, we describe an approach that addresses this deficiency. In this way, this short chapter recommends a direction of improved linking between the two literatures at a level that is more fruitful than is currently the case.

A theoretical framework for conceptual change

Conceptual change views of science learning processes have provided a powerful framework for science education research as well as for the design of instruction since the late 1970s (Duit & Treagust, 2003). Over the past four decades, conceptual change theory and literature has evolved to include epistemological, ontological, and social/affective aspects of students' conceptual change (Duit, Treagust, & Widodo, 2013).

The most common research approach is an epistemological view of conceptual change, focusing on *challenging students' understanding of particular concepts* by creating cognitive conflict with their presently held conceptions in order to raise the status of the scientific conception as an explanation in terms of its plausibility, intelligibility and fruitfulness (Posner, Strike, Hewson, & Gertzog, 1982) (e.g. heat transfer as energy flow from high to low temperature objects versus 'cold energy' transfer).

An ontological view of conceptual change, on the other hand, focuses on *students' perspectives on the nature of the conception being investigated* (Chi, 2008). From this view, conceptual change can be achieved when students appreciate the different ontological categories in which the concept exists (e.g. heat conduction in relation to kinetic particle theory to explain energy transfer versus the caloric view) and successfully interpret phenomena by invoking and applying the scientifically acceptable ontology.

Following the call by Pintrich, Marx, and Boyle (1993), researchers have steered away from an overly rational approach to pay *more attention to the affective, social domain*. As shown in Liu, Hou, Chiu, and Treagust's (2014) investigation and Berland and Reiser's (2009) study, students' emotions and attitudes as well as their peer discussion and relationships interact with their learning of science concepts. Consistent with the arguments in this chapter, Zembylas (2005) argued that emotions should act not only as moderating variables of cognitive outcomes but as variables of equal status for identifying conceptual changes.

Each of these three views of conceptual change has produced a substantial amount of literature as evidenced by the volume edited by Vosniadou (2013). Because conceptual change is a complex process, it is advisable to take multidimensional approaches and consider the epistemological, ontological and affective aspects of conceptual change (Treagust & Duit, 2008). Indeed, it is more productive to examine learning through a multidimensional approach, as for example with Venville and Treagust's (1998) research on Grade 10 students' conceptions of genes. Despite the effectiveness of multidimensional approaches for supporting students' conceptual change, recent research studies on conceptual change do not adopt such approaches explicitly.

Multiple representations as tools to support conceptual change

Science education researchers have investigated the functions of representations in supporting students' conceptual understanding and attitudes towards learning science (Ainsworth, Prain, & Tytler, 2011). Different modes of representation (such as analogies, diagrams, graphs, cartoons, formulas, text, simulations, and gestures) or different levels of representations (macro, micro, and symbolic) are adopted to develop, understand, and communicate scientific concepts in scientific discourse and science learning. Learning a new concept can be guided by the use of different representations (see Treagust & Tsui, 2013). We list some science education studies below. As a guide to navigate different representations and educational implications, in Table 12.1 we illustrate some characteristics and roles of representations in supporting students' conceptual understanding.

TABLE 12.1 Use of different representations to support students' conceptual change in selected science education studies

	Analogy and Physical Analogical Models	Diagram	Multi-Level Representations	Integration of Multiple Representations
Link to scientific practice	Communication, Idea generation, Visualization	Idea generation, Visualization, Communication	Scale/scope	Flexibility in thinking
Example studies	Treagust et al. (1996), Treagust et al. (2003), Coll et al. (2005)	Waldrip et al. (2010)	Gilbert & Treagust (2009), Treagust & Tsui (2013)	McLure et al. (2016), Won et al. (2014)
Research methods	Class observation, Interviews, Diagnostic tests	Observation, Interviews	Diagnostic tests, Interviews, Observations	Class observation, Interviews, Diagnostic tests
Domains of conceptual change investigated	Epistemological, ontological, and affective	Epistemological and affective	Epistemological and ontological	Epistemological, ontological, and affective
Representation generator/presenter	Teacher as presenter	Teacher as presenter, Students as generator in group work	Teacher or computer simulation	Teacher as presenter, Student as generator in group work
Why it works	Bridge difficult concepts with familiar object or physical models	Visualize scientific ideas	Link between the observable and scientific models/symbols	Evaluate different representations and correspondence in their understanding
Teaching strategy involved	FAR guide, Teaching with analogies	Students draw and discuss drawings	Computer simulation/ visualization	Thinking Frames Approach

Analogies and analogical models

An example of a representational cognitive tool is the analogy or analogical model. Scientists use analogies to better communicate their scientific ideas, such as Kepler using the workings of a clock to explain planetary motions. In learning science, analogies can work as a bridge between something familiar and abstract concepts. For example, biology teachers often explain homeostasis as analogous to a student walking up the down escalator; physics teachers might explain how water pressure is analogous to voltage. Despite their advantages, analogies can also cause incorrect understanding depending on the analogue–target relationship. Subsequently, researchers have investigated better ways of using analogies to induce conceptual change. Research-based teaching models, including the Focus-Action-Reflection (FAR) Guide and Teaching-With-Analogies model, provide frameworks for teachers when assisting students to learn with analogies (Coll & Harrison, 2008).

Adopting analogies for science teaching can address epistemological, ontological, and affective aspects of conceptual change but usually not all at the same time. For example, the learning of molecular structure can be enhanced by the use of physical analogical models such as the ball and stick model or space-filling models to explain features and functions of the molecule under investigation. As students use physical models discerningly, appreciating their role, purpose, and limitations, links are formed between the different analogue models and the ontology of the target concept (Harrison & Treagust, 2000). When investigating one teacher's use of an analogy to teach physics concepts, including refraction of light, Treagust, Harrison, Venville, and Dagher (1996) noted that students displayed more interest and engagement in learning science concepts, especially on a practical optics assessment task, and the teacher exhibited more enthusiasm when using analogies. However, class discussion did not comprehensively examine the ontology of the science concept in relation to the analogy.

Diagrams

Scientific images or conceptual illustrations are beneficial to generate, visualize, and communicate scientific ideas (Latour, 1986). Despite the abundance of scientific diagrams in scientific discourse, the opportunities for students to draw diagrams are limited – possibly depicting the apparatus for laboratory work (simple illustrative diagrams) or copying existing diagrams from textbooks. Rarely are students encouraged to generate their own conceptual drawings (elaborate explanatory diagrams) in science class.

When students are encouraged to visually represent their ideas, they tend to consider what to include in diagrams, how to represent their ideas, and how to communicate or justify their diagrams. This process of drawing diagrams and justifying them helps students to consider their ideas from various angles and develop more scientific understanding (Waldrip, Prain, & Carolan, 2010). Considering the significant educational benefits, science teachers need to engage students in generating scientific diagrams as thinking tools rather than simply memorizing 'correct' representations. Waldrip et al. (2010) suggest representation-centred teaching should accompany students' scientific reasoning and explanation to maximize its potential to support students' conceptual change. However, in research studies on diagram use for science learning, the focus tends to be on students' epistemological and affective aspects of conceptual learning rather than the ontological aspect (Ainsworth et al., 2011).

Multilevel representations

Science concepts encompass different scales (e.g. phenomenological and molecular) and thus involve different scopes of representation. Gilbert and Treagust (2009) note the importance of understanding chemical phenomena at three levels: a phenomenological level where the properties are observed and measured; the molecular level where models are developed to explain the behaviours of entities like ions and molecules; and a symbolic level where symbols are allocated to represent atoms and electrical charge. Treagust and Tsui (2013) included an additional cellular/microscopic level for an understanding of biology concepts. Improving students' capability to move across different levels of representation contributes to greater scientific conceptual understanding (Schwartz & Brown, 2013).

Integration of multiple representations

The capability to adopt and coordinate multiple representations flexibly is implicitly anticipated and practised in science laboratories, but science students' level of multiple representation integration tends to be limited and superficial (Kozma, 2003). In a recent study, Won, Yoon, and Treagust (2014) investigated Grade 11 students' strategies in interpreting and evaluating multiple representations in relation to their conceptual understanding of the human respiratory system. The extent to which students integrated their use of multiple representations – drawings, physical model, and text – interacted with their level of conceptual understanding.

One teaching strategy supporting students' use of multiple representations is the Thinking Frames Approach (TFA) (Newberry & Gilbert, 2007). As a structured guideline for teachers to adopt a representation-oriented teaching approach, Newberry and Gilbert (2007) suggested a teaching model, where multiple representation-based activities are systematically included. The teaching model includes five steps – set the question, brainstorm, visualize, sequence, and paragraph. Students' prior conceptions are challenged in the initial stage and students work in groups to generate, discuss, and evaluate their ideas. Two forms of representations are most notably included in this process to support students' conceptual development – diagrams and verbal/written texts. The students are also given a 'Levels Mountain' to differentiate simple descriptions from logical scientific explanations and to evaluate their own work accordingly (Newberry, Gilbert, & Hardcastle, 2005).

The TFA can be used to address all three of the domains of conceptual change from epistemological, ontological, and affective perspectives. For example, recent research by McLure, Won, and Treagust (2016) found that the TFA encouraged epistemological conceptual change by challenging a particular alternative conception held by students through demonstrations that created cognitive conflict with that conception. Students then explained their observations by visualizing the scientific conception, followed by production of verbal, pictorial, and written explanations. Students found that this iterative process in various representational formats allowed them to refine and deepen their understanding of the concept.

Although students were initially hesitant to engage in the process of generating representations using the TFA and to discuss them with their peers, they soon realized the benefit of the structured process in improving their understanding. Students reported considerable improvement in their feelings of self-efficacy in understanding new concepts and in writing elaborated explanations. Students received support from peers within the small group environment that gave them confidence in putting forward their explanations and seeking further clarification. As students defended the scientific conception, it gained in status amongst all group members, thus supporting the affective aspect of conceptual change.

Throughout the TFA process, the teacher used questioning strategies in order to direct students' thinking towards the underlying ontological model in question. After a series of lessons in each topic, which allowed students to construct elaborated understanding by applying the model in a variety of everyday situations, pre- and post-test results indicated that students dramatically improved their level of conceptual understanding in various science topics, including thermal physics, the particle theory, Newton's laws, electricity, genetics, and natural selection. Furthermore, the effect of the TFA lessons, judged by delayed post-tests, persisted long after the teaching period and resulted in persistent ontological conceptual change.

Implications

The representations discussed in this chapter are actively used by scientists in their practice. By adopting representations explicitly in science class, science teachers aim to not only emulate scientists' practice but also help students build better conceptual understanding through epistemological, ontological, and affective dimensions of conceptual change. But as illustrated above, most studies on conceptual change involve at best two of these aspects of conceptual change. Multiple representations have great potential to serve as a powerful learning and teaching tool for conceptual change by visualizing concepts or by linking a familiar idea with the abstract concept.

Research shows that representations are usually created and presented by the teacher in class rather than generated and discussed by the students. However, researchers have found that when the opportunities for representation generation are given to students themselves, students tend to build better scientific understanding and enjoy science learning more.

Successful teaching for conceptual change depends on various instructional methods and strategies involving multiple representations (Duit & Treagust, 2012).

When teaching with different kinds of representations, teachers need to find a balance between their existing teaching practices and the representations used in their teaching practices. Nevertheless, conceptual change strategies with multiple representations may not be effective or efficient unless they are embedded in a constructivist learning environment.

While it is acknowledged that the three aspects of conceptual change – epistemological, ontological, and social/affective – are worthy of research using multiple representations, disappointingly, we have found that few researchers explicitly link all three aspects in their studies on students' representations. Rather, they tend to focus on the epistemological aspect of conceptual change, without necessarily being overt about this, and some affective/social aspects. As some researchers have suggested over the years (see, for example, Venville & Treagust, 1998; Vosniadou, Baltas, & Vamvakoussi, 2007), effective conceptual change occurs when those three aspects are integrated in supporting students' understanding. In this chapter, we have tried to clarify how multiple representations can be used in science instruction to achieve all three aspects of conceptual change.

References

Ainsworth, S., Prain, V., & Tytler, R. (2011). Drawing to learn in science. *Science, 333*(6046), 1096–1097. doi:10.1126/science.1204153.

Berland, L. K. & Reiser, B. J. (2009). Making sense of argumentation and explanation. *Science Education, 93*(1), 26–55.

Chi, M. T. H. (2008). Three types of conceptual change: Belief revision, mental model transformation and categorical shift. In S. Vosniadou (Ed.), *International handbook of research on conceptual change* (pp. 61–82). New York: Routledge.

Coll, R. K., France, B., & Taylor, I. (2005). The role of models and analogies in science education. *International Journal of Science Education, 27*(2), 183–198.

Coll, R. K., & Harrison, A. (Eds.) (2008). *Using analogies in middle and secondary science classrooms: The FAR Guide-An interesting way to teach analogies.* Thousand Oaks, CA: Corwin Press.

Duit, R., & Treagust, D. F. (2003). Conceptual change: A powerful framework for improving science teaching and learning. *International Journal of Science Education, 25*(6), 671–688.

Duit, R., & Treagust, D. F. (2012). Conceptual change: Still a powerful framework for improving the practice of science instruction. In K. C. D. Tan & M. Kim (Eds.), *Issues and challenges in science education research* (pp. 43–54). Dordrecht: Springer.

Duit, R., Treagust, D. F., & Widodo, A. (2013). Teaching science for conceptual change: Theory and practice. In S. Vosniadou (Ed.), *International handbook of research on conceptual change* (pp. 487–503). New York: Routledge.

Gilbert, J. K., & Treagust, D. F. (Eds.). (2009). *Multiple representations in chemical education.* Dordrecht: Springer.

Harrison, A. G. & Treagust, D. F. (2000). Learning about atoms, molecules and chemical bonds: A case-study of multiple model use in grade-11 chemistry. *Science Education, 84*, 352–381.

Kozma, R. (2003). The material features of multiple representations and their cognitive and social affordances for science understanding. *Learning and Instruction, 13*(2), 205–226.

Latour, B. (1986). Visualisation and cognition: Drawing things together. In H. Kuklick & E. Long (Eds.), *Knowledge and society studies in the sociology of culture past and present* (Vol. 6, pp. 1–40). Greenwich, CT: JAI Press.

Liu, C.-J., Hou, I.-L., Chiu, H.-L., & Treagust, D. F. (2014). An exploration of secondary students' mental states when learning about acids and bases. *Research in Science Education, 44*(1), 133–154.

McLure, F., Won, M., & Treagust, D. F. (April, 2016). *Thinking frames approach: Improving conceptual understanding in thermal physics through student-generated diagrams and explanations.* Paper presented at the Annual Conference of the National Association of Research in Science Teaching, Baltimore, MD.

Newberry, M., & Gilbert, J. K. (2007). Bringing learners and scientific expertise together. In K. S. Taber (Ed.), *Science education for gifted learners* (pp. 197–211). London: Routledge.

Newberry, M., Gilbert, J. K., & Hardcastle, D. (2005). Visualising progression through the science curriculum in order to raise standards. *School Science Review, 86*(316), 87–96.

Pintrich, P. R., Marx, R. W., & Boyle, R. A. (1993). Beyond cold conceptual change: The role of motivational beliefs and classroom contextual factors in the process of conceptual change. *Review of Educational Research, 6*, 167–199.

Posner, G. J., Strike, K. A., Hewson, P. W. & Gertzog, W. A. (1982). Accommodation of a scientific conception: Towards a theory of conceptual change. *Science Education, 66*, 211–227.

Schwartz, R., & Brown, M. H. (2013). Understanding photosynthesis and cellular respiration: Encouraging a view of biological nested systems. In D. F. Treagust & C.-Y. Tsui (Eds.), *Multiple representations in biological education* (pp. 203–223). Dordrecht: Springer.

Treagust, D. F., & Duit, R. (2008). Conceptual change: A discussion of theoretical, methodological and practical challenges for science education. *Cultural Studies of Science Education, 3*(2), 297–328.

Treagust, D. F., G. Chittleborough, G., & Mamiala, T. L. (2003). The role of submicroscopic and symbolic representations in chemical explanations. *International Journal of Science Education, 25*(11), 1353–1368.

Treagust, D. F., Harrison, A. G., Venville, G. J. & Dagher, Z. (1996). Using an analogical teaching approach to engender conceptual change. *International Journal of Science Education, 18*, 213–229.

Treagust, D, F., & Tsui, C.-Y. (Eds.). (2013). *Multiple representations in biological education.* Dordrecht: Springer.

Venville, G., & Treagust, D. F. (1998). Exploring conceptual change in genetics using a multidimensional interpretive framework. *Journal of Research in Science Teaching, 35*, 1031–1055.

Vosniadou, S. (Ed.). (2013). *International handbook of research on conceptual change* (2nd edn.). New York: Routledge.

Vosniadou, S., Baltas, A. & Vamvakoussi, X. (2007). *Reframing the conceptual change approach in learning and instruction.* Oxford: Elsevier.

Waldrip, B., Prain, V. & Carolan, J. (2010). Using multi-modal representations to improve learning in junior secondary science. *Research in Science Education, 40*(1), 65–80. doi: 10.1007/s11165-009-9157-6.

Won, M., Yoon, H., & Treagust, D. F. (2014). Students' learning strategies with multiple representations: Explanations on the human breathing mechanism. *Science Education, 98*(5), 840–866. doi:10.1002/sce.21128.

Zembylas, M. (2005). Three perspectives on linking the cognitive and the emotional in science learning: Conceptual change, socio-constructivism and poststructuralism. *Studies in Science Education, 41*, 91–116.

SYNTHESIS II

Representation, concepts, and concept learning

Tamer G. Amin

Introduction

Research on conceptual change emerged in the 1970s out of, and in reaction to, the Piagetian constructivist stage view of cognitive development (Amin, Smith, & Wiser, 2014). Given this legacy, the focus was on the solitary learner making sense of experience and on internal cognitive representations and processes. Many researchers have now converged on the broad assumption that when studying conceptual change it is important to examine the interaction between internal and external representations.

This common assumption is reflected in the six chapters in this part. Sherin discusses how the use of (external) physics equations influence problem-solvers' application of (internal) intuitive knowledge and, conversely, how intuitions are formed to make sense of equations. Gelman and DeJesus examine how language (an external representation) activates an (internal) essentialist interpretation of natural kind categories which can invite and hinder conceptual change. Novack, Congdon, Wakefield, and Goldin-Meadow document that analysis of (external) gestures can provide information about (internal) transitional states of conceptual understanding and that gestures can contribute to changes in mathematical understanding. Brown shows that constructing an understanding of scientific explanations involves the dynamic interplay of a number of resources both internal and external. The framework he has developed to interpret student learning includes a number of internal resources—explicit imagistic representations of physical situations, implicit intuitive attributions of agency to aspects of these situations, and implicit or explicit explanatory models—and an explicit external resource, verbal-symbolic knowledge. Säljö makes a case for seeing concepts as "hybrid" entities, both inside the head and distributed over external symbolic tools. He illustrates his view using the example of students learning about the concept of the carbon footprint as they use a simulation, the Carbon Footprint Calculator. Treagust, Won, and McLure summarize a program of research that demonstrates how a variety of external representations such as diagrams, physical models, and analogies are very effective in teaching for conceptual understanding. They argue that research on the importance of multiple representations in science learning has not been adequately integrated with theories of conceptual change. They illustrate this by showing that different types of external representations (sometimes multiple representations together) can induce a variety of positive effects on students' conceptual understanding.

The chapters in this part represent distinct disciplinary traditions—including developmental psychology, the learning sciences, and education. They illustrate a range of different research methods including experimental hypothesis testing, interpretive analysis of interview protocols, and discourse analysis. They also address concepts within a variety of domains including science, mathematics, and the social sciences. The objective here is to look across this diversity to offer a synthetic view of research that addresses connections between representation and conceptual change. The approach I take is to select a sufficiently broad and comprehensive theoretical lens through which to view many distinct lines of research. In this way, I hope to show that diverse research programs not only converge in some respects, but also complement one another in interesting ways.

I have selected Carey's (2009) account of concepts and concept acquisition as my organizing framework. There are several reasons for this choice. First, Carey offers a *foundational* account, describing and defending *generic* constructs with potential for a wide scope of application. That is, she provides explicit and precise answers to basic questions like 'What is a concept?' 'How do concepts relate to beliefs?' 'How is conceptual knowledge represented?' 'What are the different kinds of changes in conceptual knowledge?' Her answers to these questions come from considering empirical and theoretical work in foundational disciplines: namely, philosophy, cognitive psychology, and developmental psychology. Second, her account is particularly relevant to the aspects of conceptual change addressed in this part. It is explicit about issues of representational format, the interplay between internal and external representations, and the roles of representations and model-based reasoning practices in the construction of novel concepts. Finally, her theoretical proposals rest on a wide-ranging empirical data base, including investigations across the lifespan from infancy to adulthood, controlled investigations in the laboratory and instructional studies in classrooms, research across different cultures and languages, and research in the history of science. A foundational theoretical structure that is explicit about representational matters and coheres with this range of empirical data must surely be a good place to start when attempting to synthesize a diverse literature on representation and conceptual change.

This synthesis is organized as follows. I begin by presenting a summary of Carey's (2009) account of concepts and concept acquisition, highlighting three aspects of her account: the nature of concepts, the formats of conceptual representation, and the kinds of concept acquisition and processes of change. I then discuss the literature on representation and concept learning in three sections.

First, I survey the different constructs used to account for how conceptual knowledge is represented—either iconically or propositionally, internal to the mind or external. I then consider briefly the tension between the "cognitivist" position of viewing concepts as *internal* mental constructs and the distributed/ discursive position of viewing concepts as also extended over external symbolic tools. Using Carey's account of concepts, I argue that we can see these views as complementary. I then discuss how representation has figured in accounts of the processes of concept learning, organizing the presentation in terms of the distinction between knowledge enrichment and conceptual change (in its narrow sense). I conclude by suggesting productive directions for future research implied by this synthesis.

An account of concepts and concept acquisition

Concepts are often described as the mental representations that specify the basis for categorizing things in the world. Carey (2009) argues that categorization is just one phenomenon among many that a view of concepts should explain. She also considers how concepts refer to entities in the world, how they support communication, the role they play in reasoning, how concepts are acquired, and the distinction between a concept and beliefs *about* it. To Carey, concepts are unitary mental symbols that obtain their content (or meaning) from two components: how a concept is causally linked to entities in the world—that is, how they refer (e.g. how the concept *gold* is reliably connected to gold objects); and the concept's inferential role, how it contributes to thought. On some views, all beliefs within which a concept participates can be seen as an aspect of its meaning. However, Carey argues that it is important to identify a subset of beliefs about a concept as contributing to its content per se.[1]

Natural kind concepts like *gold* or *dog* help us see why we need to appeal to both aspects of the content of concepts; they also clarify why only some aspects of our knowledge about a concept should be treated as part of its content. It might be thought that the content of natural kind concepts are the summary perceptual representations (e.g. prototypical features and/or prototypes) that we form as a result of encountering various instances of the category. We might argue that these representations constitute the basis upon which we pick out members of the category (reference) and the basis for reasoning about them (inferential role). But this does not seem to be correct. Superficial transformations of natural kinds do not lead adults, and even children, to change their categorizations (Keil, 1989); a gold ring is still made of gold even if painted black; a dog is still a dog even it has lost one of it four legs. As Gelman (2003; Gelman & DeJesus, Chapter 8, this volume) has shown, even children's representations of natural kind concepts incorporate an assumption of essentialism. We tend to appeal to some underlying essence that makes the entity what it is and causes it to have the properties it does, even when we know very little about what that essence actually is; we defer to experts, assuming they have this knowledge.

So how do the concepts (the mental symbols) for natural kinds refer and what is their inferential role? According to Carey (2009), the assumption of essentialism is the key to both. The mental symbol, *dog* or *gold*, is associated with the essentialist assumption and this can, for most laypersons, constitute the core of the inferential content of the concept. The essentialist assumption is also the key to understanding reference. While perceptual representations of features and/or exemplars may contribute, the essentialist assumption means that we defer to experts to fill in gaps in our knowledge; we appeal to them and their scientific practices to ensure that the things that we refer to as "gold" are in fact gold. So, in an important sense, much of the meaning of a natural kind concept is in fact outside the head. Stated more generally, both internal (mental) and external processes connect concepts to referents in the world.

With regard to the format of knowledge representation, Carey is explicit in distinguishing iconic or propositional (language-like) formats. An iconic representation is analogical: the parts and relationships between parts of the representation stand in for parts and the relationships between parts of the thing represented; the ear and the head in the picture of a dog represent the ear and the head of the dog depicted. Propositional (or language-like) representations do not have this property; the "d" in "dog" does not represent some part of a dog; the relative size of the ears and the eyes need to be represented in some language-like format—for example, *bigger than (ears, eyes)*. In Carey's account of concepts both iconic and propositional representations can be implicated in establishing reference and in characterizing the inferential role of a concept.

From this perspective, acquiring a concept is learning to use the concept (as unitary symbol) such that it refers to entities in the world and participates in a network of beliefs, supporting inferences in a way that corresponds to its use in some community. The following is a broad outline of Carey's account of acquisition. The concepts available to infants constitute the preverbal starting point of the concept acquisition process.[2] Carey assumes that most of these initial concepts such as *object*, *agent*, and *number* are represented iconically.[3] She distinguishes two types of change in conceptual knowledge. One is knowledge enrichment, which involves elaboration of knowledge in terms of existing concepts and generalizations over perceptual experiences. This type of knowledge change can include forming new conceptual categories based on existing representations or forming new beliefs that express relationships between existing concepts. The other is more dramatic; it involves change at the level of concepts themselves, creating new conceptual representations in the process; this is "conceptual change," strictly speaking.

Carey distinguishes three concept acquisition processes involving public symbols such as language. The first involves mapping public symbols to existing preverbal concepts—for example, mapping the count/mass noun distinction to the existing preverbal conceptual distinction between individuated and unindividuated entities. The second case is where a new label is encountered resulting in the construction of a concept by combining existing representations resulting in a weak effect of learning a symbol on conceptual knowledge. For example, young preverbal infants are able to distinguish dogs, cups, and tables but do not treat them as kind sortals. That is, when shown a dog and cup sequentially emerging from and returning behind a screen, young infants do not infer the presence of two objects. However, learning labels does trigger kind representations that support quantification. The role of language here is to trigger an existing conceptual capacity, it doesn't create it.

A third case is when a label is encountered that does not correspond to either an existing preverbal concept or a combination of existing conceptual representations. In this case, the symbol—usually in the context of a larger symbol structure—supports the construction of one or more concepts. This involves the mechanism of Quinian bootstrapping, where an external symbol structure stands in for concepts (and relationships between concepts) that the learner does not possess. Although only shallowly interpreted, this symbol structure serves as a placeholder for the new concept(s) yet to be constructed. Available conceptual resources, often iconically represented, will support partial interpretation of the symbol structure. Model-based reasoning (involving abductive inference) will enrich the interpretation of the symbol structure resulting in the construction of novel concepts.

A paradigm example of this mechanism is a breakthrough in understanding the concept of number made by (English-speaking) children in their fourth year. Carey's account of this breakthrough can be summarized as follows. Preverbal infants can represent individual objects iconically, using an "object file" system limited in capacity to set sizes of three. Object file representations represent the cardinal value of sets only implicitly by virtue of there being one file per item in the set. Over the course of about a year and a half (from 24 to 42 months) toddlers will use their iconic object file system to sequentially learn the words "one," "two," and then "three." While "four" and above have not yet been understood, children will have learned the count list by rote (often to about ten) without numerical understanding. This serves as a symbolic placeholder. The object file system allows a partial interpretation of the list, giving meaning to only "one," "two," and "three." Crucially, the child still does not yet understand that moving from one number word to the next means *add one*. But the rote memorization of the count procedure includes knowledge of succession ("two" comes after "one," "three" comes after "two," "four" comes after "three" etc.). The child is now in a position to make an abductive inferential leap and can interpret the succession relation as meaning *add one*. This breakthrough now allows the child to understand "four" and above. This illustrates how an external symbolic placeholder, learned initially without conceptual understanding, provides a structure that helps a learner build a richer representational repertoire that goes beyond what was already present. It also shows how propositional and iconic representations interact in this process.

In the rest of this synthesis, these broad features of Carey's account of concepts and concept acquisition are used as an organizing framework to synthesize the diverse lines of research described in the chapters in this part and the literature on representation and concept learning more broadly.

Characterizing representational resources

Carey distinguishes iconic and propositional representations and describes the roles they play in various processes of knowledge enrichment and conceptual change. I begin here by surveying the different representational resources appealed to in the chapters in this part and other related work to account for concept learning. I organize the survey using the distinction between iconic and propositional representations (both internal and external). I then turn to the contribution of these resources to processes of change.

Iconic representations

As already mentioned, in iconic representations, the parts and relationships between the parts of the representation stand in for parts and relationships of the thing represented. In contrast to propositional (language-like) representations, they support easy search for, and access to, information and support rich perceptually-based inferences (Larkin & Simon, 1987). Iconic representations can be judged more or less similar to what they represent but are not beliefs that can be judged true or false. Moreover, iconic representations can be internal (mental) or external and can vary in degree of abstraction.

Various external iconic representations have been discussed in the literature. *Physical models* are three-dimensional external iconic representations that can stand in for objects and events in the world. Treagust et al. (Chapter 12, this volume) list physical analogical models among the external representational tools that help communicate and visualize abstract scientific ideas and support idea generation. Novack et al. (Chapter 9, this volume) also discuss research that examines the role of action on three-dimensional physical objects (mathematical manipulatives) in supporting mathematical understanding, although they discuss evidence that the learning potential of actions on such concrete objects is limited.

Images are two-dimensional external iconic representations that can represent objects and events. I use the word "images" to refer to static diagrams and photographs as well as dynamic simulations and video recordings. Treagust et al. (Chapter 12, this volume) also list diagrams as helpful in science instruction for conceptual understanding because they support communication, visualization, and idea generation. They point out that getting students to actively generate diagrams and make representational decisions themselves is particularly effective for concept learning (see also Lehrer & Schauble, Chapter 14, this volume). Other researchers have documented the prevalence of photographs in textbooks and the interpretive difficulties they present to learners (Pozzer-Ardenghi & Roth, 2003, 2005). Moreover, schematic animations and highly realistic simulations are an increasingly important tool in instruction, especially in STEM subjects. In a review and meta-analysis, D'Angelo et al. (2014) found that these tools improve student learning (when compared to instruction that does not use simulations) and that they are particularly effective when enhanced, such as adding dynamic representations and/or metacognitive support.

There are also a variety of internal iconic representations discussed in literature. *Mental imagery* is the mental reenactment of prior perceptions in the absence of the things and events previously perceived. There is a long tradition of research in cognitive science documenting that mental imagery can play a role in thought (see Kosslyn, Thompson, & Ganis, 2006). Brown (Chapter 10, this volume) lists conscious images of physical situations as a reasoning resource science learners might use. Mental imagery can be challenging to study, but various methods have been devised to infer their existence and function in thought. These include analysis of drawings, verbal indicators of imagery in written and oral language use, and the analysis of gestures (Clement, 2008; Lakoff & Núñez, 2000; Marghetis & Núñez, 2010; Nersessian, 2008; Stephens & Clement, 2010). In addition, fMRI has been used to locate aspects of apparently abstract technical reasoning in brain regions typically responsible for perceptual processes (Tsang, Rosenbberg-Lee, Blair, Schwartz, & Menon, 2010). Mental imagery has been shown to ground abstract understanding and reasoning in science and mathematics in less sensorimotor knowledge and support creative leaps in these domains.

Image schemas are a more schematic form of internal iconic representation. They are generalized patterns that emerge from repeated sensorimotor experiences. They are structured wholes, or gestalts, specifying the topological relations between components (Johnson, 1987). Examples include the *container* schema with an inside, an outside, and a boundary; the *path* schema with a starting point, a goal and the path linking the two; and *forced movement* with an animate agent exerting a force on an inanimate object resulting in its movement. Crucially, image schemas *interpret* perceptions or images, categorizing elements of an image (i.e. *as* a container or *as* the locus of a force), thereby supporting inferences. Image schemas can be combined to form composite schemas and as structured gestalts they can be mapped to linguistic symbols (Mandler, 2004). The existence and nature of image schemas have been inferred from patterns in language use (Lakoff & Johnson, 1999), priming and other effects in psycholinguistic studies (Gibbs, 2005), and the analysis of gestures during reasoning and problem-solving (Novack & Goldin-Meadow, 2017; Novack et al., Chapter 9, this volume).[4]

Some contributors to this part and beyond, use the idea of image schema, but sometimes use different terminology. Many of the p-prims (e.g. *force-as-mover*) described by diSessa (diSessa, 1993; Chapter 1, this volume) as contributing to intuitive and scientific understanding are image schemas. The same can be said for the "core intuitions" Brown (1993; Chapter 10, this volume) suggests are used by learners to attribute agency to aspects of the physical situations they reason about and some of the conceptual schemas described by Sherin (2001; Chapter 7, this volume) as the semantic poles of symbolic forms used to understand equations. Novack, Goldin-Meadow and colleagues (Novack & Goldin-Meadow, 2017;

Novack et al., Chapter 9, this volume) have argued that gestures have an effect on concept learning because they activate image schematic schematizations over sensorimotor experience. Moreover, image schemas have been identified as the source domains of conceptual metaphors implicit in the language of technical domains like science (Amin, Jeppsson, & Haglund, 2015/2017) and mathematics (see Hall & Nemirovsky, 2012; Lakoff & Núñez, 2000).

Mental models are another kind of internal iconic representation. For some time, they have been recognized as important for human reasoning and reading comprehension (Johnson-Laird, 1983; Van Dijk & Kintsch, 1983). They are analogical representations of situations and events, intermediate in abstraction between imagery and propositional representations. They can result from interpreting aspects of images with image schemas; their construction can be constrained by propositional knowledge. Conceptual change researchers have shown that mental models enable explanation and prediction of natural phenomena (Brown & Clement, 1989; Clement, 2013; Vosniadou, Chapter 2, this volume; Vosniadou & Brewer, 1992; Wiser & Smith, 2013). Brown (Chapter 10, this volume) has distinguished explicit (conscious) and implicit (unconscious) explanatory mental models in learners' thinking. While these models provide learners with a degree of coherence in their thinking (which can be ephemeral or long-lasting), they are often inaccurate and need to be revised. Instruction will often need to target the construction of more canonical or useful models.

Propositional representations

Iconic representations are not beliefs about what they represent—i.e. they cannot be judged true or false. For this, propositional representations, consisting of arbitrary symbols and syntactic rules such as natural languages and mathematics, are needed. Conceptual change research aims to understand how technical knowledge is learned and how to teach it effectively. Technical knowledge is made up of propositions—mathematical theorems, empirical generalizations, and explanatory hypotheses etc.—which must be communicated to others and supported with arguments. Iconic representations are important interpretive resources and support inference generation and communication, but propositional representations are indispensable to knowledge representation and the practices of knowledge construction. Technical knowledge is realized in specialized genres that combine iconic and propositional representations systems (Martin & Veel, 1998). Therefore, concept learning will quickly involve an encounter with, and attempts to interpret, propositional representations.

Some concept learning research has explored the effects of propositional representations, such as language, on young children's conceptual representations (Gelman, 2009; Gelman & DeJesus, Chapter 8, this volume); the importance of drawing on verbal-symbolic knowledge as a resource when constructing scientific explanations (Brown, Chapter 10, this volume); how the use of physics equations shapes understanding when they are used in problem-solving

(Sherin, 2001, and Chapter 7, this volume); the challenges that the interpretation of mathematical representations present when learning mathematical concepts (Vamvakousi, Vosniadou, & Van Dooren, 2013); and the effects of narratives on concept learning in history (Carretero, Castorina, & Levinas, 2013).

This section briefly surveyed different kinds of internal and external representations considered in the conceptual change literature. Later, I discuss the suggestions that researchers have about how these representations contribute to concept learning processes. But when *external* representations are discussed in relation to concept learning, the idea that concepts might not be a purely *internal* mental construct arises. I discuss this issue briefly first.

Inferential role, reference, and locating concepts inside or outside the head

The claim that concepts are, in some sense, not entirely in the head is often made by those advocating some version of a situated, discursive, or distributed view of cognition. This view is supported by Säljö in his chapter in Part II of this volume (see also, Clark, 2003). In this section, I suggest that this claim can, in fact, cohere with Carey's account of concepts and concept acquisition. I argue that we can distinguish two different senses of the claim and that these map onto the two aspects of concept meaning: inferential role and reference.

One sense of saying that concepts are not in the head is associated with criticisms of the over-reliance on internal mental representations in cognitive science formulated by advocates of distributed (Clark, 2003) or discursive (Säljö, Chapter 11, this volume; Schoultz, Säljö, & Wyndhamn, 2001) views of cognition. From these perspectives, concepts are said to be "hybrid" entities that extend over external multimodal representational resources. That is, it is argued that there is no need to posit concepts as purely mental representations, which are then communicated via representational tools. Instead of speaking of *having* a concept they prefer to speak of the *skilled use* of various representational tools.

Carey's (2009) dual theory of concepts is formulated firmly within a cognitivist tradition, and so is the typical target of this criticism. But in Carey's account, external representations such as natural language and mathematical symbols are necessary for the representation of abstract concepts and the inferential role of these concepts is realized in terms of these external representations in coordination with internal, often iconic representations. So the idea the concepts extend over external representations seems to be consistent with Carey's account. This view is consistent with that of other contributors to this part such as Brown and Sherin, who characterize scientific reasoning and concept learning explicitly in terms of interactions between external and internal representational resources. Indeed, elsewhere Brown (2014) has pointed out that because concepts are often written about as "regular things" or "object-like" this can often lead to the view that different approaches are incompatible. Instead, he argues that when concepts are understood as dynamically emergent structures resulting from the interaction of multiple representational resources, both internal and external, these positions can be seen as more compatible.

There is a second sense of saying that concepts are not in the head. When people carry out various cognitive tasks, they use symbolic and material tools which can reduce the need for representations and processes inside the head. So learning to use an external tool can stand in, or replace the need, for acquiring a new concept. Säljö's (Chapter 11, this volume) view of concepts and his discussion of how students' learning to use the Carbon Footprint Calculator (CFC) software stands in for "acquiring" the concept of carbon footprint illustrates this perspective.

Some human activity's carbon footprint is the amount of carbon dioxide it releases into the atmosphere. Understanding this idea scientifically involves knowing how different human activities rely on the combustion of fossil fuels and how this results in the generation of some amount of carbon dioxide. Säljö and colleagues (Fauville, Andersson-Lantz, Mäkitalo, Dupont, & Säljö, 2016; Säljö, Chapter 11, this volume) have studied student interactions as they learn to use the CFC software. Students learn to input information about their lifestyle into the CFC, which generates an estimate of their carbon footprint. This allows them to make comparisons with each other and with people around the world. Säljö points out that the knowledge and skills students need to use the CFC are already available to them when they first encounter the software. As a result, it quickly becomes a tool that they can think with, shaping their actions with consequences for the environment. The hidden design of the CFC (assuming it incorporates scientists' best knowledge to date) ensures that students can use the output to actually reduce their carbon footprint. Säljö argues that the concept carbon footprint is a "hybrid" entity, distributed over the students' minds and the software itself.

This view is compatible with Carey's dual factor perspective on concepts, and brings to the fore the referential aspect of concepts. From this perspective, learning experiences with the CFC establish a causal connection between students' mental symbol *carbon footprint* with carbon footprint as a physical phenomenon. The learning intervention capitalizes on the referential aspect of the meaning of a natural kind concept, where it is the social practices (outside the head) that causally link the mental symbol to the entity in the world to which it refers. This analysis alerts us, however, to the fact that the students have not constructed much of the inferential network that constitutes the other key aspect of the concept of the carbon footprint as scientists understand it; that knowledge is embedded in the design of the software and students can learn to use the software without acquiring the knowledge embedded in its design.

The role of representation in concept learning

I turn now to the different ways in which internal and external representations of various kinds participate in the acquisition of conceptual knowledge. I will organize the discussion using the broad distinction made by Carey between knowledge enrichment and conceptual change.

Representation and knowledge enrichment

The literature on conceptual development provides evidence for a range of internal representational resources available early in life—e.g. iconic representations of objects, agents, approximate numerosity of sets; a stock of generalizations over sensorimotor experiences (image schemas); the essentialist assumption; and a conceptual representation of causality (see Carey, 2009; Gelman, 2003; Mandler, 2004). Knowledge enrichment, as mentioned above, refers to the formation of new conceptual categories and beliefs that draw on these existing representational resources. I describe here cases of knowledge enrichment shaped by external representations.

Learning to use language can guide children in constructing new conceptual categories out of existing representational resources. This is what Carey considers to be a weak effect of language on thought. For example, speakers of English and Korean exhibit subtle differences in non-linguistic spatial categorization tasks in ways that reflect differences between the two languages (McDonough, Choi, & Mandler, 2003). In Korean, the difference between a tight fit (e.g. a hand in a glove) and a loose fit (e.g. an apple in a large bowl) is marked linguistically. This is not the case in English. Mandler (2004) reviews evidence that the preverbal conceptual repertoire of infants (those destined to learn either English or Korean) includes the image schemas for both tight and loose fit. However, adult speakers of Korean are more likely to categorize spatial situations in terms of the tight-/loose-fit distinction.

Another example of this kind of weak effect of language is the effect of labels on our natural kind (e.g. dog, gold) and social (e.g. gender) conceptual categories. Gelman (2009; Gelman & DeJesus, Chapter 8, this volume) has shown that learning labels encourages essentialist interpretations of these categories. That is, labels encourage children and adults to treat category members as if there is some underlying essence that explains their observable characteristics. They make this essentialist assumption despite limited knowledge of the underlying causal mechanisms involved. Gelman and DeJesus point out that this can have both positive and negative effects on subsequent concept learning. On the one hand, the label and associated essentialist assumption serve as a placeholder for subsequent learning, inviting learners to fill in causal details. On the other, the result is an over-emphasis on between-category differences and within-category similarities (e.g. this effect hinders learning the scientific concept of *species*). While these effects on concept learning are important, they also reflect a weak language effect. Perception-based prototypical features and/or exemplars and the essentialist assumption will already have been part of the representational repertoire; the label simply triggers the essentialist interpretation of the category.

Belief formation that involves relating existing concepts to one another is also a form of knowledge enrichment. This, too, is an important aspect of learning in technical domains but may not pose a serious learning challenge. Learning more facts about a kind of animal, its behavior, and its natural habitat is an example of easy belief formation using existing conceptual resources. Similarly, communicating beliefs about key figures and events and their dates of occurrence when teaching history is unproblematic. The beliefs are formulated in terms of a repertoire of available concepts such as nation states, kings, and revolutionary leaders, and readily conveyed via lists of facts and extended narratives. Indeed, belief formation over existing concepts is the implicit assumption of traditional instruction, conceived of as the unproblematic transmission and reception of information via language. For example, Carretero et al. (2013) point out that the narratives presented to learners for the purpose of building a sense of national identity simply draw on (and reinforce) essentialist assumptions about social groups and the nation.

A classic example of belief revision in the literature is the conceptions of the Earth that elementary school children form when introduced to the idea that it is spherical (Vosniadou & Brewer, 1992). Teachers often introduce children to this idea using a three-dimensional physical model of a spherical Earth. The assumption is that children will simply adopt the belief that "The Earth is a sphere with people living on its surface." Instead they form "synthetic" models (e.g. *The Earth is a hollow sphere and with a platform inside,* supporting the belief that "People live inside the Earth"). These models result from assimilating the idea of a spherical Earth to their concept of physical objects, the idea that unsupported objects fall, and an absolute understanding of up and down. The Framework Theory of conceptual change (Vosniadou, Chapter 2, this volume) clearly distinguishes these assimilations of new information to existing conceptual structures (knowledge enrichment) from changes in concepts themselves (Vamvakoussi et al., 2013, apply this view to mathematics).

Belief formation and revision, not involving concept change, may not always be straightforward, however. Treagust, Won, and McLure (Chapter 12, this volume) review a body of research on the use of representations such as diagrams, physical models, and analogies in teaching for scientific understanding. One of the studies reviewed examined the strategies that Grade 11 students used to make sense of the multiple representations used to teach them about how breathing works (Won, Yoon, & Treagust, 2014). In this study, students were taught the scientific explanation of breathing by using a physical model of two balloons in a jar representing lungs and a rubber sheet that represents the role of the diaphragm in breathing, and a variety of diagrams. This study showed that learners used various strategies to make sense of and learn from these multiple representations. For example, they used different representations to obtain complementary information, used one representation to interpret another, and compared more than one representation to deepen their understanding.

This study showed that learning to formulate more scientific explanations of breathing was challenging and that learners needed strategies to use the multiple representations presented to them effectively. But an account of learning in this case need not appeal to the construction of novel concepts because it can assume existing concepts and beliefs: concepts of air pressure and volume and beliefs about the relationship between them; beliefs about the effects of differences in air pressure on the direction of flow of air, etc. Instead, the challenge was learning to use a variety of representations to assemble a complex explanation out of an existing set of concepts and beliefs. This kind of belief revision in science can be particularly challenging when different representations highlight different aspects of a system or mechanism and require learners to coordinate between different representations.

Representation and conceptual change

Knowledge change can involve conceptual change in its narrow sense, change in concepts per se. Conceptual change can occur at a community level sociohistorically (Nersessian, 2008; Saxe, Chapter 6, this volume). Here I focus on conceptual change in *individual learners* and emphasize the roles that representations of various kinds (internal and external) play in this process. Quinian bootstrapping is the mechanism Carey proposed as an account of how this takes place. To recap briefly, the proposal is that external representations function as placeholders for relationships between concepts; this anchors the process of acquiring new concepts. Initially, the inferential role of a new concept would be specified almost entirely in terms of the relationships expressed in the placeholder structure linking a target concept to other concepts (that themselves could be novel). Modeling activities (drawing on iconic representations) support the meaningful interpretation of the symbols of the placeholder structure, and the inferential role of a new concept is thereby enriched.

Although few researchers explicitly view their work in these terms, different strands of the literature on representation and concept learning can be seen as addressing different aspects of the process of Quinian bootstrapping. One research strand, well represented by Säljö's chapter in this part of the volume and others (Duit, Roth, Komorek, & Wilbers, 1998; Pea, 1994; Roschelle, 1992; Sfard, 2008), characterizes technical domains as specialized multimodal discourses and learning as the appropriation of these discourses. These researchers argue that good teaching involves creating opportunities for learners to negotiate the meaning of the representations that constitute knowledge in a domain. Thus, they describe the symbolic tools through which concepts are realized, use of these tools by individual learners and groups of learners, interactional formats in classrooms, the norms of communication that are encouraged by instruction, and the strategies that help interlocutors negotiate and converge in their understanding. Given this focus, the research methods used are discourse and conversational analysis. From the perspective offered here, this could be seen as saying that many concepts that learners are expected to learn are part of elaborate inferential networks formulated in terms of external symbolic representations of various kinds and that learning to use these symbols like an expert in the domain is a key target of learning. But from the present perspective, one would still want to ask how a learner can come to see novel symbols *as* meaningful. That is, we would still want to identify the *internal* resources and processes implicated in making sense of external symbols.

The learner's challenge of making sense of the symbols of technical domains is often described as the challenge of learning "abstract" concepts. A broad approach to understanding this challenge the learner faces begins by suggesting that learners must build on the knowledge available to them resulting from their everyday, sensorimotor experiences. This is the explicit orientation of those who approach concept learning from an embodied cognition perspective (Amin, Jeppsson, & Haglund, 2015; Hall & Nemirovsky, 2012) but this broad orientation is not always explicitly framed in terms of embodied cognition. For example, the use of 3-D models and 2-D visual representations to teach mathematical and scientific concepts has been a common component of good teaching for a long time. More recently, research has investigated the use of many kinds of iconic representations—such as photographs, diagrams, conceptual visual models, analogies, and, increasingly, simulations—in the teaching and learning of difficult, abstract concepts (see D'Angelo et al., 2014; Duit, Treagust, & Widodo, 2013; Treagust et al., Chapter 12, this volume, for reviews).

This large body of research on the role of iconic representations in supporting the learning of abstract concepts can be categorized with respect to that aspect of Quinian bootstrapping that each research strand tackles. Some work focuses on evaluating learning environments that incorporate iconic elements with the aim of demonstrating that significant gains in conceptual understanding can be achieved (e.g. Lindgren & Johnson-Glenberg, 2013; Lindgren, Tscholl, Wang, & Johnson, 2016). Using experimental research designs, this research documents *that* using iconic representations of various kinds—especially rich, interactive, virtual environments—are very effective teaching and learning tools. However, from a Quinian bootstrapping perspective we would be interested in learning more about the mechanism of change and ask: what *internal* iconic representations are formed through the experiences that learners have and how do those interact with external *propositional* representations to produce conceptual understanding?

Some instructional experiments have tested specific hypotheses about mechanisms of change. Research begins by determining learners' pre-instruction concepts and contrasting these with concepts in the domain of interest. Instruction is then designed around visual representations that are hypothesized to support the needed conceptual restructuring (Smith, 2007; White, 1993; Wiser & Amin, 2001). The effectiveness of the instructional intervention provides evidence for the role of the visual representations in conceptual change. In some of this work, the instructional intervention is designed to enable the explicit evaluation of the effectiveness of a number of bootstrapping techniques, such as limiting case analysis and analogical reasoning (Smith, 2007).

Other work using detailed qualitative analysis of interview protocols and classroom discourse looks at processes of change on a finer scale. This has led to novel theoretical constructs, especially dealing with the nature and role of imagery and image schemas in developing understanding in technical domains. For example, diSessa (1993) identified a large number of (image schematic) p-prims that constituted the pre-instruction "sense of mechanism." He showed how the misapplication of p-prims interferes with understanding of Newtonian mechanics but also how, after reorganization, they can contribute to scientifically sound inferences. Similarly, Brown and Clement (1989) showed that strategically selected physical situations which activated (image schematic) anchoring intuitions and bridging analogies help learners construct explanatory mental models. More recently, Clement (2009) has described how both learners and experts use imagery while performing creative bootstrapping techniques like analogical and extreme case reasoning.

Analysis of gestures has emerged as a particularly promising tool for inferring the presence of internal iconic representations and understanding their contributions to conceptual change. At least two broadly distinct lines of research on gesture can be distinguished. Foundational research in psychology, represented in Novack et al.'s contribution in this part (see also Goldin-Meadow, 2003), is establishing experimentally that gestures drive cognitive change, including conceptual change. More specifically, we have learned that gestures' key contribution is to activate image schematic representations which are used flexibly by learners across contexts because they abstract away from specific actions on objects (Novack & Goldin-Meadow, 2017). In parallel, there is a growing body of descriptive research on gesture in education and the learning sciences, which documents the use of gesture by teachers and learners as communicative and sense-making tools in instructional settings (Alibali & Nathan, 2012; Scherr, 2008). This research shows that meanings not expressed verbally are communicated by teachers during instruction; it can infer learner conceptions that may interfere with or contribute to learning, and hypothesizes the contributions gestures and associated internal iconic representations might be making to understanding abstract technical concepts.

From the research reviewed so far we learn that well designed simulations and visual representations, and the careful selection of physical situations and gestures strategically activate internal iconic representations that can support concept learning. But important to a Quinian bootstrapping account is to locate the role of iconic representations within the broader context of an inferential network, which includes the propositional representations—linguistic and mathematical—indispensable to technical knowledge.

Recently, some research programs have addressed the interactions between iconic and propositional representations that contribute to concept learning and the acquisition of expertise in technical domains. Two of these are represented by the contributions by Brown and Sherin to this part. Brown (Chapter 10, this volume) has shown how learners who have developed canonical understanding of electric current have successfully integrated (iconic) core intuitions, images of physical situations and explanatory mental models with (propositional) verbal-symbolic knowledge in electricity. Sherin (2001, and Chapter 7, this volume) has explored how image schematic knowledge elements are used (as part of symbolic forms) to interpret physics equations. He also shows how the use of equations can change the way in which learners apply p-prims in a way that supports a more scientific understanding of the concept of force. In addition, a number of researchers are examining the connection between conceptual metaphors implicit in the language of science and conceptual change (see Amin, 2015 for review). One finding from this work is that learners sometimes misinterpret the metaphorical language of science, mapping image schemas incorrectly to abstract concepts (Brookes & Etkina, 2015). Most of these examinations of the interactions between iconic and propositional representations are not presented explicitly within accounts of Quinian bootstrapping (but see Amin, 2009 for discussion). But like the research reviewed throughout this section, each can be viewed as potentially contributing to such accounts.

Finally, research on learning progressions, explicit about Quinian bootstrapping processes, suggests that interactions between internal and external representations can be seen in a broader context. Wiser and Smith (2016) chart the conceptual changes needed for children to understand atomic-molecular theory by middle school. They describe an initial knowledge state in which young children understand solid objects in terms of size, color, and function but not as made of a kind of material; where weight is understood in terms of the sensorimotor experience of heft, leading to judgments that liquids and very small objects do not have weight; where there is no understanding of amount of material; size is a global concept of bigness; and volume is not differentiated from other notions of spatial extent. There is a large gulf between this understanding and the scientific concepts of mass, material, volume, density, and weight and the conceptual changes that occur include changes in learners' metacognitive and epistemological understanding (e.g. measurement devices are better than perception as a source of knowledge about the weight of an object) (see Part IV and Smith, Synthesis IV, this volume). So Wiser and Smith describe a K-8 learning progression bridging initial and target understanding. They also describe two intermediate knowledge states, central to each is a model of matter. Instruction, centered on modeling, realizes a series of episodes of Quinian bootstrapping involving linguistic and mathematical placeholder structures interpreted using iconic representations.

This approach broadens the perspective on interactions between internal and external representations in at least two ways: it shows that it is important to describe these interactions within a broader account of the resources available to the learner at a particular point in time (including metacognitive and epistemological knowledge); and that it is important to compare understanding in a domain of knowledge to more advanced scientific understanding, characterized in terms of these interactions. While encouraging this breadth of perspective, Wiser and Smith's account is not always explicit about all the representational resources that learners draw on within key learning episodes. This means that their perspective can be enriched by drawing on the constructs and methodological tools for analyzing a broader range of internal iconic representations, especially how these interact with language and mathematical representations as described above.

Conclusions and recommendations

In this synthesis, I used Carey's (2009) account of concepts and concept acquisition to synthesize research on representation and concept learning. We saw that different research programs assumed that it is important to understand the interaction between internal and external representations and that some researchers appeal to similar types of iconic and propositional representations, even if the terminology they use is often different. I argued that the broad theoretical divide regarding concepts between cognitivists and those preferring situated/discursive views of cognition can be resolved when viewed from the perspective described here. And while the distinction is rarely made in this literature between knowledge enrichment and conceptual change, the synthesis made it possible to describe some of the different ways that researchers have described the roles of representations in these two types of knowledge change processes. That is, the framework allowed us to see how various lines of research both converge and complement each other in various respects.

Two broad recommendations follow from this discussion. First, pointing out that different researchers use different terms for similar constructs constitutes a call for researchers to unify their use of terms. Research on representation and concept learning is likely to be more cumulative if, as a community, we can recognize when our constructs overlap and we use the same terminology to signal that overlap. Second, I suggested that different lines of research can be seen as contributing to parts of a larger programmatic whole. The distinction between knowledge enrichment and conceptual change allowed us to recognize different concept learning processes and the different roles that representations play in these processes. Moreover, we saw that different lines of research could be seen as addressing different aspects of the Quinian bootstrapping process. Recognizing these complementarities is important because it allows us to situate the contribution of each line of research within the larger collective program and helps us identify what research is still needed. For example, this discussion reveals that research on concept learning rarely examines interactions between representations in the context of a broader account of concept learning that acknowledges changes in how a concept refers *and* its inferential role. In addition, research has also not examined how external representations of different types (e.g. language, equations *and* gesture) interact together and with internal representations in the process of concept learning.

In conclusion, I would like to offer two caveats with regard to the organizing framework offered here. First, this synthesis assumed a sharp distinction between knowledge enrichment and conceptual change. But since concepts are characterized in part in terms of inferential role, the difference between belief revisions and concept change needs to be seen as a subtle one despite the profound implications of the distinction for learning and teaching. Carey (2009) and Wiser and Smith (2016) suggest that the distinction blurs when successive knowledge states are characterized at a finer scale. Second, when discussing belief revision, I did not address the distinction between changes in conceptual understanding and belief acceptance, but other research on conceptual change has shown it to be relevant (see Hofer, Chapter 19, this volume; Lombardi & Sinatra, Chapter 20, this volume; Smith, Synthesis IV, this volume). How these subtleties complicate our understanding of representation and concept learning must be examined as the field moves forward. Ultimately, this framework is a working hypothesis and should be modified as needed, but its value is in reminding us of the larger program to which we are all contributing.

Acknowledgments

I would like to thank David Brown, Olivia Levrini, and Carol Smith for their comments on an earlier version of this synthesis. I also gratefully acknowledge the European Institutes for Advanced Study (EURIAS) Fellowship Programme/Marie-Curie Actions, 7th Framework Program and the Hanse-Wissenschaftskolleg (HWK) (Institute for Advanced Study), Delmenhorst, Germany for a 2016–17 fellowship during which this synthesis was written.

Notes

1 An extended discussion of this issue is beyond the scope of this synthesis (but see Carey, 2009, chapter 13). One of Carey's arguments for her position concerns the possibility of disagreement about specific beliefs. I might have a belief that there are white tigers, but you do not. For this disagreement concerning a belief about tigers to be possible, we must share some *concept* of tigers.

2 Carey posits a number of innate concepts, which she refers to as "core cognition," as the foundation for later conceptual development. While her arguments are compelling, innate concepts need not be assumed as part of the organizing framework for this synthesis.

3 Carey views concepts such as *object*, *agent* and (approximate) *number* as the mandatory output of modular perceptual systems, and therefore, are not revisable. Moreover, while she assumes they are represented iconically, they have conceptual content—i.e. their content goes beyond spatiotemporal information.

4 A number of different kinds of gestures have been distinguished (Alibali & Nathan, 2012): deictic gestures indicate something in the context of speech (e.g. by pointing); iconic gestures, which resemble something being thought about (e.g. a spiral gesture when referring to spiral staircase); metaphoric gestures, where the gesture is metaphorically related to the idea expressed (e.g. a forward gesture indicating a time in the future); and beat gestures with no meaningful content that are aligned with prosodic features of speech. The first three kinds of gestures ("representational" gestures) have been studied in research concerned with concept learning.

References

Alibali, M. W., & Nathan, M. J. (2012). Embodiment in mathematics teaching and learning: Evidence from learners' and teachers' gestures. *Journal of the Learning Sciences*, 21, 247–286.

Amin, T. G. (2009). Conceptual metaphor meets conceptual change. *Human Development*, 52, 165–197.

Amin, T. G. (2015). Conceptual metaphor and the study of conceptual change: Research synthesis and future directions. *International Journal of Science Education, 37*(5–6), 966–991.

Amin, T. G. Jeppsson, F., & Haglund, J. (Eds.) (2015). Special issue entitled: Conceptual metaphor and embodied cognition in science learning. *International Journal of Science Education, 37*(5–6), 745–991.

Amin, T. G., Smith, C., & Wiser, M. (2014). Student conceptions and conceptual change: Three overlapping phases of research. In N. Lederman & S. Abell (Eds.), *Handbook of research on science education* (vol. 2, pp. 57–81). New York: Routledge.

Brookes, D. T., & Etkina, E. (2015). The importance of language in students' reasoning about heat in thermodynamics processes. *International Journal of Science Education, 37*(5–6), 759–779.

Brown, D. E. (1993). Refocusing core intuitions: A concretizing role for analogy in conceptual change. *Journal of Research in Science Teaching, 30*(10), 1273–1290.

Brown, D. E. (2014). Students' conceptions as dynamically emergent structures. *Science & Education, 23*(7), 1463–1483.

Brown, D. & Clement, J. (1989). Overcoming misconceptions via analogical reasoning: Abstract transfer versus explanatory model construction. *Instructional Science, 18*(4), 237–261.

Carey, S. (2009). *The origin of concepts.* Oxford: Oxford University Press.

Carretero, M., Castorina, J. A., & Levinas, L. (2013). Conceptual change and historical narratives about the nation: A theoretical and empirical approach. In S. Vosniadou (Ed.), *International handbook of research on conceptual change* (2nd ed., pp. 269–287). London: Routledge.

Clark, A. (2003). *Natural-born cyborgs: Minds, technologies, and the future of human intelligence.* New York: Oxford University Press.

Clement, J. (2008). *Creative model construction in scientists and students: The role of imagery, analogy and mental simulation.* Dordrecht: Springer.

Clement, J. (2009). The role of imagistic simulation in scientific thought experiments. *Topics in Cognitive Science, 1,* 286–710.

Clement, J. (2013). Roles for explanatory models and analogies in conceptual change. In S. Vosniadou (Ed.), *International handbook of research on conceptual change* (2nd ed., pp. 412–446). London: Routledge.

D'Angelo, C., Rutstein, D., Harris, C., Bernard, R., Borokhovski, E., & Haertel, G. (2014). *Simulations for STEM learning: Systematic review and meta-analysis.* Menlo Park, CA: SRI International.

diSessa, A. A. (1993). Toward an epistemology of physics. *Cognition and Instruction, 10*(2&3), 105–225.

Duit, R., Roth, W.-M., Komorek, M., & Wilbers, J. (1998). Conceptual change cum discourse analysis to understand cognition in a unit on chaotic systems: Towards an integrative perspective on learning in science. *International Journal of Science Education, 20*(9), 1059–1073.

Duit, R., Treagust, D. F., & Widodo, A. (2013). Teaching science for conceptual change: Theory and practice. S. Vosniadou (Ed.), *International handbook of research on conceptual change* (pp. 487–503). New York: Routledge.

Fauville, G., Andersson-Lantz, A., Mäkitalo, Å., Dupont, S., & Säljö, R. (2016). The carbon footprint as a mediating tool in students' online reasoning about climate change. In O. Erstad, K. Kumpulainen, Å. Mäkitalo, K. Schröder, P. Pruulman-Vengerfeldt, & T. Jóhannsdøttir (Eds.), *Learning across contexts in the knowledge society* (pp. 179–202). London: Sense.

Gelman, S. (2003). *The essential child: Origins of essentialism in everyday thought.* Oxford: Oxford University Press.

Gelman, S. (2009). Learning from others: Children's construction of concepts. *Annual Review of Psychology, 60,* 115–40.

Gibbs, R. (2005). *Embodiment and cognitive science.* Cambridge: Cambridge University Press.

Goldin-Meadow, S. (2003). *Hearing gesture: How our hands help us think.* Cambridge, MA: Harvard University Press.

Hall, R., & Nemirovsky, R. (2012). Introduction to the special issue: Modalities of body engagement in mathematical activity and learning. *Journal of the Learning Sciences, 21*(2), 207–215.

Johnson, M. (1987). *The body in mind: The bodily basis of meaning, imagination, and reason.* Chicago, IL: University of Chicago Press.

Johnson-Laird, P. N. (1983). *Mental Models: Towards a cognitive science of language, inference, and consciousness.* Cambridge: Cambridge University Press.

Keil, F. C. (1989). Concepts, kinds, and cognitive development. Cambridge, MA: MIT Press.

Kosslyn, S. M., Thompson, W. L., & Ganis, G. (2006). *The case for mental imagery.* Oxford: Oxford University Press.

Lakoff, G., & Johnson, M. (1999). *Philosophy in the flesh.* New York: Basic Books.

Lakoff, G., & Núñez, R. E. (2000). *Where mathematics comes from: How the embodied mind brings mathematics into being.* New York: Basic Books.

Larkin, J. H. & Simon, H. A. (1987). Why a diagram is (sometimes) worth ten thousand words. *Cognitive Science, 11,* 65–99.

Lindgren, R., & Johnson-Glenberg, M. (2013). Emboldened by embodiment: Six precepts for research on embodied learning and mixed reality. *Educational Researcher, 42*(8), 445–452.

Lindgren, R., Tscholl, M., Wang, S., & Johnson, E. (2016) Enhancing learning and engagement through embodied interaction within a mixed reality simulation. *Computers and Education, 95,* 174–187.

Mandler, J. (2004). *The foundations of mind: The origins of the conceptual system.* Oxford: Oxford University Press.

Marghetis, T. & Núñez, R. (2010). *Dynamic construals, static formalisms: Evidence from co-speech gesture during mathematical proving.* Technical Report, Vol. 22, No. 1. San Diego: Center for Research in Language, University of California.

Martin, J. R., & Veel, R. (Eds.) (1998). *Reading science.* London: Routledge.

McDonough, L., Choi, S., & Mandler, J. M. (2003). Understanding spatial relations: Flexible infants, lexical adults. *Cognitive Psychology, 46,* 229–259.

Nersessian, N. (2008). *Creating scientific concepts.* Cambridge, MA: MIT Press.

Novack, M. A., & Goldin-Meadow, S. (2017). Gesture as representational action: A paper about function. *Psychonomic Bulletin and Review, 24*(3), 652–665. doi:10.3758/s13423-016-1145-z.

Pea, R. D. (1994). Seeing what we build together: Distributed multimedia learning environments for transformative communications. *Journal of the Learning Sciences, 3*(3), 285–299.

Pozzer-Ardenghi, L. L. & Roth, W.-M. (2003). Prevalence, function, and structure of photographs in high school biology textbooks. *Journal of Research in Science Teaching, 40,* 1089–1114.

Pozzer-Ardenghi, L. L. & Roth, W.-M. (2005). Making sense of photographs. *Science Education, 89,* 219–241.

Roschelle, J. (1992). Learning by collaborating: Convergent conceptual change. *Journal of the Learning Sciences, 2*(3), 235–276.

Scherr, R. E. (2008). Gesture analysis for physics education researchers. *Physical Review Special Topics—Physics Education Research, 4,* 010101.

Schoultz, J., Säljö, R., & Wyndhamn, J. (2001). Heavenly talk: Discourse, artifacts, and children's understanding of elementary astronomy. *Human Development, 44,* 103–118.

Sfard, A. (2008). *Thinking as communicating: Human development, development of discourses, and mathematizing.* Cambridge: Cambridge University Press.

Sherin, B. (2001). How students understand physics equations. *Cognition and Instruction, 19*(4), 479–541.

Smith, C. (2007). Bootstrapping processes in the development of students' commonsense matter theories. *Cognition and Instruction, 25*(4), 337–398.

Stephens, L., & Clement, J. (2010). Documenting the use of expert scientific reasoning processes by high school physics students. *Physical Review Special Topics—Physics Education Research, 6*(2), 1–15, doi:/10.1103/PhysRevSTPER.6.020122.

Tsang, J. M., Rosenberg-Lee, M., Blair, K. P., Schwartz, D. L., & Menon, V. (2010, June). *Near symmetry in a number bisection task yields faster responses and greater occipital activity.* Poster presented at the 16th annual meeting of the Organization for Human Brain Mapping, Barcelona, Spain.

Vamvakousi, X., Vosniadou, S., & Van Dooren, W. (2013). The framework theory approach applied to mathematics learning. In S. Vosniadou (Ed.), *International handbook of research on conceptual change* (2nd ed., pp. 305–321). London: Routledge.

van Dijk, T. A., & Kintsch, W. (1983). *Strategies of discourse comprehension.* New York: Academic Press.

Vosniadou, S., & Brewer, W. E. (1992). Mental models of the earth: A study of conceptual change in childhood. *Cognitive Psychology, 24*(4), 535–585.

White, B. (1993). ThinkerTools: causal models, conceptual change, and science education. *Cognition and Instruction, 10*(1), 1–100.

Wiser, M., & Amin, T. (2001). "Is heat hot?" Inducing conceptual change by integrating everyday and scientific conceptions. *Learning and Instruction, 11,* 331–355.

Wiser, M., & Smith, C. (2013). Learning and teaching about matter in the middle-school years; How can the atomic-molecular theory be meaningfully introduced. In S. Vosniadou (Ed.), *International handbook of research on conceptual change* (2nd ed., pp. 177–194). London: Routledge.

Wiser, M., & Smith, C. (2016). How is conceptual change possible? Insights from science education. In D. Barner & A. S. Baron (Eds.), *Core knowledge and conceptual change* (pp. 29–51). Oxford: Oxford University Press.

Won, M., Yoon, H., & Treagust, D. F. (2014). Students' learning strategies with multiple representations: Explanations on the human breathing mechanism. *Science Education, 98*(5), 840–866. doi:10.1002/sce.21128.

PART III

Modeling, explanation, and argumentation in conceptual change

Editor: Clark A. Chinn

Orientation

This section of the book examines the intersections between conceptual change and three practices that are central to inquiry: modeling, explanation, and argumentation. The six chapters in this section, together with the concluding synthesis, describe a variety of instructional interventions and research programs that help us understand the central role that these three practices can play in conceptual change.

The first three chapters take a higher-level view, presenting overviews of instructional approaches that integrate modeling, explanation, argumentation, and conceptual change. The other three chapters provide a more detailed examination of the thinking and discourse that emerge when learners engage with particular inquiry tasks and problems. Together, the six chapters provide a rich portrait of both the higher-level and fine-grained processes that must be integrated to promote effective inquiry and conceptual change.

In the first contribution, Sibel Erduran, Ebru Kaya, and Pinar Seda Cetin (building on earlier work by Erduran and Dagher) present heuristics for organizing and understanding inquiry instruction. The Benzene Ring Heuristic highlights the interconnections among prediction, explanation, and modeling and shows how these interface with data, class activities, and the real world. Argumentation is a core discourse used in representing ideas and in reasoning with explanations, models, and data. Richard Lehrer and Leona Schauble present an overview of their ambitious instructional project to engage students in a curriculum of modeling activities. Their chapter presents a very rich array of ideas to guide instructional efforts to promote increasingly sophisticated conceptions and scientific modeling practices by students. María Pilar Jiménez-Aleixandre and Pablo Brocos present a contrastive analysis of the conditions that promote conceptual change in two contexts—developing explanations and models, and making decisions about socio-scientific issues. Their evidence from two studies documents how argumentation and conceptual change proceed in distinguishable ways across these contexts.

Turning to the more micro-perspectives on conceptual change, Leema Berland and Rosemary Russ examine how argumentation and explanation are related in children's inquiry. They contend that argumentation is complex and often proceeds with irrational moves and lack of explicit awareness, and that these features must be taken into account when understanding conceptual change. Laurence Viennot and Nicolas Décamp argue that improvement in conceptions depends on learners' critical attitude, which allows them to recognize incompleteness or internal inconsistency in the explanations that they encounter. This critical attitude can thus spur changes in conceptions to overcome these problems. Finally, the chapter by Shulamit Kapon discusses three dimensions of a metric for sense-making—intuitive knowledge, understanding of mechanisms, and the situation's framing. These dimensions interact to influence how argumentation, explanation, and modeling unfold to promote conceptual change.

The concluding synthesis begins with a conceptual analysis of what is meant by the terms *modeling, explanation,* and *argumentation.* Then, like Synthesis IV by Smith in Part IV metacognition and epistemology in conceptual change, it uses the AIR model of epistemic cognition (developed by Chinn, Rinehart, and Buckland)—which contrasts epistemic aims, ideals, and reliable processes—as a lens for understanding the contributions of the chapters to our understanding of how conceptual change proceeds and how instruction can be designed to foster it. The six chapters collectively point to the critical role of argumentation in propelling changes in students' models and explanations of natural phenomena.

13

CONSOLIDATION OF CONCEPTUAL CHANGE, ARGUMENTATION, MODELS AND EXPLANATIONS

Why it matters for science education

Sibel Erduran, Ebru Kaya and Pinar Seda Cetin

Introduction

There has been a significant body of research in science education focusing on conceptual change since the 1980s. As separate bodies of literature, research on argumentation, models and explanations has taken root in science education since the 1990s. In their seminal work on conceptual change, Posner, Strike, Hewson and Gertzog (1982) proposed a framework that explained how "people's central, organizing concepts change from one set of concepts to another set, incompatible with the first" (p. 211). Their analyses pointed out two types of conceptual change: assimilation and accommodation. In assimilation, which is also called weak knowledge structuring or conceptual capture (Duit & Treagust, 2003), existing concepts are used to deal with new phenomena. In accommodation or radical knowledge structuring, students' existing knowledge is insufficient to grasp new phenomena, therefore, they must replace or reorganize their central concepts. As learners encounter new knowledge, which is not compatible with their previous knowledge, they use their conceptual ecology to decide whether the new knowledge is rational, believable, internally consistent and has explanatory and predictive power. Hence, an individual decides that the new knowledge is worthy of learning only when these criteria are met (Hewson & Hewson, 1988).

Argumentation in science education, on the other hand, has highlighted the role of engagement in scientific discourse and practices in the acquisition of scientific reasoning (Erduran & Jiménez-Aleixandre, 2007). Argumentation can be defined as the "justification of knowledge claims with evidence" (Jiménez-Aleixandre & Erduran, 2007) and includes a variety of discursive practices such as "assessing alternatives, weighing evidence, interpreting texts, and evaluating the potential viability of scientific claims" (Driver, Newton, & Osborne, 2000, p. 288). The literature on models and modeling in science education led to substantial insights into how learners construct knowledge representations. Models are forms of knowledge that can be defined as abstract representations of reality and can be "an idea, object, event, process, or system" (Justi & Gilbert, 2000, p. 994). Modeling enables an unknown reality (target) to be explained with a more familiar reality (source) (Duit & Glynn, 1996). As models focus on the specific aspects of a phenomenon, they simplify it (Ingham & Gilbert, 1991).

Finally, considering the dominance of scientific explanations in school science curricula, it is not surprising that explanations have a long history in science education research (Kim, 1994; McCain, 2015). A scientific explanation is often considered to be how and why something happens (Chinn & Brown, 2000). Typically, scientists explain phenomena by determining how and why they occur along with the conditions surrounding the observed events (Nagel, 1961). In science education, considerable emphasis is placed on developing students' ability to substantiate their explanations using reasons and evidence. Explanations can be articulated relative to disciplinary conceptual frameworks (Dagher & Erduran, 2014) highlighting variations in how explanations are defined in different fields of science.

In the rest of this chapter, we will review two example heuristics that help consolidate the definitions of conceptual change, argumentation, models and explanations into a framework that can have some utility in science education. We refer to two particular heuristics (i.e., the Benzene Ring Heuristic and the Theories-Laws-Models or TLM heuristic) proposed by Erduran and Dagher (2014) that not only synthesize perspectives about these concepts but also provide visual tools for summarizing and communicating them. The visual imagery is likely to facilitate the pedagogical applications of a consolidated framework that brings together some rather difficult and sometimes unfamiliar strategies (e.g., argumentation) for teachers. After reviewing the heuristics and making explicit their affordances for representing conceptual change, argumentation, models and explanations in a simplified form, we illustrate how the Benzene Ring Heuristic has been used in in-service science teacher education and what teachers have produced as example lesson ideas.

Consolidating conceptual change, argumentation, models and explanations

As the preceding discussion illustrates, the research literatures on conceptual change, argumentation, models and explanations have emerged as separate bodies of knowledge with limited links, particularly from an epistemic perspective. Heuristics proposed by Erduran and Dagher (2014) have the potential to interrelate these concepts and, thus, provide a holistic account that might have some educational applications. Even though these authors do not specify such interrelationships, the heuristics are generative in their nature and potentially yield new connections between the concepts of conceptual change, argumentation, models and explanations.

The first heuristic proposed by Erduran and Dagher (2014) brings together separate theoretical accounts of scientific practices as a whole. The Benzene Ring Heuristic (see Figure 13.1) represents the various epistemic and cognitive aspects of science at the corners of the hexagon, and social contexts and practices are shown as mediating factors around the ring. The components are not arranged in a linear fashion but can rather be related to each other in a multidirectional manner. The heuristic emphasizes modeling of data generated through a set of activities such as experimentation, observation and classification. Modeling serves to explain and predict the phenomena under investigation. The models help explain different scientific concepts. For example, the atomic model can help explain concepts such as electrons, protons and neutrons. Furthermore, it illustrates the connections between these concepts. In the example of the atomic model, the Bohr model of the atom can help predict chemical bonding between different atoms and explain chemical properties. Argumentation is a mediating process that interlinks the epistemic and cognitive aspects of science such as prediction and explanation. For example, chemists can use atomic models to make predictions about what products can be expected in a chemical reaction given the use of particular reactants. In other words, they could be arguing for why a reaction is likely to occur given the atomic structures of the reactants. Various stages of modeling, predicting and explaining can involve argumentation or the justification with evidence of the claims being made.

The second heuristic proposed by Erduran and Dagher (2014) focuses on scientific knowledge that is inclusive of a coherent framework of theories, models and explanations (see Figure 13.2). According to these authors, theories, laws and models (TLM) are forms of scientific knowledge that work together to generate and/or validate new knowledge. For example, the atomic theory, the periodic law of elements and molecular models help understand the structure of matter. TLM share a special characteristic: explanation. All theories, laws and models

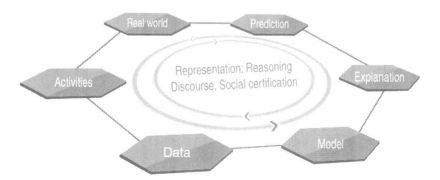

FIGURE 13.1   Benzene Ring Heuristic of scientific practices.
Source: Adapted from Figure 4.2 from Erduran, S., & Dagher, Z. (2014). *Reconceptualizing the nature of science for science education: Scientific knowledge, practices and other family categories.* Dordrecht, The Netherlands: Springer.

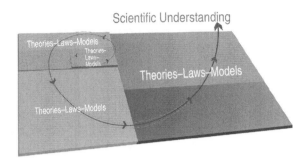

FIGURE 13.2 TLM, growth of scientific knowledge and scientific understanding.
Source: Adapted from Figure 6.1 from Erduran, S., & Dagher, Z. (2014). *Reconceptualizing the nature of science for science education: Scientific knowledge, practices and other family categories.* Dordrecht, The Netherlands: Springer.

help explain a particular phenomenon. Explanations are the "glue" that tie TLM together because explanations, underpinned by TLM, have to be consistent and coherent with one another. For example, a model of a molecule cannot be inconsistent with the atomic theory in how it is used to explain a function. Scientific knowledge growth involves the joint and progressive development of theories, laws and models which amount to particular paradigms such as the atomic theory. If at some point a drastic paradigm shift occurs, this gives rise to new cycles of knowledge growth. The history of science is full of examples of paradigm shifts, such as from the phlogiston theory in chemistry to Lavoisier's theory of chemical reactions, and from pangenesis in biology to Mendelian inheritance (Erduran & Dagher, 2014). As Thagard (1990) explains, "scientific knowledge often grows slowly with gradual additions of laws and concepts. But sometimes science undergoes dramatic conceptual changes when a whole system of concepts and laws are replaced by new ones" (p. 183).

The first heuristic involves the fine-grained level of modeling activity when data are collected and interpreted, whereas the second heuristic positions models at a more meta-level of scientific knowledge as they change over time. Both heuristics involve (a) models as forms of scientific practices and knowledge, (b) argumentation as a mediating process of justification, (c) explanations as the virtues of scientific practices and knowledge, and (d) conceptual change either as specific scientific concepts that are part of models, in the case of the first heuristic or as systems of concepts as in the case of paradigms and/or paradigm shifts, as implied by the TLM framework. Although both heuristics are underpinned by conceptual change, concepts are related to each component in different ways. For example, in the case of TLM, there is a system or a collective of concepts that compound theories, laws and models. In the case of the Benzene Ring Heuristic, concepts are used to make predictions, and models are tools for explaining concepts.

Although Erduran and Dagher (2014) did not explicitly relate conceptual change to the Benzene Ring Heuristic and TLM, both heuristics are underpinned by conceptual change because all scientific practices and knowledge are developed, evaluated and revised through incremental or radical changes in conceptual frameworks. The Benzene Ring Heuristic illustrates the processes of concept development, whereas the TLM illustrates the higher-level paradigmatic organization and change of concepts. Both heuristics can account for both domain-general and domain-specific concepts. For instance, all sciences might utilize models and, thus, the generic aspects of modeling can be discussed; in addition, the heuristics allow for articulation of domain-general features of models, for instance models of the solar system, the atom or the cell division with related conceptual frameworks (e.g., the planets, the sub-atomic particles and organelles) that help define them.

Applying the consolidated framework to science education

Although there has been a significant body of research in science education focusing on conceptual change, argumentation, models and explanations, these literatures have rarely been synthesized. Our extension and adaptation of Erduran and Dagher's (2014) heuristics, linking them to conceptual change, is an effort towards consolidating these disparate bodies of literature in order to generate some educationally useful frameworks. Although earlier calls have been made for providing teachers with frameworks explaining the growth of scientific knowledge as pedagogical tools (Duschl & Erduran, 1996), science curriculum materials and teaching continue to ignore this important metacognitive dimension of science learning. For example, Duschl and Erduran (1996) had proposed that visual tools such as Toulmin's Argument Pattern, Duschl's Goal of Science Hierarchy and Gowin's V Heuristic could be used to organize teaching of higher order thinking skills (i.e., the cognitive dimension of knowledge growth) and to reflect the development of scientific knowledge in the disciplines (i.e., the epistemic dimension of knowledge growth).

How would a consolidated framework of conceptual change, argumentation, models and explanation manifest itself in a science lesson? How can teacher education help coordinate these ideas for teachers given that they are not traditionally well connected in teaching nor coordinated in science learning environments? An example will be provided here to illustrate (a) how teacher education can help guide the articulation of conceptual change, argumentation, models and explanations together through the use of the Benzene Ring heuristic; (b) what resources teachers can, thus, generate to apply their learning to develop lesson materials; and (c) how such activities can be extended for further meta-cognitive learning goals that can be guided by the TLM heuristic.

The first author used the Benzene Ring Heuristic (Erduran & Dagher, 2014) and Toulmin's argument framework (Toulmin, 1958) in professional development workshops with in-service teachers in Singapore in 2015. A group of chemistry teachers were being trained as part of the new curricular developments in Singapore to infuse scientific practices and nature of science into their teaching. The workshop consisted of two primary activities. One workshop activity engaged groups of teachers in the Benzene Ring Heuristic by giving an example from acid-base chemistry. The different components of the heuristic were explained by showing how models of acids and bases can explain and predict neutralization through activities such as classification of sensory properties. The teachers were then asked to think of an example relevant to their teaching and develop the components of the Benzene Ring Heuristic as applied to that topic. The teachers were also encouraged to draw examples from everyday life to make the lesson resources relevant and motivating from a student's perspective. This aspect of the resources was also important in making the link to the "real world" component of the heuristic. The second workshop activity introduced teachers to Toulmin's argument pattern and asked teachers to supplement the earlier Benzene Ring characterization by writing down some potential claims and supporting evidence statements around the topic. In summary, the teacher training workshops were underpinned by the Benzene Ring Heuristic, which incorporated models and explanations explicitly in a particular conceptual context, creating an affordance for conceptual change. A simplified version of Toulmin's framework in terms of claims and evidence helped clarify the key arguments.

Figure 13.3 illustrates an example framework for lesson resources developed by a group of teachers. The lesson activity for students focused on polymer chemistry and included a cartoon entitled "Evolution of the Diapers." This activity is developed to teach polymer chemistry concepts by using the Benzene Ring Heuristic. In the activity, first students are asked to make a prediction by answering the question "Where does the water go in a diaper?" Students construct different claims to answer this question. For example, some students say that "water has reacted with the super polymer," some say that "water has been absorbed into the polymer," and some say that "water has been adsorbed onto the polymer." In fact, these claims focus on different scientific concepts such as chemical reaction, absorption and adsorption. Then students are asked to justify their claims by collecting data and using the data to propose models. Using the Benzene Ring Heuristic (Erduran & Dagher, 2014), the teacher could plan a lesson that covers aspects of scientific practices such as modeling and argumentation. For example, the teacher could produce a set of claims and a set of evidence statements that either support or refute the claims. The students could then be expected to discuss which evidence supports what claim. As part of the evidence statements, alternative models can be included that help explain why water disappears in the diaper. Here, the aim is to engage students in scientific practices that potentially help change their misconceptions about ideas in polymer chemistry that are applicable to everyday life. The Diaper Activity can be extended for further meta-cognitive learning goals that can be guided by the TLM heuristic. For example, the topic of polymer chemistry in the context of superabsorbent polymers lends itself to the valence bond theory. A teacher can choose to use the TLM heuristic to seek out ways of making links between models of adsorption versus absorption and the valence bond theory. There is also the possibility to use the TLM to highlight how models and theories of these phenomena have changed over time in the history of chemistry.

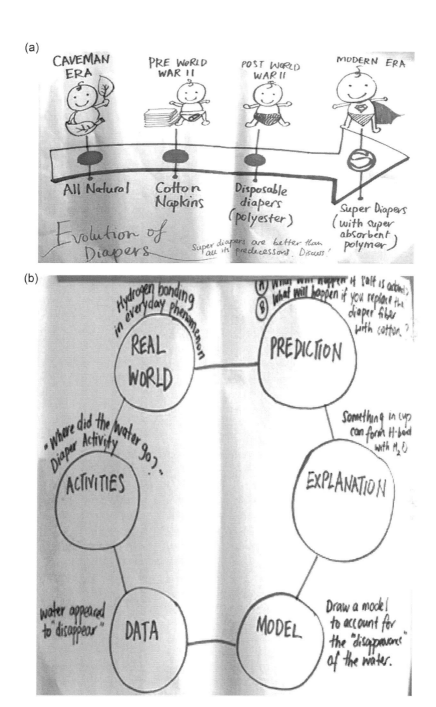

FIGURE 13.3 Diaper Activity example consolidating conceptual change, modeling, argumentation and explanation.

Source: Permission to use these images has been granted by the teachers in Singapore who participated in this research.

(c)

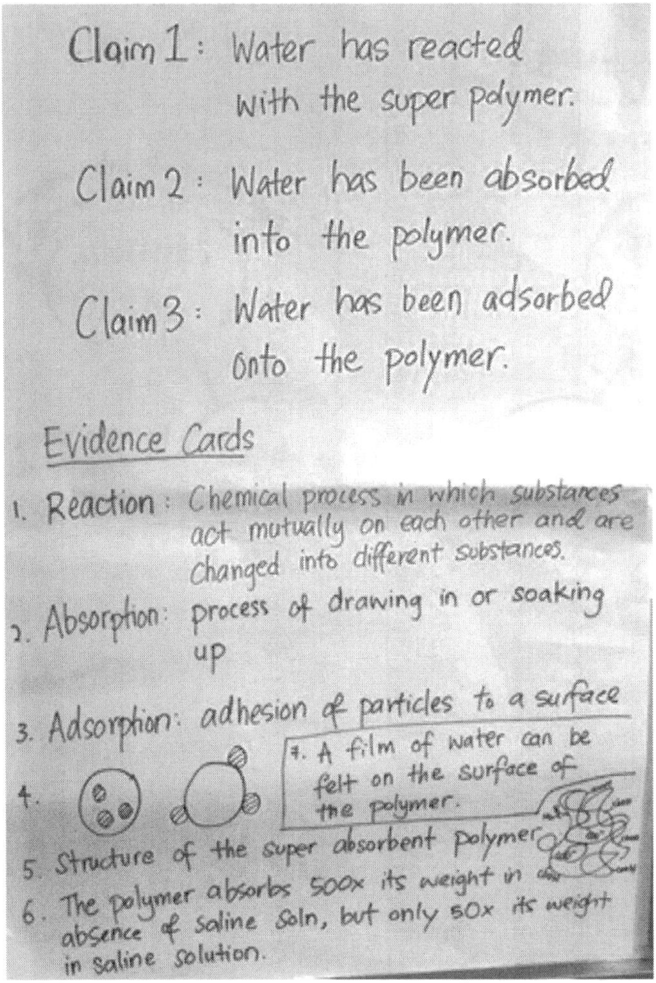

Claim 1: Water has reacted with the super polymer.

Claim 2: Water has been absorbed into the polymer.

Claim 3: Water has been adsorbed onto the polymer.

Evidence Cards

1. Reaction: Chemical process in which substances act mutually on each other and are changed into different substances.

2. Absorption: process of drawing in or soaking up

3. Adsorption: adhesion of particles to a surface

4.

4. A film of water can be felt on the surface of the polymer.

5. Structure of the super absorbent polymer

6. The polymer absorbs 500x its weight in absence of saline soln, but only 50x its weight in saline solution.

FIGURE 13.3   (Continued).

Conclusions

In this chapter, we capitalized on existing heuristics to consolidate the traditionally disparate notions of conceptual change, argumentation, models and explanations, such that they can have some utility in science education. Such consolidation is important for science education purposes because without a coherent framework that embraces these important concepts, each concept is not likely to reach its full potential in being articulated for the teaching and learning of science. For example, targeting argumentation without any awareness or focus on conceptual change is likely to promote one skill (i.e., the skill of justifying claims with evidence) at the expense of another (i.e., the skill of conceptual understanding). In a similar vein, if models and explanations are not linked to conceptual change and argumentation in science teaching, it is likely that students will remain in the dark about how models and explanations emerge in the first place. While conceptual change and argumentation can be vehicles for emphasizing the processes of scientific reasoning, models and explanations may be conceived as examples of scientific knowledge. Taken together, when these concepts are represented in visual form, they illustrate processes of knowledge construction, validation and revision in science at the level of particular scientific practices and also at the meta-level of scientific paradigms and paradigm shifts. Students' effective learning of science has to take into consideration these various levels of knowledge and knowledge growth in a connected and coordinated fashion. Though limited at this stage, teachers' engagement with visual heuristics has provided us with a preliminary empirical application of consolidated frameworks on conceptual change, argumentation, models and explanations.

Acknowledgments

The authors wish to acknowledge the contribution of Singapore teachers to the materials presented in Figure 13.3.

References

Chinn, C., & Brown, D. E. (2000). Learning in science: A comparison of deep and surface approaches. *Journal of Research in Science Teaching, 37*(2), 109–138.

Dagher, Z., & Erduran, S. (2014). The role of disciplinary knowledge in science education: The case of laws and explanations in biology and chemistry. In M. Matthews (Ed.), *Handbook of research on history, philosophy and sociology of science* (pp. 1203–1234). Dordrecht: Springer.

Driver, R., Newton, P., & Osborne, J. (2000). Establishing the norms of scientific argumentation in classrooms. *Science Education, 84*(3), 287–312.

Duit, R., & Glynn, S. (1996). Mental modelling. In G. Welford, J. Osborne, & P. Scott (Eds.), *Research in science education in Europe: Current issues and themes* (pp. 166–176). Bristol, PA: Farmer Press.

Duit, R., & Treagust, D. F. (2003). Conceptual change: A powerful framework for improving science teaching and learning. *International Journal of Science Education, 25*(6), 671–688.

Duschl, R., & Erduran, S. (1996). Modeling the growth of scientific knowledge. In G. Welford, J. Osborne, & P. Scott (Eds.), *Research in science education in Europe: Current issues and themes* (pp. 153–165). London: Falmer Press.

Erduran, S., & Dagher, Z. (2014). *Reconceptualizing the nature of science for science education: Scientific knowledge, practices and other family categories*. Dordrecht: Springer.

Erduran, S., & Jiménez-Aleixandre, M. P. (Eds.) (2007). *Argumentation in science education: Perspectives from classroom-based research*. Dordrecht: Springer.

Hewson, P. W., & Hewson, M. G. (1988). An appropriate conception of teaching science: A view from studies of science learning. *Science Education, 72*(5), 597–614.

Ingham, A. I., & Gilbert, J. K. (1991). The use of analogue models by students of chemistry at higher education level. *International Journal of Science Education, 13*(2), 203–215.

Jiménez-Aleixandre, M. P., & Erduran, S. (2007). Argumentation in science education: An overview. In S. Erduran & M. P. Jiménez-Aleixandre (Eds.), *Argumentation in science education: Perspectives from classroom-based research* (pp. 3–27). Dordrecht: Springer.

Justi, R., & Gilbert, J. K. (2000). History and philosophy of science through models: Some challenges in the case of "the atom". *International Journal of Science Education, 22*(9), 993–1009.

Kim, J. (1994). Explanatory knowledge and metaphysical dependence. *Philosophical Issues, 5*, 51–69.

McCain, K. (2015). Explanation and the nature of scientific knowledge. *Science & Education, 24*, 827–854.

Nagel, E. (1961). *The structure of science: Problems in the logic of scientific explanation*. New York, NY: Harcourt, Brace and World.

Posner, G. J., Strike, K. A., Hewson, P. W., & Gertzog, W. A. (1982). Accommodation of a scientific conception: Toward a theory of conceptual change. *Science Education, 66*, 211–277.

Thagard, P. (1990). The conceptual structure of the chemical revolution. *Philosophy of Science, 57*(2), 183–209.

Toulmin, S. (1958). *The uses of argument*. Cambridge: Cambridge University Press.

14

THE DYNAMIC MATERIAL AND REPRESENTATIONAL PRACTICES OF MODELING

Richard Lehrer and Leona Schauble

Explanation, modeling, and argumentation are integrally connected, but we take modeling to be the conceptual anchor. Indeed, explanation and argument are intrinsic to modeling practices. Philosophers agree that modeling is the characteristic form of explanation in science (e.g., Nersessian, 2008), but uncertainty is inherent in scientific modeling. Uncertainty arises materially, in that modeling always involves particular configurations of instruments, measures, and conditions of observation that undergird model formation and test. Uncertainty also arises conceptually, as one attempts to establish the explanatory coherence of a model in light of potential alternatives. As a result, modeling always occurs against a background of model competition and critique (Ford, 2015). These aspects of modeling are sometimes overlooked because educators have tended to focus more intently on students' conceptions of models than on their participation in the practice of modeling. *Model*, of course, is a two-faced word that refers both to an analogical system of objects and relations that represents a particular natural phenomenon, and to the practice of model generation and revision. When used as a noun, *model* refers to the products of scientific practice; most of the conceptual change research has been concerned primarily with changes in student understanding of scientific models in that sense. However, *model* is also a verb, emphasizing student involvement in model generation, critique, and test, and not simply the acquisition of science's final form products (Duschl, 1990). Moreover, model generation proceeds against a backdrop of competing models, so that critique and argument are inherently entailed. Thus, modeling communicates (to students, among others) the interconnectedness of science concepts and scientific practices, as well as the interrelations among practices, such as modeling, explanation, and argument, which are often considered and treated as distinct.

These considerations influence how we think about the purpose of science education. In particular, we do not regard science education as being primarily about promoting conceptual change. We find it more useful to conceive of our goal as apprenticing students into the practice of modeling nature. Conceptual change theories emphasize reorganization in the private mental structures of individual thinkers. Yet for purposes of expression, communication, and public evaluation, scientific concepts are instantiated in the form of models. Moreover, models are visible and shareable. They organize scientific activity and argument— their meaning and function depend on the shared history, agreed-upon methods, and knowledge accepted as legitimate within a community, what Knorr Cetina (1999) refers to as an epistemic culture. For that reason, modeling is consistent with a theory of domain learning that presumes that practices derive meaning from their epistemic function within knowledge-making communities and that concepts are embedded within this matrix of making. This perspective also shapes our perspective on education. Classrooms are communities, too, implying that the pedagogical challenge is to find ways of supporting classrooms in which modeling, explanation, and argument are accepted as legitimate ways to build structured bases of shared knowledge about core ideas in science.

To achieve and study these goals, we take a design study approach that encompasses a longer-term view than is usually applied in studies of conceptual change. A guiding question is how best to catalyze the extended *development* of modeling practices with young students. Therefore, most of our work is conducted in public schools where we work intensely with teachers in cross-grade teams. Together, we, and teachers, seek to learn how best to instructionally support modeling phenomena such as biomechanical motion, ecosystem functioning, and organismic/population growth. Subsequently, we study learning longitudinally as students progress through their schooling (usually the elementary to middle school grades, although we have also taken brief forays into high school). Findings from our research inform changes to instructional design, and in turn, questions about instructional variation inform the research. We have worked in science in two public school systems, one in the Midwest and another in the Midsouth. The two systems differ in their resources for schooling and in their traditions and expectations about the professional roles of teachers. Large proportions of students in both sites are English language learners and/or minority. In both sites, we worked with multiple schools and with several (up to 4 dozen) teachers within each of the participating schools.

Consistent with design study methodologies, we do not usually adopt experimental comparison as our primary approach (although experiments are occasionally embedded within our work). We are more likely to focus on replicating forms of instruction with variation across classrooms and timescales, in an attempt to understand which variants of the learning ecology (including, for example, tools, forms of talk, notations, and activity structures) are potentially necessary and sufficient to support desired forms of development. Analysis of classroom interaction and talk, student engagement and work, structured assessments, and in-depth student interviews help us track changes in thinking at both the classroom and individual student levels. As we support and study student learning, we keep three trajectories in sight. First, we seek to characterize student resources for making conceptual progress on the specific science "big ideas" under study. Big ideas refer to historically generative conceptual systems that can be potentially addressed by young students, yet have no ceiling in the sense that they are both meaningful and challenging for people of all levels of expertise, even disciplinary experts. Second, we focus on the development of students' modeling practices as methods for sustaining student inquiry and investigation of these big ideas. Children's ideas are often not canonical, but their initial conceptions can be fruitful resources for building further understanding. Third, we investigate how these two forms of development reciprocally influence each other.

In the absence of a context in which participants are generating scientific knowledge, legitimate scientific practices are unlikely to be operating (what is most frequently seen are variants of "doing school"). Therefore, a first goal is to organize classroom activity around building scientific knowledge, not in the sense that the findings are genuinely novel discoveries, but that they are new to students. We accomplish this by immersing children in long-term investigations of a bounded, but rich set of domain ideas (for example, comparatively exploring "Who lives here?" in a local pond, prairie, and woodland). Students need opportunities to grow a structured base of knowledge over an extended period, because scientific knowledge and scientific practices co-develop and bootstrap each other. Asking interesting questions, proposing alternative explanations, and evaluating counterevidence for a claim, among other forms of reasoning, do not usually appear until students have sufficient knowledge to support these processes. In addition, developing knowledge is bound to developing representational, meta-representational, and material competencies.

We find that a foundational site to initiate the development of modeling is representation. Students' representational resources range from physical microcosms to symbolic systems, such as scientific drawings and mathematical expressions. The selective and amplifying functions of representations are not immediately evident to students. That is, children do not immediately understand that representations often leave out redundant or theoretically irrelevant information; nor is it evident why representations often feature conventions that portray things that are not directly visible or enhance things that are difficult to see. Students especially dislike omitting information and initially seem to prefer veridical copies of the real world. However, we find that children's representations evolve as they begin to deploy these representations to support explanations and arguments. Indeed, representational choices are central in all forms of modeling. For example, first graders studied decomposition by designing compost columns to study factors that influence "rot" (Lehrer, Carpenter, Schauble, & Putz, 2000). The compost columns were motivated by the fact that winter was coming on, and although the class had been observing their Hallowe'en pumpkins decomposing on the playground, cold weather had brought the process to a halt. The studies began with debates over which attributes of the environment to include or omit in the columns to simulate the processes children were observing outside. Children readily suggested adding water from time to time to represent the process of rain. It seemed reasonable to them to expose some of the columns to sunlight or heat sources, because they had observed that the process of decomposition was faster in warm weather. The debate focused on whether to include gum wrappers. Some children pointed out that they had seen gum wrappers on the ground in the schoolyard, but others argued that these were unlikely to play a role in rates of decomposition. It is important to let discussions like these, about the depictive status of a representation, play out, so that children have opportunities to understand that models are not copies but rather, are exemplifications (after Goodman, 1976).

Experts read representations transparently, but it takes time and thinking for children to decide which aspects of a situation are relevant to the question being investigated and how those features should be symbolically incorporated into the representation. To help youngsters maintain correspondence between the representation and the represented aspects of the world, it is often a good idea to begin with representations that resemble their referents in some literal way. For example, lengths of string are cut and arranged below a line that represents the ground to record changes in the length of plant roots; over time, these may be re-represented as graphs that display quantitative units of length, with the units represented, as is conventional, in bars (conventionally, a case value plot) that rise above the X-axis. Educators ask questions and provoke comparisons that motivate representations that increasingly rely less exclusively on literal resemblance to their referents. Starting with drawings and physical models, children gradually progress to other less depictive representational forms, such as maps, diagrams, mathematical expressions, distributions, models of chance, and agent-based simulations. As the symbolic complexity of their models increases, the kinds of questions students can address also increase in power and sophistication.

From the earliest grades, students are encouraged to invent a diversity of representations and to compare and contrast their qualities, and especially, to discuss what the variants invented by the class members "show and hide." Educators avoid assigning representations as an exercise; they are always positioned as tools to support answers to questions. Because children hold varying and sometimes conflicting ideas and represent them in diverse ways, representations become a focus for scientific argumentation. Moreover, because representations are developed in support of inquiry, children decide which features of a natural system should be amplified and which reduced, and thus representations also function as explanations.

A critical requirement for supporting representational competence is a strong, conceptually based approach to mathematics instruction in which students are routinely encouraged to make sense of the world by mathematizing it. Mathematics and statistics are powerful and general symbolic languages for describing and supporting inference about the world. However, although these conceptual tools certainly have domain-general utility, domain experts do not simply deploy them in algorithmic ways; rather, they are selected, employed, tuned, and evaluated based on domain-specific assumptions about the purposes and the relevant content at hand (Cobb & Moore, 1997). Therefore, from a student's perspective, scientific knowledge-building is primarily a domain-specific enterprise, even as we encourage students to capitalize on a history of experiences with mathematics and other models that can be regarded in some sense as domain general.

Although representations are symbolic, Nature is material. Thus, a second major focus is engaging students with the material side of science. Many psychological descriptions of science portray it primarily as a form of reasoning, and struggles to arrange the material world in ways so that it can be studied and understood are largely absent from these accounts. In fact, much of science is devoted to finding a reliable way to measure air pressure, set up a lens so that it splits light in a desired manner, or build a system that detects gravitational waves. In our view, engaging with the material side of science is not only an important aspect of the discipline; it is also critical for interpreting the meaning and trustworthiness of data. As a starting point, our teachers focus on developing a robust theory of measurement (Lehrer, 2003). This includes helping students understand the variety of complex concepts involved in measuring an apparently straightforward quality, like length; but it also includes debates about how to identify and combine the necessary components in a compound measurement, such as devising a measure of the sustainability of an aquatic system. Measuring and conceiving are integrally related; establishing a way to measure a quality deeply influences (and often changes) one's conception of that quality (van Fraasen, 2008).

Investigations may provoke a need to invent or adapt tools, for example, using GPS images to develop a map of vegetation in the schoolyard. Students should play a role in designing and agreeing on standard ways to produce data, such as developing observational protocols and comparisons (including experiments). For example, second graders were comparing soils from the prairie, woodland, and wetland. They wanted to devise a standard way to describe the rate at which water filters through each of the soil types. Students decided to fill coffee filters with a common volume of soil of each type, add a constant amount of water, and measure the time it took for the water to pass completely through the filter. Each component of this arrangement—the mechanical filtering system, the amounts of soil and water, how to decide when the water had "gone completely through," and time as the final dependent measure—were fertile sites for decision and debate. Thus, they were a source of the uncertainty that we alluded to earlier, which produces an "open texture" to models (Hesse, 1963).

Many models have a material quality that confronts and resists those who wish to learn from them. For example, sixth graders who were studying two retention ponds near their school pursued ideas about the interactions between biotic and abiotic features by attempting to construct and study sustainable aquatic systems in one-gallon glass jars (Lehrer, Schauble, & Lucas, 2008). Each student identified and assembled the kind of substrate, plants, and animals to include, and prepared to study growth, reproduction, and change over time in the system.

However, the efforts of students were often thwarted; several of the jars promptly became overwhelmed with algal growth and crashed. Over the ensuing weeks, children struggled to achieve what Pickering (1995) calls a "mechanic grip" on their aquatic systems, meaning that they sought to wrestle Nature into a position so that she could be studied. As they did so, they learned a great deal about interactions between water chemistries and the jar inhabitants. This substantial program of work on the "mechanics" of the model had deep conceptual resonance. Over the course of their investigation, students compared and contrasted ingredients and changes in their own jar to the jars of other students as they pursued questions about issues such as rates of plant reproduction, effects of the "crowdedness" of jars on dissolved oxygen, and relationships between the density of indicator species like daphnia and system sustainability. Students pondered whether and how their simulations were adequate representations of the actual ponds they were concurrently studying. Many noted that, although the processes and interactions were similar, the jars were much more volatile systems than the ponds—that is, more rapidly disrupted by apparently minor modifications.

In this work, students' material practices and representational practices intersected and evolved together. These aspects of scientific practice are usually stripped out of science education activities, presumably to increase efficiency or perhaps to reduce complexity. But each of the decisions made along the way—about measurement, method, material components and simulations, protocols, and comparisons—undergirds scientific data and scientific argumentation. Each is open to critique and to defense, and thus broadens the range of scientific argumentation, which more traditionally in education is constrained to the formal relations between claims and evidence.

Here, then, is a top-level summary of our findings about supporting scientific modeling with young students (a more detailed argument is delineated in Lehrer & Schauble, 2015). First, supporting scientific practices requires that students be genuinely involved in scientific knowledge-building, ideally during investigations that last over sufficient time so that knowledge-building culminates in a well-structured conceptual system. It is not necessary that every student hold precisely the same knowledge; an advantage of this approach is that students can "specialize" in developing expertise in a personal interest in, say, lichen or mussels, or the various ways that aquatic insects employ to move through the water. In this way, the knowledge of the class exceeds the knowledge of any one individual student. Activity structures for sharing and critiquing knowledge (such as research meetings and reviews of data representations) are critical for building and sustaining contexts where knowledge-building becomes accepted as the business of the day (Lucas, Broderick, Lehrer, & Bohanan, 2005).

Second, it is important to avoid underestimating the representational demands involved in understanding a scientific drawing, graph, or simulation. Symbolic products often rely on conventions that are not familiar to novices, and they make sense to a community only against the backdrop of a system of shared goals, which themselves take time to create. Students have impressive resources for generating and interpreting representations, but the process should not be rushed. Third, it is good practice to begin instruction by capitalizing on students' existing representational resources. But then it is necessary to gradually and continually up the ante by pressing for increased precision, asking questions that require taking a deeper look, and supporting interpretation, comparison, and contrast between representational inventions produced by class members. Children's modeling capacity is built on their emerging representational repertoire.

Fourth and finally, science is material as well as symbolic and logical. Much of the work of scientists involves wrestling Nature into a position so that she reveals her secrets. This may mean inventing or adapting tools and instruments, designing protocols and experiments, devising and testing simulations and models, and staging conditions in which events of theoretical interest are likely to occur. It usually means struggling with measure, which always entails thinking deeply about the nature of the construct being measured. These aspects of science, which are frequently effaced from school science, should be experienced by students because they are the means by which scientific knowledge is created.

In our view, these *are* the processes of most interest to educators. What is less well known is where, when, and how these foundational experiences and understandings can best be recruited as resources as students move into high school and increasingly encounter scientific ideas that are necessarily farther from their own personal invention. In short, we know quite a bit about what the beginning of this educational trajectory entails, but we know less about its outlying destinations. That is mainly because the conditions have not yet existed for moving multiple groups of students longitudinally through classrooms where this kind of instruction is consistently pursued. It will require extended developmental research in contexts convivial to these forms of instruction to shed light on that question.

References

Cobb, G. W., & Moore, D. (1997). Mathematics, statistics, and teaching. *The American Mathematical Monthly, 104*, 801–823.

Duschl, R. A. (1990). *Restructuring science education: The importance of theories and their development*. New York: Teachers College Press.

Ford, M. J. (2015). Educational implications of choosing "practice" to describe science in the next generation science standards. *Science Education, 99*(6), 1041–1048.

Goodman, N. (1976). *Languages of art*. Indianapolis, IN: Hackett Publishing Company, Inc.

Hesse, M. B. (1963). *Models and analogies in science*. London: Sheed and Ward.

Knorr Cetina, K. D. (1999). *Epistemic cultures: How the sciences make knowledge*. Cambridge, MA: Harvard University Press.

Lehrer, R. (2003). Developing understanding of measurement. In J. Kilpatrick, W. G. Martin, & D. E. Schifter (Eds.), *A research companion to principles and standards for school mathematics* (pp. 179–192). Reston, VA: National Council of Teachers of Mathematics.

Lehrer, R., Carpenter, S., Schauble, L., & Putz, A. (2000). Designing classrooms that support inquiry. In J. Minstrell & E. Van Zee (Eds.), *Inquiring into inquiry learning and teaching in science* (pp. 80–99). Washington, DC: American Association for the Advancement of Science.

Lehrer, R., & Schauble, L. (2015). Developing scientific reasoning: The role of epistemic practices. In R. Lerner, L. S. Liben, & U. Mueller (Eds.), *Child psychology and developmental science, 7th Edition, Volume 2: Cognitive processes* (pp. 671–714). Hoboken, NJ: John Wiley & Sons.

Lehrer, R., Schauble, L., & Lucas, D. (2008). Supporting the development of the epistemology of inquiry. *Cognitive Development, 24*, 512–529.

Lucas, D., Broderick, N., Lehrer, R., & Bohanan, R. (2005). Making the grounds of scientific inquiry visible in the classroom. *Science Scope, 29*(3), 39–42.

Nersessian, N. J. (2008). *Creating scientific concepts.* Cambridge, MA: The MIT Press.

Pickering, A. (1995). *The mangle of practice: Time, agency, and science.* Chicago, IL: University of Chicago Press.

van Fraasen, B. C. (2008). *Scientific representation.* New York: Oxford University Press.

15

SHIFTS IN EPISTEMIC STATUS IN ARGUMENTATION AND IN CONCEPTUAL CHANGE

María Pilar Jiménez-Aleixandre and Pablo Brocos

Introduction: processes driving conceptual change

In this chapter, we discuss the interrelations between argumentation and conceptual change. Conceptual change requires modification of the epistemic status of learners' ideas, such as changes in whether some ideas are accepted or not. This chapter discusses the role of argumentation—that is, knowledge evaluation—in promoting change in the epistemic status of ideas during conceptual change. We use an expanded notion of conceptual change (CCh) including: (a) modification of models and explanations, or CCh in the strict sense; and (b) changes in decisions about scientific dilemmas of social relevance, which may be considered as modification of positions or beliefs, but also involves making sense of concepts, as is the case with (a). As diSessa (2002) argued, it is necessary to address a variety of types of mental entities in CCh research.

From a range of factors and processes driving conceptual change, we focus on the relative epistemic status of competing explanations or options and on the influence of argumentative interactions in the processes of *modification of these epistemic statuses*, which results in changes either to conceptual models or in decisions related to scientific dilemmas. These processes combine cognitive, epistemic, and social dimensions in an approach suggesting that science education should place at its center the development and modification of epistemic claims. Chinn and Rinehart (2016) argued that emotion is central to epistemic cognition, and we also consider the role of emotions in argumentation and conceptual change.

In the processes of evaluating and revising ideas, the scientific practices of argumentation and developing explanations are intertwined. The distinction between epistemic and scientific practices is addressed elsewhere (Jiménez-Aleixandre & Crujeiras, 2017); epistemic practices are understood as a broader construct and scientific practices as epistemic practices in the context of specific learning contexts or content areas within science.

Rationale: argumentation and emotions meet conceptual change

This section reviews the conceptualization of argumentation, conceptual change, and epistemic status, and recent perspectives about emotions in argumentation.

Argumentation is a complex scientific practice involving both justification—or the *evaluation* of knowledge claims by combining available evidence and relevant theory—and the *persuasion* of an audience. Therefore, our focus is on social or dialogic processes rather than on individual ones. We draw from approaches viewing argumentative interactions as processes involving negotiations and conceptual change (Baker, 2002, 2009), which can promote the social construction of knowledge. In this perspective, argumentative interactions are characterized as "attempts to decide on alternative solutions by transforming attitudes towards them" (Baker, 2009, p. 133).

Conceptual change is viewed from a perspective considering concepts and representations as discursive tools in the context of social practices. We view such changes as occurring in two contexts: developing models and explanations, and making decisions about socio-scientific issues (SSI). Although CCh in these two contexts differs, as discussed below, we argue that shifts in epistemic status play a crucial role in both. Since the influential paper by Pintrich, Marx, and Boyle (1993), research on CCh has addressed motivational, affective, and situational processes, as well as cognitive processes. In addition to these processes, decisions in SSIs involve a range of dimensions besides scientific knowledge, such as values, ethical concerns, cultural habits, or emotions; a complexity recognized in research about decision-making.

In their seminal paper, Posner, Strike, Hewson, and Gertzog (1982) were the first to draw attention to the role of the epistemic status of students' ideas in learning. They proposed four conditions for CCh related to the intellectual (now termed *epistemic*) status of students' ideas: whether new ideas were intelligible, plausible, and fruitful, and whether old ones were unsatisfactory. Hewson and Thorley (1989) stated that CCh is about "changing, i.e., raising or lowering, the status of conceptions" (p. 542), pointing out that it is a distortion to consider that the conditions are met when teachers judge it to be so from responses about content. Students' thinking (and talking) about the status of their ideas is a central component of the enactment of epistemic practices as argumentation. Hewson (1985) also noted the role of students' epistemological commitments or evaluative standards, which is related to the shifts in status of their ideas and positions.

Designs of argumentative learning environments often promote the generation of alternatives with different epistemic status (Jiménez-Aleixandre, 2008). We argue that *epistemic status* has a range of meanings in diverse argumentative contexts: in developing explanations it refers to the plausibility and explanatory power of alternative models, and in decision-making to the degree of acceptability of options. Along these lines, Baker (2002) proposed five conditions for argumentative interactions: (1) a diversity of proposals (solutions, methods); (2) proposals distributed across interlocutors; (3) proposals having, from the point of view of participants, different epistemic status, as more or less plausible, believable, acceptable; (4) the requirement to choose between them; and (5) that in order to choose, "the interlocutors establish (…) arguments and counterarguments, the creation of which potentially modify the epistemic statuses of the initial proposals" (Baker, 2002, pp. 306–307).

Relationships between argumentation and emotions are understudied. Emotions are absent in Toulmin's (1958) well-known work, for example. In most of the argumentation literature, when emotions are mentioned at all, they are often treated as having a negative or fallacious impact on reasoning. In argumentation about SSI, emotive and rational patterns have been contrasted. Christian Plantin (2011) took a novel approach to these relationships, conceiving *emotions as argumentative resources* that are mobilized alongside knowledge. The focus is not on determining the authentic psychological emotions the participants feel (the "emotional"), or the validity of their arguments, but rather on understanding how people mobilize emotions as ("emotive") resources within their discourses for argumentative purposes. Thus, for instance, when participants appeal to death and life issues, or when they argue that a meat diet is part of their national identity, they are using emotions as argumentative resources. We argue that emotive resources may have an important role in the modification of the epistemic status of ideas.

Features of the processes of change in epistemic status

The processes of change in epistemic status share some common features across contexts, but other features depend on the context. As Chinn and Rinehart (2016) proposed, epistemic cognition is situated. An instance of this situatedness is that evidence, expertise, or values may be weighed differently in different argumentative contexts.

In arguments about scientific explanations, shifts in epistemic status are linked to evidence and to relevant theory. In this context, the practices of argumentation and explanation are intertwined, for changes in explanations may relate to the generation and interpretation of evidence, and to the connections between evidence and explanation through justifications. However, in arguments about SSI, a range of dimensions are mobilized besides scientific knowledge, such as values or emotions. Thus, we suggest that, in the SSI context, shifts in acceptability are related to dynamic interactions among emotions, appeals to scientific evidence, and other dimensions such as cultural identities or ethical concerns.

The differences between the meanings of the three conditions for CCh related to the epistemic status of ideas and options in the two contexts are summarized in Table 15.1, where the second column incorporates a summary of conditions of CCh discussed in Hewson and Thorley (1989). We leave out the fourth condition, dissatisfaction with previous ideas, as it is defined in terms of low levels of plausibility and/or fruitfulness for the learner, which makes these ideas susceptible to having their status changed.

TABLE 15.1 Differences in the meanings of the conditions for conceptual change in the two contexts of developing scientific explanations and socio-scientific decision-making

Contexts/ Conditions	Developing Explanations and Models (Individual Focus)	Decision-Making about Socio-Scientific Issues (Social Focus)
Intelligible	The learner knows what the conception means	Participants socially share or negotiate the meaning of the issue
	The pieces of the conception fit together for the learner	Participants assess the coherence or contradiction among dimensions (evidence, values, etc.) of the issue
	The learner can find a way of representing the conception	Participants represent and share options and dimensions of the issue
	The learner can explore the possibilities inherent in it	Participants can predict or anticipate implications of the options
Plausible/ Acceptable	The learner believes that the conception is true	Participants believe that it is individually or socially possible to carry out the option
	The conception is consistent, and can be reconciled, with others accepted by the learner	The option is consistent with other conceptions and values individually or socially accepted
	The conception is consistent with evidence (for the learner)	The option is consistent with evidence (for the participants)
Fruitful	For the learner:	For participants:
	The conception has explanatory power	The option has potential to address several dimensions of the dilemma
	The conception achieves something of value	The option achieves something of value, individually or socially
	The conception solves insoluble problems, suggests new possibilities, directions	The option solves the dilemma, suggests new possibilities, directions

The main differences between both contexts in our approach, as summarized in Table 15.1, are:

1   In developing explanations, the focus is on the individual learner, whereas in decision-making it is on participants in a social interaction as they work collectively to make sense of the issue and the alternative options.
2   Intelligibility refers to the intelligibility of the conception in the first case, whereas in the second it includes the social negotiation of meanings, ranging from the comprehension of the issue and the variety of dimensions involved, to the available options and their implications.
3   Plausibility is met when the learner can reconcile the conception with other high-status, well-established ideas, and available evidence, accepting it as true. In the case of decision-making about SSI, we propose replacing this term with acceptability, which indicates not only the degree of feasibility of the options considered, in light of the available evidence and previous ideas,

but also their accordance with personal and social values. In plausibility/ acceptability, we have introduced, in both contexts, the consistency with evidence, although Hewson and Thorley place this issue within the conceptual ecology, rather than in the conditions for CCh.

4   Fruitfulness is related to usefulness, in the sense of achieving something of value for the learner. We argue that for scientific explanations this condition is linked to the explanatory power of concepts and models. For socio-scientific contexts, the fruitfulness of an option depends on the degree to which it can solve problems or dilemmas, according to individual and social values.

Examining shifts in explanations and in acceptability of options

To this point, we have presented a theoretical overview of argumentation and conceptual change in scientific and SSI contexts. We illustrate these processes in the two case studies below, first in a scientific context and then in an SSI context.

Changes in kindergarteners' explanations about the mouthpieces of snails

This case is drawn from a study about kindergarteners' (5–6 years old) use of first-hand evidence and purposeful observation to revise their understandings, in the context of a six-month project about snails (Monteira & Jiménez-Aleixandre, 2016). The study seeks to identify entry points for argumentation in kindergarten. Because evidence evaluation is a central component of argumentation (Jiménez-Aleixandre, 2008), the focus was on the scientific practice of engaging in argument from evidence. After the children had observed the snails for two weeks but not gathered data about their organs, the teacher asked them to draw "what they thought was inside the snail's mouth." All of the 20 drawings returned represented something like a human tongue, with a semi-elliptical shape, and 10 of them with teeth around it. Two months later, in a critical revision representative of the teacher's use of recurrence, the children were asked to discuss those drawings and to explain why they had drawn it that way: 14 children said, with slightly different wording "I thought it was like ours," which we interpret as a reference to intelligibility (of the previous idea). Then, when asked by the teacher to compare the drawings with the new data, they acknowledged that none of them were right when imagining what it was like, and that now they would draw it differently "shaped like a ribbon," an analogy that fits that mouthpart (the "radula").

What were these new data that prompted children's dissatisfaction with their previous conception? One source of data was the repeated observation of deep holes or "tunnels" in food like carrots, which suggested a different kind of teeth:

TEACHER: We need to study what their teeth are like. Because they are not like ours: Are they?

ELENA: Oh my, if they have them, we don't know that yet.

TEACHER: True, we don't know that yet.
ALBERTO: They are smaller.
MARTA: I think they do have teeth, because otherwise they could not make these tunnels.

In this classroom, there is a culture promoting argumentation, with a norm that claims should be backed up with evidence. Elena claimed that they don't know if snails have teeth. To this Marta responded with a piece of evidence, the tunnels, supporting her claim that they did have teeth. In other words, she considered it plausible. Other evidence, used in their arguments, came from watching snails eating flour from below a glass plate, and in a video, seeing them thrusting their radula in and out.

The status of anthropomorphic conceptions was lowered in this process: They exchanged terms as "teeth" for "spikes," and they explained that snails "scrape off" food, rather than chewing it. Critical to this process were the revision of their drawings, mentioned above, and the explicit comparison of previous and new ideas as prompted by the teacher. The children also expressed their emotions about the video:

MARTA: They [*the spikes*] had hooks [*shape*]
ROBERTO: We were impressed! [*by the video*]
TEACHER: How did it work?

In answer to this, the children mimicked the radula's movements, sticking their tongues in and out, identifying with the snails. In the seventh session involving this issue, they had the opportunity to directly observe a limpet's radula. In the subsequent revision of ideas, the teacher focused on the new notions, prompting them to propose explanations about how this mouthpart, with such tiny spikes, could make holes.

TEACHER: And what would they do in order to make holes?
ESTER: They would stretch it, pick up food, and withdraw it into the mouth.
MARTA: True, like butterflies.
ALBERTO: Certainly while the radula is spinning it is digging because it makes deep holes.

The plausibility of Ester's proposal, consistent with evidence and with other accepted notions, was acknowledged by Marta, who expressed her belief in the explanation's truthfulness. She compared it with how butterflies feed. Then Alberto proposed a mechanism accounting for the deep holes observed in food. This reveals the advances in these young children's thinking, for explanations that include mechanisms are very challenging for students to construct. Monteira and Jiménez-Aleixandre (2016) suggested that the process of change intertwined with argumentation using evidence is related to an environment where the teacher promoted epistemic talk and argumentative discourse.

Shifts in the acceptability of vegetarian diets by pre-service teachers

This case is drawn from the doctoral study of the second author with pre-service teachers (85 distributed over 20 small groups). They were asked to construct an argument about which diet would be better, using a complex data set involving information about five dimensions: nutrition, ecology, ethics, economy, and personal-cultural. It needs to be noted that in Spain vegetarians are a minority, estimated between 1.5 percent and 3 percent of the population, and there is social stereotyping considering them "weird."

One issue emerging from the analysis of the 20 written arguments and the oral debates in four groups (represented here as groups A, B, C, D) is an increase in the acceptability of vegetarian diets. This does not mean that participants were deciding that a vegetarian diet was best, but that they were acknowledging the advantages of vegetarian diets on some dimensions (e.g., healthier, more sustainable, and more ethical). This is reflected in the written reports, with ten proposing omnivorous diets with reduced meat amounts, seven omnivorous, two vegetarian, and one vegan diet. We interpret the ten "reducing meat" proposals as attempts to reach a compromise attending to conflicting information from different dimensions.

The status of vegetarianism was raised due to the evaluation of scientific evidence about nutrition and ecology, such as evidence on energy efficiency and water footprints. There were also appeals to ethical considerations about sentience and animal welfare. The issue was emotively framed, for instance, in the surprise and annoyance expressed by participants when finding out the benefits of vegetarian diets, which correspond to Plantin's (2011) displayed emotions, or when Alicia said about animal farming, "I feel pity for them [*animals*]," corresponding to spoken emotions. Emotive resources were used for expressing the acceptability of vegetarianism and in particular of veganism. For example, Blas comments: "For instance, for me ... veganism is an abomination."

This shifting of status was not a linear process in the debates. Instances of acknowledgment of the benefits of vegetarian diets occur in the four groups, as when Carlos said, "Wow... right now I tell you that the vegetarian one is winning on every aspect." The option was consistent with evidence, but not always with other conceptions and values that were individually and socially accepted. This conflict was voiced in all the groups, sometimes appealing to unsupported ideas:

AARON: But all these data [*ecology*] will always support a vegetarian diet, but still it is not enough to ... to have a decent health.

DAVID: ... [*vegetarian is*] much healthier. But being healthier doesn't mean being balanced.

In the final decisions, greater weight was assigned to the cultural habits, which resulted in a compromise about "reducing meat." This weight, which lowered the status of vegetarianism, was explicitly acknowledged in the written reports:

> "Our society also opts for an omnivorous diet, because most people eat it. If a majority would have a vegetarian diet we would choose it" (A).

> "Meat plays a cultural role in 'traditional' Galician diet, so a proposal for a change of diet that would dispense with it would be very difficult because of the important loss of a consolidated symbolic expression that makes part of our heritage" (B).

The role of the epistemic status of ideas in conceptual change is an understudied issue. We wanted to highlight the relevance of scientific evidence and arguments in modifying the status of conceptions in the context of developing explanations. In the context of SSI, the modification of the status of options may also be related to ethical values and to social cultural habits, in situated evaluations. We suggest that when promoting conceptual change more attention is needed to the processes of status modification.

Acknowledgments

Work supported by the Spanish Ministerio de Economía y Competitividad (MINECO); Contract grant numbers: EDU2012-38022-C02-01 and EDU2015-6643-C2-2-P. Pablo Brocos' work is supported by the Spanish Ministerio de Educación, Cultura y Deporte, scholarship code FPU14/03755.

References

Baker, M. (2002). Argumentative interactions, discursive operations and learning to model in science. In P. Brna, M. Baker, K. Stenning, & A. Tiberghien (Eds.), *The role of communication in learning to model* (pp. 303–324). Mahwah, NJ: Lawrence Erlbaum.

Baker, M. (2009). Argumentative interactions and the social construction of knowledge. In N. Muller Mirza & A.-N. Perret-Clermont (Eds.), *Argumentation and education: Theoretical foundations and practices* (pp. 127–144). Dordrecht: Springer.

Chinn, C. A., & Rinehart, R. W. (2016). Epistemic cognition and philosophy: Developing a new framework for epistemic cognition. In J. A. Greene, W. A. Sandoval, & I. Bråten (Eds.), *Handbook of epistemic cognition* (pp. 460–478). New York, NY: Routledge.

DiSessa, A. (2002). Why "conceptual ecology" is a good idea. In M. Limón & L. Mason (Eds.), *Reconsidering conceptual change. Issues in theory and practice* (pp. 29–60). Dordrecht: Kluwer.

Hewson, P. W. (1985) Epistemological commitments in the learning of science: Examples from dynamics. *European Journal of Science Education, 7,* 163–172.

Hewson, P. W., & Thorley, R. (1989). The conditions of conceptual change in the classroom. *International Journal of Science Education, 11,* 541–553.

Jiménez-Aleixandre, M. P. (2008). Designing argumentation learning environments. In S. Erduran & M. P. Jiménez-Aleixandre (Eds.), *Argumentation in science education: Perspectives from classroom-based research* (pp. 91–115). Dordrecht: Springer.

Jiménez-Aleixandre, M. P., & Crujeiras, B. (2017). Epistemic practices and scientific practices in science education. In B. Akpan, & K. Taber (Eds.), *Science education: An international comprehensive course companion* (pp. 69–80). Rotterdam: Sense Publishers.

Monteira, S. F., & Jiménez-Aleixandre, M. P. (2016). The practice of using evidence in kindergarten: The role of purposeful observation. *Journal of Research in Science Teaching, 53*(8), 1232–1258. doi:10.1002/tea.21259.

Pintrich, P. R., Marx, R. W., & Boyle, R. B. (1993). Beyond cold conceptual change: The role of motivational beliefs and classroom contextual factors in the process of conceptual change. *Review of Educational Research, 63*, 167–199.

Plantin, C. (2011). *Les bonnes raisons des émotions* (The good reasons of emotions). Bern: Peter Lang.

Posner, G. J., Strike, K. A., Hewson, P. W., & Gertzog, W. A. (1982). Accommodation of a scientific conception: Toward a theory of conceptual change. *Science Education, 62*, 211–227.

Toulmin, S. (1958). *The uses of argument.* Cambridge: Cambridge University Press.

16

CONCEPTUAL CHANGE THROUGH ARGUMENTATION

A process of dynamic refinement

Leema K. Berland and Rosemary S. Russ

In this chapter, we have been charged with the task of exploring the question: What does conceptual change during argumentation look like? From the outside, it seems like this should be a fairly straightforward task. (We certainly thought it would be when we agreed to write the chapter!) If we were to answer this question straightforwardly, we would look at some argumentative discourse and isolate moments of conceptual change in discourse.

So why aren't we going to do that? Well, the conceptual change literature offers us a cognitive understanding of how learning occurs: individual students have ideas and then—by some process—come to recognize that those ideas are flawed and so they change their ideas/concepts. However, engaging in scientific argumentation is a social practice. As such, the learning can only be located in the interactions between the participants. Thus, it is unsurprising that there are few individual "ah-ha" moments of conceptual change in the argumentation we have studied and that it can be challenging to identify explicit points of conceptual change.

Here we explore theoretically why this question (i.e., what does conceptual change during argumentation look like?) is problematic and consider an alternative framework for characterizing conceptual change through argumentation that is consistent with what we see in data from classroom discussions. Specifically, we argue this initial framing of the chapter assumes that both conceptual change and argumentation are rational, deliberate processes that are capable of being localized in people and in time. We suggest instead that understanding conceptual change in and around argumentation requires embracing the irrationality and complexity of these processes and tracking their co-refinement across students and time.

Frameworks for characterizing conceptual change

Within science education, research focusing on *concepts* and *conceptual change* emerged in the 1970s and 1980s. At an intuitive level, conceptual change embodies the idea that people's understandings of the world change over time. Here we describe two different frameworks for characterizing conceptual change—the rational and the refinement frameworks.

Rational conceptual change

Within literature on conceptual change, there is diversity in the *content* of the conceptions researchers have attributed to students. However, the literature typically shares a set of standard assumptions about the *form* that knowledge takes in the minds of students (Sherin, Sherin, & Madanes, 2000). Generally speaking, there is some tacit agreement around a depiction of knowledge that parallels "theories" in the professional scientific community. Specifically, students are thought to have coherent theories about a domain they consistently use to reason about related problems.

This notion of knowledge as mini-theories affords thinking of knowledge change—or conceptual change—as akin to Thomas Kuhn's (1970) paradigm shifts in professional science (e.g., Carey, 1985). Posner, Strike, Hewson and Gertzog (1982) expand this metaphor, arguing that students replace conceptions with new conceptions when they become dissatisfied with the original conception and find the new conception intelligible, plausible, and potentially fruitful for reasoning.

This rational framework necessitates metacognition and rationality. First, it assumes people are consciously aware of their current concepts, problems with those current concepts, possible alternatives, and strengths of the alternatives. Second, it assumes once students are aware of these things, they engage in logical analyses of the pros and cons of each of the conceptions.

Dynamic refinement change

Other science education scholars suggest knowledge does not always exist in coherent theories, and conceptual change often does not involve full-scale, conscious, replacement of one theory with another (diSessa, 1993). Instead, these scholars adopt a dynamic refinement framework for characterizing conceptual change, based in a network model of mind.

Network models of mind (e.g., Minstrell, 1992) represent knowledge not as internally consistent theories but instead as a large set of moderately small elements that become temporarily "connected" to one another when we reason about the world. With the network model of mind, learning (or conceptual change) does not occur as a process localized in time and place in which the learner explicitly recognizes a deficit in his own knowledge and then logically decides between alternatives (Hammer, 1996). Instead, learning is a process of successive, dynamic refinement in which learners come to use different knowledge in different contexts, and new connections between knowledge are gradually formed so their reasoning becomes more and more productive within new contexts.

In this view, even though researchers might observe successful learning events in one context (students answering questions correctly), they do not assume conceptual change has occurred. Instead, they expect learning to be piecemeal and to occur gradually as networks are broken and reformed over and over in different contexts within different communities. So what may look like conceptual change in one context may not be apparent in another context. Further, and importantly for our work here, they do not expect students to be aware of this process as it takes place; metacognition and rationality are neither required nor expected in the refinement framework.

Frameworks for characterizing learning through scientific argumentation

The term *scientific argumentation* describes learners—scientists and students— generating, defending, and evaluating claims about how the world works. Research examines both the discursive process in which claims are critiqued, defended, and improved, and the final product of the claim (Berland & McNeill, 2010). Researchers argue that students can and should learn with and through the discursive process of constructing argumentative products (cf. Osborne, 2010). The argumentative products, therefore, represent the students' understandings. Science education policy and research often emphasize that students' science understandings should take the form of models and explanations (National Research Council, 2012), thus looking for learning involves looking for change in the models and explanations expressed in and through the argument. In what follows, we examine how the rational and refinement frameworks for characterizing conceptual change apply to learning through argumentation.

Rational conceptual change through argumentation

The expectation that students can and should learn through scientific argumentation (often implicitly) draws on images of learning that are consistent with the rational view of conceptual change. In this work, learners are expected to evaluate new, contradictory information rationally, and to revise their understandings (or claims) accordingly. Osborne (2010) summarizes this position:

> learning is often the product of the difference between the intuitive or old models we hold and new ideas we encounter. Through a cognitive process of comparison and contrast, supported by dialogue, the individual then develops new understanding. Consequently, learning requires opportunities for students to advance claims, to justify the ideas they hold, and to be challenged [i.e., opportunities for argumentation].
>
> *(p. 464)*

This perspective depicts learning as a rational process of conceptual change. From this perspective, the claim is that the students' "theory" and changes to it are evidence of learning. If we focus on models and explanations as key learning outcomes, then the claim would be that the evidence of learning would be in the changes to those products.

Dynamic refinement change through argumentation

This depiction of rational conceptual change through argumentation largely ignores the social nature of argumentation, which often results in an irrational experience. That is, when we engage in arguments about topics in which we are invested, we are rarely convinced by logical counterarguments; instead we interpret counterarguments through our biases. In short, we do things that others would consider non-rational.

In fact, viewing argumentation as non-rational can explain many challenges associated with individuals learning through argumentation: we may not offer rebuttals to counterarguments (Osborne et al., 2004) because we want to focus on the veracity of our own ideas rather than attend to alternatives; we exhibit confirmation biases against counter-evidence (D. Kuhn, 1989) because we are motivated to find evidence that supports, not disputes, our own claims; and we rarely revise our claims in light of alternatives (Berland & Lee, 2012) when we are invested in convincing others.[1]

For example, in some of Berland's (2008) prior work, when investigating and constructing explanations of a computer model, the 7th graders concluded that "everyone's evidence seemed evident enough to prove their statements." Thus, these students found a way to avoid the rational conclusion that one of the groups needed to change their claim: rather than trying to resolve competing claims and come to consensus, these students determined that they must have been examining different computer programs. In a similar case, we saw a student who gradually and silently adopted his classmate's claims, never admitting that he changed his position (Berland & Lee, 2012). This student actively participated in argumentation (including the evaluation of counterarguments) but did not show explicit evidence of rational revision of his claims (i.e., conceptual change).

Despite the fact that we rarely see rational, explicit revision of claims in our studies of argumentation, there exists ample evidence that participating in scientific argumentation supports student learning scientific concepts (e.g., Asterhan & Schwarz, 2009; Osborne, 2010). We argue that understanding learning in argumentation to be a gradual, potentially tacit, process of refining ideas explains this disconnect.

For example, in an analysis of middle school and adult pre-and post-arguments, as well as the dyadic interactions that occurred between those written products, Kuhn, Shaw, and Felton (1997) found few participants changed their claims—or exhibited strong conceptual change. However, almost all participants qualitatively improved their arguments (i.e., introducing new evidence, explicitly rebutting counterarguments, etc.). Further, discourse analysis suggests this was the result of the participants gradually refining their ideas throughout their interactions.

Understanding learning through argumentation as a process of refinement requires taking a microgenetic approach in which *ideas* are the object of study, rather than *individuals*. This framework builds on the understanding that it takes time and interaction to learn. Using a refinement framework, learning might include instances of:

- Individual students drawing on a range of different types of knowledge as they seek to construct and defend claims *without explicit recognition that they are doing so* (Sherin, Krakowski, & Lee, 2012).
- Students seeking to connect others' arguments into their own *without explicit recognition that they are doing so* (Roth, 2014).
- Students following the implications of one piece of knowledge to construct a claim or new question *without explicit recognition that they are doing so* (Russ, Scherr, Hammer, & Mikeska, 2008).

In this depiction of learning through argumentation, evidence of learning is seen when claims *and justifications* change. Thus, the focal outcome of science education—the students' models and explanations—can appear as claims or justifications. Below we explore an episode of classroom discourse, analyze it using both the rational and refinement frameworks for characterizing learning, and use it to demonstrate this perspective on the conceptual change through argumentation.

An example

The discussion we unpack begins when a teacher from a large suburban school district on the East Coast of the USA asks her 1st graders: "Do you think seeds can grow in sand?" (Russ, 2006). Over the course of the next 10 minutes, students co-generate a number of claims and justifications.

Matthew offers the first, tentative answer to this question: "I think that, I think that seeds will not grow in sand because I wrote that it doesn't have the protein [food] that soil does for the seeds ..." Aidan quickly agrees with Matthew. Figure 16.1 depicts their argument.

Aidan adds another justification to the argument. He suggests seeds cannot grow in sand because sand absorbs water, effectively keeping the water from the seed.

> And cause sometimes when I see some stuff come out of my mouth that's wet and when it drops on the sand I see a little round dot of water and and the sand is like sucks *UP* the water. [Like??] keeps it to itself like takes the water away from the seed and the seed doesn't have any water but the sand does.

Elisabeth then implicitly agrees seeds cannot grow in sand because they do not get enough water. However, she offers a different mechanism.

> Because the soil is like hard and the water is like, pssshhh, blocked. Like with all those sticks and stuff—it's real hard so the water won't get through.

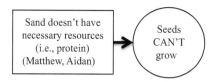

FIGURE 16.1   Initial argument focusing on sand providing necessary resources.

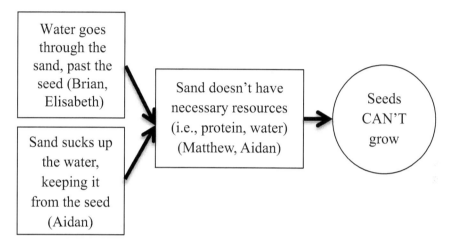

FIGURE 16.2   Developing argument that sand withholds water.

> But in sand since usually sand will be blown away not sticks into the sand—
> it's easy that it's not blocked so it just goes—shhhhhhwweeee. (Motions
> with both hands water flowing down.)

Another student, Brian, uses gesture to mime water going through sand to agree
with Elisabeth.

As shown in Figure 16.2, Elisabeth, Brian, and Aidan agree the seed would
not grow, however, they disagree on why: Aidan describes sand absorbing the
water while Elisabeth and Brian depict water flowing through sand.

Finally, Jorge introduces a third argument.

> I think it would grow because, because the water goes through it, and if the
> water goes through it might receive some water.

Here, Jorge agrees with Elisabeth and Brian's understanding that water flows
through the sand but he disagrees with their claim: Jorge believes seeds have
access to water that moves through sand and, hence, can grow (see Figure 16.3).
Jorge does not explicitly acknowledge this claim is different from his peers,
though the teacher does point it out.

The introduction of Jorge's alternative claim based on Elisabeth's justification
leads to some explicit disagreement, shown in Table 16.1.

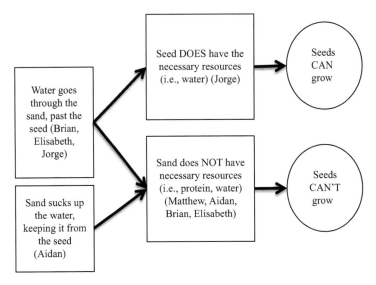

FIGURE 16.3 Developing argument questioning whether sand withholds water.

TABLE 16.1 Students disagree about the claim

Speaker	Quote
Kyle	[Jorge is saying] That the water can go through the sand. So um, so the plants can grow.
Elisabeth	*Can't* grow. [Emphasis hers]
Kyle	No they can grow they need water to grow. Why do you say they can't grow?
Elisabeth	Because if the water is going through it's not exactly where the seed is if you put it near the top... 'Cause the water is going near the bottom— and if it's going near the bottom it's not near the seed it's by the top.

The teacher does not push the class to resolve the disagreement in this moment, and they move on to discuss a possible experiment about seeds growing in sand.

How can we make sense of the conceptual change and argumentation in this episode of student discourse?

Applying a rational framework to the example

If we adopt a rational framework, the episode does not meet the criteria for argumentation or conceptual change. In terms of argumentation, it isn't until the very end of this exchange—when Jorge, Kyle, and Elisabeth discuss whether water passing through sand will enable the seed to grow—that students explicitly disagree. Thus, while there are instances of students stating components of an argument (i.e., claims and justifications), the exchange does not look like the prototypical scientific argument.

Similarly, in the rational framework, the strongest evidence of conceptual change would be the student(s) changing their claims, and/or recognizing their ideas have changed. However, we do not see that. For example, even though Aidan offers multiple explanations for why seeds cannot grow in sand, he does not explicitly recognize how those ideas change over time.

Applying a dynamic refinement framework to the example

In contrast, if we adopt a refinement framework we find ample evidence of learning through argumentation in this episode. The argumentation occurs because the ideas are "tentative" (Osborne & Patterson, 2011)—students are unsure of their claims and how to defend them. This lack of certainty results in a collaborative interaction with ample evidence of student learning.

In fact, we see many moments of successive refinement of claims and ideas we would expect from a non-rational understanding of learning through argumentation.

*   Individual students (i.e., Aidan) draw on multiple types of knowledge, including factual knowledge (i.e., seeds need water) and everyday experiences (i.e., sand soaking up spit), to construct and defend claims.
*   Students connect others' arguments to their own (i.e., Elisabeth building on Matthew's argument which builds on Aidan's).
*   Students following the implications of one piece of knowledge to construct a new claim or question (i.e., Jorge's conclusion that water passing through sand means seeds can grow).

Further, students do the above *without explicit recognition of what they are doing*. If conceptual change through argumentation was rational, we would expect Aidan to notice when he draws on different types of knowledge or for Elisabeth to notice she is modifying Aidan's account. Instead, we see the whole class dynamically refining their ideas over the course of the conversation.

Finally, in this argument there are two possible claims students defend with explanations. Thus, if we consider their explanation as a key outcome, then the changes of note are occurring throughout the argument, not just at the level of claims. This is consistent with a dynamic refinement framework for learning, but less consistent with a rational framework.

Last comments

Understanding conceptual change and argumentation as a process of idea refinement rather than a specific moment of change, is not controversial. In fact, we wonder if this reality has (implicitly) pushed researchers of argumentation (ourselves included) to bifurcate; some of us define learning through argumentation in terms of the concepts students learned through the argumentation as evidenced on pre-/post-tests rather than their discourse, and others focus on the learning of *how* and *why* to engage in argumentation as evidenced in their discourse rather than their conceptual understandings. In contrast, the dynamic refinement framework offers us alternative approaches to evaluating student learning through the argumentation. For example, preparation for future learning assessments (Schwartz & Martin, 2004), and trajectories of successive refinement during the arguments themselves both become appropriate measures of learning.

Acknowledgment

The data for the case study presented in this work comes from NSF ESI-9986846, "Case Studies of Elementary Student Inquiry in Physical Science" Project (PIs David Hammer and Emily van Zee).

Note

1 Many researchers, ourselves included, have addressed these challenges by focusing on the students' goals for their argumentative interactions (Asterhan & Schwarz, 2009; Berland & Reiser, 2011; Felton, Garcia-Mila, & Gilabert, 2009). For example, goals related to deliberation (Asterhan & Schwarz, 2009; Felton, Garcia-Mila, & Gilabert, 2009) and sense-making (Berland & Reiser, 2011) are more likely to support students in what could be considered conceptual change. However, consistent with its philosophical roots (Walton, 1998), this approach assumes rationality: that the individuals engaged in the argument will rationally act in ways to achieve their end goal.

References

Asterhan, C., & Schwarz, B. (2009). Argumentation and explanation in conceptual change: Indications from protocol analyses of peer-to-peer dialog. *Cognitive Science*, *33*(3), 374–400.

Berland, L.K. (2008). *Understanding the composite practice that forms when classrooms take up the practice of scientific argumentation.* (Unpublished Dissertation). Northwestern, Evanston, IL.

Berland, L.K., & Lee, V.R. (2012). In pursuit of consensus: Disagreement and legitimization during small-group argumentation. *International Journal of Science Education*, *34*(12), 1857–1882.

Berland, L.K., & McNeill, K.L. (2010). A learning progression for scientific argumentation: Understanding student work and designing supportive instructional contexts. *Science Education*, *94*, 765–793.

Berland, L.K., & Reiser, B.J. (2011). Classroom communities' adaptations of the practice of scientific argumentation. *Science Education*, *95*, 191–216.

Carey, S. (1985). *Conceptual change in childhood.* Cambridge, MA: MIT Press.

diSessa, A. (1993). Toward an epistemology of physics. *Cognition and Instruction*, *10*, 105–225.

Felton, M., Garcia-Mila, M., & Gilabert, S. (2009). Deliberation versus dispute: The impact of argumentative discourse goals on learning and reasoning in the science classroom. *Informal Logic*, *29*(4), 417–446.

Hammer, D. (1996). Misconceptions or P-Prims: How may alternative perspectives of cognitive structure influence instructional perceptions and intentions? *Journal of the Learning Sciences, 5,* 97–127.

Kuhn, D. (1989). Children and adults as intuitive scientists. *Psychological Review, 96,* 674–689.

Kuhn, T.S. (1970). *The structure of scientific revolutions* (2nd edition). Chicago, IL: University of Chicago Press.

Kuhn, D., Shaw, V., & Felton, M. (1997). Effects of dyadic interaction on argumentative reasoning. *Cognition and Instruction, 15,* 287–315.

Minstrell, J. (1992). *Facets of students' knowledge: A practical view from the classroom.* Presented at the Annual Meeting of the American Educational Research Association, San Francisco, CA.

National Research Council. (2012). *A framework for K-12 science education: Practices, crosscutting concepts, and core Ideas.* Washington, DC: National Academies Press.

Osborne, J. (2010). Arguing to learn in science: The role of collaborative, critical discourse. *Science, 328*(5977), 463–466.

Osborne, J., Erduran, S., & Simon, S. (2004). Enhancing the quality of argumentation in school science. *Journal of Research in Science Teaching, 41,* 994–1020.

Osborne, J., & Patterson, A. (2011). Scientific argument and explanation: A necessary distinction? *Science Education, 95*(4), 627–638.

Posner, G.J., Strike, K.A., Hewson, P.W., & Hertzog, W.A. (1982). Accommodation of a scientific conception: Toward a theory of conceptual change. *Science Education, 66,* 211–227.

Roth, W.-M. (2014). Science language Wanted Alive: Through the dialectical/dialogical lens of Vygotsky and the Bakhtin circle. *Journal of Research in Science Teaching, 51*(8), 1049–1083.

Russ, R.S. (2006). A framework for recognizing mechanistic reasoning in student scientific inquiry (Unpublished doctoral dissertation). Retrieved from http://hdl.handle.net/1903/4146.

Russ, R.S., Scherr, R.E., Hammer, D., & Mikeska, J. (2008). Recognizing mechanistic reasoning in student scientific inquiry: A framework for discourse analysis developed from philosophy of science. *Science Education, 92,* 499–525.

Schwartz, D.L., & Martin, T. (2004). Inventing to prepare for future fearning: The hidden efficiency of encouraging original student production in statistics instruction. *Cognition and Instruction, 22,* 129–184.

Sherin, B., Krakowski, M., & Lee, V.R. (2012). Some assembly required: How scientific explanations are constructed during clinical interviews. *Journal of Research in Science Teaching, 49*(2), 166–198.

Sherin, M.G., Sherin, B., & Madanes, R. (2000). Exploring diverse accounts of teacher knowledge. *Journal of Mathematical Behavior, 18*(3), 357–375.

Walton, D. (1998). *The new dialectic: Conversational contexts of argument.* Toronto, ON: University of Toronto Press.

17

CONCEPT AND CRITIQUE

Two intertwined routes for intellectual development in science

Laurence Viennot and Nicolas Décamp

Introduction

The point of departure for the views presented here is an epistemological position: physics is a science that aims at a coherent and parsimonious description of the world, in which a limited number of laws account for a large set of phenomena within a specified range of validity. Within this framework, coherence should be a pillar of physics education. Coherence can be defined (in a compelling if somewhat negative way) as *not claiming both a thing and its contrary*. In particular, this means not claiming something contrary to any laws of a physical theory that would, at the same time, be admitted as valid (such as Newton's laws or any personal 'theory') for the model adopted. Here, the word 'model' refers to a reductive description of the situation at hand, in which some features are chosen a priori as relevant. In particular, it would be incoherent to continue to adhere to the same model and theory where a prediction does not conform to an experimental fact. In such cases, either the model or the theory must be changed.

On this definition, coherence can be seen as a criterion for assessing the accuracy of a learner's view or line of reasoning. In more positive terms, coherence can be understood as a kind of compass that orients a student's scientific formation; this is to characterize intellectual development in science as a pathway that leads learners to a more coherent analysis of the material world. A major question then arising is how to document learners' intellectual development and the conditions most likely to favor it. In the first place, this requires more precise analysis of what constitutes intellectual development—a need reinforced by recent developments in science education—with a needed focus on coherence.

In recent years, science teaching objectives for secondary education have placed more emphasis on skills than on concepts (e.g., European Commission, 2015), risking a relative disregard of conceptual structuring. Indeed, there is already alarming evidence to this effect, as, for instance, in Norway and Sweden

(Lie, Angell, & Rohatgi, 2012). On the other hand, a critical attitude is an essential part of the practice of argumentation which is a core skill in science. In this context, it seems important to explore the interplay between the development of conceptual understanding and the critical attitude needed for argumentation, and to ask whether students can really develop either without the other (Henderson, MacPherson, Osborne, & Wild, 2015). This constitutes the main research question for the series of investigations outlined below. By way of grounding, the components of intellectual development will first be discussed.

Standpoints on intellectual development

To begin, we would like to take a step back from the idea of intellectual development as a succession of conceptual changes. As is well documented, how people reason in science—students, teachers, authors, lay people—is sensitive to the particular context, physical situation, and language in which a question is posed. Such reasoning has therefore been characterized as the emergence of 'knowledge in pieces' (diSessa, 1993). But because such occurrences are transversal, extending to other domains (e.g., linear causal reasoning, Viennot, 2001, chapter 5), they may be seen as theory-like (Vosniadou, 2002). More importantly, and perhaps because of their transversal character, such lines of reasoning survive local changes in a person's views. This is why we prefer to speak of conceptual *development* rather than conceptual *change*.

That said, intellectual development is not reducible to conceptual development; clearly, the development of a critical attitude is also an essential component of intellectual development. For present purposes, then, the key question is whether students can develop a critical attitude, independent of conceptual understanding. To address this question, we focus on the issue of coherence as defined above. We also investigate the extent to which students detect incomplete explanations, which is one aspect of exercising a critical attitude. In so restricting our investigation, we exclude much of what is characterized as critical thinking by cognitive scientists, whose definitions are much wider. For instance, we do not consider here students' ability to criticize public accounts of science with respect to possible asymmetric relationships of power, nor do we consider other abilities such as those listed by Jiménez-Aleixandre and Puig (2012).

It is worth noting that adopting a critical stance to any explanation—a prerequisite for relevant argumentation—requires awareness of one's own state of comprehension, a metacognitive dimension that indicates something of what it is to learn science. Although the connection between critical thinking and metacognition is not always acknowledged (e.g., Zohar & Barzilai, 2013), some authors (e.g., Vermunt, 1996) explicitly link the two. We share this view of critical stance as a component of metacognition—that is, as an essential condition for active self-regulation of one's own learning processes. Enacting a critical attitude is also a means of expressing dissatisfaction; in this light, such a stance can also be viewed as a search for intellectual satisfaction (Feller, Collins, & Viennot, 2009; Mathé and Viennot, 2009; Viennot, 2006, 2014). Consequently, the inquiries reported below deploy some markers of intellectual satisfaction. We further consider that posing questions that directly challenge an explanation indicates an active search for meaning beyond an attitude of mere doubt, perhaps relating to psychological factors such as self-esteem or self-efficacy (Bandura, 2001). Because these metacognitive and affective components of critical attitude seem a priori difficult to unravel, they are designated here as 'metacognitive-critical-affective' (MCA).

Studies of the co-development of conceptual understanding and critical attitude in advanced physics students

Main features

To document possible links between conceptual understanding and critical attitude, taking account of MCA factors, we chose to conduct in-depth case study investigations based on extended individual interviews. For each study, we designed conditions for a 'concept-driven-interactive pathway' (CDIP; see Viennot & de Hosson, 2015). A CDIP takes the form of a series of events—inputs from the interviewer and responses from the student, possibly involving experiments, questions or requests and discussion—oriented toward concept acquisition. As in the teaching experiment method (Komorek & Duit, 2004), the interaction is structured and guided to allow students to express their initial thoughts and reactions to various events. A CDIP is also progressive, in that what is understood at a given step may serve to construct the next stage of knowledge, and it offers students opportunities to critique presented textual or iconic explanations.

Within this framework, knowledge that is 'already there' may be reorganized and extended during the interview. Although resembling a teaching–learning format, this interaction is used as a research tool—not to evaluate a learning sequence but to address specific research questions. We examined how MCA factors might evolve in conjunction with conceptual comprehension by capturing students' *intellectual dynamics* during their interaction with the interviewer—that is, the interplay between conceptual and MCA factors. In each case, the sample comprised between 7 and 14 third- or fourth-year university students. Each study was centered on a different physics topic, such as hot air or helium balloons, radiocarbon dating, or survival blankets. In assessing critical development, we explored interviewees' capacity to detect and analyze incoherent or incomplete explanations.

First example: radiocarbon dating

The topic of radiocarbon dating is well suited to our purposes, in that it seems well known, but its details are far from obvious, and many incomplete explanations can be found in popular accounts. In fact, beyond the exponential decay of radiocarbon in dead organisms and the role of ^{14}C half-life (5730 years), a *relatively* complete and coherent explanation of this process should at least include the following conceptual nodes:

1 The need to know the initial proportion of radiocarbon to ordinary carbon in an organism at the time of its death;
2 The uniformity of this quantity in the atmosphere and living beings;
3 The constancy in time of this quantity;
4 The process of formation of radiocarbon;
5 The process of radioactive decay of radiocarbon;
6 How the balance between the corresponding numbers per second of radiocarbon atoms involved in these two processes results in a steady value of $[^{14}C/^{12}C]$ in the atmosphere;
7 The constancy of the total number of nuclei (radio carbon + nitrogen);
8 The multiplicative effect of the existing numbers of radiocarbon and nitrogen nuclei in the destruction and creation of ^{14}C nuclei, respectively;
9 How this multiplicative structure explains the stable proportion of radiocarbon to ordinary carbon in the atmosphere.

For this investigation (Décamp & Viennot 2015), we selected five documents from the Internet that provided incomplete explanations as compared to the above list. Using conceptual nodes 7, 8 and 9, we also designed a sixth document to explain how a steady state ^{14}C population can be reached and maintained from an unbalanced initial situation. Ten prospective teachers were then presented with these documents in order of increasing completeness. For each document, the interviewee was invited to state to what extent they were satisfied, or whether they would need further information. An example of a response considered to exhibit a critical attitude would be 'How is it that there is a constant proportion of radiocarbon in the atmosphere? Is there no radiocarbon decay in the atmosphere?'

Transcripts were processed at two levels of analysis: a conceptual level (which is not commented on here) and MCA aspects. Our MCA indicators included levels of agreement, types of questions posed (i.e., anecdotal or 'crucial,' as above) and levels of intellectual satisfaction or frustration. The findings indicated that most students need to reach a threshold of comprehension *beyond mere logical necessity* before activating their critical potential. For instance, there is no need to know how radiocarbon dating works to ask, after the most incomplete text, why the concentration of ^{14}C atoms in the atmosphere would be constant in time, as if there was no radioactive decay in the atmosphere. However, it was observed that such a question was not raised by students until a certain degree of comprehension of the phenomenon was reached. Once this (student-dependent) threshold was reached, agreement, moderate satisfaction, and anecdotal questions disappeared, being replaced by frustration, crucial questions, critiques (including self-critiques), and an active search for comprehension until the student was finally satisfied with the most complete explanation. We describe this dynamics of co-development as 'delayed critique.'

For a minority of participants (2/10), we also observed a persistent absence of critique, regardless of the incompleteness of the explanation at hand. Contrary to the cases of 'delayed critique' just described, these students already knew the topic very well. They were happy with their own responses and (therefore?) neglected to consider the texts for what they were—that is, deeply incomplete. It may be that they unconsciously completed what they were reading; we describe this syndrome as 'expert anesthesia of judgment.'

To sum up, this investigation illuminates how student teachers manage their intellectual resources when interacting with an expert. Here, activation of interviewees' critical potential according to their level of intellectual frustration and/or self-confidence was found to be linked to their comprehension of the topic. Two intellectual dynamics were identified—'delayed critique' and 'expert anesthesia'—thus providing strong support for the thesis of a direct interplay between conceptual and critical aspects of student teachers' development.

Previous and subsequent studies: converging results

The findings of this investigation align with previous results and are built on in subsequent investigations. Specifically, 'expert anesthesia of judgment' had already been observed and analyzed in physics teachers. For instance, a hot air balloon is nearly always presented as isobaric (see, for instance, Giancoli, 2005) when calculating the internal temperature needed for take-off. If teachers see no objection to this hypothesis ($N = 129/130$, Viennot, 2014), it is not because the textbook writers or teachers have ignored the law of fluid statics. Their knowledge in this domain should suffice to indicate that an isobaric situation inevitably results in a crash, given that all kinds of flotation link to a gradient of pressure, or that the same pressure on both sides of an envelope cannot result in a force exerted on this envelope. In this case, the observed critical passivity may reflect the fact that this inconsistent hypothesis leads to a correct solution via the calculation of Archimedes' upthrust, which falls within teachers' expertise.

Another experiment looked at a popular commentary on the world freefall record. It was said that the hero ascended to an altitude of 40,000 meters in a helium balloon before jumping out and was then in freefall, given 'the absence of an atmosphere.' Twenty-three PhD students and six in-service teachers were asked individually whether they would pose any questions to grade 10 students to help them comprehend this text (Viennot, 2013). Despite their sufficient expertise, none of the participants mentioned that a helium balloon cannot reach a place where there is no air.

With regard to 'delayed critique,' some instances were also observed in an investigation involving 14 third-year university students of scientific mediation (Mathé and Viennot, 2009). These prospective journalists were asked for their opinions about an article explaining how a hot air balloon works. This paper mentioned the usual inconsistent hypothesis, and while interviewees did criticize the paper after realizing that the hypothesis was absurd, there was, in most cases, a notable delay in doing so.

In one subsequent investigation, a small group ($N = 7$) of prospective teachers in fourth year at university were interviewed about phenomena related to a survival blanket (Viennot and Décamp, 2016a). Again, we observed a dynamics of 'delayed critique' (6/7). In this case, unlike the previous studies, a preconception strongly influenced students' judgments—that the best possible way to protect against cold with a survival blanket was to ensure the maximum reflection of heat toward the body. Not surprisingly, then, participants were found to have difficulty in critiquing texts presenting the same view. In one case, however, an element of information available from the start (that the gold side is more emissive and less reflective than the silver side) was used to trigger an 'early critique,' confirming that this dynamics was logically possible. In contrast, none of the students were subject to 'expert anesthesia of judgment,' given that none were experts on this topic. Very similar results were obtained with a last research piece about osmosis (Viennot & Décamp, 2016b).

These two investigations confirm that the most frequent intellectual dynamic that we have identified, 'delayed critique,' is also relevant concerning these topics. The absence of expert anesthesia does not invalidate our previous interpretations in this regard, given that the topics—survival blanket and osmosis—were unfamiliar to all our interviewees. It is also interesting to observe in each investigation a case of 'early critique'—in other words, a very short delay before the activation of a critical attitude despite a very incomplete comprehension of the phenomenon at hand. These (very infrequent) cases designate a possible objective for teacher development, that is, to express one's frustration even in the absence of complete comprehension.

Concluding remarks

This chapter synthesized a series of investigations based on in-depth interviews about several physical situations, bearing on what appears to be the *co-development* of conceptual comprehension and critical attitude. The way a given potential of critique is activated or not may strongly depend on students' evolving comprehension of a topic in conjunction with some psychological aspects. These studies highlight the metacognitive, critical and affective aspects of interviewees' comments, and several dynamics of co-development are characterized. 'Delayed critique' is perhaps the most frequent dynamic in the case of non-obvious topics, where a threshold of comprehension has to be reached, beyond mere logical necessity, before students activate their critical potential. The case of 'early critique,' probably infrequent for non-obvious topics, arises where a student makes use of what they already know, to pose relevant questions without inhibition, despite their incomplete comprehension of the topic. In contrast, 'expert anesthesia' of judgment designates a lack of activation of the critical attitude, despite a high level of conceptual structuring. On this (still exploratory) basis, we suggest that further research should continue to explore the entangled processes of conceptual and critical development in students and teachers. In particular, it seems relevant to investigate how to foster an 'early critique' in students, that is, how to help them to use what they already know—a kind of 'conceptual parsimony'—to activate their critical potential. To this end, we suggest that correlation-based studies will probably not suffice. Instead, our findings support the need for in-depth analyses of students' *intellectual dynamics*—that is, of intervening *processes* during interaction with a teacher or with other students in constructing critical judgments of the coherence and completeness of scientific explanations.

References

Bandura, A. (2001). Social cognitive theory: An agentic perspective. *Annual Review of Psychology, 52,* 1–26.

Décamp, N., & Viennot, N. (2015). Co-development of conceptual understanding and critical attitude: Analysing texts on radiocarbon dating. *International Journal of Science Education, 37,* 2038–2063, doi:10.1080/09500693.2015.1061720.

diSessa, A. A. (1993). Toward an epistemology of physics. *Cognition and Instruction, 10*(2–3), 105–225.

European Commission. (2015). *Science education for responsible citizenship.* Report EUR 26893 EN chair Hellen Hazelkorn Brussels.

Feller, I., Colin, P., & Viennot, L. (2009). Critical analysis of popularization documents in the physics classroom: An action-research in grade 10. *Problems of Education in the 21st Century, 17,* 72–96.

Giancoli, D. C. (2005). *Physics* (6th ed.). Instructor Resource Center CD-ROM. Upper Saddle River, NJ: Prentice Hall.

Henderson, J. B., MacPherson, A., Osborne, J., & Wild, A. (2015). Beyond construction: Five arguments for the role and value of critique in learning science. *International Journal of Science Education, 37*(10), 1668–1697, doi: 10.1080/09500693.2015.1043598.

Jiménez-Aleixandre, M. P., & Puig, B. (2012). Argumentation, evidence evaluation and critical thinking. In B. J. Fraser, K. Tobin, & C. McRobbie (Eds.), *Second international handbook of science education* (pp. 1001–1015). Dordrecht: Springer, doi: 10.1007/978-1-4020–9041-7.

Komorek, M. & Duit, R. (2004). The teaching experiment as a powerful method to develop and evaluate teaching and learning sequences in the domain of non-linear systems. *International Journal of Science Education, 26*(5), 619–633.

Lie, S., Angell, C. & Rohatgi, A. (2012). Interpreting the Norwegian and Swedish trend data for physics in the TIMSS Advanced Study. *Nordic Studies in Education, 32,* 177–195.

Mathé, S., & Viennot, L. (2009). Stressing the coherence of physics: Students', journalists' and science mediators' reactions. *Problems of Education in the 21st Century, 11*(11), 104–128.

Vermunt, J. D. (1996) Metacognitive, cognitive and affective aspects of learning styles and strategies: A phenomenographic analysis. *Higher Education, 31,* 25–50, doi:10.1007/BF00129106.

Viennot, L. (2001) *Reasoning in physics.* (chap. 5) Dordrecht: Kluwer.

Viennot, L. (2006) Teaching rituals and students' intellectual satisfaction. *Physics Education*, 41, 400–408.

Viennot, L. (2013) Les promesses de l'Enseignement Intégré de Science et Technologie (EIST): de la fausse monnaie?, *Spirale* n° 52, 51–68.

Viennot, L. (2014) *Thinking in physics: The pleasure of reasoning and understanding*. Dordrecht: Springer.

Viennot, L., & de Hosson, C. (2015) From a subtractive to multiplicative approach, a concept-driven interactive pathway on the selective absorption of light. *International Journal of Science Education*, 37(1), 1–30. doi: 10.1080/09500693.2014.950186.

Viennot, L., & Décamp, N. (2016a). Co-development of conceptual understanding and critical attitude: Toward a systemic analysis of the survival blanket. *European Journal of Physics*, 37(1), 015702, doi: 10.1088/0143–0807/37/1/015702.

Viennot, L., & Décamp, N. (2016b). Conceptual and critical development in student teachers: First steps towards an integrated comprehension of osmosis. *International Journal of Science Education*, 38(14), 2197–2219, doi:10.1080/09500693.2016.1230793.

Vosniadou, S. (2002). On the nature of naive physics. In M. Limon & L. Mason (Eds.), *Reconsidering conceptual change: Issues in theory and practice* (pp. 61–76). Dordrecht: Kluwer.

Zohar, A., & Barzilai, S. (2013). A review of research on metacognition in science education: Current and future directions. *Studies in Science Education*, 49(2), 121–169, doi: 10.1080/03057267.2013.847261.

18

EVALUATING SELF-GENERATED EXPLANATIONS IN THE PROCESS OF UNDERSTANDING

Shulamit Kapon

Conceptual change, in my view, is an ongoing process of reorganization and recontextualization of a complex knowledge system (diSessa, 1993). During this process, when it is carefully crafted, learners gradually start to use the scientific ideas and models that they learn in school independently as interpretive frameworks for making sense and explaining phenomena in the natural world, and as a basis for innovative design. Employing scientific ideas and models in this way involves a complex process of sense-making in which learners construct and reconstruct a series of self-explanations that evolve, change, replace one another, or merge into new self-explanations; the evolution of self-explanations involves an ongoing tacit evaluation of their relative soundness. This iterative construction, evaluation, and reconstruction of self-explanations must take place even after the learner "hears" a well-crafted instructional explanation (Kapon & diSessa, 2012); otherwise, no meaningful learning occurs. I study this tacit evaluation: how individuals temporarily decide to prefer one self-generated explanation for a phenomenon in the physical world over another, decide upon the tacit criteria to be used in the evaluation process and how these criteria evolve with formal schooling in the physical sciences.

This chapter is part of a section that discusses the role of explanation, argumentation, and modeling in the process of conceptual change. I consider these constructs as closely related but very different in their nature and function. The function of an explanation for something is to make this something clearer and more reasonable by clarifying the causes, context, and consequences of the thing to be explained. Argumentation is the process of reasoning systematically in support of an idea, action, or theory. Thus, the function of argumentation is to persuade others. Explanation and argumentation are closely related. Asking students to argue—to be very explicit about their and others' claims, the grounds and warrants for these claims, to identify the limits of the claims (rebuttals), etc.—also serves to clarify these claims, and thus forces students to generate self-explanations, and enhances their understanding.

Modeling, in my view, is the design of representations (physical, mathematical, graphical, computational, etc.) and highly idealized descriptions of a system or process in a way that afford the generation of predictions and explanations based on these representations. Models are instrumental in the creation of an explanation because they explicate the causes, context, and consequences of the thing to be explained. They are instrumental in argumentation because they can provide a rationale (i.e., warrant) for an argument, while argumentation can be used to justify the validity of a model. This chapter aims to illustrate how conceptual change can be seen as an evolution of self-generated explanations and to discuss the roles that the interrelations and functions of explanation, argumentation, and modeling play in this process.

A multidimensional metric for sense-making

I think of the tacit evaluation of self-explanations, which I consider as sense-making, as taking place simultaneously along a multidimensional metric that is sensitive to the content, the structure, and the context of the explanation. In science, the noun *metric* denotes a system of measurement. Here I use the term metaphorically to describe a system by which the soundness of the self-generated explanation is assessed. I operationalize three central dimensions in this metric: intuitive knowledge, mechanism, and framing (Kapon, 2017). Although these are not the only dimensions, they are central in the reasoning of learners of science and continue to evolve and play a role in experts' thinking. When I metaphorically refer to intuitive knowledge, mechanism, and framing as central dimensions of the metric for sense-making, I mean that each has a metaphoric magnitude, which allows individuals to evaluate the soundness of their self-generated explanations along this dimension. The composition of these evaluations *together* is what forms our sense that the explanation is sound and that we understand it.

The intuitive knowledge dimension

The intuitive knowledge dimension of the metric is sensitive to the content of the explanation. Fischbein (1987) described intuition and perception as types of cognition, where intuition implies extrapolation beyond the directly accessible information (i.e., mere perception). For example, if a teacher unintentionally drops a piece of chalk while speaking, no one would pay attention to this event. However, if by some miracle, the chalk floated in the air, students would notice; it is their intuition that suggests that the chalk *should* have fallen when it was dropped (i.e., an extrapolation), and thus when it did not, they were surprised.

Fischbein argued that systematic instruction may result in the formation of new intuitive knowledge that leads to intuitive evaluations and insights. He termed this type of intuitive knowledge "secondary intuition" as opposed to "primary intuition" that develops independently through our experience with the world. Hence, formal knowledge of science can be transformed into intuitive knowledge during the process of learning.

Let us assume that every self-explanation a person believes at a particular moment is based on the activation of a chunk of intuitive knowledge and that some intuitions are stronger than others, in the sense that we trust them more in a particular context. If we think of intuitive knowledge as one dimension in the metric for sense-making, then the metaphorical magnitude of this dimension can be defined as the extent to which we trust this particular piece of intuitive knowledge.

We can model a specific relevant chunk of intuitive knowledge as a complex knowledge element that we term explanatory-primitive, or e-prim (Kapon & diSessa, 2012). E-prims are self-explanatory accounts of how things are (e.g., things fall downwards). Their source can be our experience with the physical world, education, language, or interaction with other people; they can be encoded both verbally and non-verbally, and they can have different levels of complexity.

The relative strength of an e-prim is described by the term "priority" (diSessa, 1993). High priority implies that the e-prim is cued more frequently in particular contexts, and when activated, it is less likely to be deactivated when its related inference seems to contradict inferences based on other cued e-prims. Relative priorities are constantly negotiated in the process of learning by their (1) explanatory hierarchy—when an e-prim can explain another activated e-prim; (2) consistency—when the implications of an e-prim are consistent with other activated e-prims and ideas; (3) context—contextual features that affect the classification of objects and the framing of situations; (4) the nature of the explanans—agency-based e-prims might be "stronger" than agency-free e-prims; (5) developmental history—e-prims that were abstracted from frequent varied experiences in the physical world will probably have higher priority than e-prims that were abstracted from the use of language or education (Kapon & diSessa, 2012).

The mechanism dimension

In the history and philosophy of science literature, mechanistic explanations have often been considered more advanced and sophisticated than teleological explanations. Mechanistic explanations have been regarded in educational and psychological studies as surpassing causal explanations since they explain *how* a cause created an effect by explicating the process by which it occurred. Note that some e-prims provide a sense of how things work, a sense of mechanism. Thus, the activation of a particular e-prim affords, at least potentially, the articulation of a particular mechanism.

Mechanism as a dimension in a metric of sense-making reflects sensitivity to the structure of mechanisms. Specifically, people will be able to notice a "more" mechanistic explanation compared to a lesser one, and rich mechanistic explanations, by the merits of their structure, will support a sense of understanding (Ahn, Kalish, Medin, & Gelman, 1995).

Based on a review of the literature in the philosophy of science, Russ, Scherr, Hammer, and Mikeska (2008) highlighted seven structural components of mechanistic explanations that are hierarchically organized: (1) description of the target phenomenon; (2) identification of setup conditions; (3) identification of entities; (4) identification of activities; (5) identification of the properties of the entities; (6) identification of the organization of entities; and (7) chaining backward and forward (see Russ et al. for more details). Russ et al. also identified two additional components: (1) the use of analogies to similar mechanisms in other contexts; (2) the use of external animated models (gestures, body movements, etc.) to illustrate how certain entities act in the mechanism. This framework could be considered as identifying discourse markers to infer the self-evaluation of the relative strength of the mechanism of a given explanation by assessing the number and nature of different structural components that reflect a mechanistic explanation and that are present in that explanation. Note that these markers are only sensitive to the structure of the explanation, not to scientific correctness (i.e., content), and thus the mechanism provides a complementary dimension to the intuitive knowledge dimension in the metric.

The framing dimension

The idea that the context of reasoning and the nature of the interaction affect the evaluation of explanations is not new. When participants in an interaction perceive the nature of this interaction in a particular way (e.g., whether it is a play, a social gathering, an academic lecture, etc.), and thus interpret the utterances, gestures, and actions that take place, as well as the nature of their participation in the interaction accordingly, we say that they *framed* the interaction in a particular way (Bateson, 1972). Framing forms an additional dimension of the metric for sense-making. It complements the intuitive knowledge and the mechanism dimensions, because it is explicitly sensitive to the context within which the explanation is generated. Hence, the tacit assessment of self-explanations is also affected by the framing of the social interaction within which the explanation is generated, because this framing implies a set of expectations. For instance, many students feel that the explanations provided in a physics class (a social frame) must include references to formulas (Hammer, Elby, Scherr, & Redish, 2005).

Inferring the relative strength of a self-generated explanation along the framing dimension involves identifying the particular frames that define the interaction and the mutual alignment and relative positioning of the participants in each frame. For instance, in the typical social frame of a classroom, the teacher is positioned as more knowledgeable than the students, and thus the students' evaluation of the soundness of their self-generated explanations may include a consideration of the extent to which it coheres with what they think the teacher would consider a good explanation. We can identify the overlapping frames that define the interaction by: (1) figuring out the larger contexts (i.e., an interview, a homework assignment, etc.); (2) noting explicit markers in people's surface linguistic forms of sentences that can be used as cues to identify frames (i.e., omissions, repetitions, etc.); (3) noting linguistic registers such as conventional lexical, syntactic, and prosodic choices (e.g., motherly tone) that are used to convey the interactive frame to other participants and the relative alignment of the participants in this frame; and (4) the way a speaker physically aligns herself to another person and manipulates the objects in the environment as she explains (Tannen, 1993; Tannen & Wallat, 1987).

Illustrative case

To illustrate the interrelations between intuitive knowledge, mechanism, and framing dimensions, and (briefly) how each can be inferred from students' discourse, below I apply the model to analyze a case of students' reasoning. The illustrative case discussed here is based on 18 minutes that were drawn from a 90 minute interview with two 7th graders, Reut and Nathalie (pseudonyms), conducted by Orit Parnafes and Lital Ditchi-Kedar in 2009. In the interview, Parnafes and Ditchi-Kedar were discussing the results of a demonstration which they just witnessed with the girls: a plastic bottle was connected to a pump. As air was pumped out of it, the bottle shrank. The girls started to explain to one another what was happening, drew a representation of what was happening on paper, explained the phenomenon based on this drawing, and came up with a mutually agreed-upon explanation.

Roughly speaking, the girls generated two distinct explanations for the phenomenon of the shrinking bottle that were expressed somewhat differently by each girl. The first was that the bottle shrank to fill the vacuum. The second was that the bottle shrank because the pressure of the particles outside the bottle overcame the pressure of the particles inside the bottle. These explanations were considered separately and were only connected toward the end of the session. A full microgenetic analysis that provides a detailed account of each dimension in the metric, and captures the individual dynamical reasoning of each girl, appears elsewhere (Kapon, 2017). Here I provide a summary of the analysis to illustrate the points of this chapter.

Reasoning along the intuitive knowledge dimension

In the case of both girls, the core of the first explanation was the e-prim "a vacuum has to be filled," whereas the core of the second explanation was the e-prim "overcoming," the intuitive schematization of one force or influence that overpowers another (diSessa, 1993). The priority shift between "a vacuum has to be filled" and "overcoming" was different for each girl and it is illustrated here with Nathalie. At first, she preferred "a vacuum has to be filled" over "overcoming" since it explicitly cohered with her observations. The shift occurred when she tried to explain to Reut why the particles move in the first place into the vacuum. This was a step toward a more explicit mechanism, and "overcoming" garnered further contextual priority since it afforded the articulation of this explanation by using force and pressure differences. Hence, for Nathalie, the reason for the priority shift was the achievement of explanatory hierarchy and consistency (Kapon & diSessa, 2012). Note that the specific articulation of each mechanism was initiated by the activation of a particular e-prim.

Reasoning along the mechanism dimension

Mechanism was another dimension that played a role in the girls' preferences for the second explanation. The second explanation that each girl generated was more mechanistic than the first one. In Nathalie's case, each of the two explanations she generated had all the required components of mechanistic explanation, including the highest order component, chaining backwards. However, a closer examination of the *content* of each code revealed that Nathalie's second explanation was indeed more mechanistic than the first one. The activities in which the entities were engaged (i.e., code #4), for instance, were better articulated in the second explanation. More importantly, the chaining backwards category (code #7) was richer, with additional explicit connections between the first explanation and the second. Further, the move from the first to the second explanation was an evolution, in contrast to the case of Reut, in which the shift was a replacement.

Reasoning along the framing dimension

The third dimension of evaluation that was examined was the frames each girl used to make sense of the interaction. In this case, there were two larger contexts that dictated the girls' structures of expectations: the context of participating in an interview and the context of science and science in school. Science and science in school were found to be the dominant frames in the interaction. This finding can explain the high regard for the mechanism dimension, as well as the preference for "scientific" entities, such as force and pressure in the explanation, thus highlighting the multidimensional nature of sense-making. The examination of the interactive frames and the relative alignment of the girls and the interviewers in these frames (Tannen & Wallat, 1987) revealed two interactive frames. The first was sense-making, and the second was providing the right answer (as in oral exams). The linguistic and non-linguistic registers suggested that although there were times in the interview when the girls were looking for reassurance from the interviewers that they were heading in the right direction, the dominant frame was sense-making. This frame reinforced the power of the intuitive knowledge dimension, showing that a particular framing can privilege a particular intuitive knowledge element (assign it a higher priority).

On the interrelations of explanation, argumentation, and modeling in students' reasoning

What role did the interrelations and function of explanation, argumentation, and modeling play in the local conceptual change processes described in the previous example? The previous analysis focused on explanation. Yet models were central to the explanations that Reut and Nathalie developed. Encouraged to draw to show their explanations, both girls drew silently for a full eight minutes and then extensively referred back to the drawings throughout the session, even though the interviewer's instructions were to explain. The girls' drawings were not pictorial representations of the process, because they included entities that the girls did not see in the demonstration (e.g., particles), but rather were simple models of the process that they witnessed. Throughout, the girls not only referenced their own drawings but also one another's drawings. At one point, Reut turned to Nathalie and asked "Can I try to explain? … Let's say that this is a bottle …" and she started to draw while explaining what she was doing. In the new drawing (model) there were also arrows that indicated the forces that the particles exerted on the walls of the bottle. Nathalie intervened at some point by deleting one of the arrows inside the bottle so there were more arrows on the outside, to explain why the bottle shrunk. At this point, the girls' turns were overlapping and they were completing each other's sentences. The shared model provided a shared vocabulary to describe and think together about the phenomenon.

In the above case, modeling and reasoning while using the model refined the generated explanation, resulting in greater understanding and a sense of understanding of the phenomenon in question. What role, if any, did argumentation play in the learning processes discussed here? In the specific case of the two 7th graders who reasoned about the shrinking bottle (Kapon, 2017), in my view, there was no explicit engagement in argumentation. The girls were not engaged in making claims or justifying these claims. They were engaged in a sense-making process in which they were trying to figure out why a specific phenomenon occurred. Hence, the phenomenon to be explained (that the bottle shrank when air was pumped out of it) was not in doubt. What the girls were trying to do was to explain to themselves why, and later how, this explanandum came to be. On the other hand, in a case of K11–K12 physics students who were working on long-term open-ended research projects (Kapon, 2016) argumentation became central when the students started to write their research reports in which they had to share their findings with others. There, the need to formulate strong arguments that justified and explained their models and claims was crucial. Hence, although explanation, argumentation and modeling are closely related, and all play a role in the process of conceptual change, the nature and function of each construct in this process is different.

References

Ahn, W., Kalish, C. W., Medin, D. L., & Gelman, S. A. (1995). The role of covariation versus mechanism information in causal attribution. *Cognition, 54*(3), 299–352.

Bateson, G. (1972). A theory of play and fantasy. In G. Bateson (Ed.), *Steps to an ecology of mind: Collected essays in anthropology, psychiatry, evolution, and epistemology* (pp. 177–193). London: Intertext Books.

diSessa, A. A. (1993). Toward an epistemology of physics. *Cognition and Instruction, 10*(2&3), 105–225.

Fischbein, E. (1987). *Intuition in science and mathematics: An educational approach*. Dordrecht: Reidel.

Hammer, D., Elby, A., Scherr, R., & Redish, E. (2005). Resources, framing, and transfer. In J. Mestre (Ed.), *Transfer of learning from a modern multidisciplinary perspective* (pp. 89–120). Greenwich, CT: Information Age Publishing Inc.

Kapon, S. (2016). Doing research in school: Physics inquiry in the zone of proximal development. *Journal of Research in Science Teaching*, *53*(8), 1172–1197. doi:10.1002/tea.21325.

Kapon, S. (2017). Unpacking sensemaking. *Science Education*, *101*(1), 165–198. doi:10.1002/sce.21248.

Kapon, S., & diSessa, A. A. (2012). Reasoning through instructional analogies. *Cognition and Instruction*, *30*(3), 261–310.

Russ, R. S., Scherr, R. E., Hammer, D., & Mikeska, J. (2008). Recognizing mechanistic reasoning in student scientific inquiry: A framework for discourse analysis developed from philosophy of science. *Science Education*, *92*(3), 499–525.

Tannen, D. (1993). What's in a frame? Surface evidence for underlying expectations. In D. Tannen (Ed.), *Framing in discourse* (pp. 14–56). New York: Oxford University Press.

Tannen, D., & Wallat, C. (1987). Interactive frames and knowledge schemas in interaction: Examples from a medical examination/interview. *Social Psychology Quarterly*, *50*(2), 205–216.

SYNTHESIS III

Modeling, explanation, argumentation, and conceptual change

Clark A. Chinn

This part of the volume comprises six chapters presenting theoretical frameworks and empirical research connecting conceptual change to two or more of these practices: modeling, explanation, and argumentation. My charge here is to synthesize ideas on the interrelations among conceptual change and these three practices. This charge includes examining what these six chapters have to say, but also stepping back to consider broader literatures bearing on these interrelations.

To this end, the outline of this synthesis is as follows. In the first section, I will discuss each of the three practices (modeling, explanation, and argumentation)—analyzing what each involves, how they are interrelated, and how they are related to conceptual change. In this discussion, I will draw on philosophical as well as educational research, including the six chapters in this part. The goal is to develop a set of working definitions of what these constructs are and how they are interrelated.

The second section then uses these ideas to examine empirical research—with a strong focus on the chapters in this part—on the interrelations of modeling, explanation, argumentation, and conceptual change in content understanding. I will consider the empirical claims that emerge from the six chapters in this part and what the implications are for conceptual change in the classroom.

The third section addresses an additional dimension of conceptual change in connection with the three practices: Learning to engage in the practices involves conceptual change in the practices themselves—that is, conceptual change in students' very understanding of modeling, explanation, and argumentation.

Conceptual interrelations among modeling, explanation, argumentation, and conceptual change

To understand the practices of modeling, explanation, and argumentation (and thus how they might be related to conceptual change), a useful starting point is to examine the conceptual relations among models, explanations, and arguments—the products produced by modeling, explanation, and argumentation. Understanding these interrelations is complicated by the fact that philosophers and other analysts have not reached consensus on the best way to conceptualize models, explanations, and arguments, let alone their interrelations. But I will nonetheless endeavor to sketch a few key points.

Throughout, the terms *conceptual change* and *change(s) in conceptions* are used interchangeably to refer to fundamental or significant alterations in concepts and their interrelations. Alterations in conceptions are "significant" if the new conceptions challenge in some way previous ideas or if the resources to grasp the new ideas are initially lacking. I do not intend to presuppose any particular theory of conceptual change when using the term.

Models, modeling, and conceptual change

First, as several of the authors in this part emphasize, modeling is a central practice of science (Duschl & Grandy, 2008). Modeling involves constructing, revising, and evaluating models. But what are models, and how are they to be distinguished from other scientific entities such as theories?

On some analyses, such as the semantic view of models and theories (Suppes, 1960), models can be viewed as roughly similar to theories. But on other analyses, models are distinct representations from theories and other language-based representations (e.g. Godfrey-Smith, 2006; Weisberg, 2013). One critical distinction is that theories or propositional claims in science can be evaluated in terms of truth or falsity, whereas models have a different relationship to the world. One does not properly say that a model (e.g. a model of human memory) is true or false. Or, rather, if one *does* evaluate truth values, one must say that it is false: All models are false, because models are deliberate idealizations and oversimplifications of the world which are not intended to fully represent the world. Instead, models are properly evaluated in terms of similarity to the world in the desired respects (Giere, 1988; Godfrey-Smith, 2006; Weisberg, 2013).

Many philosophers treat models as intermediate in some fashion between theories and data, although they differ on the exact sense in which they are intermediate. Giere (1988) treated models as situation-specific specifications of a theory; for instance, a model of oscillation with a range of damping factors included is an application of the theory of mechanics to a particular case. A theory can be tested against the world only when specified as a model; in this way, a theory can be compared to the world. Further, a theory can thus be viewed as a family of such specific models. In contrast, Godfrey-Smith (2006) viewed models as including new information not part of theories. On Godfrey-Smith's view, the construction of the model of an oscillator in a complex setting incorporates new principles and concepts that are not part of the theory of mechanics proper. In both treatments, however, the locus for testing theoretical constructs against data is the intermediate model, not the theory as a whole.

As deliberate oversimplifications and idealizations, models are constructed for particular purposes, and different modelers may have different purposes. In some fields (such as hydraulics), engineers use models known to be based on faulty underlying theories because they are computationally tractable and useful approximations that can guide engineering design. As another example of how different purposes can lead to different models, two groups of scientists might construct very different models of climate change. One model could simply be intended to make accurate predictions without caring about whether the details of the model captured underlying mechanisms, whereas the other model might have explanatory purposes of representing all the underlying mechanisms as well as making predictions. How the model is evaluated will obviously depend on the purposes: Given its purposes, the former model would not be evaluated against data related to the mechanisms of climate change, whereas the latter model would. (To be sure, climate scientists have increasingly come to demand that their models do capture these underlying mechanisms accurately, but this is simply to say that the scientists have come to prefer one purpose over another.)

There are many types of models. Weisberg (2013) distinguished between concrete models, mathematical models, and computational models. Others have made other distinctions, such as models that describe structures, models that predict, and models that explain (Godfrey-Smith, 2006). Scientists also construct models *of* data, as well as models that explain data (Suppes, 1960). For example, as Lehrer and Schauble (Chapter 14, this volume) point out, deciding how to numerically represent plant growth involves modeling quantitatively how plants have grown—deciding which dimensions to represent such as height, how to represent height, and so on.

Modeling (as a practice) encompasses all the processes involved in constructing and justifying models. These include processes such as generating ideas for models, developing tests for testing models, evaluating models, revising them, justifying them through arguments, and so on. All these processes are centered on models as an epistemic product.

Models could be involved in conceptual change in at least three ways. One way, corresponding roughly to the theory-change view of conceptual change, involves fundamental changes in the components and processes of the models, as when a creationist model of speciation is replaced by an evolutionary model; this seems to fit some historical changes in science (T. S. Kuhn, 1962) and seems to be one view adopted in the chapter by Jiménez-Aleixandre and Brocos (Chapter 15, this volume). Another way involves gradual changes, which over time may end up in large-scale qualitative differences, as when small changes over time in understanding of atoms and electrons eventually lead to a very different model from the earlier models (Shapere, 1989); this corresponds to a gradual view of how conceptual change occurs (Chinn & Brewer, 1998); Jiménez-Aleixandre and Brocos (Chapter 15, this volume) also describe change that appears to fit this approach. A third way is less a matter of changing models than changing the understanding of the situation to which models apply. According to Rodrik (2015), economists generally do not reject one economic model in favor of another, but rather change their understanding of the situations to which various models apply, while essentially retaining *all* the models as applicable to one situation or another. This approach seems to correspond to the knowledge-in-pieces view (diSessa, Chapter 1, this volume; diSessa, Gillespie, & Esterly, 2004) that many of the authors of these six chapters adopt.

Explanations, models, and conceptual change

Three approaches to analyzing explanation have been prevalent in the philosophy of science (Godfrey-Smith, 2003). The first is the covering law approach, which treats explanation as the subsumption of a phenomenon to be explained under a general law (also called a "covering law"). According to this approach, for example, one can explain the length of the shadow of a flagpole using laws combining the height of the flagpole and the angle at which the light of the sun strikes the pole. This approach is widely regarded as a failure because one could use the same laws to explain the height of the flagpole in terms of the length of its shadow and the position of the sun. To most, this seems intuitively wrong: One can explain the length of the shadow using the position of the sun and the height of the flagpole, but not the height of the flagpole using the length of the shadow (Godfrey-Smith, 2003; Salmon, 1989). What seems to be missing is that the height of the flagpole plays a causal role in determining the length of the shadow (given the position of the sun), but not *vice versa*.

Accordingly, a second prominent account of explanation has been the causal account, which treats causation as central to explanation (Salmon, 1989). One has provided an explanation when one has provided a causal account of how a phenomenon was produced. Such causal accounts can answer "why" questions or "how possibly" questions (Achinstein, 1983). In order to account for the full range of causal explanations found in the natural and social sciences, one needs to incorporate probabilistic notions of causality, so that a cause makes an effect more likely but does not make its occurrence certain (Salmon, 1989).

The third account of explanation is the unification approach, such as that of Kitcher (Kitcher, 1989). Unification approaches treat explanation as providing general schemas for argument patterns that unify diverse phenomena. Kitcher tracked changes in Mendelian explanations from Mendel through Watson-Crick in terms of the schemas used to provide explanation. For example, an intermediate refined Mendelian schema involved specifying loci and alleles at these loci, accounting for individuals with particular sets of alleles as having particular traits, and specifying a process by which distribution of progeny are obtained. Although some have treated the unification as not bound to include causality, others have viewed the causal and unifying approaches to be, at least some of the time, compatible with each other (Godfrey-Smith, 2003).

Further, although the covering law explanation fails as a general account of explanation, some explanations in the history of science seem to take the form of covering law explanations, such as explaining the movement of objects according to the law of gravitation, even though there is no causal mechanism to confer real understanding. Initially, many scientists said that this did not provide a real explanation, but later there was a shift toward accepting this as an explanation, showing that what counts as an explanation shifts within science itself (T. S. Kuhn, 1962). Godfrey-Smith (2003) argued further that there are many forms of explanation in different fields and subfields of science, and that one should not expect a single account of explanation to cover all these forms and should look at all the particular ways in which scientists use the term *explain* in different settings. Sometimes scientists use the term in a mathematical way (e.g. explaining variance). Other times they may mean that a detailed process or mechanism has been specified, which could be viewed as a kind of description as well as an explanation.

Recent work on understanding—an important aim of epistemic processes—has emphasized its connection to explanation. Explanations help provide a subjective sense of understanding in those who encounter and comprehend these explanations (Grimm, Baumberger, & Ammon, 2017; Kvanvig, 2003); understanding can be conferred either through the unificatory role or the causal role of explanations. Kapon (Chapter 18, this volume) emphasizes the role of explanation in providing a subjective sense of understanding.

The processes of explanation (*explaining* as a verb rather than as a noun) are analogous to the processes involved in modeling (as a verb). The process of explanation may involve generating ideas for explanations, revising explanations, testing and evaluating explanations, and justifying them through argumentation—that is, all the processes needed to generate, refine, and establish explanations within a community.

What is the relationship between explanations and models? Given my earlier analyses of models, I conclude that some models do not function as explanations. For example, models that function as predictions only, models that show structures but not processes (e.g. a model of the structure of a cell), and models of data are types of legitimate models that do not provide explanations in any of the senses discussed above. Thus, contrary to those who suggest that all models are explanations, some but not all models function as explanations. Furthermore, the same model might be used by one scientist for the purpose of explanation, and for another for the purpose merely of prediction. Thus, the purpose also depends on the intent of the modeler.

Conversely, some but not all explanations are models. As discussed above, models are not identical to theories on many analyses. Yet theories are also regarded as providing explanations (Godfrey-Smith, 2003; Thagard, 1992) and can do so without appealing to models. Godfrey-Smith (2006) described the case of Buss's (1987) *The Evolution of Individuality* as an instance of exemplary evolutionary theorizing that did not employ models.

> There are no formal mathematical models in Buss' book. And further, there are no overt models of any other kind. Buss' entire argument is based

on the causal roles and consequences of actual cellular machineries, actual environmental circumstances, and actual developmental sequences. ... But there is no significant role for deliberate consideration of fictional, idealized, or merely schematic organisms, and the distinction between cautious exposition and deliberate fiction is a crucial one here.

(Godfrey-Smith, 2006, p. 731)

Godfrey-Smith pointed out that one could reconfigure Buss's work in terms of models, but then it would be a different science than it was. "Buss' explanations do have some modal 'reach,' but are generally more closely tied to contingent features of actual organisms" (Godfrey-Smith, 2006, p. 732). Godfrey-Smith argued further that Darwin's *Origin of Species* had the same character.

In contrast, in Maynard Smith and Szathmáry's (1995) *The Major Transitions in Evolution*, models were used extensively. According to Godfrey-Smith, this work developed more general models that, "if they work at all, would work just as well in a range of nearby possible worlds that happen to be inhabited by different organisms" (Godfrey-Smith, 2006, p. 732). Thus, models differ from non-model forms of explanation in their explicit intent to go a level up in abstraction and generality, and in their deliberate oversimplification to highlight just some aspects, and not to function just as causal accounts of particular organisms. Thus, on this analysis, some but not all explanations are models, and some but not all models are explanations. There is an important implication for instruction that follows from the interrelationship of models and explanations, which I will discuss in the next section summarizing important principles emerging from empirical work.

Finally, what is the relationship between explanation and conceptual change? The proposal for the three possible forms of change in models also applies well to explanations (which include the explanatory models discussed above). That is, explanations may change (a) by one paradigmatic explanation being replaced by another (*replace*), (b) by gradual changes over time that cumulatively lead to major changes (*gradual change*), and (c) by shifting the contexts to which different explanations apply (*dynamic contextual shift*). (See Amin, Synthesis II, this volume, for additional discussion of these issues.)

Whether writing of models or explanations, the chapters in this part have varied in their perspective on conceptual change. Among those who take the most explicit stances, the chapter by Jiménez-Aleixandre and Brocos appears to adopt the first perspective. The chapter by Kapon espouses, at least in part, a gradualist view. The chapter by Berland and Russ appears to take the dynamic contextual shift approach. (It is possible that these authors might actually espouse multiple perspectives in combination as best representing their approaches.)

It's not my intent to try to resolve the long-standing disagreements in the field in these issues. My own perspective is that different theories of conceptual change are likely to apply in different learning settings, and that multiple perspectives might apply at different phases of a particular instance of ongoing conceptual change. For example, when learning about natural selection, a student might weigh the explanation that species are immutable against a gradually constructed alternative explanation that change occurs over generations via natural selection processes. Weighing one against the other, the student might conclude at one point that the natural explanation is better and replace her immutability view with a natural explanation view.

When learning about another topic, the shift may be a gradual shift in extending an explanatory element from one situation to another. For example, a learner can work out that the explanatory element she uses to explain why a book feels heavy when it is held (push heavy things up) also applies to a table on which the book rests (Clement, Brown, & Zietsman, 1989). Gradual changes or contextual shifts are not necessarily easy to make; they, too, may be strongly resisted. Students may resist applying the explanatory element that is readily understood to apply to holding a book up to the situation of the table holding the book up.

Argumentation, models, explanations, and conceptual change

Now we turn to the third focal practice of this section: argumentation. Argumentation can be conceived as individuals constructing arguments or as dialogic argumentation among multiple people, arguing simultaneously in a dialog (e.g. argumentation among research team members about how to interpret the results of an experiment) or arguing in a distributed fashion across time and place (e.g. a series of arguments across many publications over several years for and against a newly promulgated explanation). Conceptually, an individual argument takes the form of reasons that support a claim, together (optionally) with elaborations that explain why the reasons support the claim. A dialogic argument can additionally include a complex network of additional support for reasons and linking elaborations, rebuttals of reasons, or linking elaborations, counterarguments against a position, arguments for contrary positions, and so on (Chinn & Clark, 2013).

There has been some interchange between terms in the field and ways of relating the terms that can be misleading. *Explanation* is sometimes used in the sense that I have just used the term *argument*. I fully endorse the position and arguments made by Osborne and Patterson (2011) for distinguishing clearly between *argument* and *explanation* in the way I have done in this synthesis. A scientific explanation (to take science as an example) provides a causal or unificatory account of a body of evidence, whereas an argument provides reason to believe a claim or position. An argument is an explanation only in the sense that an argument provides the arguer's cognitive explanation for why he or she believes that the claim is true (hence, when assessments wish to ask for a student's argument, they may prompt the student to *explain their reason*). But this is a totally different thing—it is not a scientific explanation that accounts for the scientific phenomena under consideration. Arguments are not scientific explanations, nor are explanations arguments.

Loosely, it may make sense to say that people can advance arguments to support models. However, this is not so. A model is not a proposition and so cannot be the claim that is supported by reasons. One can incorporate a model into a proposition and then construct an argument supporting or opposing that proposition (such as the proposition that a given model of photosynthesis provides a comprehensive explanation of the available evidence, or the claim that a model of climate change closely resembles the real world in specified respects). Similarly, if we follow common practice and say that an explanation is an answer to a *why* question or a *how* question, then one can say that an argument can be constructed to support or oppose, not the explanation by itself but, rather, the broader claim that the explanation is indeed an answer (or a good answer, or the best answer, etc.) to that question.

The reasons given in arguments to support explanations and explanatory models can be evidence, but they are not limited to evidence. One can, to be sure, argue for the verisimilitude of a model or the adequacy of an explanation by invoking evidence as reasons to accept these claims. But one can also make arguments on the basis of a variety of other kinds of explanatory ideals (i.e. the criteria or standards that good explanations should fulfill; see Toulmin, 1972). These ideals include the internal consistency of the explanation, its elegance, its fruitfulness, its fit with other accepted explanations, and so on (see also Chinn, Rinehart, & Buckland, 2014).

Argumentation can provide one basis for changing one's epistemic stances— that is, changing stances such as believing, accepting, knowing, conviction, taking something to have a presumption in its favor, entertaining, and so on (Chinn, Buckland, & Samarapungavan, 2011). This is a point emphasized by Jiménez-Aleixandre and Brocos in their chapter in this part, and it is also consistent with the stance taken by Kapon in her chapter. For example, if one believes creationist theory and then encounters very strong evidence-based arguments for evolutionary theory, one might then change one epistemic stance and accept evolutionary theory and reject creationist theory, or one might move at least to the stance of entertaining evolutionary theory and reducing the degree of belief in creationism; this can be viewed as a significant epistemic and conceptual change, though certainly not a full conceptual change.

Full conceptual change involves meeting two epistemic goals: one must both believe (or accept, or take some other stance indicating a degree of intellectual commitment) the new set of conceptions, and one must understand them (Chinn & Samarapungavan, 2001). Argumentation can promote both goals. First, ample research shows that argumentation can change belief, though they do not always do so, both in professional academic communities and in learners (Asterhan & Schwarz, 2007; Goldman et al., 2016; Longino, 1990). Arguments can provide a body of reasons to support change in epistemic stances, as Darwin's arguments in *On The Origin of Species* did for many creationists of his era (Chinn & Buckland, 2011). Second, arguments can also promote better understanding of a new idea. For example, the argument that some whales have bones of vestigial legs not only provides reason to believe that whales evolved from mammals; it also can enable students to understand how evolution works more fully—earlier forms may remain in later species, something they might not have understood before reflecting on this evidence.

Multiple routes to conceptual change

Now that I have clarified the constructs and examined conceptual relations among modeling, explanation, argumentation, and conceptual change, I discuss some empirical findings on their interrelationships from the six chapters in this part. The fundamental theme that I draw from these findings—and a theme that can be discerned in the conceptual change literature more broadly—is that there is not a single route to changing conceptions, but rather multiple routes. These chapters illustrate that there are diverse processes that are successful at enabling a change in learners' conceptions.

In my discussion of these different routes, I distinguish three aspects of them, drawing on a recent model that specifies three critical components of epistemic cognition: (1) one's *aims* or goals, (2) the *ideals* or standards used to evaluate models, explanations, and arguments, and (3) the specific *processes* seen as reliable means to develop models and explanations (Chinn et al., 2011; Chinn & Rinehart, 2016; Chinn et al., 2014). Smith (Synthesis IV, this volume) suggests that this framework can be useful in organizing epistemic research on conceptual change, and I use it here to highlight important aspects of modeling, explanation, and argumentation.

The chapters present different aims and ideals that can guide the development of new conceptions, as well as processes that can reliably achieve them. None of the chapters present comparison data that pit different aims, ideals, or processes against each other. Rather, each chapter presents empirical examples that demonstrate that there are multiple aims, ideals, and processes that can foster changes in conceptions—thus, there are multiple routes to conceptual change. The use of this epistemic framework points to the close connections between this part of the volume (modeling, explanation, and argumentation) and the part on epistemology and metacognition (Smith, Synthesis IV, this volume).

Aims associated with changes in conceptions

The authors of the six chapters in this part all discuss instruction that has the outcome of promoting shifts in learners' scientific conceptions. One point on which all the authors in these chapters appear to agree is that *conceptual change* is not the salient aim for students in their interventions. Rather, the aims include seeking to simply developing good explanations or models; any conceptual change occurs as a "by-product" of focusing on these other aims. Lehrer and Schauble are very explicit about this, but the conclusion is consistent with all the chapters.

Several chapters emphasize the centrality of explanation as the aim that students should focus on (sometimes with models as a vehicle for explanation). Jiménez-Aleixandre and Brocos show that a drive to explain unusual holes in carrots leads children to change their ideas about the mouthpieces of snails and how snails eat. Kapon discusses an episode with two girls in which a drive to explain the collapse of a plastic bottle with air removed promotes productive discourse and new explanatory ideas; Kapon's analysis also points to the centrality of models as a vehicle for explanations, as the two girls relied heavily on drawings that served as models carrying their explanations. Making explanation a central aim is consistent with much research on conceptual change (Chinn, Duncan, Dianovsky, & Rinehart, 2013; Posner, Strike, Hewson, & Gertzog, 1982; Smith & Unger, 1997).

Lehrer and Schauble emphasize another important aim: focusing on developing students' representational competence as they engage in modeling. They also emphasize the value of developing models of data as well as explanatory models, as when children work out how to measure the sustainability of an aquatic system. By engaging in both kinds of modeling (data modeling and explanatory modeling) on topic after topic, children can develop a strong sense of how science at all levels involves developing models as deliberate oversimplifications and overgeneralizations to achieve their particular purposes. Students thus have an opportunity to grasp the powerful role of their own purposes in shaping the form of models, both models of data and models of science. Developing models is central to other contemporary accounts of conceptual change (Chinn et al., 2013).

Other significant aims featured in these chapters include prediction, entertaining, and persuasion. Erduran, Kaya, and Cetin show that teachers design units on chemical adsorption with the intent that when students' predictions are not supported, this will prompt changes in ideas, an emphasis in theories of conceptual change since Posner et al. (1982). Berland and Russ note that the students who engaged in discussions about whether plants can grow in sand seemed to be engaged in talk that was exploratory; students can be viewed, then, not as seeking final "knowledge" but as seeking "plausible" ideas (Lombardi, Sinatra, & Nussbaum, 2013) that are worth entertaining. Finally, both Berland and Russ and Jiménez-Aleixandre and Brocos emphasize that when learners engage in argumentation, the purpose is often to persuade, not rationally co-construct, knowledge and yet this goal is nonetheless consistent with knowledge change (including changes substantial enough to be regarded as conceptual change) within a community of arguers.

Ideals used to evaluate conceptions

In line with philosophers' claims about how scientists evaluate explanations, the authors in this part have implicitly and explicitly emphasized a variety of different explanatory ideals (or criteria) used to evaluate explanations (including explanatory models). These ideals can be used to evaluate alternative models during processes of conceptual change. All of the chapters invoke *fit with evidence* at least implicitly as one criterion that learners use to evaluate their explanatory models. For example, Jiménez-Aleixandre and Brocos show that first graders are keenly committed to developing an explanation of how snails eat that is consistent with the evidence they have seen. The press to align models with evidence is also evident in the teacher lesson plans described by Erduran et al. to develop understanding of chemical reactions, adsorption, and absorption; students are expected to develop models that are consistent with the evidence seen and gathered. Developing conceptions that fit evidence is widely seen as central in conceptual change.

Other ideals feature in these chapters, as well, which is appropriate given that the evaluation of explanations in scientific communities is influenced by multiple criteria (Samarapungavan, 1992). The chapter by Viennot and Décamp emphasizes the central importance of two other criteria: completeness of ideas and internal consistency. Viennot and Décamp point out that even those who are knowledgeable of physics fail to engage other knowledge when evaluating explanations on topics, such as radiocarbon dating, that fail to meet these criteria. Lehrer and Schauble show that elementary school children are able to make models accountable to their purposes, as when a model of data must emphasize those aspects of the data that are most important for the purpose at hand (e.g. representing the height of plants and not their actual appearance). This requires children to learn that irrelevant features should be left out of their models (such as leaving flowers out of a model showing plant height). Kapon shows that adolescents are also sensitive to the ideal of including mechanisms (e.g. pressure exerted by unseen particles when explaining why a bottle collapses when the air inside is removed); this is consistent with other recent empirical work on how children develop conceptions (Russ, Scherr, Hammer, & Mikeska, 2008).

Jiménez-Aleixandre and Brocos analyze how three criteria (intelligibility, plausibility, and fruitfulness) vary across two explanatory contexts—developing a causal explanation versus taking and defending a socioscientific position. For example, in a context of developing causal models, the criterion of plausibility means that the conception is consistent with others accepted by the learners, whereas in the context of socioscientific decision-making, plausibility means consistent with social and individual values as well as conceptions. It is important for learners to develop an appreciation of how ideals should vary across contexts (Chinn et al., 2014).

Processes for achieving changes in conceptions

The chapters also describe a very broad range of processes that can produce productive changes in conceptions. In most cases, these processes are *social* processes, deployed as groups or communities of students work together. Many of the processes—but not all—involve argumentation. The discussion below highlights some of the prominent processes discussed in the chapters.

Explanation and modeling without argumentation

Kapon argues that one of the examples she discusses shows that learners can produce new ideas without disagreeing. In her example, two girls discussing the collapse of a plastic bottle when air was removed did so without disagreeing with each other or presenting explicit reasons for or against ideas; rather, they jointly constructed an explanation by building on each other's ideas. Kapon refers to this process as *sense-making*. This example suggests that change can proceed without argumentation, and that explanation does not always involve explicit argumentation.

Erduran et al. emphasize that change can be produced not only by evidence-based argumentation, but also by argumentation that elucidates relations between theories and concepts. Such argumentation can be used, for instance, to explain how the model organizes its components (electrons, protons, neutrons) and their interrelations.

Developing explanations and models through argumentation grounded in evidence

Other chapters emphasize that conceptual change (broadly construed as in the preceding discussions) is promoted through arguments grounded in evidence. This point is made explicitly by Erduran, Kaya, and Cetin; Jiménez-Aleixandre and Brocos; Lehrer and Schauble; and Kapon. At least two major alternatives are described as effective. Erduran et al. describe instruction in which teachers explicitly have students consider evidence for alternative models. This is a widely used approach to promote change in conceptions (Chinn, Duncan, & Rinehart, in press). In contrast, Jiménez-Aleixandre and Brocos and Kapon describe processes in which students revise a model over time. For example, in the Jiménez-Aleixandre and Brocos study, first graders who were developing new conceptions of snails' mouthpieces seemed to add or revise ideas one by one to a model being developed by the class as a community.

The efficacy of argumentation grounded in evidence for promoting conceptual development is consistent with large bodies of research on the use of evidence to promote conceptual change (Chinn & Brewer, 1993; Clement, 2013). Chinn et al. (2013) showed that such argumentation can promote both acceptance of (or belief in) new ideas and understanding of these ideas. In their chapter, Erduran et al. also emphasize these two roles of argumentation.

Argumentation with and without metacognition about change

Berland and Russ conclude that the first graders in their study engaged in a form of argumentation in which some changed conceptions about whether plants can grow in sand, but the children were not aware that their ideas were changing. This suggests that such awareness is not needed for change in conceptions. But Jiménez-Aleixandre and Brocos point to the efficacy of the opposite type of process. They show that the first graders in their study were aware that their earlier ideas about snails' mouthpieces (as like human teeth) differed from their later conceptions (of a spinning radula). The chapters in this part suggest that both processes can be effective. However, Smith (Synthesis IV, this volume) summarizes evidence indicating that deep learning (such as conceptual change) is promoted through use of more extensive metacognitive processes.

Emotions and virtues in argumentation and reasoning

Jiménez-Aleixandre and Brocos make emotional aspects of argumentation a centerpiece of their analysis of how change occurs. It is not just that arguments can be emotional (e.g. expressing anger when making an argument); rather, the emotions people feel are incorporated into the arguments for supporting or opposing a claim (e.g. opposing veganism because it is part of our national identity—"eating meat is a core part of our culture"). Jiménez-Aleixandre and Brocos argue further that warm aspects of argumentation are particularly important when students engage in decision-making about socioscientific issues. These illustrations are consistent with a large body of research on warm aspects (e.g. emotions and motivation) of conceptual change (Duit, Treagust, & Widodo, 2013; Sinatra & Pintrich, 2003).

Viennot and Décamp also emphasize warm aspects of argumentation in their emphasis on the importance of a critical attitude underlying effective argumentation. Their analysis indicates that a critical attitude may be essential to creating the dissatisfaction needed to improve ideas; for instance, a critical attitude can spur a reader to notice gaps or contradictions in a text on how hot-air balloons float that need to be repaired. This critical attitude can be viewed as an epistemic virtue (Chinn et al., 2014) that supports a change in conceptions.

Focusing on developing representations as part of models

To highlight a final productive change-producing process, Lehrer and Schauble argue persuasively in their chapter that educators can focus students productively on processes of developing representations (see also Lehrer & Schauble, 2004). By addressing questions such as, "What does each representation show, and what does it hide," students will gain an understanding of the purposes of modeling and will learn different affordances of different models of data as well as different explanatory models. An important aspect of representation is developing ways to measure complex constructs, which involves the development of representations. Smith (Synthesis IV, this volume) also emphasizes the epistemic importance of measurement, and Amin (Synthesis II, this volume) summarizes research on representations as a way of facilitating conceptual change.

Summary

In summary, the six chapters in this part of the book highlight a diverse array of routes to conceptual change. The routes vary according to their aims (e.g. explanations, predictions, persuasion), the ideals that guide the products developed (e.g. evidential fit, coherence with other ideas, plausibility, internal consistency), and the processes used (e.g. sense-making, argumentation in various forms, developing representations for models). None of the papers test different aims, ideals, or processes against each other, but they are broadly consistent with the notion that there are multiple productive routes to conceptual change.

Conceptual change *in* modeling, explanation, and argumentation

To this point, I have examined how the practices of modeling, explanation, and argumentation are related to conceptual change in the content of science. But there is one more sphere of interrelations between these three practices and conceptual change. Specifically, the development of reasoning involves conceptual change *in* these reasoning practices (Chinn et al., 2013), including modeling, explanation, and argumentation. Through education, students will need not only to mobilize these practices to support conceptual change in content understanding (e.g. understanding natural selection or genetics), they will also need to change their conceptual understanding *of* these practices. This is one reason why conceptual change can be so difficult: The reasoning processes needed to support conceptual change must themselves undergo change (Chinn et al., 2013; Sinatra & Chinn, 2012). Thus, unlike the history of science—in which there is evidence that major changes in reasoning practices and content do not happen at the same time (Chinn et al., 2013)—learning in classrooms can involve conceptual change simultaneously in content and in reasoning practices.

Below, I discuss possible areas of conceptual change in modeling, explanation, and argumentation. In each dimension, I take broadly a facets or knowledge-in-pieces approach to conceptual change in epistemic practices. That is, I do not suppose that learners change from one "theory" to another of what modeling, explanation, or argumentation is. Rather, I envision that students undergo a shift in the range of resources that they recruit. These resources may be organized in terms of the same dimensions discussed in the previous section and discussed by Smith (Synthesis IV, this volume): (1) *aims* or goals, (2) the *ideals* or standards used to evaluate models, explanations, and arguments, and (3) the specific *processes* seen as reliable means to engage in these processes (Chinn et al., 2011; Chinn & Rinehart, 2016; Chinn et al., 2014). Conceptual change involves, of course, a change in conceptions, and these resources all involve a way of conceptualizing the practices of science and other disciplines. Arguments, for example, have a conceptual structure that students can understand (or misunderstand); on one analysis, this involves components of claims, evidence, and reasoning to connect claims to evidence (Berland & McNeill, 2010).

Conceptual change in modeling

A substantial body of research indicates that children have ideas about models and modeling that differ substantially from the normative practices of fields such as biology, economics, and psychology (e.g. Treagust, Chittleborough, & Mamiala, 2002). In terms of understanding the *aims* of models, students may think that models are intended to be an exact copy of some aspect of the world, thus misunderstanding the essential oversimplifying nature of models. They may also fail to appreciate the diversity of aims of models (as discussed earlier). They may see models as true or false, rather than as bearing a similarity relationship to the world. Consequently, they may appreciate that models highlight which-ever aspects of the world are important for the purposes of the modeler. All of these ideas may involve a significant shift in how models and their aims are understood.

Modeling involves the use of epistemic *ideals* (or criteria) that can be used to evaluate models. Pluta, Chinn, and Duncan (2011) reported that, collectively, seventh graders who had not yet learned modeling practices proposed ideals for evaluating explanatory scientific models that closely paralleled lists of ideals advanced by philosophers of science as the ideals used by scientists to evaluate models. These ideals included fitting the evidence, providing an explanation, being accurate, and being understandable. However, only about a quarter of the students spontaneously proposed evidential criteria, suggesting that a move in modeling practice to a strong emphasis on evidentiary ideals as the foremost ideal will represent a conceptual change for many students. Another ideal that may involve conceptual shifts is the ideal of avoiding extraneous details. In both explanatory models and data models, extraneous details that are superfluous to the purposes of the model are omitted (e.g. flowers are not included in expert models of photosynthesis, or in data models such as bar graphs of the height of plants). But children often seek to include such details in their early models; learning that such extraneous details can be left out represents another conceptual change by students, as discussed by Schauble and Lehrer in their chapter (see also Lehrer & Schauble, 2004).

Finally, growth in reasoning may also involve conceptual change in students' grasp of reliable practices related to modeling. Godfrey-Smith (2006) has argued that modeling involves using processes of explanatory inference (inference to the best explanation) as well as imagination; Godfrey-Smith explicitly relates the imagination needed to construct a model to the imagination needed to construct the world of a novel. Although I am not aware of any research that directly addresses these issues, reliable methods of explanatory inference will involve consideration of alternative models, and much research indicates that both children and adults tend not to consider alternatives regularly (Arkes, 1991). And there is evidence that students often generally do not see science as any kind of creative enterprise (Bell, Blair, Crawford, & Lederman, 2003). Thus, these strategies are candidates to be involved in conceptual change.

Conceptual change in explanation

Like modeling, the practices of developing, refining, and evaluating explanations may involve conceptual change as students advance epistemically. As I discussed earlier, there is overlap between models and explanations, because some models serve as explanations; in such cases, the facets of modeling that may involve conceptual change will carry over to explanations. In this section, we focus on other facets of explanation that may involve conceptual change.

Beginning with *aims* of explanation, we discussed earlier that explanations take a diversity of forms, depending on the aims or purposes of those who explain. It seems likely that most students will lack an appreciation of this diversity, so that developing awareness of the different aims and forms of explanations will be an area that potentially involves conceptual change. Understanding the causal nature of explanations may come early, but understanding non-causal or more complex causal forms of explanation may also require students to develop new ideas about what explanation can be (cf. Grotzer, 2003; see also Smith, Synthesis IV, this volume).

In a review of developmental literatures on children's grasp of explanation, Brewer, Chinn, and Samarapungavan (1998) argued that there are continuities between explanation as understood by children and explanation in science. In particular, children seem to share certain explanatory ideals such as preferring explanations with broader evidential scope and better fit with other established knowledge (Samarapungavan, 1992). However, there are other ideals that are important in science but that are likely not to be part of the repertories of resources used by younger children. In science, Brewer et al. (1998) suggested the ideal of fruitfulness as a candidate for such an ideal, as children are unlikely to appreciate that future potential of an explanation may be important in its present evaluation. Similarly, I am not aware of any evidence that children appreciate the ideal of a very precise quantitative fit between evidence and a theory, when this is possible. In history, there is evidence that history students fail to appreciate the value of corroboration or contextualization when evaluating historical documents; they even fail to evaluate sources of documents, which suggests that their everyday repertoire of ideals for evaluating what they read does not include source trustworthiness as a salient ideal used regularly (Wineburg, 2001).

Finally, the processes used by practitioners in different disciplines to construct, evaluate, and revise explanations include processes that will be conceptually novel to many students who are being enculturated into those processes. For example, in history, the processes used by historians to construct historical explanations include taking historical actors' perspective through systematic use of empathy (Breisach, 2007) and the use of highly developed counterfactual scenarios (Weinryb, 2011). For novices, perspective-taking is inaccurate and very difficult (Gehlbach, 2004), and there is no evidence that I am aware of that children can engage in advanced forms of counterfactual reasoning. Thus, learning these processes will likely involve the development of new conceptualizations of perspective-taking, how to support claims, and what explanation in history involves. In science, learning about observation involves coming to conceptualize observation in new ways (Eberbach & Crowley, 2009). Thus, learning to engage in reliable epistemic processes involves developing new ways of understanding basic processes of reasoning, such as observation.

Conceptual change in argumentation

Mastery of argumentation—the third focal practice of this part of the volume—is also likely to involve significant conceptual changes as students' understanding of what argumentation is and how to engage in it changes. In terms of the aims of argumentation, younger students often view the aims of argumentation to be winning a dispute, not the rational, collaborative improvement of ideas (Chinn & Clark, 2013). Indeed, in one study, high school students viewed argumentation as something to be *avoided*, not engaged in, in knowledge construction (Bendixen, Zemp, Keller-Johnson, Winsor, & Feucht, 2011). Thus, reconceptualizing the aims of argumentation is one facet of conceptual change in this practice.

In understanding of criteria for evaluating argumentation (written and oral), children frequently fail to include clear descriptions of evidence in their arguments, along with the reasoning that connections evidence to claims (Berland & McNeill, 2010); thus, these are ideals that are not a part of children's repertoire of resources. Similarly, children and novice adults do not spontaneously include consideration of alternative positions or counterarguments (Berland & McNeill, 2010), also suggesting that this ideal is not significant for them. Developing a new conceptualization of the ideals of argumentation is part of learning to argue.

Finally, growth in argumentation also involves shifts in processes used. One dimension of this is during discursive argumentation. Studies of growth of argumentation over time have shown growth in a number of specific processes, such as asking for clarification, incorporating evidence into argumentation, using more rebuttals and more varied rebuttals (D. Kuhn & Udell, 2003; Ryu & Lombardi, 2015). All of these suggest a growing grasp of the different parts of arguments and how to use them.

Conclusion

Changing conceptions regularly involves processes of modeling, explanation, and argumentation. In this synthesis, I have first outlined an analysis of the inter-relations among models, explanations, and arguments (and the parallel processes of modeling, explanation, and argumentation). Models and explanations overlap but are not identical, and argumentation is a component of the processes of modeling and explanation, but arguments are neither models nor explanations. Given that changing conceptions frequently involves the use of conceptions in models and in explanations, conceptual change is bound to be intimately connected to modeling, explanation, and argumentation.

In the second section, I argued that there are multiple routes to conceptual change, which are amply illustrated by the diverse routes discussed in the six chapters in this part. These routes can be distinguished by their aims, the ideals used to judge whether the aims are achieved, and the reliable processes for achieving these aims. I discussed a diverse range of aims, ideals, and processes for which the chapters in this part provide empirical illustrations.

Finally, during an extended period of conceptual change, learners' grasp of reasoning can itself change. Again using aims, ideals, and reliable processes as my conceptual lens, I pointed to a number of significant conceptual changes that can be expected as learners gain a better grasp of modeling, explanation, and argumentation.

Acknowledgments

I thank the editors, Tamer Amin and Olivia Levrini, for their excellent, insightful feedback on multiple drafts of this synthesis. I am also very grateful to Na'ama Av-Shalom, Sarit Barzilai, Hebbah El-Moslimany, Andy Elby, Brandon Mauclair-Augustin, and Randi Zimmerman for their very helpful comments on an earlier draft.

References

Achinstein, P. (1983). *The nature of explanation.* New York: Oxford University Press.

Arkes, H. R. (1991). Costs and benefits of judgment errors: Implications for debiasing. *Psychological Bulletin, 110,* 486–498.

Asterhan, C. S. C., & Schwarz, B. B. (2007). The effects of monological and dialogical argumentation on concept learning in evolutionary theory. *Journal of Educational Psychology, 99,* 626–639.

Bell, R. L., Blair, L. M., Crawford, B. A., & Lederman, N. G. (2003). Just do it? Impact of a science apprenticeship program on high school students' understanding of the nature of science and scientific inquiry. *Journal of Research in Science Teaching, 40,* 487–509.

Bendixen, L. D., Zemp, L. M., Keller-Johnson, J., Winsor, D. L., & Feucht, F. C. (2011). *Epistemic cognition across age groups and domains.* Paper presented at the annual meeting of the American Educational Research Association, New Orleans, LA.

Berland, L. K., & McNeill, K. L. (2010). A learning progression for scientific argumentation: Understanding student work and designing supportive instructional contexts. *Science Education, 94,* 765–793. doi:10.1002/sce.20402.

Breisach, E. (2007). *Historiography: Ancient, Medieval, & Modern* (3rd ed.). Chicago, IL: University of Chicago Press.

Brewer, W. F., Chinn, C. A., & Samarapungavan, A. (1998). Explanation in scientists and children. *Minds and Machines, 8,* 119–136.

Buss, L. (1987). *The evolution of individuality.* Princeton, NJ: Princeton University Press.

Chinn, C. A., & Brewer, W. F. (1993). The role of anomalous data in knowledge acquisition: A theoretical framework and implications for science instruction. *Review of Educational Research, 63,* 1–49.

Chinn, C. A., & Brewer, W. F. (1998). Theories of knowledge acquisition. In B. J. Fraser & K. G. Tobin (Eds.), *International handbook of science education* (Vol. 1, pp. 97–113). Dordrecht: Kluwer.

Chinn, C. A., & Buckland, L. A. (2011). Differences in epistemic practices among scientists, young earth creationists, intelligent design creationists, and the scientist creationists of Darwin's era. In R. Taylor & M. Ferrari (Eds.), *Epistemology and science education: Understanding the evolution vs. intelligent design controversy* (pp. 38–76). New York: Taylor & Francis.

Chinn, C. A., Buckland, L. A., & Samarapungavan, A. (2011). Expanding the dimensions of epistemic cognition: Arguments from philosophy and psychology. *Educational Psychologist, 46*, 141–167. doi:10.1080/00461520.2011.587722.

Chinn, C. A., & Clark, D. B. (2013). Learning through collaborative argumentation. In C. E. Hmelo-Silver, C. A. Chinn, C. K. K. Chan & A. M. O'Donnell (Eds.), *International handbook of collaborative learning* (pp. 314–332). New York: Routledge.

Chinn, C. A., Duncan, R. G., Dianovsky, M., & Rinehart, R. (2013). Promoting conceptual change through inquiry. In S. Vosniadou (Ed.), *International handbook of research on conceptual change* (2nd ed., pp. 539–559). New York: Taylor & Francis.

Chinn, C. A., Duncan, R. G., & Rinehart, R. W. (in press). Epistemic design: Design to promote transferable epistemic growth in the PRACCIS project. In E. Manalo, Y. Uesaka & C. A. Chinn (Eds.), *Promoting spontaneous use of learning and reasoning strategies: Theory, research, and practice for effective transfer*. New York: Routledge.

Chinn, C. A., & Rinehart, R. W. (2016). Epistemic cognition and philosophy: Developing a new framework for epistemic cognition. In J. A. Greene, W. A. Sandoval & I. Bråten (Eds.), *Handbook of epistemic cognition* (pp. 460–478). New York: Routledge.

Chinn, C. A., Rinehart, R. W., & Buckland, L. A. (2014). Epistemic cognition and evaluating information: Applying the AIR model of epistemic cognition. In D. Rapp & J. Braasch (Eds.), *Processing inaccurate information: Theoretical and applied perspectives from cognitive science and the educational sciences* (pp. 425–453). Cambridge, MA: MIT Press.

Chinn, C. A., & Samarapungavan, A. (2001). Distinguishing between understanding and belief. *Theory into Practice, 40*, 235–241.

Clement, J. (2013). Roles for explanatory models and analogies in conceptual change. In S. Vosniadou (Ed.), *International handbook of research on conceptual change* (2nd ed., pp. 412–446). New York: Taylor & Francis.

Clement, J., Brown, D. E., & Zietsman, A. (1989). Not all preconceptions are misconceptions: Finding "anchoring conceptions" for grounding instruction on students' intuitions. *International Journal of Science Education, 11*, 554–565.

diSessa, A. A., Gillespie, N. M., & Esterly, J. B. (2004). Coherence versus fragmentation in the development of the concept of force. *Cognitive Science, 28*, 843–900.

Duit, R., Treagust, D. F., & Widodo, A. (2013). Teaching science for conceptual change. In S. Vosniadou (Ed.), *International handbook of research on conceptual change* (2nd ed., pp. 487–503). New York: Taylor & Francis.

Duschl, R. A., & Grandy, R. E. (Eds.). (2008). *Teaching scientific inquiry: Recommendations for research and implementation*. Rotterdam, NL: Sense Publishers.

Eberbach, C., & Crowley, K. (2009). From everyday to scientific observation: How children learn to observe the biologist's world. *Review of Educational Research, 79*, 39–68.

Gehlbach, H. (2004). A new perspective on perspective taking: A multidimensional approach to conceptualizing an aptitude. *Educational Psychology Review, 16*, 207–234.

Giere, R. N. (1988). *Explaining science: A cognitive approach*. Chicago, IL: University of Chicago Press.

Godfrey-Smith, P. (2003). *Theory and reality: An introduction to the philosophy of science.* Chicago, IL: University of Chicago Press.

Godfrey-Smith, P. (2006). The strategy of model-based science. *Biology and Philosophy, 21*, 725–740.

Goldman, S. R., Britt, M. A., Brown, W., Cribb, G., George, M., Greenleaf, C.,... Project READI. (2016). Disciplinary literacies and learning to read for understanding: A conceptual framework for disciplinary literacy. *Educational Psychologist, 51*, 219–246.

Grimm, S. R., Baumberger, C., & Ammon, S. (Eds.). (2017). *Explaining understanding: New perspectives from epistemology and philosophy of science.* New York: Routledge.

Grotzer, T. A. (2003). Learning to understand the forms of causality implicit in scientifically accepted explanations. *Studies in Science Education, 39*, 1–74.

Kitcher, P. (1989). Explanatory unification and the causal structure of the world. In P. Kitcher & W. C. Salmon (Eds.), *Scientific explanation* (Vol. 13, pp. 410–505). Minneapolis: University of Minnesota Press.

Kuhn, D., & Udell, W. (2003). The development of argument skills. *Child Development, 74*, 1245–1260.

Kuhn, T. S. (1962). *The structure of scientific revolutions.* Chicago, IL: University of Chicago Press.

Kvanvig, J. L. (2003). *The value of knowledge and the pursuit of understanding.* Cambridge: Cambridge University Press.

Lehrer, R., & Schauble, L. (2004). Modeling natural variation through distribution. *American Educational Research Journal, 41*, 635–679.

Lombardi, D., Sinatra, G. M., & Nussbaum, E. M. (2013). Plausibility reappraisals and shifts in middle school students' climate change conceptions. *Learning and Instruction, 27*, 50–62.

Longino, H. E. (1990). *Science as social knowledge: Values and objectivity in scientific inquiry.* Princeton, NJ: Princeton University Press.

Maynard Smith, J., & Szathmáry, D. (1995). *The major transitions in evolution.* Oxford: Oxford University Press.

Osborne, J. F., & Patterson, A. (2011). Scientific argument and explanation: A necessary distinction? *Science Education, 95*, 627–638. doi:10.1002/sce.20438.

Pluta, W. J., Chinn, C. A., & Duncan, R. G. (2011). Learners' epistemic criteria for good scientific models. *Journal of Research in Science Teaching, 48*, 486–511.

Posner, G. J., Strike, K. A., Hewson, P. W., & Gertzog, W. A. (1982). Accommodation of a scientific conception: Toward a theory of conceptual change. *Science Education, 66*, 211–227.

Rodrik, D. (2015). *Economics rules: The rights and wrongs of the dismal science.* New York: W. W. Norton.

Russ, R., Scherr, R. E., Hammer, D., & Mikeska, J. (2008). Recognizing mechanistic reasoning in student scientific inquiry: A framework for discourse analysis developed from philosophy of science. *Science Education, 92*, 499–525.

Ryu, S., & Lombardi, D. (2015). Coding classroom interactions for collective and individual engagement. *Educational Psychologist, 50*, 70–83.

Salmon, W. C. (1989). Four decades of scientific explanation. In P. Kitcher & W. C. Salmon (Eds.), *Scientific explanation* (Vol. 13, pp. 3–219). Minneapolis: University of Minnesota Press.

Samarapungavan, A. (1992). Children's judgments in theory choice tasks: Scientific rationality in childhood. *Cognition, 45*, 1–32.

Shapere, D. (1989). Evolution and continuity in scientific change. *Philosophy of Science, 56*, 419–437.

Sinatra, G. M., & Chinn, C. A. (2012). Thinking and reasoning in science: Promoting epistemic conceptual change. In K. R. Harris, S. Graham & T. Urdan (Eds.), *APA educational psychology handbook: Vol 3. Application to learning and teaching* (pp. 257–282). Washington, DC: American Psychological Association.

Sinatra, G. M., & Pintrich, P. R. (Eds.). (2003). *Intentional conceptual change*. Mahwah, NJ: Erlbaum.

Smith, C., & Unger, C. (1997). What's in dots-per-box? Conceptual bootstrapping with stripped-down visual analogs. *The Journal of the Learning Sciences, 6*, 143–181.

Suppes, P. (1960). A comparison of the meaning and uses of models in mathematics and the empirical sciences. *Synthese, 12*, 287–301.

Thagard, P. (1992). *Conceptual revolutions*. Princeton, NJ: Princeton University Press.

Toulmin, S. E. (1972). *Human understanding: The collective use and evolution of concepts*. Princeton, NJ: Princeton University Press.

Treagust, D. F., Chittleborough, G., & Mamiala, T. L. (2002). Students' understanding of the role of scientific models in learning science. *International Journal of Science Education, 24*, 357–368.

Weinryb, E. (2011). Historical counterfactuals. In A. Tucker (Ed.), *A companion to the philosophy of history and historiography* (pp. 109–119). Malden, MA: Wiley-Blackwell.

Weisberg, M. (2013). *Simulation and similarity: Using models to understand the world*. Oxford: Oxford University Press.

Wineburg, S. (2001). *Historical thinking and other unnatural acts: Charting the future of teaching the past*. Philadelphia, PA: Temple University Press.

PART IV

Metacognition and epistemology in conceptual change

Editors: Carol L. Smith and Marianne Wiser

Orientation

This section examines the relations among metacognition, epistemic-thinking, and conceptual change. The contributions show that metacognition and epistemic-thinking are multifaceted phenomena that can be analyzed at both individual and social levels, and that there are multiple mechanisms by which they interact with content-specific conceptual change.

The first contributor, Barbara Hofer, lays out a multifaceted model of epistemic-thinking, situated in a multifaceted model of metacognition. On this view, individuals vary in their explicit beliefs about knowledge and knowing, that affect what they attend to in learning situations, the goals and strategies they select, and how they react to conflicting information in deciding what to believe. We learn that college students are more likely to understand and accept counter-intuitive theories like evolution by natural selection, if they have both epistemic trust in scientists and an epistemology in which beliefs are critically evaluated, based on evidence. Doug Lombardi and Gale Sinatra, the second contributors, focus on the multiple factors that influence how students evaluate the plausibility of competing explanatory models. We learn that students can make these judgments, either implicitly or with attention to explicit epistemic standards, and that students are more likely to accept controversial models (such as human-caused climate change) if prompted to reappraise them based on fit with scientific evidence.

The third contributor, David Hammer, presents excerpts from an extended case study of a college student learning physics to highlight the dynamic interactions between epistemic-thinking and conceptual change. We learn that students have multiple epistemic resources that can be activated unconsciously by features of the social and cultural situation that implicitly frame their approach to learning. By scaffolding the activation, elaboration, and discussion of more productive epistemic frames, teachers can help their students develop a better conceptual understanding of physics and of their own learning. William Sandoval, the fourth contributor, foregrounds the social roots of epistemic-thinking. He argues that epistemic-thinking necessarily develops in a community of practice, with shared knowledge-building goals and norms. We learn that even elementary school children can develop epistemic goals and norms for seeking evidence to justify their beliefs, through a classroom that fosters explicit dialog around evaluating claims for challenging science topics. The fifth contributor, Frank Keil, explores what young children know about their reliance on others in knowledge-building and how knowledge clusters in other minds. We learn that young children overestimate what they can learn on their own and typically think others' knowledge clusters around superficial goals. However, as children learn about the deeper causal principles in science, they become more aware of how much of their knowledge depends on others, especially content experts, whose knowledge clusters around these causal principles.

In her synthesis chapter, Carol Smith identifies three broad classes of models that have informed research on the interactions among metacognition, epistemic-thinking, and conceptual change and discusses the ways they are complementary. In addition, she points out how these classes of models converge. One convergence is the recognition that some aspects of epistemic-thinking may be implicit, non-symbolic, and experiential, while others are explicit, symbolically represented, and socially shared. A second is the recognition that increasing students' metacognitive awareness of epistemic-thinking, and making this thinking explicit, is important in promoting conceptual change.

19

IDENTIFYING THE ROLE OF EPISTEMIC COGNITION AND METACOGNITION IN CONCEPTUAL CHANGE

Barbara K. Hofer

The relation among epistemic thinking, metacognition, and conceptual change has been conceptualized in different ways. My own entry point for this conversation is through a body of work on what has been broadly described as personal epistemology (Hofer & Pintrich, 1997, 2002) or epistemic cognition (Chinn, Buckland, & Samarapungavan, 2011; Greene, Sandoval, & Braten, 2016; Hofer, 2016), generally viewed as a set of mental processes that involve the development and employment of individual conceptions of knowledge and knowing (Hofer, 2016). How individuals think and reason epistemically can influence how they learn, how they resolve competing truth claims, what they count as worthy evidence, and the degree to which they place trust in authority, expertise, and their own experiences. These epistemic processes have power in day-to-day decisions about health and well-being, in decisions made as citizens, and in the public understanding of science, an area fraught with concern in debates about such topics as climate change, with broad implications for the planet (Sinatra & Hofer, 2016).

Epistemic processes appear to operate at both the cognitive and metacognitive level (Barzilai & Zohar, 2016; Hofer, 2004, 2005, 2016; Kuhn, 2000), and several researchers have described the relation among the two (Barzilai & Zohar, 2014; Hofer & Sinatra, 2010; Mason & Bromme, 2010), with competing details that are beyond the scope of this brief chapter. The model we have developed and tested in my lab (Hofer, 2000, 2004; Hofer, Harris, & Goldstein, April 2011) has been one that locates epistemological awareness within metacognition, building on multidimensional models of metacognition (Pintrich, Wolters, & Baxter, 2000; Schraw, 1998) and expanding them to include epistemic components. This advances metacognition from "thinking about thinking" to also encompass "thinking about knowing," which allowed for a test of the dimensionality of the epistemic belief model (Hofer & Pintrich, 1997). For example, the category of metacognitive knowledge (e.g., knowledge of cognition, strategies, and tasks) was expanded to include beliefs about knowledge (e.g., its certainty and simplicity), as well as beliefs about the self as knower (e.g., need for epistemic closure). To the category of metacognitive judgments and monitoring we added beliefs about the nature of knowing (e.g., the source and justification for knowing), so the individual moves from "Do I know this?", a metacognitive reflection, to "How do I know this?" "Do I judge this to be credible?" "Is there evidence to support this claim?" Similarly, the metacognitive component of self-regulation and control of learning advances from "Do I need to read this again in order to understand it?" to such internal questions as "Do I know what I need to know or do I need to know more?" We developed think-aloud studies to assess how students learned online, and were able to identify the key dimensions of epistemic metacognition in the process (Hofer, 2004).

Epistemic cognition and conceptual change

Studies over the last 15 years or so have shown that epistemic cognition influences conceptual change (Gill, Ashton, & Algina, 2004; Mason, 2000, 2010; Mason & Boscolo, 2004; Stathopoulou & Vosniadou, 2007). Conceptual change has been defined in multiple ways, but will be referred to here as a restructuring of knowledge consistent with scientific understanding (Sinatra, Kienhues, & Hofer, 2014). Notably, in one study, only the more advanced epistemic beliefs were related to lasting knowledge restructuring (Mason, 2010), an outcome seldom investigated. Epistemic thinking also exists at varying degrees of generality (Hofer, 2000, 2006; Muis, Bendixen, & Haerle, 2006), as individuals have beliefs that are domain general (e.g., "knowledge is a collection of facts"), domain specific ("to know history is to know the dates when important events took place"), and topic specific ("human causes of climate change can't be certain because only 97% of climate scientists agree").

Research on conceptual change typically describes occurrences at the topic level only, but both general- and domain-level epistemic cognition could be influential in conceptual change. For example, our research shows that adolescents with a concrete, objectivist form of epistemic knowing, when asked about how to understand the causes of a war, privileged the account of a contemporary ("a person who happened to live at the time") over that of a historical expert (Hofer et al., April 2011). Those with more evaluativist epistemologies understood that the view of a historian would likely offer substantive and evaluated evidence. Similarly, objectivists judged direct experience as the best source for scientific knowledge, even in situations that did not permit it, citing absence of such access as the reason for lack of scientific certainty. For example, when asked whether scientists could know for certain how bees communicate, several students said no, because they can't talk to the bees, and one went so far as to suggest "they would need a bee decoder." Thus, epistemic conceptual change—a change in one's epistemic orientation—may in some cases need to precede or accompany conceptual change and may be a fruitful line of inquiry (Sinatra & Chinn, 2012).

Evolutionary theory: epistemic cognition and conceptual change

Several studies my students and I have conducted indicate that epistemic cognition plays a role in the understanding and acceptance of evolutionary theory. Understanding evolutionary theory is critically important for an educated citizenry, who can then make sense of such issues as why it is problematic to overuse antibiotics, how viruses such as HIV began in chimpanzees, and whether genetically modified organisms are an issue for genetic diversity of crops, and why that might matter. Yet only a minority of Americans fully accept evolution through natural selection and 34 percent reject it entirely, claiming that humans and other living things have always existed in their present form (Masci, February 12, 2016). Evolutionary theory occupies a distinct role in conceptual change research as issues of understanding and acceptance can be studied separately (unlike gravity, photosynthesis, etc.), as well as the relation between the two.

Understanding of a scientific theory typically involves knowledge of the scientific concepts and processes. Acceptance of a theory implies a recognition that this is the best explanation available, based on existing evidence. In the case of evolution, one might understand the theory but not accept it. Consider, for example, the individual with religious training that fosters denial of evolution, but who learns enough about scientific explanations to pass a biology test. Similarly, one might accept the theory, knowing there is strong scientific evidence and consensus, but not fully understand the mechanisms by which evolution operates. Correlations between understanding and acceptance differ, depending on the population studied and measures used (Sinatra, Southerland, McConaughy, & Demastes, 2003). The direction of the relation also differs. Some science educators argue for addressing acceptance of evolution prior to teaching for scientific understanding, as rejection of the concept might serve as a barrier to understanding (Smith, 1994). In other words, students would first be taught that there is a preponderance of evidence and that scientists are confident in their assessment, and then would be taught how evolution works. More recently, in regard to the topic of climate change, a series of experimental studies suggests that the inverse may be effective, as fostering understanding can lead to acceptance (Ranney & Clark, 2016).

In our initial pilot research on students' understanding and acceptance of evolutionary theory (Hofer, Lam, & DeLisi, 2011), building on elements of the Sinatra et al. (2003) study, we surveyed 89 undergraduates with a web-based questionnaire that included multiple measures of understanding of evolutionary theory, including a vignette-based assessment (Settledge & Jenson, 1996) and multiple measures of acceptance, including the Measure of Acceptance of the Theory of Evolution (MATE). In this study, understanding and acceptance were correlated. In addition, using a topic-specific assessment of epistemic development, we found that individuals who were multiplists (i.e., those with a subjective view of knowledge, who think one opinion is as good as another) were less likely to accept evolution than those in the transition to evaluativism. Further, those most likely to accept the theory were evaluativists (i.e., those who coordinate subjective and objective views of knowledge, weigh evidence, evaluate the source of authority, and understand the relative nature of truth claims). Acceptance of the theory was positively correlated with conflict about the theory ("Do you personally experience any conflict in accepting the theory of evolution?"), reaffirming the role that cognitive conflict plays in conceptual change, an important reminder to instructors about its value in learning.

In the next iteration of the study (n = 333 college undergraduates) we continued our focus on a "hot cognition" model of conceptual change (Pintrich, Marx, & Boyle, 1993; Sinatra, 2005). Drawing on similar work with other topics that included affective variables (Gill et al., 2004), we assessed the degree to which evolution was perceived as a personally and emotionally significant issue (e.g., "How important is the issue of evolution to you personally?", "How emotionally significant is this topic to you?"). We also examined domain-specific measures of epistemic thinking in science, their perceived certainty of scientists' position on evolutionary theory, and a number of other variables, including students' understanding of the meaning of the word "theory." Understanding and acceptance were again positively correlated, and personal significance of the topic was correlated with acceptance. In regard to epistemic cognition, a general pattern of results emerged: advanced, topic-specific epistemological positions and advanced science-specific epistemic beliefs were both positively associated with an acceptance of evolution, and understanding was positively correlated with domain-specific epistemic beliefs about science. Students showed a naïve and colloquial conception of the word "theory," with most students assuming it meant a hypothesis or untested assumption, indicating a particular challenge in understanding and acceptance.

Our third study focused more directly on conceptual change. This longitudinal study of a subset of students (n = 122) from the previous study identified factors associated with changes in understanding and acceptance of evolution over a two-year period (Hofer, DeLisi, & Lam, April 2009). This enabled us to move beyond the short-term and context-bound concerns researchers have raised about the effects identified in most conceptual change studies (Sinatra & Chinn, 2012). We found that an increase in the emotional salience of evolution between Times 1 and 2 was associated with both an increase in understanding and acceptance of evolution, supporting the role of affective variables in the process of conceptual change. Most notably, increased understanding of evolution was associated with an advancement in beliefs about science between time 1 and 2. As students move from a more limited understanding of the nature of science to greater epistemic competence, they also advance to a more thorough understanding of evolution, lending support to the role of epistemic conceptual change proposed by Sinatra and Chinn (2012).

In addition, those who increased in their understanding of evolution from Time 1 to 2 were those who tended to rate scientists as more certain about evolution at Time 1. This suggests that if they think this is indeed a body of accepted knowledge they are more likely to engage in understanding the scientific theory. Similarly, Time 1 acceptance was positively correlated with an increase in understanding of evolutionary theory, providing additional support for Smith's (1994) proposition that it could be fruitful to address acceptance first and then address understanding.

Although students need to understand the tentative nature of scientific findings (Sinatra et al., 2014), they also need to learn to discriminate which findings have been well substantiated. This finding suggests a role that epistemic trust in science plays in how college students think about learning science. Scientists can be perceived as experts whose consensus offers a sociocultural variable in conceptual change. Sociocultural conceptual change theorists assert that when a new idea replaces an old one, it is because the new idea is reflective of a larger, "normative" view of a given community (Murphy, Alexander, Greene, & Edwards, 2007). Students in our sample who assessed the scientific consensus to be more certain at Time 1 showed an increase in their understanding of evolution two years later.

Future research and educational implications

More research is clearly needed on the role of epistemic metacognition in conceptual change. One avenue would be to investigate the role that perceptions of scientists' certainty and epistemic trust play in mediating conceptual change in science, as well as how such trust develops. Research also needs to focus on the process of change, which may require more microgenetic studies (Siegler, 2006). Conceptual change is unlikely to be abrupt and simple, yet current methods tend to capture outcomes more than process. Our longitudinal study, for example, gives only blunt testimony to the connection between epistemic cognition and conceptual change over time, and more work is needed that examines this linkage at a fine-grained level. This could also foster intervention studies, an additional area for fruitful research.

Science educators may want to focus on teaching a nuanced understanding of the epistemic foundations of science, how it is that scientists know, what counts as evidence, and what role theories play in understanding science. Such teaching helps students move beyond seeing issues such as evolution or climate change as something that scientists "believe," and helps them understand the scientific foundations of knowledge and the empirical grounds for acceptance. Current research suggests that teachers need to work toward the building of epistemic competence (Murphy & Alexander, 2016), assisting students in the skills of evaluating the source and worthiness of evidence. Fundamentally, these skills need to be viewed as a key aspect of critical thinking (Greene & Yu, 2016) and researchers working at the intersection of epistemic cognition, metacognition, and conceptual change need to help bolster the case for including such awareness within the teacher education curriculum.

References

Barzilai, S., & Zohar, A. (2014). Reconsidering personal epistemology as metacognition: A multifaceted approach to the analysis of epistemic thinking. *Educational Psychologist, 49*(1), 13–15.

Barzilai, S., & Zohar, A. (2016). Epistemic (meta)cognition: Ways of thinking about knowledge and knowing. In J. A. Greene, W. A. Sandoval, & I. Braten (Eds.), *Epistemic cognition*. New York: Routledge.

Chinn, C. A., Buckland, L. A., & Samarapungavan, A. (2011). Expanding the dimensioins of epistemic cognition: Arguments from philosophy and psychology. *Educational Psychologist, 46*(3), 141–167.

Gill, M. G., Ashton, P. T., & Algina, J. (2004). Changing preservice teachers' epistemological beliefs about teaching and learning in mathematics: An intervention study. *Contemporary Educational Psychology, 29*, 164–185.

Greene, J. A., & Yu, S. B. (2016). Educating critical thinkers: The role of epistemic cognition. *Policy Insights from the Behavioral and Brain Sciences, 3*, 45–53.

Greene, J. A., Sandoval, W. A., & Braten, I. (2016). *Epistemic cognition*. New York: Routledge.

Hofer, B. K. (2000). Dimensionality and disciplinary differences in personal epistemology. *Contemporary Educational Psychology, 25*, 378–405.

Hofer, B. K. (2004). Epistemological understanding as a metacognitive process: Thinking aloud during online searching. *Educational Psychologist, 39*, 43–55.

Hofer, B. K. (2005). The legacy and the challenge: Paul Pintrich's contributions to personal epistemology research. *Educational Psychologist, 40*, 95–105.

Hofer, B. K. (2006). Domain specificity of personal epistmology: Resolved questions, persistent issues, new models. *International Journal of Educational Research, 45*, 85–95.

Hofer, B. K. (2016). Epistemic cognition as a psychological construct: Advancements and challenges. In J. A. Greene, W. A. Sandoval, & I. Braten (Eds.), *Handbook of episemic cognition*. New York: Routledge.

Hofer, B. K., & Pintrich, P. R. (1997). The development of epistemological theories: Beliefs about knowledge and knowing and their relation to learning. *Review of Educational Research, 67*, 88–140.

Hofer, B. K., & Pintrich, P. R. (Eds.). (2002). *Personal epistemology: The psychology of beliefs about knowledge and knowing*. Mahwah, NJ: Erlbaum.

Hofer, B. K., & Sinatra, G. M. (2010). Epistemology, metacognition, and self-regulation: Musings on an emerging field. *Metacognition and Learning, 5*, 113–120.

Hofer, B. K., DeLisi, A., & Lam, C. F. (April 2009). *Evolutionary theory and students' conceptual change: The role of epistemic beliefs and emotional salience*. Paper presented at the American Educational Research Assocation, San Diego, CA.

Hofer, B. K., Harris, A., & Goldstein, L. (April 2011). *Adolescent epistemological development: History and science*. Paper presented at the American Educational Research Association, New Orleans, LA.

Hofer, B. K., Lam, C. F., & DeLisi, A. (2011). Understanding evolutionary theory: The role of epistemological development and beliefs. In R. Taylor & M. Ferrari (Eds.), *Epistemology and science education: Understanding the evolution vs. intelligent design controversy* (pp. 95–110). New York: Routledge.

Kuhn, D. (2000). Metacognitive development. *Current Directions in Psychological Science, 9*, 178–181.

Masci, D. (February 12, 2016). On Darwin Day, 5 facts about the evolution debate. Retrieved from http://www.pewresearch.org/fact-tank/2016/02/12/darwin-day/.

Mason, L. (2000). Role of anomalous data and epistemological beliefs in midde school students' theory change about two controversial topics. *Eurpean Journal of Psychology of Education, XV,* 329–346.

Mason, L. (2010). Beliefs about knowledge and revision of knowledge: On the importance of epistemic beliefs for intentional conceptual change in elementary and middle school students. In L. D. Bendixen & F. C. Feucht (Eds.), *Personal epistemology in the classroom: Theory, research, and practice* (pp. 258–291). Cambridge: Cambridge University Press.

Mason, L., & Boscolo, P. (2004). Role of epistemological understanding and interest in interpreting a controversy and in topic-specific belief change. *Contemporary Educational Psychology, 29,* 103–128.

Mason, L., & Bromme, R. (2010). Situating and relating epistemological beliefs into metacognition: Studies on beliefs about knowledge and knowing. *Metacognition and Learning, 5,* 1–6.

Muis, K. R., Bendixen, L. D., & Haerle, F. C. (2006). Domain generality and domain specificity in personal epistemology research: Philosophical and empirical reflections in the development of a theoretical model. *Educational Psychology Review, 18,* 3–54.

Murphy, P. K., Alexander, P., Greene, J. A., & Edwards, M. N. (2007). Epistemological threads in the fabric of conceptual change research. In S. Vosniadou, A. Baltas, & X. Vamvakoussi (Eds.), *Reframing the conceptual change approach in learning and instruction,* Oxford: Elsevier.

Murphy, P. K., & Alexander, P. A. (2016). Interrogating the relation between conceputal change and epistemic beliefs. In J. A. Greene, W. A. Sandoval, & I. Braten (Eds.), *Epistemic cognition.* New York: Routledge.

Pintrich, P. R., Marx, R. W., & Boyle, R. A. (1993). Beyond cold conceptual change: The role of motivational beliefs and classroom contextual factors in the process of conceptual change. *Review of Educational Research, 63*(2), 167–199.

Pintrich, P. R., Wolters, C. A., & Baxter, G. P. (2000). Assessing metacognition and self-regulated learning. In G. Schraw & J. C. Impara (Eds.), *Issues in the measurement of metacognition.* Lincoln, NE: Buros Institute of Mental Measurements.

Ranney, M. A., & Clark, D. (2016). Climate change conceptual change: Scientific information can transfrom attitudes. *Topics in Cognitive Science, 8,* 49–75.

Schraw, G. (1998). Promoting general metacognitive awareness. *Instructional Science, 26,* 113–125.

Settledge, J., & Jenson, M. S. (1996). Investigating the inconsistencies in college student responses to natural selection test questions. *The Electronic Journal of Science Education.* Available at: http://ejse.southwestern.edu/article/view/7553/5320.

Siegler, R. S. (2006). Microgenetic analyses of learning. In W. Damon, R. Lerner, D. Kuhn, & R. S. Siegler (Eds.), *Handbook of child psychology: Vol. 2. Cognition, perception, and language* (6th edition). Hoboken, NJ: WIley.

Sinatra, G. M. (2005). The "warming trend" in conceptual change research: The legacy of Paul R. Pintrich. *Educational Psychologist, 40,* 107–115. doi:10.1207/s15326985ep4002_5.

Sinatra, G. M., & Chinn, C. A. (2012). Thinking and reasoning in science: Promoting epistemic conceptual change. In K. R. Harris, S. Graham, & T. Urdan (Eds.), *APA educational psychology handbook: Vol. 3. Application to teaching and learning* (pp. 257–282). Washington, DC: American Psychological Association.

Sinatra, G. M., & Hofer, B. K. (2016). Public understanding of science: Policy and educational implications. *Policy Insights from the Behavioral and Brain sciences. 3*(2), 245–253. doi:10.1177/2372732216656870.

Sinatra, G. M., Kienhues, D., & Hofer, B. K. (2014). Addressing challenges to public understanding of science: Epistemic cognition, motivated reasoning, and conceptual change. *Educational Psychologist, 49*, 123–138.

Sinatra, G. M., Southerland, S. A., McConaughy, F., & Demastes, J. W. (2003). Intentions and beliefs in students' understanding and acceptance of biological evolution. *Journal of Research in Science Teaching, 40*, 510–528.

Smith, M. U. (1994). Counterpoint: Belief, understanding, and the teaching of evolution. *Journal of Research in Science Teaching, 31*, 591–597.

Stathopoulou, C., & Vosniadou, S. (2007). Exploring the relationship between physics-related epistemological beliefs and physics understanding. *Contemporary Educational Psychology, 32*, 255–281.

20

DON'T BELIEVE EVERYTHING YOU THINK

Reappraising judgments about conceptions

Doug Lombardi and Gale M. Sinatra

Misconceptions are notoriously robust and resistant to change, particularly in science, and helping individuals reconstruct knowledge toward scientifically accurate conceptions may require a multifaceted approach. Often, conceptual change requires improving the clarity and coherence of the content to make it more comprehensible. It may require providing students with key background knowledge that supports the content. But, affording opportunities to reappraise judgments about knowledge and knowing (i.e., epistemic judgments) may also be necessary for conceptual change.

Plausibility, an epistemic judgment that we have defined as an evaluation of the potential truthfulness of a novel conception (Lombardi, Nussbaum, & Sinatra, 2016), is especially relevant for controversial and complex topics, such as human-induced climate change, where there is a gap between what laypersons and scientists find plausible, that is, what we call a *plausibility gap* (Lombardi, Sinatra, & Nussbaum, 2013). Individuals often make such *epistemic judgments* implicitly and automatically. However, judgments of plausibility are characteristically tentative and changeable with explicit and purposeful thinking. Instruction also has the potential to improve students' plausibility appraisals and reappraisals when confronted with scientific information. We discuss how to bridge this plausibility gap by promoting explicit reappraisals through metacognitive and epistemological processes. Our research shows that sustained classroom instruction encouraging plausibility reappraisal contributes to the development of a scientific habit of mind (e.g., being critically evaluative about the connections between evidence and explanations). Further encouraging these practices contributes to both conceptual change and epistemic conceptual change (i.e., changes in views about the nature of knowledge and knowing; Lombardi et al., 2013). For example, conceptual change about global warming may involve shifting from a sun-centered causal model to a human-centered causal model, with a related epistemic conceptual change in an individual's ideas about causal processes.

Plausibility Judgments in Conceptual Change model

Individuals naturally make judgments about the nature of knowledge and knowing, or, *epistemic judgments*, and such judgments may include plausibility of an explanation, validity of a data set, and/or credibility of a source. Individuals may make epistemic judgments without much conscious thought, and in situations of conceptual change learning, may involve the novel message (e.g., the to-be-learned conception). We have recently created a theoretical model that specifically examines plausibility judgments of explanations. The model explains how reappraising plausibility may facilitate conceptual change, and also posits how such reappraisals may lead to epistemic conceptual change. Central to this model of *Plausibility Judgments in Conceptual Change* (PJCC) is the mechanism of the judgment, which may involve implicit processing (i.e., low awareness and low cognitive effort), explicit processing (i.e., high awareness and high cognitive effort), or in some cases both types of processing. Because implicit processing is often a default cognitive mode (Stanovich, 2010), plausibility judgments are often implicit. These judgments depend on a degree of evaluation, which is influenced by skilled intuition, individuals' dispositions, and/or the social or instructional context that could prompt individuals to be more critical.

We posit that people cognitively pre-process information prior to forming a plausibility judgment based on their perceptions. For example, perceptions of a source's credibility (e.g., the trustworthiness and/or expertise of the source) may depend on corroborative and coherent alignment with prior knowledge and beliefs, as well as message characteristics such as perceived degree of conjecture or uncertainty. Such perceptions may draw on implicit cognitive processes that are not reflective and purposeful about the source of the novel conception (Bråten, Braasch, Strømsø, & Ferguson, 2015). Our theoretical position about pre-processing has received some empirical support where perceptions of an author's trustworthiness predict plausibility and not vice-versa (Lombardi, Seyranian, & Sinatra, 2014). Thus, we proposed that perceptions based on the source of incoming information occur prior to implicit or explicit evaluations involved in forming plausibility judgments (Lombardi, Nussbaum et al., 2016).

Our PJCC model builds upon a long line of theoretical work in conceptual change (see, for example, Dole & Sinatra, 1998), and also incorporates other philosophical and psychological perspectives to provide a detailed explanatory model of the factors that form judgments of plausibility, as well as components that predict how and when plausibility reappraisals result in conceptual change (for details, please see Lombardi, Nussbaum et al., 2016). From a conceptual change viewpoint, the core of the PJCC explains how explicit and critical evaluations of novel explanations may influence reappraisals of plausibility, which in turn, might influence knowledge reconstruction. Reappraising plausibility may be particularly important for facilitating conceptual change about controversial socio-scientific concepts where there is a gap between what laypersons and scientists find plausible (Lombardi et al., 2013). In developing the PJCC, we were informed by the empirical work we have been conducting on judgments of plausibility over the last decade.

Empirical studies of plausibility and conceptual change

Prior to our series of studies, researchers had made few attempts to empirically investigate the role of plausibility in conceptual change. Our first plausibility study examined the relation between undergraduate students' plausibility judgments of human-induced climate change and knowledge of weather and climate distinctions (Lombardi & Sinatra, 2012). Two groups of students enrolled in general education science courses (one course focused on a semester-long examination of climate change and the other course broadly examining physical geography topics, with only a brief mention of climate change) experienced significant increases in their knowledge about weather and climate distinctions over the course of a semester. But more importantly, in terms of plausibility, this study showed that greater plausibility ratings of eight scientific statements about human-induced climate change[1] resulted in a significant drop in students' confusions about weather and climate differences at semester's end. This study, along with another examining the relations between topic emotions, epistemic motives, and plausibility, prompted us to consider the connections between cognitive evaluations of scientific evidence and explanations with plausibility, which motivated a detailed comparative conceptual change study (Lombardi et al., 2013). In this quasi-experimental study, grade 7 students weighed the connections between four lines of evidence and two alternative models of climate change (Model A: the scientifically accepted model of human-induced climate change, and Model B: a plausible but non-scientific explanation of sun-induced climate change). We specifically used a Climate Change Model-Evidence Link (MEL) diagram to help students weigh these connections. Clark Chinn and his colleagues at Rutgers University originally developed MEL diagrams for middle grades life science instruction (Chinn & Buckland, 2012), and we adapted the scaffold's structure and mode in constructing the Climate Change MEL. The results of our quasi-experimental study showed shifts in plausibility judgments toward the scientific model in students who engaged in the activity, as well as significant and strong conceptual change about climate, sustained six months after instruction. Interestingly, a comparison group that engaged in an instructional task that was similar in structure and content, but did not have students explicitly weigh alternative explanations, showed no plausibility shifts or conceptual change.

Instructional activities, such as the Climate Change MEL, which allow students to critically examine what they know and how they know, could prompt reappraisal of plausibility judgments. Such critical comparisons could involve "metacognitive reflection, rethinking ... old beliefs and comparing them with ... new ideas in order to judge the new ideas as more plausible and fruitful" (Pintrich, Marx, & Boyle, 1993, p. 174). Pintrich et al. (1993) specifically noted that engaging in metacognitive reflection involves rethinking beliefs in order to make plausibility judgments. Reappraisal involves rethinking the plausibility of conceptions. When individuals explicitly reflect on the certainty and correctness of these conceptions (factors that shape plausibility judgments), then they are engaging in what Barzilai and Zohar (2016) call epistemic metacognition.

The potential connection between plausibility reappraisal and epistemic cognition, along with our first few empirical studies informed our conceptualization of the PJCC, where we posited that explicit, critical, and evaluative thinking would promote reconsiderations of earlier judgments of plausibility. Lombardi, Danielson, and Young (2016) recently tested this notion experimentally in a study involving undergraduate students. Lombardi, Danielson et al. (2016) found that students who read a refutation text were critically evaluative, which in turn shifted their judgments of plausibility and reconstructed their knowledge toward the scientific explanation that humans are causal contributors to current changes in the climate. In comparison, reading an expository text did not activate critical evaluation, and post-reading knowledge was more strongly related to background knowledge (i.e., expository text readers retained their existing conceptions).

Lombardi, Danielson et al. (2016) showed a relation between critical evaluation and plausibility reappraisal, but we speculate that in certain instructional situations a refutation text may not call for as much epistemic heavy lifting as an MEL diagram. A recent study by Lombardi, Brandt, Bickel, and Burg (2016) supports this speculation through a more careful qualitative analysis of students' written evaluation when engaging in the Climate Change MEL. Students who made reflective evaluations after being exposed to a line of evidence collected over a decade that clearly shows our Earth receiving less energy from the Sun, while at the same time, global temperatures rising at an accelerated rate, were able to see a contradiction with the alternative explanation that current climate change is caused by increasing amounts of energy from the Sun. Lombardi, Brandt, et al. (2016) also showed, quantitatively, how such reflective evaluations lowered the plausibility of this alternative conception. Students who wrote about lines of evidence showing a sharp increase in human emissions of carbon and corresponding temperature increases experienced an increase in the plausibility of the scientific explanation of human-induced climate change. Such evaluations characterize a reappraisal of plausibility, and how such reappraisals might facilitate conceptual change (i.e., from the sun-induced conception to the human-induced conception). But conceptual change would only occur if the plausibility of the novel conception exceeded the plausibility of the existing conception.

It is important to note, however, that other factors (e.g., social context, motivated reasoning) might promote change or retention in the existing conception (Sinatra, Kienhues, & Hofer, 2014), which may override plausibility reappraisals.

Ongoing studies, future directions, and concluding thoughts

Our current project is examining how more sustained critical evaluation supports plausibility reappraisal, knowledge reconstruction, and epistemic conceptual change. In this three-year project, Lombardi and colleagues have specifically designed MEL diagrams and associated instructional materials that cover controversial and/or abstract Earth and space sciences topics (i.e., climate change, fracking, and earthquakes, water resources and land use, and formation of the Moon). The project's Year 2 results suggest a robust connection between participants' level of evaluation and their plausibility reappraisal (i.e., greater evaluation facilitates shifts in plausibility; Lombardi, Bickel, Bailey, & Burrell, in press). We are hesitant to speculate that this is reflective of epistemic conceptual change at this time because these findings are context- and topic-specific. Our hope is that the Year 3 data, which includes quasi-experimental comparison groups, will allow us to determine the effect of evaluation isolated from context and topic, and thereby give clearer evidence of whether epistemic conceptual change (changes in students' evaluations and epistemic judgments) has occurred. Year 2 results are also providing some preliminary evidence that students who regularly engage in instruction promoting critical evaluation and plausibility reappraisal are undergoing epistemic conceptual change. Over the course of a school year, some participants are more critically evaluative in an argument that supports their position on school recycling. But this evidence is not particularly strong because the pro/con recycling task is somewhat distal from the instructional activities and topics that students covered throughout the school year.

Other classroom instructional strategies and activities, in addition to MEL diagrams, may also support changes in epistemic judgments about plausibility. Such activities include use of critical questions and argument vee diagrams (Nussbaum & Edwards, 2011), and openness to alternatives (Meyer & Lederman, 2013). However, our research in actual classrooms suggests that to promote reappraisal of plausibility, students need to explicitly and purposefully consider how they are judging scientific explanations. Sinatra and Taasoobshirazi (2018), in a review of metacognitive and self-regulated learning in support of conceptual change, make three instructional recommendations. First, they recommend constructing the type of learning environment where individuals must consider alternative theories as seen in Lombardi et al. (2013). Second, they recommend that instruction be designed by promoting epistemic conceptual change, as we have argued here and elsewhere, as key to promoting conceptual change (Sinatra & Chinn, 2011). In these learning contexts, instructors ask students to justify their knowledge, critically evaluate sources, and reflect on what they know as well as how they know it. And third, Sinatra and Taasoobshirazi (2018) recommend the incorporation of emotion regulation into the self-regulation of science learning because many topics requiring conceptual change are controversial in the minds of students and may evoke strong, negative emotions. In sum, instruction that prompts students to be metacognitive and self-regulated, that evokes and prompts evaluations of background knowledge as does critical evaluations and reappraisal of plausibility, promotes conceptual change.

Our focus has been on judgments about the plausibility of explanations, and specifically our work has centered on the potential truthfulness of scientific explanations compared to plausible, but non-scientific explanations (Lombardi, Nussbaum et al., 2016). However, individuals typically have poor understanding about the distinctions between evidence and explanations, and epistemic judgments outside the purview of plausibility may be required to facilitate epistemic conceptual change. For example, Duschl (2008) notes that when individuals consider how scientists use raw data to build lines of evidence and predictive models, they might need to make "epistemic judgments about 'what counts'" in terms of reliability and validity. Chinn, Rinehart, and Buckland (2014) would classify this as a judgment of what constitutes a reliable process for achieving an epistemic end (i.e., a plausible explanation). However, such judgments of validity may not necessarily correspond with plausibility, but may rely on another type of epistemic judgment about evidence, such as source credibility. This notion is certainly speculative and warrants further research.

Individuals' judgments about knowledge and knowing can result in misconceptions. Individuals often make epistemic judgments without explicit thought. Therefore, individuals should be skeptical of what they know and how they know; in other words, we should not believe everything we think. Before knowledge reconstruction can occur, individuals must critically evaluate what and how they know, and explicitly reappraise the quality and validity of their judgments. Carefully crafted instruction can help make epistemic judgments explicit and purposeful, and such instruction can not only deepen understanding through conceptual change, but also facilitate reappraisal of why individuals think the way they do. Promoting epistemic conceptual change should be at the forefront of our educational enterprise because individuals need to understand how scientists construct understanding in order to successfully confront societal challenges of increasing complexity.

Acknowledgments

Part of the research discussed in this chapter was supported by the US National Science Foundation (NSF) under Grant No. DRL-131605. Any opinions, findings, conclusions, or recommendations expressed are those of the authors and do not necessarily reflect the NSF's views.

Note

1 In our empirical studies, participants rated the plausibility of scientific statements about climate change (Lombardi & Sinatra, 2012, 2013), or alternative explanations about the causes of current climate change (Lombardi et al., 2013; Lombardi, Danielson, & Young, 2016), on a 1–10 Likert scale (1 = greatly implausible or even impossible and 10 = highly plausible). This method closely followed earlier plausibility measures developed by Connell and Keane (2004).

References

Barzilai, S., & Zohar, A. (2016). Epistemic (meta) cognition: Ways of thinking about knowledge and knowing. 409–424. In J. A. Greene, W. A. Sandoval, & I. Bråten (Eds.) *Handbook of epistemic cognition* (pp. 409–424). New York: Routledge.

Bråten, I., Braasch, J. L., Strømsø, H. I., & Ferguson, L. E. (2015). Establishing trustworthiness when students read multiple documents containing conflicting scientific evidence. *Reading Psychology, 36*(4), 315–349. doi: 10.1080/02702711.2013.864362.

Chinn, C. A., & Buckland, L. A. (2012). Model-based instruction: Fostering change in evolutionary conceptions and in epistemic practices. In K. S. Rosengren, E. M. Evans, S. Brem, & G. M. Sinatra (Eds.), *Evolution challenges: Integrating research and practice in teaching and learning about evolution*. New York: Oxford University Press.

Chinn, C. A., Rinehart, R. W., & Buckland, L. A. (2014). Epistemic cognition and evaluating information: Applying the AIR Model of epistemic cognition. In D. N. Rapp & J. L. G. Braasch (Eds.), *Processing inaccurate information: Theoretical and applied perspectives from cognitive science and the educational sciences* (pp. 425–454). Cambridge, MA: MIT Press.

Connell, L., & Keane, M. T. (2004). What plausibly affects plausibility? Concept coherence and distributional word coherence as factors influencing plausibility judgments. *Memory & Cognition, 32*, 185–197. doi:10.3758/BF03196851.

Dole, J. A., & Sinatra, G. M. (1998). Reconceptualizing change in the cognitive construction of knowledge. *Educational Psychologist, 33*, 109–128. doi:10.1080/00461520. 1998.9653294.

Duschl, R. (2008). Science education in three-part harmony: Balancing conceptual, epistemic, and social learning goals. *Review of Research in Education, 32*(1), 268–291. doi:10.3102/0091732X07309371.

Lombardi, D., Bickel, E. S., Bailey, J. M., & Burrell, S. (in press). High school students' evaluations, plausibility (re) appraisals, and knowledge about topics in Earth science. *Science Education*. doi: 10.1002/sce.21315.

Lombardi, D., Brandt, C. B., Bickel, E. S., & Burg, C. (2016). Students' evaluations about climate change. *International Journal of Science Education, 38*(8), 1392–1414. doi:10.1080/ 09500693.2016.1193912.

Lombardi, D., Danielson, R. W., & Young, N. (2016). A plausible connection: Models examining the relations between evaluation, plausibility, and the refutation text effect. *Learning and Instruction, 44*, 74–86. doi:10.1016/j.learninstruc.2016.03.003.

Lombardi, D., Nussbaum, E. M., & Sinatra, G. M. (2016). Plausibility judgments in conceptual change and epistemic cognition. *Educational Psychologist, 51*(1), 35–56. doi:10. 1080/00461520.2015.1113134.

Lombardi, D., Seyranian, V., & Sinatra, G. M. (2014). Source effects and plausibility judgments when reading about climate change. *Discourse Processes, 51*(1/2), 75–92. doi: 10.1080/0163853X.2013.855049.

Lombardi, D., Sibley, B., & Carroll, K. (2013). What's the alternative? Using model-evidence link diagrams to weigh alternative models in argumentation. *The Science Teacher, 80*(5), 36–41. doi:10.2505/4/tst13_080_05_50.

Lombardi, D., & Sinatra, G. M. (2013). Emotions about teaching about human-induced climate change. *International Journal of Science Education, 35*, 167–191. doi:10.1080/09500693.2012.738372.

Lombardi, D., & Sinatra, G. M. (2012). College students' perceptions about the plausibility of human-induced climate change. *Research in Science Education, 42*, 201–217. doi:10.1007/s11165-010-9196-z.

Lombardi, D., Sinatra, G. M., & Nussbaum, E. M. (2013). Plausibility reappraisals and shifts in middle school students' climate change conceptions. *Learning and Instruction, 27*, 50–62. doi:10.1016/j.learninstruc.2013.03.001.

Meyer, A. A., & Lederman, N. G. (2013). Inventing creativity: An exploration of the pedagogy of ingenuity in science classrooms. *School Science and Mathematics, 113*(8), 400–409. doi:10.1111/ssm.12039.

Nussbaum, E. M., & Edwards, O. V. (2011). Critical questions and argument stratagem: A framework for enhancing and analyzing students' reasoning practices. *Journal of the Learning Sciences, 20*, 443–488. doi:10.1080/10508406.2011.564567.

Pintrich, P. R., Marx, R. W., & Boyle, R. B. (1993). Beyond cold conceptual change: The role of motivational beliefs and classroom contextual factors in the process of conceptual change. *Review of Educational Research, 63*, 167–199. doi:10.3102/00346543063002167.

Sinatra, G. M. & Chinn, C. (2011). Thinking and reasoning in science: Promoting epistemic conceptual change. In K. Harris, C. B. McCormick, G. M. Sinatra, & J. Sweller (Eds.), *Critical theories and models of learning and development relevant to learning and teaching, Volume 1* (pp. 257–282). In K. Harris & S. Graham (Eds.), *APA educational psychology handbook series*. Washington, DC: APA Publications.

Sinatra, G. M., Kienhues, D., & Hofer, B. K. (2014). Addressing challenges to public understanding of science: Epistemic cognition, motivated reasoning, and conceptual change. *Educational Psychologist, 49*(2), 123–138. doi:10.1080/00461520.2014.916216.

Sinatra, G. M. & Taasoobshirazi, G. (2018). The self-regulation of learning and conceptual change in science: Research, theory, and educational applications. In D. Shunk & J. A. Greene (Eds.), *Handbook of self-regulated learning and performance* (2nd edition, pp. 153–165). New York: Routledge.

Stanovich, K. E. (2010). *Decision making and rationality in the modern world.* New York: Oxford University Press.

21

THE INTERACTING DYNAMICS OF EPISTEMOLOGY AND CONCEPTUAL UNDERSTANDING

David Hammer

The editors ask that I focus on clarifying my position, "rather than trying to be persuasive." It's an unusual assignment, and my sense of the line between clarifying and persuading shifts as I write, and as I get the editors' feedback. My framing shifts, in other words, my sense of what I'm doing, and as it does so, so do the ideas I express and the ways I try to express them.

That, in brief, is the position I'll try to convey: Thinking involves a complex mix of awareness and intentions, personal history and social context. It's dynamic, for me in this moment revising my draft, as for students thinking about natural phenomena. For a case in point, I'll borrow data from research Jen Radoff, Lama Jaber, and I have carried out (Radoff, Jaber, & Hammer, 2016).

Marya's reasoning and my position

"Marya" was in my "General Physics I," which is a significant departure from traditional expectations, especially in emphasizing students "learning how to learn." Lectures, problem sets, labs, and exams all challenged students to think in new ways.[1] Jen was Marya's teaching assistant (TA).

Marya approached both Jen and me early in the semester for help with homework and to express her intense anxiety about the course. She was not doing well, treating physics as equations to memorize, disconnected from tangible experience. Several weeks in, though, she was making progress, and by the end it was dramatic, in how she approached and felt about learning. Jen suggested we study how it happened, using data from the course and an interview. Marya agreed, and Lama, who was not involved in the course, interviewed her the afternoon after the final exam.

The interaction of conceptual reasoning and epistemology

I'll start with Marya's response to one of the "checkpoint questions" students answered online before every lecture, from smartPhysics (Gladding, Selen, & Steltzer, 2014). The question shown in Figure 21.1 was in the first week of the course:

Marya answered the farther ship, #2, gets hit first:

> I think enemy ship 1 has the greater speed because its parabolic trajectory shows a steeper positive slope than does enemy ship 2. If we were to go back to the two time values at which the projectiles are at zero, the second value (where the projectile hits the ship) is dependent on the initial speed and the gravitational pull [(2 × initial velocity)/g]. The greater the speed in the nominator, the greater the result of the fraction meaning the greater the time. Enemy ship 2 will be hit first because it has the lower speed.

It is an occasion for instructional sense-making.

The hardest part is her inference that the projectile aimed at ship 1 has a greater speed, because its "trajectory shows a steeper positive slope." She'd seen that steeper slope means greater speed in a graph of position over time, that week, and probably also in high school. Evidently, she took "steeper slope means greater speed" and applied it to the projectile's trajectory. The rest is clear: She used a formula from the smartPhysics video "prelecture" for the time a projectile spends in the air, $t = 2v_0/g$: If the first shell has a greater initial speed v_0, it spends more time in the air.

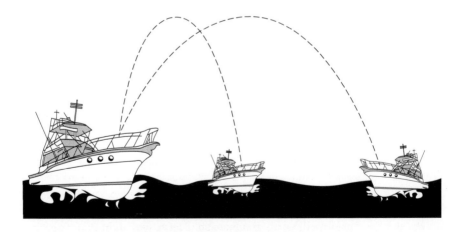

FIGURE 21.1 "A destroyer simultaneously fires two shells with different initial speeds at two different enemy ships. The shells follow the parabolic trajectories shown. Which ship gets hit first?"

Source: Adapted from *FlipIt Physics*, Gladding et al., Copyright 2014.

There is a rationality to her response, which is important to appreciate. But what does it indicate about Marya? Accounts of conceptual change have traditionally focused on identifying and addressing students' misconceptions. To me, though, her response does not indicate she has a misconception.

I see conceptual understanding as involving a complex myriad of resources in many forms, including p-prims (diSessa, 1993), and symbolic forms (Sherin, 2001), remembered facts, and simple associations. Some researchers focus on pinning down specific properties of particular forms; I focus on the many-ness of resources and their variable, contextual activation, to think about what that means for learning and teaching. After collaborating with David Brown (Brown & Hammer, 2008), who introduced me to Thelen's and Smith's models of dynamic systems, I've come to see resources more as recurrent, dynamic stabilities—more like Bartlett's account of schemas as "active organized settings" (Bartlett, 1932/1995), and less like intact cognitive objects with well-defined properties.

Thelen and Smith (2006) present two themes in applying dynamic systems theory to human development: (1) continuity of system, "from the molecular to the cultural," and (2) continuity of timescale, "from milliseconds to years" (p. 258). Patterns appear in moments; some recur and shift and grow, developing greater stability, the pattern formation as ontogenesis. The pattern of infants' moving legs in alternation, for example, first emerges in particular situations, and, over time it becomes a stable part of walking. I take patterns of connecting speed, time, and displacement (Frank, 2009) as other examples, first emerging in moments of childhood and over time, becoming stable resources.

My research generally focuses on dynamics from the scale of minutes, such as in classroom episodes, to scales of weeks and months. And I see theoretical continuity of system, from an individual to an "ensemble" (Conlin & Hammer, 2016).

So, in making sense of Marya's response, I consider the dynamics of the moment. They involve resources I can attribute to Marya, including her sense of slope: I'm sure she sees slope easily, in terrain, in images, across many contexts. She has a sense of time as a duration, which she applies in reasoning that larger t for #1 means #2 hits first. There's also evidence she has the symbolic form "prop+" (Sherin, 2001), by which she reads the expression $t = 2v_0/g$ as saying that larger v_0 means larger t.

But her response as a whole is a local "soft-assembly" (Thelen & Smith, 2006) of a system that extends beyond Marya herself. The set of activations and connections nests within and involves features of the situation: She's responding to checkpoint questions after watching a formula-intensive prelecture within a required course she finds intimidating. It is part of that soft-assembly that Marya misconceives as an association of slope with speed, but only a part: It would be a mistake to attribute that to her as a misconception she has as an individual. In just about any other situation involving motion, Marya would think differently. It's hard to imagine her on a tennis court explaining that she'd need to hit the ball more slowly to lob it a greater distance.

Attributing reasoning to Marya ought to mean it is stable in her, easily recurrent and persistent across diverse situations. I'm confident in supposing that in many many situations, Marya easily and persistently expects that either increasing distance or decreasing speed means taking a longer time. That's why her answer to the checkpoint is a moment for instructional sense-making: It's idiosyncratic. How does it last long enough for her to write it down as her answer without activating resources that are robust parts of her everyday thinking?

I've started to explain my answer to that question: Marya's reasoning holds together because it's nested within the physics course. That matters in part because of her epistemology. Across her work early in the course, Marya framed (Hammer, Elby, Scherr, & Redish, 2005) what was taking place with respect to knowledge in ways I and others have described at length (Hammer, 1994). Thus she saw the relevant knowledge as the facts and formulas delivered by the instructor and materials, and her role was to use them: Greater slope means greater velocity, $t = 2v_0/g$. Her framing excluded her own experience in the physical world, much as someone playing chess excludes their knowledge of actual knights, kings, and queens (cf. Ford, 2005). In that respect, she did show stability, across contexts of this course and, by her own account, other courses as well.

Following through on my little thought experiment—suppose she were talking about hitting balls on the tennis court—she would automatically, easily expect that knowledge comes from her experience, and she would apply her more stable patterns of reasoning about distance, speed, and time. In this way, the dynamics of Marya's thinking about physical phenomena involve both conceptual and epistemological resources. They also involve affect—that's what Jen, Lama, and I are writing about—and a great deal more, including her history in other courses, the smartPhysics graphics, and the institutional role of grades.

This all contrasts with traditional accounts of individuals' stable cognitive structures. From a dynamic systems perspective, the stability is often of a system larger than the individual, much as described in accounts of situated and distributed cognition (e.g., Greeno, 1997), and it can be momentary or long-lasting.

Progress in learning physics

The question shown in Figure 21.2 was from Thursday of the seventh week:

FIGURE 21.2   "Two balls of equal mass are thrown horizontally with the same initial velocity. They hit identical stationary boxes resting on a frictionless horizontal surface. The ball hitting box 1 bounces back, while the ball hitting box 2 gets stuck. Which box ends up moving faster?"

Source: Adapted from *FlipIt Physics*, Gladding et al., Copyright 2014.

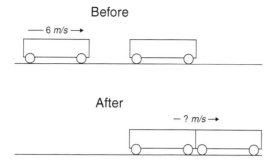

FIGURE 21.3 Problem set question.

Marya answers that box 1 moves faster because the "the interaction in situation 1 would not take away as much of the kinetic energy as the situation in 2." That makes her wonder, "Is there loss in kinetic energy in the box 1 scenario?"

> I can imagine the ball slowing down after the hit but I also feel that it would speed up. Actually, I take that back. I just watched a video of billiard balls being hit and the ball that does the hitting changes directions and slows down. [...] I just hit a ball against the wall and I varied the speeds. It seemed to me that the ball bounced back with the same speed that I hit it with. I tried but I couldn't make it go faster than its original speed no matter how hard I hit. At least, it looked that way to me.

The following Tuesday she handed in a problem set. It included a question about two carts colliding inelastically, asking for their speeds and kinetic energies, before and after colliding as shown in Figure 21.3, and then for those quantities with a 2 kg stationary cart. Marya finished the problem and continued:

> Interesting! So it seems that when the cart collides with an object with the same mass, half the initial kinetic energy is lost. When it collides with an object twice its mass, two thirds of the KE energy will be lost. So there's a relationship between the KE lost and the fraction of the mass of the stationary object and the total mass of the system. Specifically

$$KE_{lost} = KE_i \times \left(m_{stationaryobject} / m_{totalsystem} \right)$$

She checks it for a stationary cart of mass 4 kg: "So the relationship holds true!!" She then reflects on its meaning, for inelastic collisions and the conservation of energy.

Marya's responses again illustrate the interacting dynamics between epistemology and conceptual understanding.

On the checkpoint question, she looked for coherence with her experience and intuition, considering what she could visualize and what she could observe, both in video data and in her own informal experiments. She didn't use any formulas from the prelecture or even mention its topic, the conservation of momentum, in clear contrast with her response to the ships question earlier. On the carts problem, she looked for the conceptual implications of her mathematical calculations and thought to generalize from them; she composed a formula of her own. In each, she explored her own questions beyond the assignment, and her responses involve explicit metacognition, as she narrates the flow of her reasoning.

In her interview, Marya contrasted what she had been doing, "throwing symbols all over the place," with trying to "honestly have a good grasp of what was going on." "Rather than depending on a teacher to give you the right answer or a professor to tell you that's right, [...] we were approaching physics as if we were just discovering physics."

It was a shift of epistemological framing, evidenced by and supporting her tapping into her knowledge and experience, such as of bouncing or of finding new patterns and relationships. I believe the influence goes the other way as well: Thinking about her experience of bouncing, for example, helps maintain her sense of what she's doing.[2]

There's also evidence of her interest and excitement ("So the relationship holds true!!"); Marya told Lama about how she "got so excited" to have found that relationship. That's the focus of the article we're writing (Radoff, Jaber, & Hammer, 2016). But the focus here is conceptual change, as the editors remind me.

Energy is the salient concept in Marya's responses above, and the evidence shows local dynamics. On the checkpoint question, Marya considered the possibility of the ball speeding up when it bounces, which would mean a gain in kinetic energy. Watching a video of billiard balls and bouncing a ball off a wall dissuaded her from that idea, but she ended her response not quite sure the ball can't speed up. She didn't consider that possibility on the carts problem, which did not involve bouncing, nor on the next problem in the set, which did. I believe her presuming conservation on those problems reflects their organization around mathematical expressions that do not afford adding energy. It is also possible she had become convinced energy is conserved, but she did not mention coming to that conclusion.

There are continuities in Marya's understanding of energy across these problems: that there is such a thing, that it can be "lost," that it is associated with speed. So it may be reasonable to say "Marya understands moving objects have energy." In other respects, the substance seems to be a soft-assembly involving features of the situation. She participates in that assembly, but from one situation to another the assemblies only partially align, so it would be a mistake to attribute them to her as an individual. Over time, as she participates in these assemblies, patterns of her thinking in them will recur and shift and develop stability in her. And, I believe, that stability will involve epistemology, in her sense of energy as a concept with consistent meaning, serving physics as a pursuit of understanding.

Attributing a concept of energy to Marya, again, ought to mean stability in her, easily recurrent and persistent across situations. There is evidence from her later work that Marya made progress in that direction, although obviously it was all within the context of the course. In the end, though, I can't say "Marya understands energy," at the level of introductory mechanics.

I *can* say Marya frames learning differently. There is evidence of new stability in how she approaches and feels about learning, easily recurrent and persistent across situations, both within the course and, we have evidence, beyond it: In her interview with Lama, Marya said she was "doing the same things" now in Calculus. And, in a follow-up interview with Jen two years later, Marya said what she learned in physics transformed how she approached and felt about learning across her program.

More than conceptions

Science educators have generally seen conceptual change as the main objective, assessing learning mainly by gains on conceptual inventories, designing learning progressions to arrive at canonical concepts. But when I think of what happened for Marya in my course, I see her progress as a learner as far more important. I would like to understand how to help that happen more often—it's the reason for our case study (Radoff, Jaber, & Hammer, 2016).

Some of that, we argue, was in how Marya experienced conceptual change, supporting and supported by her shift of epistemology and, entangled with that, her feelings about uncertainty. Some, it is clear, had to do with our emphasis in the course, prioritizing students' learning how to learn, at times over their arriving at correct understandings.

Looking forward, I think it's important to engage further with the complexity of the dynamics—what Amin, Smith, and Wiser (2014) called the "third phase" of research. That may include reconsidering conventional practices of aggregating data, on the possibility of chaotic dynamics in learning (see Hammer & Sikorski, 2015).

Finally, for me it includes examining the messy complexity of knowledge and reasoning as I experience it in myself. I'm not suggesting anyone rely on introspection, any more than I would suggest physics students should rely on their experience of physical phenomena. But I do think our theories and our experiences should speak to each other.

Acknowledgments

This work is funded by the Gordon and Betty Moore Foundation through Grant #3475.01. I am grateful for their support, and to Lama Jaber, Jen Radoff, Carol Smith, and Marianne Wiser for helpful comments.

Notes

1 For a glimpse into lecture and references for further reading, see http://students doingscience.tufts.edu/sp_cpt/block-and-cylinder/.
2 An analogy: Having the ingredients for my salad out on the table helps maintain my sense of what I'm doing.

References

Amin, T. G., Smith, C. L., & Wiser, M. (2014). Student conceptions and conceptual change: Three overlapping phases of research. In N. G. Lederman & S. K. Abell (Eds.), *Handbook of research on science education*, Vol II (pp. 57–81). New York: Routledge.

Bartlett, F. C. (1932/1995). *Remembering: A study in experimental and social psychology.* Cambridge: Cambridge University Press.

Brown, D. E., & Hammer, D. (2008). Conceptual change in physics. In S. Vosniadou (Ed.), *International handbook of research on conceptual change* (pp. 127–154). New York: Routledge.

Conlin, L., & Hammer, D. (2016). Commentary: From the individual to the ensemble and back again. In A. A. DiSessa, M. Levin, & N. J. S. Brown (Eds.), *Knowledge and interaction: A synthetic agenda for the learning sciences* (pp. 311–325). London: Routledge.

diSessa, A. A. (1993). Towards an epistemology of physics. *Cognition and Instruction, 10*(2–3), 105–225.

Ford, M. J. (2005). The game, the pieces, and the players: Generative resources from two instructional portrayals of experimentation. *Journal of the Learning Sciences, 14*(4), 449–487.

Frank, B. W. (2009). *The dynamics of variability in physics students' thinking: Examples from kinematics.* (Doctoral Thesis), University of Maryland, College Park.

Gladding, G., Selen, M., and Stelzer, T., and W.H. Freeman (2014). smartPhysics (Now "FlipIt Physics.") www.FlipItPhysics.com.

Greeno, J. (1997). On claims that answer the wrong questions. *Educational Researcher, 26*(1), 5–17.

Hammer, D. (1994). Epistemological beliefs in introductory physics. *Cognition and Instruction, 12*(2), 151–183.

Hammer, D., Elby, A., Scherr, R. E., & Redish, E. F. (2005). Resources, framing, and transfer. In J. Mestre (Ed.), *Transfer of learning from a modern multidisciplinary perspective* (pp. 89–119). Greenwich, CT: Information Age Publishing.

Hammer, D., & Sikorski, T.-R. (2015). Implications of complexity for research on learning progressions. *Science Education, 99*(3), 424–431.

Radoff, J., Jaber, L.Z., & Hammer, D. (2016) Meta-affective learning in an introductory physics course. In D. L. Jones, L. Ding, & A. L. Traxler (Eds.), *Physics Education Research Conference 2016 Proceedings.* doi 10.1119/perc.2016.pr.060.

Sherin, B. L. (2001). How students understand physics equations. *Cognition and Instruction, 19*(4), 479–541.

Thelen, E., & Smith, L. B. (2006). Dynamic systems theories. In W. Damon & R. Lerner (Eds.), *Handbook of child psychology, Volume 1, Theoretical models of human development, 6th Edition* (pp. 258–312). Hoboken, NJ: John Wiley & Sons, Inc.

22

SITUATING PRACTICES OF EPISTEMIC COGNITION

William A. Sandoval

Conceptual change and metacognition are typically theorized as processes of individuals. The basic cognitive constructivist position is that individuals interpret their experiences in the world by constructing concepts in the mind, that are then applied to subsequent experience. Over the last two decades, interest in how people think about knowledge, epistemic cognition, has been recognized increasingly as important to efforts to learn, especially in school disciplines. Like conceptual change and metacognition, epistemic cognition has typically been studied from a cognitive perspective that argues that beliefs about the nature of knowledge, and knowing, drive efforts to learn, that is, efforts at conceptual change.

An alternative to the classic cognitive position is the situative view (Greeno & The Middle School Mathematics Through Application Project Group, 1998; Lave & Wenger, 1991). A situative theory of cognition argues that a full understanding of how people think requires close attention to how thinking occurs in interaction with the material and social resources present in all human activity. A situative view of cognition generally, and epistemic cognition specifically, emphasizes that processes of knowledge construction and evaluation are inherently social, tied to goals that emerge from activity (Saxe, 1988). I describe here my approach to developing a situated theory of epistemic cognition, an approach recently taken up in different forms by others (e.g., Chinn & Rinehart, 2016; Hammer & Elby, 2002; Kelly, 2016).

Principles of a situative account of epistemic cognition

The situative view of cognition is derived from Vygotsky's (1978, 1994) claim that "higher" psychological functions, including the development of concepts, are fundamentally cultural and historical, as cognition is situated within cultural activity. Conceptual change for an individual, from this view, is the appropriation of cultural concepts, the individual re-presentation of concepts first encountered through social interaction. Concepts themselves are developed through and tied to cultural practices, ways of acting meaningfully within cultural activity. The first principle of a situative account of epistemic cognition is the basic one that all cognition entails the individual-in-interaction with the social and/or material resources of a particular situation (Greeno, 2015; Greeno & The Middle School Mathematics Through Application Project Group, 1998). Therefore, any conception of knowledge or knowing invoked by an individual in a particular situation is tied in some way to the particulars of that situation.

A second principle is that all knowledge and knowledge practices are fundamentally social (Chinn, Buckland, & Samarapungavan, 2011; Chinn & Rinehart, 2016; Kelly, McDonald, & Wickman, 2012). Claims to knowledge do not become knowledge until some community of practice ratifies them as such, and ratification occurs through social practices of knowledge evaluation local to particular communities. Excellent discussions of the epistemological arguments for this principle can be found in Chinn & Rinehart (2016) and Kelly (2016). For the present argument, the crucial point is that practices of epistemic cognition, including the conceptions involved, are appropriated by individuals through their participation in particular activities of knowledge construction and evaluation, located within particular communities of practice.

A third principle is that participation in activity has cognitive consequences for individuals; individuals internalize their own versions of social practices and the conceptions attached to them (Gutierrez & Rogoff, 2003). Crucially, conceptions are contextually linked to the practices they enable and the situations where those practices are used. This principle is similar to the epistemological resources framework of Hammer and Elby (Hammer & Elby, 2002; Louca, Elby, Hammer, & Kagey, 2004), although they have focused on labeling particular resources and their surrounding frames (Elby & Hammer, 2010). One implication of this principle for conceptual change is that observations of changing performance on some task may indicate that the person so observed has constructed some new conception that enables a different performance, or it may mean that they have attuned some prior conception to the task situation, as described by Greeno and The Middle School Mathematics Through Application Project Group (1998).

A fourth principle is that epistemic cognition is conditioned by the goals a person pursues while constructing or evaluating knowledge. Such goals might include epistemic aims, a term used by Chinn et al. (2011) to connote goals related to knowledge, per se, as well as non-epistemic aims like maintaining relationships (Kawasaki, DeLiema, & Sandoval, 2014). This distinction acknowledges that people rarely seek knowledge for knowledge's sake. We need to know things in order to do things. Lave and Wenger (1991) argued that learning is a part of all activity, not a separate activity unto itself. In the same way, knowing is an aspect of all activity. Consequently, efforts to learn new things necessarily include epistemic and non-epistemic aims.

Epistemic cognition as situated practice

To illustrate how a situative view on epistemic cognition can be useful, I focus here on practices of justification and their development. Justification is both a crucial aspect of disciplinary knowledge construction and of conceptual change. Reliable processes of justification have been a central concern in epistemology since its origins (Chinn et al., 2011; Chinn & Rinehart, 2016). Conceptual change models rely on the proposition that individuals appropriate new conceptions when they can be justified as both plausible and fruitful. Practices for reliably justifying claims emerge in early childhood, from scrutinizing the trustworthiness of others' testimony to making sense of evidence (see Sandoval, Sodian, Koerber, & Wong, 2014). Yet, the reliability of the processes children develop prior to school are limited, for example, in their ability to help people evaluate the trustworthiness of claims they may read in the media (Strømsø & Kammerer, 2016), or making sense of concepts in academic disciplines. The justification practices children appropriate prior to school do not seem much improved by schooling (Sandoval et al., 2014).

Practices of justifying both claims to knowledge and methods for producing them develop through the pursuit of particular sorts of goals. For example, the canonical control of variables strategy of experimentation in science is a means for producing justified causal claims and derives its value from achieving that goal (Sandoval, 2005). Here, I draw out the features of a situative analysis from a longitudinal interaction analysis of a year's worth of science lessons in a mixed grade 3–4 classroom, using video records of more than 70 hours of instruction over 30 weeks (Ryu & Sandoval, 2012).

In this classroom, the teacher, Ms. Green (a pseudonym), consistently asked her students how they could convince someone of a claim. This started almost immediately at the start of the school year and continued throughout. Ms. Green posted persuasion as an important goal, as being a means to satisfy a larger goal she put forward as a goal of science: to reach consensus on the best possible answer. Children, in various ways, suggested that one has to be able to "back up" a claim. As they then began to do science work in their classroom, Ms. Green consistently reminded them of this need to back up, which in turn created a problem: what does it mean to "back up" a claim? Children suggested backing up entailed "showing evidence," but again as this new epistemic aim to show evidence was taken up by the class it became problematic. The children in the class had to devise ways to produce and "show" evidence in ways their peers found persuasive. The teacher's role in this was primarily to remind students of what their current aims were and hold them accountable to them, but the means through which epistemic aims could be appropriately satisfied, that is, the acceptable practices of knowledge production in the classroom, originated from the students. Ryu and Sandoval show how Ms. Green re-voiced students' language in consistent ways that were then taken up by the children collectively. During the course of the year, in their own group work, children spontaneously used versions of Ms. Green's demands with each other. They asked each other, "How do you know?" and "Was it a fair test?" They argued about appropriate questions to ask, methods for answering them, representations of data, and conclusions. Over the course of a school year, individual children showed, through their performance on argument construction and evaluation tasks, that they had appropriated the practices of evidence citation and justification that had emerged during their science instruction.

This example shows both the attunement of prior epistemic conceptions to specific task situations, and the development of new epistemic conceptions tied to emergent demands of collective activity. An earlier study with these same children showed that they preferred data as the strongest kind of justification for causal claims (Sandoval & Çam, 2011). Yet, when we asked them why they preferred data they told us that the person who had data was more credible, rather than locating credibility in the data, per se. As they began their science work the following year, then, this preference for evidence (data) became attuned to their own efforts to make claims about the science they were studying. Yet, as the concept of "showing evidence" became obviously problematic, these children had to develop new practices that would allow them to answer the questions that arose during their work, which entailed coming to think about evidence in new ways. Since they all "had data," that in itself no longer lent credibility to particular claims. Instead, to solve their collective problem of reaching consensus, children had to ask new questions and come up with new means to answer them: What evidence needs to be shown? What makes evidence good? How much evidence is enough? And so on. The data provided by Ryu and Sandoval (2012) make clear that the refinement of children's justification practices emerged in a reciprocal relation to epistemic aims. The demand to "back up" claims by "showing evidence" led students to suggest and refine new practices, for example to conduct "fair tests." Ambiguities surrounding what makes tests fair and how to settle conflicting interpretations of data led to a goal of "provide justification," which then led explicitly to efforts to justify claim–evidence relations in ways that would persuade classmates. The practices that emerged in collective activity were appropriated by individual children and supported their efforts to accomplish science in the classroom.

Advantages of a situative approach to studying epistemic cognition

Research into learning in the disciplines has for several decades been concerned with how learners' conceptions of the epistemology of a discipline might affect how they make sense of disciplinary conceptions; for example, how ideas about the nature of science might influence how one makes sense of concepts of matter, or evolution, or climate change. Conceptions of epistemology that productively align with a discipline tend to relate positively to conceptual change in history, math, and science (Depaepe, De Corte, & Verschaffel, 2016; Elby,

Macrander, & Hammer, 2016; VanSledright & Maggioni, 2016). Yet, traditional cognitive accounts, that posit the construction of beliefs about knowledge that are then applied to reasoning contexts, have struggled to explain an array of empirical findings that demonstrate highly contextualized epistemic thinking that refute predictions from most accounts (Sandoval, 2005). Further complicating matters is that seemingly stable developmental trends turn out, under scrutiny, to be much less stable than typical cognitive theories of epistemic cognition predict (Sandoval, Greene, & Bråten, 2016).

The studies just described (Ryu & Sandoval, 2012; Sandoval & Çam, 2011) suggest a developmental account that traces individual changes in cognition through participation in collective practice. It is an effort to tease out the intrinsic relations (Saxe, 2012) between culture and cognition—the ways in which each mutually constitutes the other. Saxe also argues for conceiving of culture and cognition both as processes. In Ms. Green's classroom, for example, the culture of science that develops is a process of work practices geared toward achieving consensus explanations through persuasion, with crucial epistemic practices of justification emerging in relation to figuring out what makes some arguments more persuasive than others.

The broad aim of this recent work is to trace how individual competence develops from engagement in collective practices. Meeting this aim requires methods to trace the meanings individuals develop from their activity. The studies of the children in Ms. Green's classroom and the development of their epistemic cognition in science rely on three prongs of analysis (Sandoval, 2012): observations of participation in collective activity, analyses of artifacts produced during that activity or in closely related settings, and individuals' reflections on their practice. This is an approach that ties measures of individual cognition closely to contexts of practical activity, both in how they are experienced by research participants and in how they are interpreted by researchers.

Common measures of epistemic conceptions (or beliefs) are problematic for shedding light on reasoning in the disciplines. Assessments of science epistemology, for example, tend to obscure specific conceptions while assigning respondents to coarse positions or stances (e.g., naïve v. sophisticated), and generally fail to consistently match conceptions elicited through other means or contexts (Sandoval, 2005). Measures of more general epistemic conceptions tend either to suffer from poor psychometrics or fail to take the differences between disciplinary epistemologies seriously (Sandoval et al., 2016). In contrast, the assessments used by Ryu and Sandoval (2012) were not just grounded in the discipline, they were closely related to the forms of scientific work children engaged in during the school year. Consequently, changes to children's ideas of justification, both in terms of a higher awareness of the value of justification and improvements in providing justifications, could be traced straightforwardly from their participation in collective efforts to persuasively justify claims to their peers.

The approach to studying epistemic cognition I sketch here is allied with recent efforts to look more closely at how children reason about the epistemic standards within and across disciplines. Middle school students posit a range of criteria for what makes a good scientific model that are aligned with expert perspectives (Pluta, Chinn, & Duncan, 2011). Upper elementary students can describe differences between forms and standards of evidence across history and science (Herrenkohl & Cornelius, 2013). Even very young students recognize sources of uncertainty in their own empirical work consistent with scientific practice (Metz, 2011). These are all examples of emergent epistemic competence tied to disciplinary learning that are overlooked by general assessments of epistemic belief that routinely paint children as unsophisticated and naïve, while developmental research would suggest children develop nuanced strategies for evaluating sources and thinking about evidence (Sandoval et al., 2014).

The situative approach suggested here starts with contexts of practice, with settings where people are actively engaged in trying to produce or evaluate knowledge. School is one such place, of course, but not the only one, by any means. In relation to conceptual change, the situative approach asks a number of questions that remain to be answered. Ryu and Sandoval (2012) did not look at how the refinement of epistemic aims and practices influenced children's understanding of the science topics they studied during the year, nor how changing epistemic conceptions influenced children's changing conceptions of the world. Further, much more research is needed on how schooled knowledge, and the epistemic practices developed to learn it, are related to epistemic practices employed out of school. The situative approach suggests tracing the generalization of practices through analyses of the individual-in-interaction across multiple settings (Jurow, 2004). In this analysis, the aim has less to do with documenting what individuals believe about the nature of knowledge and knowing, and more to do with tracing how individuals display conceptions of knowledge and knowing in relation to practices of knowledge production and evaluation. This assumes contextual variability from the start, rather than the consistency predicted by more cognitive models (Sandoval, 2012). Changes in epistemic cognition, then, include both changing attunements of prior conceptions to new settings and the appropriation of new conceptions within settings of use.

Conclusion

A situative perspective on epistemic cognition can productively focus research attention on how individuals appropriate practices of knowledge-building and evaluation and how such appropriation leads to conceptions about both particular aspects of the world (disciplinary knowledge) and about what knowledge is and how one knows. Cognitive constructivist theories do not seem able to explain the range of contradictory empirical findings of epistemic cognition research (Sandoval, 2012). Of course, assuming epistemic cognition is highly situated raises the question of how and to what extent individuals might generalize specific epistemic conceptions across settings of activity and over time, and how those change with changes in practice. Pursuing such research will improve theoretical accounts of epistemic cognition, while potentially clarifying how aspects of epistemic cognition promote or impede conceptual change.

Acknowledgments

The work described here was supported in part by the National Science Foundation (DRL award #0733233), although the views expressed here are not necessarily shared by the agency. Thanks to Noel Enyedy, Elizabeth Redman, and Sihan Xiao for their part in the work. Special thanks to Carol Smith and Marianne Wiser for helpful comments on earlier versions of this chapter.

References

Chinn, C. A., Buckland, L. A., & Samarapungavan, A. (2011). Expanding the dimensions of epistemic cognition: Arguments from philosophy and psychology. *Educational Psychologist, 46*(3), 141–167.

Chinn, C. A., & Rinehart, R. W. (2016). Epistemic cognition and philosophy: Developing a new framework for epistemic cognition. In J. A. Greene, W. A. Sandoval, & I. Bråten (Eds.), *Handbook of epistemic cognition* (pp. 460–478). New York: Routledge.

Depaepe, F., De Corte, E., & Verschaffel, L. (2016). Mathematical epistemological beliefs: A review of the research literature. In J. A. Greene, W. A. Sandoval, & I. Bråten (Eds.), *Handbook of epistemic cognition* (pp. 147–164). New York: Routledge.

Elby, A., & Hammer, D. (2010). Epistemological resources and framing: A cognitive framework for helping teachers interpret and respond to their students' epistemologies. In L. D. Bendixen and C. F. Florian (Eds.), *Personal epistemology in the classroom: Theory, research, and implications for practice* (pp. 409–434). Cambridge: Cambridge University Press.

Elby, A., Macrander, C., & Hammer, D. (2016). Epistemic cognition in science: Uncovering old roots to turn over new leaves. In J. A. Greene, W. A. Sandoval, & I. Bråten (Eds.), *Handbook of epistemic cognition* (pp. 113–127). New York: Routledge.

Greeno, J. G. (2015). Commentary: Some prospects for connecting concepts and methods of individual cognition and of situativity. *Educational Psychologist, 50*(3), 248–251.

Greeno, J. G., & The Middle School Mathematics Through Application Project Group. (1998). The situativity of knowing, learning, and research. *American Psychologist, 53*(1), 5–26.

Gutierrez, K., & Rogoff, B. (2003). Cultural ways of learning: Individual traits or repertoires of practice. *Educational Researcher, 32*(5), 19–25.

Hammer, D., & Elby, A. (2002). On the form of a personal epistemology. In B. K. Hofer & P. R. Pintrich (Eds.), *Personal epistemology: The psychology of beliefs about knowledge and knowing* (pp. 169–190). Mahwah, NJ: Erlbaum.

Herrenkohl, L. R., & Cornelius, L. (2013). Investigating elementary students' scientific and historical argumentation. *Journal of the Learning Sciences, 22*(3), 413–461. doi:10.1080/10508406.2013.799475.

Jurow, A. S. (2004). Generalizing in interaction: Middle school mathematics students making mathematical generalizations in a population-modeling project. *Mind, Culture, and Activity, 11*(4), 279–300.

Kawasaki, J., DeLiema, D., & Sandoval, W. A. (2014). The influence of non-epistemic features of settings on epistemic cognition. *Canadian Journal of Science, Mathematics and Technology Education, 14*(2), 207–221. doi:10.1080/14926156.2014.903319.

Kelly, G. J. (2016). Methodological considerations for the study of epistemic cognition in practice. In J. A. Greene, W. A. Sandoval, & I. Bråten (Eds.), *Handbook of epistemic cognition* (pp. 392–408). New York: Routledge.

Kelly, G. J., McDonald, S., & Wickman, P.-O. (2012). Science learning and epistemology. In B. J. Fraser, K. G. Tobin, & C. J. McRobbie (Eds.), *Second international handbook of science education* (pp. 281–291). Netherlands: Springer.

Lave, J., & Wenger, E. (1991). *Situated learning: Legitimate peripheral participation*. Cambridge: Cambridge University Press.

Louca, L., Elby, A., Hammer, D., & Kagey, T. (2004). Epistemological resources: Applying a new epistemological framework to science instruction. *Educational Psychologist, 39*(1), 57–68.

Metz, K. E. (2011). Disentangling robust developmental constraints from the instructionally mutable: Young children's epistemic reasoning about a study of their own design. *Journal of the Learning Sciences, 20*(1), 50–110.

Pluta, W. J., Chinn, C. A., & Duncan, R. G. (2011). Learners' epistemic criteria for good scientific models. *Journal of Research in Science Teaching, 48*(5), 486–511.

Ryu, S., & Sandoval, W. A. (2012). Improvements to elementary children's epistemic understanding from sustained argumentation. *Science Education, 96*(3), 488–526.

Sandoval, W. A. (2005). Understanding students' practical epistemologies and their influence on learning through inquiry. *Science Education, 89*, 634–656.

Sandoval, W. A. (2012). Situating epistemological development. In J. van Aalst, K. Thompson, M. J. Jacobson, & P. Reimann (Eds.), *The future of learning: Proceedings of the 10th international conference of the learning sciences* (Vol. 1, pp. 347–354). Sydney: International Society of the Learning Sciences.

Sandoval, W. A., & Çam, A. (2011). Elementary children's judgments of the epistemic status of sources of justification. *Science Education, 95*(3), 383–408.

Sandoval, W. A., Greene, J. A., & Bråten, I. (2016). Understanding and promoting thinking about knowledge: Origins, issues, and future directions of research on epistemic cognition. *Review of Research in Education, 40*(1), 457–496.

Sandoval, W. A., Sodian, B., Koerber, S., & Wong, J. (2014). Developing children's early competencies to engage with science. *Educational Psychologist, 49*(2), 139–152. doi:10.1080/00461520.2014.917589.

Saxe, G. B. (1988). Candy selling and math learning. *Educational Researcher, 17*(6), 14–21.

Saxe, G. B. (2012). *Cultural development of mathematical ideas*. Cambridge: Cambridge University Press.

Strømsø, H. I., & Kammerer, Y. (2016). Epistemic cognition and reading for understanding in the internet age. In J. A. Greene, W. A. Sandoval, & I. Bråten (Eds.), *Handbook of epistemic cognition* (pp. 230–246). New York: Routledge.

VanSledright, B., & Maggioni, L. (2016). Epistemic cognition in history. In J. A. Greene, W. A. Sandoval, & I. Bråten (Eds.), *Handbook of epistemic cognition* (pp. 128–146). New York: Routledge.

Vygotsky, L. S. (1978). *Mind in society: The development of higher psychological processes*. Cambridge, MA: Harvard University Press.

Vygotsky, L. S. (1994). The cultural development of the child. In R. van der Veer & J. Valsiner (Eds.), *The Vygotsky reader* (pp. 57–72). Oxford: Blackwell.

23

DEVELOPING AN UNDERSTANDING OF THE LIMITS OF KNOWING

Frank C. Keil

While considerable research has focused on changes in epistemological understanding in adolescents and college students, less attention has been paid to epistemic changes during the elementary school years. If, however, epistemological understanding is construed as including a sense of the special nature of "knowing" as opposed to "thinking," prior research suggests that even preschoolers have some grasp of the distinction by associating knowing something with the belief that it is true (Johnson & Maratsos, 1977). In addition, several lines of work have shown that a sense of knowing becomes more refined during the elementary school years. For example, elementary schoolers become increasingly sophisticated in realizing that knowing x entails a certainty of belief about x (Montgomery, 1992).

Several lines of work have documented extensive changes in how children understand the distribution of knowledge in other minds as well as their ability to assess the limits of their own understanding. Two different patterns of change are considered here and their implications for broader themes of the development of epistemological understanding and metacognition. One pattern concerns an early tendency to see more knowledge as acquired first-hand through direct experience than secondhand through testimony. The second pattern consists of changing views of how knowledge is distributed in other minds, with a tendency to increasingly value the role of central causal patterns in inferring knowledge domains. Taken together, these patterns of change may reflect underlying conceptual changes in epistemology that cover not just beliefs about knowledge in isolation but also views of how knowledge is connected to the causal structure of the world. In particular, changes in views of the structure and distribution of knowledge, a form of metacognition, may be linked to a growing understanding of the privileged nature of certain causal patterns in making sense of the world. In addition, changing theories of mind may also be involved as children come to appreciate that the knowledge-bearing capacities of any one mind are intrinsically limited. All of this ultimately may have implications for how local conceptual change occurs in the science classroom.

An individualism bias in views of knowledge ownership

One developmental trend concerns the tendency to see most of one's knowledge as having been acquired through first-hand experience as opposed to being acquired through the testimony of others. We can call this tendency an "individualism bias" (Gelfert, 2011), based on the idea that all of us, but especially young children, overestimate how much we are lone individuals gathering information directly about the world. Conversely, we underestimate the extent to which we are dependent on knowledge gathered by other minds and often passed between individuals through extensive chains. Young children are not completely unable to distinguish directly acquired information from indirectly acquired information. When children were told about other individuals growing up on deserted islands, even kindergarteners were able to distinguish knowledge that was acquired directly as distinct from knowledge acquired indirectly (Lockhart, Goddu, Smith, & Keil, 2016). Thus, they judged that such individuals were likely to have knowledge that the sky is blue or that one sleeps when one is tired (direct) but less likely to know that germs can make you sick or that dinosaurs were big (indirect). However, even as the youngest children were able to distinguish directly from indirectly acquired knowledge, they also tended to see a greater percentage of indirect knowledge as directly acquirable. In short, the individualism bias is never absolute among school-age children, with even kindergarteners having some ability to sense what kinds of information are learned from others. More importantly, however, it declines substantially with increasing age even as it continues to be present to a lesser extent, even in adults.

Such a bias may be partly related to an overoptimism bias in that children who overrate their knowledge acquisition capacities might as a consequence overrate their abilities to acquire complex information on their own (Lockhart, Chang, & Story, 2002; Lockhart, Nakashima, Inagaki, & Keil, 2008). This pattern is found across a range of tasks and settings (also Boseovski, 2010; Diesendruck & Lindenbaum, 2009). The individualism bias may also arise for reasons to do with source-monitoring failures (Drummey & Newcombe, 2002) and misattributions concerning where knowledge is actually located. If one fails to keep track of how one acquired a piece of knowledge, when in doubt, one may default to assuming not only that one acquired that knowledge directly but also that other information entailed by that knowledge is also individually known.

More broadly, younger children may have their knowledge acquisition more richly scaffolded in ways that are not always obvious. For example, while asking a child about animals that the child observed on a recent zoo trip, a parent may pose the questions in the context of having a picture book laid out with pictures of animals. The child may list a large set of features for several distinct animals thinking that she has recalled completely from memory when in fact she is only recalling small fragments and then is recovering the rest from the pictures that are laid out in front of her.

This tendency to think one knows a great deal as an autonomous individual can wax and wane even in adults as a result of local supporting contexts. When adults are asked to search for information on the Internet, they subsequently rate their knowledge of other unrelated information at higher levels than those who acquire the same information without an internet search (Fisher, Goddu, & Keil, 2015). A series of follow-up studies suggested recent search-related behavior causes a greater sense of knowing of content unrelated to the specific target of a search. In an analogous manner, young children, who are constantly supported in the knowledge acquisition by others, may develop an inflated sense of how much they know on their own.

These inflated senses of individually acquired information are not completely off the mark. If an individual has ready and reliable access to information in other minds, that person might be forgiven for saying that she "knows" that information. After all, it might be even adaptive in terms of memory management to forget information that one can instantly access later for various pointers (Sparrow, Liu, & Wegner, 2011). Although, in dramatic cases, one can easily distinguish between having knowledge (knowing one's zip code) and knowing where to find it (knowing how to look up any person's zip code), there is a tendency in adults, and especially in children, to attribute unclear or boundary cases to one's own internal knowledge.

As just noted, while the individualism bias perseveres on into adulthood, it does diminish. What factors account for this reduction in the bias? One possibility is an increasing awareness of patterns of deference, namely a growing sense of the breadth and depth of knowledge in other minds and the ways that even experts must rely on each other. Simply grasping that deference is a norm in the culture at large, may feed back onto a metacognitive awareness of one's own acts of deferring and hence a better sense of one's own knowledge limits. While the trust and testimony literature reveals that even preschoolers recognize that some sources are to be trusted more than others, there are also developmental changes in the manner in which children choose to trust and defer to others (Harris, 2012). Younger children tend to defer primarily to parents and other caregivers, while all children start to be more sensitive to the ways in which there are different reservoirs of expertise in the world around them (Henrich & Broesch, 2011). This shift may reflect an early heuristic to blindly trust close caregivers, a heuristic that simplifies cognitive load for the young child. It does not require an ability to assess whether knowledge is justified but merely requires a sense of whether an informant is likely to be benign. This heuristic makes adaptive sense if young children have difficulties in figuring out whether informants have legitimate grounds for making their assertions. With increasing age, children move away from evaluating sources in terms of such traits as warmth and group membership to considering how others might actually know more than them because of greater mastery of the relevant material (Landrum, Mills, & Johnston, 2013). A second factor concerns a growing ability to reflect on their own knowledge limitations and to realize more fully just how shallow their own explanatory understanding is (Aguiar, Stoess & Taylor, 2012; Mills & Keil, 2004). This awareness emerges gradually during the early school years, but seems to change most dramatically between kindergarten and grade four. Finally, as they enter formal education, students may more clearly see markers of deference in academic materials and in the ways information is transmitted by teachers. Such markers might be as overt as phrases like "scientists have shown that …" and as subtle as increasing use of citations and footnotes.

Shifting views of knowledge clusters

As children become ever more aware that much of their knowledge is learned secondhand through others, they start to explore more deeply how knowledge is organized in other minds. In particular, they develop a richer understanding of how knowledge is clustered in different communities of specialists and experts. Although even preschoolers have a crude sense that there are different experts for different domains (Lutz & Keil, 2002), considerable subtleties remain concerning the possible ways that knowledge might be distributed in other minds. People can come to have special areas of expertise due to very different factors. One might become an expert in an area because of an interest in acquiring knowledge that serves a highly practical goal. A shoe salesman might have greater than average knowledge about the latest fashions, variations in foot shapes, orthopedics of feet, durability of different materials, and techniques for convincing customers. All of these forms of expertise might advance the goal of selling shoes. Alternatively, a person may be seen as having expertise in the form of understanding deep underlying causal principles that can explain a diverse array of surface phenomena, or "discipline-based expertise" (Danovitch & Keil, 2004). Thus, an expert on mechanics might be expected to understand the core principles involved in the movements of objects and their physical interactions.

Young children may have a crude sense of these different forms of expertise but they weigh them differently by favoring goal-based forms over discipline-based forms when put in competition against each other. For example, children were told to suppose they wanted to know why sidewalks are kept clean by people who want to be nice to others. They were then asked who would provide better help in answering the question: someone who knows why people get angry if someone is mean to them or someone who knows why salt melts ice on people's icy driveways but sugar does not. Younger children, those below the third grade, were more prone to pick the salt melting person (related to the goal of keeping sidewalks clean) while older children and adults were more prone to pick the anger-related person (shared psychology discipline) (Danovitch & Keil, 2004).

This shift in which expertise types are preferred is at least partly caused by increasing appreciation of the causal factors that underlie phenomena and make them cohere even though they may differ at the surface level. Indeed, it is possible to show that increasingly elaborated causal schemas often are drivers of better insight into discipline-based forms of expertise (Keil, Stein, Webb, Billings, & Rozenblit, 2008). Thus, one can present children with knowledge that bears a surface schema relation to another domain but lacks a deeper causal commonality, and knowledge that lacks surface similarity but shares a deeper causal commonality, to see on what basis they generalize. For example, children were told about an expert who knows all about a physics fact involving bounded objects in motion (e.g., why a hammer drives a nail better when you swing the hammer faster). The children were then asked which of two topics that person also knows a lot about: (a) a cognitive psychology fact that had something to do with bounded objects in motion (e.g., why people do better catching a ball with two eyes open instead of one); and (b) a physics fact that had little to do with bounded objects in motion (e.g., why big bridges need really big supports). Each child therefore received two choices: a surface schema-consistent but discipline-inconsistent case and a surface schema-inconsistent but discipline-consistent case. Children shifted during the elementary school years from favoring surface schema-consistent but discipline-inconsistent cases to favoring surface schema-inconsistent but discipline-consistent cases.

A more general developmental pattern may be at work here. The growth from favoring surface schema-consistent cases to deeper discipline-consistent ones resonates with other studies showing that children look more and more beyond surface features with increasing age. For example, a related shift may occur when younger children believe experts based on simple verification of obvious features while older children start to put more emphasis on general claims even when those claims are more difficult to verify and may rely on knowledge of invisible properties and features (Koenig et al., 2015).

Other factors that may influence shifts in which forms of expertise are favored are linguistic environments and developing theories of mind. With respect to developing theories of mind, more sophisticated understandings of beliefs may result in shifts of judgment about which informants to trust in certain domains (Van Reet, Green, & Sobel, 2015). Thus, preschoolers who succeed on false belief tasks at higher levels will endorse statements by a confederate with a more developed sense of false belief over a confederate with a less well-developed sense. Analogously, as school-age children begin to succeed on higher order theory of mind tasks in which they have to navigate such complexities as third and fourth order false beliefs (Osterhaus, Koerber, & Sodian, 2016), they may show relevant shifts in their opinions of which informants are trustworthy.

Finally, children shift in how they understand the breadth and depth of expert knowledge; and they shift in ways that seem to be related to a gradually growing understanding of how knowledge must be limited by real-world interactions between minds and information (Landrum & Mills, 2015). Younger children attributed to specialists greater knowledge about both details and principles, but older children and adults judged that generalists, while having less specific trivia knowledge might still have knowledge of general principles equal to or even exceeding specialists. What develops may be an understanding that some forms of expertise warrant attributing knowledge of principles but not details. Thus, older children see more limits to knowledge even in expert minds. This in turn may be related to a growing understanding of factors that define and stabilize categories (Landrum & Mills, 2015). If a category is broad enough (e.g., animals), the factors that define and enable stable categorization of its members may be largely driven by biological principles, whereas for a lower-level category (e.g., toy poodles), those factors may arise from highly specific trivia-like details.

Next steps

We have seen how converging factors may precipitate epistemological conceptual changes that are responsible for developmental trajectories concerned with the individualism bias and the discernment of knowledge clusters. In addition, as epistemological views become more sophisticated and pay more attention to how knowledge is connected to the causal structure of the world, conceptual change in the realm of understanding those causal structures becomes relevant. Thus, one's own changing concepts of the world feed back on changing beliefs about how knowledge is connected to the world. Future studies need to unpack these factors. In particular, there is a need to explore how metacognitive sophistication and epistemological insights are linked to a growing appreciation of how minds can and cannot track the causal structure of the world. These factors may interact in iterative cycles wherein increasing awareness of causal structures enhances understandings of the cognitive challenges of grasping those structures, which in turn may lead to more optimal deployment of individual and shared cognitive resources to causal inquiry. A greater understanding of these cycles may be critically relevant to learning in science classrooms where instruction may be most effective when it focuses on both epistemological conceptual change and changing concepts about the causal structure of the world.

References

Aguiar, N. R., Stoess, C. J., & Taylor, M. (2012). The development of children's ability to fill the gaps in their knowledge by consulting experts. *Child development, 83*(4), 1368–1381.

Boseovski, J. J. (2010). Evidence for "rose-colored glasses": An examination of the positivity bias in young children's personality judgments. *Child Development Perspectives, 4*(3), 212–218.

Danovitch, J. H., & Keil, F. C. (2004). Should you ask a fisherman or a biologist? Developmental shifts in ways of clustering knowledge. *Child Development, 75*, 918–931.

Diesendruck, G., & Lindenbaum, T. (2009). Self-protective optimism: Children's biased beliefs about the stability of traits. *Social Development, 18*(4), 946–961.

Drummey, A. B. & Newcombe, N. S. (2002). Developmental changes in source memory. *Developmental Science, 5,* 505–513.

Fisher, M., Goddu, M. K., & Keil, F. C. (2015). Searching for explanations: How the internet inflates estimates of internal knowledge. *Journal of Experimental Psychology: General, 144*(3), 674.

Gelfert, A. (2011). Expertise, argumentation, and the end of inquiry. *Argumentation, 25,* 297–312.

Harris, P. L. (2012). *Trusting what you're told: How children learn from others.* Cambridge, MA: Harvard University Press.

Henrich, J., & Broesch, J. (2011). On the nature of cultural transmission networks: Evidence from Fijian villages for adaptive learning biases. *Philosophical Transactions of the Royal Society of London B: Biological Sciences, 366*(1567), 1139–1148.

Johnson, C. N., & Maratsos, M. P. (1977). Early comprehension of mental verbs: Think and know. *Child Development, 48,* 1743–1747.

Keil, F., Stein, C., Webb, L., Billings, V. D., & Rozenblit, L. (2008). Discerning the division of cognitive labor: An emerging understanding of how knowledge is clustered in other minds. *Cognitive Science, 32*(2), 259–300.

Koenig, M. A., Cole, C. A., Meyer, M., Ridge, K. E., Kushnir, T., & Gelman, S. A. (2015). Reasoning about knowledge: Children's evaluations of generality and verifiability. *Cognitive psychology, 83,* 22–39.

Landrum, A. R., & Mills, C. M. (2015). Developing expectations regarding the boundaries of expertise. *Cognition, 134,* 215–231.

Landrum, A. R., Mills, C. M., & Johnston, A. M. (2013). When do children trust the expert? Benevolence information influences children's trust more than expertise. *Developmental Science, 16*(4), 622–638.

Lockhart, K. L., Chang, B., & Story, T. (2002). Young children's beliefs about the stability of traits: Protective optimism? *Child Development, 73*(5), 1408–1430.

Lockhart, K. L., Goddu, M. K., Smith, E. D., & Keil, F. C. (2016). What could you really learn on your own? Understanding the epistemic limitations of knowledge acquisition. *Child Development, 87*(2), 477–493.

Lockhart, K. L., Nakashima, N., Inagaki, K., & Keil, F. C. (2008). From ugly duckling to swan? Japanese and American beliefs about the stability and origins of traits. *Cognitive Development, 23*(1), 155–179.

Lutz, D. J., & Keil, F. C. (2002). Early understanding of the division of cognitive labor. *Child Development, 73,* 1073–1084.

Mills, C. M., & Keil, F. C. (2004). Knowledge the limits of one's understanding: The development of an awareness of an illusion of explanatory depth. *Journal of Experimental Child Psychology, 87,* 1–32.

Montgomery, D. (1992) Young children's theory of knowing: The development of a folk epistemology. *Developmental Review, 12,* 410–430.

Osterhaus, C., Koerber, S., & Sodian, B. (2016). Scaling of Advanced Theory-of-Mind Tasks. *Child Development, 87*(6), 1971–1991.

Sparrow, B., Liu, J., & Wegner, D. M. (2011). Google effects on memory: Cognitive consequences of having information at our fingertips. *Science, 333,* 776–778.

Van Reet, J., Green, K. F., & Sobel, D. M. (2015). Preschoolers' theory-of-mind knowledge influences whom they trust about others' theories of mind. *Journal of Cognition and Development, 16*(3), 471–491.

SYNTHESIS IV

Conceptualizing the interactions among epistemic thinking, metacognition, and content-specific conceptual change

Carol L. Smith

Epistemic thinking and its interaction with metacognition and content-specific conceptual change have recently been modeled in multiple ways. These models are not mutually exclusive, but rather highlight different aspects of the phenomena under study. Here I outline three classes of models that view the interaction as part of (a) metacognitive processes underlying self-regulated learning; (b) cognitive processes that are both situated in particular contexts and distributed across artifacts and other minds; and (c) content-specific processes of model construction and revision in long-term learning progressions. I first consider the distinctive contributions of each perspective, then how these perspectives may be complementary and converge, and finally promising areas for further research.

Contrasting perspectives on the interaction of epistemic thinking, metacognition, and content-specific conceptual change

Metacognitive models

Consider first models that draw on our understanding of the interactions of cognitive and metacognitive processes in self-regulated learning. Metacognition is traditionally defined both by its content (cognition about cognition) and its function (the monitoring and control of cognition in the service of improved self-regulation), rather than by its form or conscious status. That is, metacognition like all cognition can vary in whether it takes declarative or procedural forms and whether we are consciously aware of it or not. Indeed, conscious awareness may not be essential for exerting metacognitive control, although it may be important for learning that involves overriding past habits and rethinking entrenched beliefs.

In his pioneering work on metacognition, Flavell (1979) proposed a model of cognitive monitoring in which four components interact: (a) metacognitive knowledge; (b) metacognitive experiences; (c) goal-setting processes; and (d) actions or strategies undertaken to achieve those goals. Metacognitive knowledge is knowledge about individual differences and similarities in cognitive processing, how tasks vary in their cognitive requirements, what strategies are effective in these tasks, and how persons, tasks, strategies, and goals may interact. Metacognitive experiences are conscious experiences that accompany any intellectual activity, including feelings of puzzlement or ease of processing, and awareness of metacognitive beliefs. These experiences trigger goal-setting processes that, in combination with metacognitive knowledge, influence the selection of particular strategies. These goals and strategies operate on either a cognitive or a metacognitive level: *Cognitive* goals and strategies involve making intellectual progress on some task (e.g. improve one's understanding of a text by rereading); *metacognitive* goals and strategies involve monitoring or assessing the extent to which one is making progress on some task (e.g. monitor or assess one's understanding of a text by self-testing), which allows one to target specific areas of understanding that need improvement, and to select appropriate cognitive goals and strategies.

Early work on metacognition focused on meta-memory: how the development of students' knowledge about how their memory works affects their ability to predict and monitor their memory difficulties, and supports the development of new memory strategies to enhance memory performance. Later work explored the development of meta-conceptual knowledge, skills, and strategies in additional areas such as text comprehension, problem-solving, writing, and reasoning. Although students undergo considerable metacognitive development in these areas, there is extensive individual variation in achievements. This finding led to the design of interventions, such as using reciprocal teaching, to teach explicit comprehension-monitoring strategies (Palincsar & Brown, 1984). Overall, researchers have found that metacognitive knowledge and skills can be taught, that they make distinctive (and larger) contributions to predicting academic achievement than intellectual ability, and that enhancing such knowledge and strategies can compensate for intellectual deficits (Veenman, van Hout-Wolters, & Afflerbach 2006).

Hofer's work (Chapter 19, this volume) exemplifies this approach by extending multi-part metacognitive models to include (a) epistemic knowledge (e.g. beliefs about the nature of knowledge and the self as knower), (b) epistemic judgments and monitoring processes (e.g. monitoring and evaluating the sources and justifications for knowledge), and (c) epistemic self-regulation and control processes (e.g. processes that guide goal-setting, selection of strategies, and planning in knowledge-building efforts). These aspects work together and in interaction with other metacognitive processes to regulate knowledge building that occurs on a cognitive level (e.g. forming new beliefs, changing beliefs, integrating a set of beliefs into a situation model, etc.) Thus, for Hofer and others, like Barzilai and Zohar (2014), epistemic metacognition differs from other aspects of metacognition in its *content* (thinking about *knowledge and knowing* rather than about *memory and memorizing,* or *comprehension and understanding*) but not in its form or level. They embrace the idea that epistemic thinking could be understood within a basic cognitive and metacognitive architecture and that epistemic metacognition, like other aspects of metacognition, has multiple interrelated components that have diverse forms.

One challenge is how to describe the *content* of epistemic knowledge across different knowledge domains and the mechanisms by which it affects learning. In their review of developmental models of epistemic thinking derived from interviews with college students, Hofer and Pintrich (1997) proposed that epistemic knowledge could be described along four dimensions that concern the simplicity, certainty, sources, and justification of knowledge. For each dimension, naïve and sophisticated poles were identified, which embraced opposite beliefs. Students progressed from a *naïve objectivist epistemology* that assumes knowledge is simple and certain, comes from outside sources, and is passively absorbed without critical evaluation, to a (more sophisticated) *constructivist and evaluativist epistemology* that assumes knowledge is complex, open to revision, has both internal and external sources, and requires active interpretation and critical evaluation of evidence. The same four dimensions could describe knowledge in any domain, although students may vary in the degree of sophistication in different domains. More sophisticated epistemic beliefs facilitate learning and conceptual change in multiple ways: by affecting what students attend to (e.g. underlying concepts and relations among ideas vs. surface form and isolated facts), what sources they value and trust (e.g. knowledgeable experts and data from well-designed studies vs. anecdote and personal experience), their motivation (e.g. high vs. low levels of effort and persistence), affective responses to conflict or uncertainty (e.g. interest and curiosity vs. avoidance and anxiety), and degree of metacognitive engagement. In this way, student epistemological beliefs were integrated into "warmer" models of conceptual change (Pintrich, 1999) in which motivation, interest, and emotion are also important.

Another challenge is how to *assess* various aspects of epistemic thinking in order to test their effects on conceptual change. In keeping with the importance attached to explicit epistemic beliefs, many studies have used self-report questionnaires in which students rate their degree of agreement with statements about the simplicity, certainty, sources, and justification of knowledge, using Likert scales. One advantage of these measures is they are objective and easily scored quantitatively, permitting large-scale studies of relations among epistemic beliefs and other variables, such as self-reported goals, use of strategies, and learning outcomes.

Hofer (Chapter 19) cites a series of her studies with college students, which found that students with more sophisticated epistemic beliefs about science and evolution were more likely to understand and accept evolution by natural selection and that change in understanding of evolution was associated with change in epistemic beliefs. Other studies with younger students and a range of conceptual content have found constructivist epistemic beliefs are associated with greater conceptual change when learning from refutation texts (Mason, 2010; Qian & Alvermann, 1995), from traditional classroom instruction (Stathopoulou & Vosniadou, 2007) and from inquiry-based instruction using computer models or simulations (Songer & Linn, 1991). Although none tested whether the effects were mediated through effects on goals and strategies, the studies by Mason and Stathopoulous and Vosniadou did show that students with constructivist beliefs were more meta-conceptually aware of their initial beliefs, conflicts between those beliefs and scientists', and the changes they had made. Still other studies have found that constructivist beliefs are associated with a greater use of mastery goals and knowledge integration and comprehension-monitoring strategies (see Mason, Boscolo, Tornator, & Roncini, 2013 for a review) and that greater use of mastery goals is associated with greater conceptual change (Linnenbrink & Pintrich, 2003).

While Hofer's work extends metacognitive models to embrace diverse aspects of epistemic thinking, Lombardi's and Sinatra's contribution in this volume focuses on the diverse factors that affect a *particular* kind of epistemic judgment— judging the plausibility of a claim. Crucially, their model specifies plausibility judgments can be made using implicit (System 1) processing, explicit (System 2) processing, or both.[1] Students make plausibility judgments implicitly by processing a variety of factors (e.g. fit with prior knowledge, message complexity, source credibility), quickly and in parallel with low cognitive effort and without awareness of the bases for these judgments. However, students can also make plausibility judgments with more effort, using explicit epistemic criteria (e.g. evaluating whether evidence supports or refutes a model), especially when topic interest and epistemic motives are high or when prompted. Such explicit reappraisals draw on metacognitive knowledge of epistemic standards and students' ability to exert metacognitive control of a judgment process. They are crucial in conceptual change, because students who understand a new idea need to be convinced that it is more plausible than alternatives, before accepting it.

Lombardi and Sinatra tested their model through a series of studies that used quasi-experimental or experimental designs and that assessed students' judgments of the plausibility of different models of climate change and their climate knowledge with Likert-rating scales. For example, one study manipulated 7th graders' metacognitive engagement with epistemic issues. The experimental group discussed the role of falsifiability in changing scientists' plausibility judgments, and used written model-evidence link diagrams to evaluate whether new evidence supported, contradicted, or was irrelevant to each model. The comparison group took the same time (2 days) and examined the same evidence, within an inquiry approach that did not explicitly address these epistemic issues. They found significant change in plausibility judgments and climate knowledge only for the experimental group, a change that was maintained six months later as well (Lombardi, Sinatra, & Nussbaum, 2013). Further regression analyses showed that both plausibility judgments and correct evaluation of contradictory evidence predicted post climate knowledge scores, consistent with change in climate knowledge being mediated through plausibility reappraisals spurred on by the model-evidence link activity (Lombardi, Brandt, Bickel, & Burg, 2016).

In summary, metacognitive models see conceptual change as making revisions to one's beliefs. They propose that more sophisticated epistemic beliefs and a high degree of meta-conceptual engagement are needed to facilitate the deep processing and sustained effort needed for belief revision. Further, relevant epistemic knowledge is typically described in general ways that would allow its application across a broad range of conceptual content.

Situated and distributed models

A second class of models emphasizes that epistemic thinking, like all cognition, is situated and distributed in nature, which has implications for how knowledge representations and inquiry skills are conceptualized. These models stress that individual concepts or beliefs are not hard atoms residing in individual minds, but assembled from smaller pieces on the fly in particular contexts, where what is assembled is influenced by larger physical, social, and cultural contexts. Thus, the knowledge needed to perform tasks is situated in particular contexts and distributed across internal and external representations (physical and symbolic artifacts) and across minds (self and more knowledgeable others). Further, inquiry skills are not conceptualized as individual cognitive achievements, but as socially embedded *practices* that are learned through participation in communities that share particular knowledge-building goals and epistemic norms. Thus, much of students' epistemic knowledge is *implicitly* represented in their knowledge-building practices rather than in explicit, generalizable beliefs, which has important implications for how epistemic understanding should be studied and assessed. At the same time, they recognize the importance of making such knowledge explicit in order to support individual reflection, shared discussion, and conceptual change.

Hammer and Elby (2002) were the first to take this perspective in modeling epistemic thinking. In contrast to those who saw children as having fixed beliefs organized in a unitary objectivist epistemology (i.e. believing that knowledge is simple, certain, and comes from external sources), they argued that even young children have multiple resources that allow them to think about knowledge in different ways, in different contexts. For example, in some contexts, students treat knowledge as *transmitted stuff*; in others, they consider it something that has been *invented* or even *constructed* by themselves from component parts or clues. These resources are of a smaller grain size than beliefs and are activated in different combinations in different contexts to form locally coherent *epistemic frames*. Such frames organize student expectations about what information to use in answering questions and typically operate outside of conscious awareness (Hammer, Elby, Scherr, & Redish, 2010). Given the implicit and context sensitive nature of student thinking, they argue that detailed interpretive *case studies* are needed to understand the interaction of epistemic thinking and conceptual change.

In his contribution to this volume, Hammer uses excerpts from a recent case study of Marya, a student in his college physics course, to illustrate these dynamics. Initially, Marya, like many students, used a (less availing) *formal calculation frame* when confronting projectile motion problems, a frame she probably developed and connected to science learning from her prior experiences with science and math. This frame locates physics knowledge in formulas and numbers, rather than networks of underlying physics concepts, and blinds her both to her role as meaning-maker and to the relevance of her prior everyday experiences. One of Hammer's goals as a teacher is to help students activate more productive frames through changing situational dynamics. For example, he helps students activate an initially weaker *intuitive sense-making frame* by asking students to draw on their personal experiences and by showing respect for their everyday ideas. This frame, shown to be more availing in his prior research, treats physics knowledge as constructed stuff, and highlights the importance of the student's efforts in reasoning and looking for coherence across situations. Later excerpts show how Marya increasingly approaches problems from this sense-making frame and takes the initiative in posing her own questions, leading her to experience more enthusiasm, confidence, and excitement about her learning. By course's end, Marya discusses how her new approach to learning is empowering and generalizable to many other academic learning contexts.

Overall, Hammer's dynamic systems account stresses not only the many-ness of students' epistemological resources, but also of their resources for building specific conceptual understanding, and how the two always dynamically interact. Rather than assuming students have well entrenched physics misconceptions that need to be challenged and replaced, Hammer assumes that students have many valuable but loosely organized low-level physical intuitions about specific situations that need to be organized and integrated into the conceptual framework of modern physics. On this account, conceptual change is difficult and takes time, in part because so many physical situations and physical intuitions are involved, and in part because organizing and reconciling divergent intuitions takes time and the "right kind of" mental work. Marya's shift in epistemological framing does not eliminate the extensive work needed to develop robust physics concepts, but makes progress, in developing such concepts, possible.

Hammer's case study foregrounds Marya: her words, efforts, experiences, emotions, and reflections in the course of working on classroom physics problems.

Lurking in the background, but equally important, are the many changes he made in his teaching approach. (See Redish & Hammer, 2009, for extensive discussion of these changes. These include introducing new vocabulary for various frames, such as "sense-making," "shopping for ideas," "seeking coherence" in order to make the epistemological framing of their courses explicit.)

Sandoval tackles the importance of changes in classroom practice head-on in his contribution to this volume. He embraces the view that "all knowledge and knowledge practices are fundamentally social... Claims to knowledge do not become knowledge until some community of practice ratifies them as such, and ratification occurs through social practices of knowledge evaluation local to particular communities" (p. 254, Chapter 22, this volume). In a series of studies, he documented the progress made by a group of elementary school students, in understanding the practice of providing justification based on evidence, using methods that combined individual assessments with in-depth observation and analysis of classroom discussion. Individual assessments with these children in 3rd grade revealed that, although they preferred arguments based on data to ones based on authority, they had limited understanding of what makes good evidence for a claim (Sandoval & Çam, 2011). However, through participation in a classroom community the following year in which they sought to convince each other of answers to self-generated questions under the guidance of a knowledgeable and experienced teacher, they were able to internalize more sophisticated norms of argumentation in order to be persuasive. These norms progressed from simply trying to convince others by providing some backing for claims, to recognizing the need to show some evidence, but where the evidence is seen as self-evident and unproblematic, to ultimately recognizing the need to articulate exactly how the evidence provides justification for a claim (Ryu & Sandoval, 2012). Developing classroom epistemic norms involved making them the object of discussion as students negotiated the meaning of key terms and discussed what it means to convince others, show evidence, and provide justification for how evidence bears on claims as the class pursued first-hand investigations about magnetism, electricity, and the Earth's materials, over a full year. Evidence that children had internalized new norms and developed a new concept of *evidence* (a case of epistemic conceptual change) came from comparing pre/post performance on argument construction and evaluation tasks with novel content. They found that students improved both their ability to cite relevant evidence and to explain how that evidence was relevant to the claims they were making.

Keil's contribution (Chapter 23, this volume) explores a different implication of situated and distributed models: namely, if knowledge is socially distributed, then it follows that both experts and novices must rely on appropriate patterns of deference to others in order to learn and solve problems. Thus, he investigates whether children appreciate their dependence on others for their knowledge, the criteria they use to place epistemic trust in others, and what they know about how knowledge clusters in other minds. He probes their understanding of these issues implicitly by asking them to judge what other people are likely to know in different scenarios, and analyzing their judgment patterns, without requiring justifications. His studies reveal that even preschool children aren't clueless about these issues: they realize that they wouldn't be likely to have certain kinds of knowledge if socially isolated, they would trust some individuals more than others, and they would recognize there can be different kinds of expertise. However, during the elementary school years, they develop more insight about how much knowledge is second hand, a greater awareness of domain experts whose knowledge clusters around underlying causal principles rather than surface goals, and greater recognition of the importance of relying on domain experts, rather than simply someone with whom you have an emotional bond and personal connection. He speculates that these developments may serve as an important resource for learning from others in academic environments and that developing greater content knowledge in school about deeper causal schemas for different topics may be needed to support these new epistemological insights.

Overall, situated models have called attention to the *complexity and multiplicity* of the epistemic resources even young children have, how epistemic knowledge may be *implicit* in their knowledge-building practices, and how students can use their epistemic and metacognitive resources to become more effective learners by gaining greater metacognitive understanding of relevant norms and practices. Although such models highlight context dependence and specificity, the epistemic frames and practices they have focused on are of potentially wide scope and could apply across a broad range of content (e.g. frames that highlight sense-making and coherence-seeking; practices that involve the use of evidence in argumentation; or patterns of deference to more knowledgeable experts). Less attention has been paid to ways the influence of epistemology on conceptual change might *vary for different conceptual content* and to *the reverse type of influence* (i.e. how more sophisticated conceptual understandings might facilitate further epistemological progress). In the next section, I consider how both of these issues are directly addressed in content-specific models of long-term learning progressions.

Content-specific models of long-term learning progressions

Central questions in conceptual change research concern how to individuate concepts, characterize what counts as a conceptual change, and understand what makes conceptual change more difficult than other forms of learning. In a recent review, Amin, Smith, and Wiser (2014) argued the field had converged on a systemic view of concepts and conceptual change, by which they meant concepts are part of knowledge networks that involve relations among multiple interacting elements, often at different levels of analysis. They argued it is increasingly recognized that concepts are grounded in perception and action and that the use of language and other external symbols helps overcome the limitations of image schematic representation. They also noted that, in order to understand how concepts can be both *participants* in beliefs as well as *constituted* by them, it is important to distinguish the *mental symbol* that stands for a concept and is linked to symbols for other concepts in the network, from the *content* of the concept itself—a set of relations linking that symbol with many other elements in the network, which (taken together) is the meaning attached to that symbol (see Amin's synthesis on Representation, Concepts, and Concept Learning, Part II, this volume for further discussion of these issues).

More recently, Wiser and Smith (2016) argued that not all beliefs involving a concept are meaning determining. Rather, three classes of beliefs are particularly important: (a) beliefs that specify the role of the concept in explanations, (b) ontological commitments (e.g. weight is a force), and (c) epistemological beliefs inherent in determining how the concept applies to the world (e.g. reliable information about weight requires scale measurement). By assuming only a subnetwork of beliefs involving a concept are meaning determining, they preserved the distinction between conceptual change and other forms of learning. Most learning involves elaborating on existing relations among concepts. Conceptual change, in contrast, is a more radical form of learning because it involves changing the explanatory role of the concept and its ontological and epistemological commitments. Further, because the content of concepts is constituted by beliefs that relate them to other concepts, concepts don't change in isolation from each other. Rather, conceptual changes involve coordinating adjustments in how multiple concepts are articulated and applied to the world, and changing epistemological commitments is an inherent feature of (most) conceptual changes.

Consider, for example, changes in children's concept of weight as children move from considering weight a perceptual quantity (felt weight) to an objective force and measured quantity (scale weight) that plays an explanatory role in models of materials. These changes not only involve changes in the type of entity they take weight to be, but also in epistemological assumptions about how to reliably determine something's weight, and in the role of weight in their explanations. Initially, children associate weight with the perceptual experience of hefting objects. Variation in the weight of objects helps explain how objects behave (e.g. a heavy object is harder to lift and can cause more damage if dropped), but is not itself explained. However, as children's knowledge network expands to include new concepts (e.g. the kind and amount of material), they can develop an explanatory account of an object's weight (e.g. the weight of an object depends upon both the kind and amount of material it is made of), which supports thinking of weight as an objective and invariant quantity. Further, relating weight to balance scales and learning to measure weight, gives them new ways to determine an object's weight, which can conflict with felt weight judgments. Reconciling these conflicting weight judgments thus requires addressing and changing underlying epistemological assumptions. Whereas students initially trust felt weight judgments because of their *familiarity and immediacy*, they need to recognize the greater validity, precision, and reliability of weight measurement, and learn to trust model-based inferences and thought experiments over misleading perceptual experiences (e.g. judging that a tiny piece of clay weighs something, even though it feels weightless, because all stuff must weigh something).

In keeping with this more content-specific approach, conceptual change researchers have investigated how a variety of epistemic commitments about the nature and form of good explanations and evidence, support common student misconceptions about specific scientific topics. On the one hand, whereas scientists limit their explanations of natural events to physical causes, students consider a *broader range of explanations* and often favor non-material causes in particular contexts. The favoring of intentional, teleological, or supernatural explanations over mechanistic explanations is particularly salient in student thinking about how living things have become adapted to their environments (Evans, 2007). On the other hand, when focusing on physical causality, students have and favor *more limited and simpler causal models* than scientists (Perkins & Grotzer, 2005). For example, students favor: models where the causes *resemble* the observed phenomena more than ones that provide mechanistic explanations in terms of *unseen events or entities* with different properties; models that assume linear causality rather than ones with multiple linear, mediating, interactive, or constraint-based causes; deterministic models over probabilistic models; and models with a central causal agent to those with distributed processes and emergent causality. Given that the concepts underlying atomic-molecular theory or the theory of evolution by natural selection not only require a commitment to mechanistic and naturalistic explanations, but also reasoning about probabilistic and chance elements, and interactive and emergent causality, they are particularly challenging.

Learning progression researchers have been particularly interested in how content-specific conceptual changes require building the epistemological sophistication needed for particular scientific models. These researchers have drawn on analyses of the conceptual challenges posed by scientific big ideas (e.g. atomic-molecular theory, evolution by natural selection), what we know about student starting ideas, common misconceptions, and effective instruction, in order to hypothesize a *sequence of conceptual changes* in long-term learning progressions (LPs) that would allow students to successfully bridge from their initial knowledge state (lower anchor) to an understanding of the scientific idea (upper anchor) with appropriate instruction. Two key insights of the LP approach are (a) that the gap between starting and target ideas is too great to be bridged in one step, hence the need to identify *intermediate knowledge* states that serve as stepping stones for further learning; and (b) that students need to be engaged in knowledge-building *practices* involving the progressive construction and revision of a series of more explanatorily adequate models, where content knowledge, practices, and epistemology develop together and mutually support each other (Duncan and Rivet, 2013). Each new model introduces new concepts, ontological distinctions, and epistemological commitments that are "within range" of understanding, given student attainment of a prior model, while helping students move forward by putting the next model "within range." Thus, two-way interactions between building conceptual and epistemological sophistication are at the heart of LP accounts (see Wiser & Smith, 2016, for further discussion).

The idea that conceptual change is promoted by engaging students with iterative cycles of model construction, evaluation, and revision has been supported by much research (see Part III on Modeling, Explanation, and Argumentation in Conceptual Change, this volume). Further, multiple teaching studies have shown that directly addressing unspoken epistemological presuppositions promotes greater conceptual change. For example, Perkins and Grotzer (2005) found that adding explicit teaching about relevant complex causal schemas to "best practices" conceptual change curricula units on electric circuits (Grade 4) and density (Grade 8) made them more effective in promoting content-specific conceptual change. Stewart, Cartier, and Passmore (2005) found that asking high school students to compare and contrast the explanatory power of models of adaptation that made different epistemological assumptions (e.g. Paley's model of a supernatural designer, Lamarck's need-based model, and Darwin's mechanistic model of natural selection) improved students' understanding and acceptance of Darwin's model. Finally, Schwartz and White (2005) found that their Model-enhanced Thinkertools curriculum simultaneously enhanced middle-school students' meta-knowledge about the nature and purpose of models, their physics understanding of force and motion, and their ability to engage in physics inquiry; it also led to better performance on some far transfer problems and writing conclusions compared to students with a prior version of the Thinkertools curriculum.

These studies also suggest that limitations in students' understanding of specific models and their epistemological foundations, as revealed in prior interview studies (see Driver, Leach, Millar, & Scott, 1996 for a review) may reflect limitations in their typical science teaching experiences rather than inherent limitations in their ability to engage with these issues. Direct evidence that even elementary children can develop both a deep conceptual and an epistemological understanding of science comes from studies of the progress made by students in Sister Gertrude's classroom over a six-year period, whose work foreshadowed a learning progressions approach. Her classroom pedagogy focused on learning counterintuitive conceptual content through progressive construction and revision of content-specific models, while negotiating shared scientific norms and standards for evaluating those models, and metacognitively reflecting on the status of new ideas and their own process of conceptual change. By the end of 6th grade, most of her students had not only developed an understanding of the particulate nature of matter, the Earth as a cosmic body, and Newton's laws of motion, but also developed a genuinely constructivist view of learning and of science, as evidenced both by their reflective "mini-essays" on learning and science and their responses in nature of science interviews (Smith, Maclin, Houghton, & Hennessey, 2000). Her students saw the goal of science as developing ever more adequate explanatory ideas involving unseen entities, recognized the need for testing those ideas against multiple sources of evidence, and appreciated the complex role of ideas in the learning process, including how prior ideas lead to resistance to change—insights that go well beyond those commonly articulated by much older high school or college students.

Convergences and complementarities across models

I have already mentioned numerous *differences* in what these models highlight and attend to. Here, let me summarize those differences, lay out why they may reflect complementarities rather than incompatibilities, and highlight possible areas of *convergence*.

Metacognitive models of epistemic thinking emphasize the *individual* mental processes underlying self-regulated knowledge building: distinguishing those that work on a *metacognitive* level to assess and control progress from those that work on a *cognitive* level to make that progress. They extend existing metacognitive frameworks to identify the *multiple components* of epistemic metacognition that work together and in interaction with other cognitive and metacognitive processes to support learning. They focus on general beliefs about knowledge and knowing that apply across a broad range of topics and use multiple methods (such as self-report scales, think-alouds, or interviews) well suited for tapping explicit epistemic beliefs. They characterize conceptual change as involving belief revision and are often tested by studies of the impact of students' *existing* epistemic beliefs on briefer learning episodes (e.g. understanding and integrating information presented in texts or computer simulations).

In contrast, situated and distributed models emphasize the social and contextual nature of epistemic thinking. They focus on *external discourse* around epistemic issues rather than the internal processes of monitoring, planning, and self-assessment to highlight the social origins of that internal dialog and the *normative* aspects of epistemic thinking. They also draw on analyses of cognition that emphasize its experiential roots in perception and activity, its multifaceted, context-dependent nature, and its implicit, sub-conceptual aspects that are unconscious and unverbalized, that provide valuable resources for learning. Rather than seeing conceptual change as involving the *revision* of explicit beliefs, they see it as involving the *organization of* many resources into more coherent, explicit structures supported by new symbolic representations. Given the social, implicit, and context-dependent nature of epistemic thinking, their studies use interpretive methods, intensive case studies, and inferences from observation of problem-solving or classroom dialogs, and often study teaching contexts designed to transform those epistemic understandings.

Finally, content-specific models of long-term learning progressions focus on the *implicit epistemic commitments* underlying specific conceptual content and epistemic practices. They build on conceptual change models that assume concepts must be understood in the context of complex conceptual ecologies that include both imagistic and symbolic elements, and that the meaning of concepts depends in part on relations among elements in knowledge networks. Conceptual change involves both change in specific beliefs and in the concepts used to formulate those beliefs. They see conceptual change as difficult and time-consuming because it involves not only changing specific beliefs but also what conceptual distinctions are made, and reorganizing relations among many elements in the network, including epistemological and ontological commitments. They use interpretive methods and conceptual analyses and study the impact of extensive (multi-year) innovative teaching interventions that are designed to develop explicit epistemic and conceptual insights not commonly observed among students at any age.

To see how these models offer complementary insights about the *content* of epistemic thinking, consider the recent AIR model proposed by Chinn, Rinehart, and Buckland (2014). Working from a situated/distributed view of epistemic cognition and drawing on the recent work of epistemologists, they show how the goals and content of epistemic knowledge are more diverse and content-specific than acknowledged in metacognitive models. Their model has three main components: (a) the epistemic *aims* (*A*) one might pursue and the values placed on these aims; (b) the epistemic *ideals* (*I*) one holds which are used as standards to evaluate whether one has achieved one's epistemic aims; and (c) the knowledge of *reliable processes* (*R*) that can be used to achieve epistemic ends. Each component includes *many* subcomponents, which may be applied in different ways in different conceptual contexts. For example, epistemic aims not only include the goal of having knowledge (or true beliefs), but also having understanding, useful models, and explanations of phenomena. Individuals may pursue different epistemic aims in different contexts, weigh these aims differently, or adopt non-epistemic aims entirely (such as avoiding effort or finishing quickly). In addition, there are five broad classes of epistemic ideals that can vary in form or weighting in different contexts. These include ideals about the form (or internal structure) of an explanation, connections with other knowledge, connections with empirical evidence, standards for believing the testimony of others, and good communication. Finally, individuals must acquire a large number of schemas about reliable processes for producing knowledge (e.g. the conditions under which processes as diverse as one's perception, memory, reasoning, personal, or formal evidence-gathering using measurements, statistical analyses and study designs, and testimony from others, produce reliable knowledge, as well as how emotion and epistemic virtues and vices affect the reliability of information).

The AIR model is compatible with metacognitive models as its three components are part of what is needed for effective epistemic self-regulation and coordination with others: epistemic goals and values, knowledge of epistemic ideals (needed to monitor and judge whether epistemic aims have been achieved), and knowledge of reliable processes (needed for achieving epistemic aims). (Not included, but also needed are monitoring and evaluation skills, capacity for metacognitive awareness and conscious experiences, and actual skills at using those reliable processes.) The five classes of explanatory ideals incorporate (in reorganized form) some of the beliefs about the simplicity, certainty, source, and justification of knowledge highlighted by Hofer and Pintrich. Further, the detailed schemas specifying the conditions under which different processes produce reliable knowledge are exactly the kind of conditional knowledge schemas that Flavell argued were an important part of metacognition.

The AIR model also contains elements that align well with content-specific models of learning progression as it implies that there will be substantive differences in the relevant epistemic knowledge for different domains and topics. For example, epistemic ideals about the form of explanations would vary for different content, fitting nicely with Perkins and Grotzer's proposal about how different conceptual content draw on causal schemas that vary in form and complexity. Similarly, different content may require different schemas about reliable processes (e.g. schemas about weight measurement and perceptual felt weight judgments).

Although the AIR model provides a general framework for thinking about the dimensions of epistemic cognition, it doesn't lay out specific developmental trajectories for different academic domains (e.g. science, history) or topics within domains (e.g. evolution, climate science), or discuss broad similarities across topics. Here, there could be contributions from both the metacognitive and learning progressions perspectives, respectively, in shedding light on those broader patterns. For example, the four general dimensions identified by Hofer and Pintrich (1997) might be helpful in capturing general ways experts differ from novices across domains. For example, experts in a domain are likely to be more aware than novices of the complex structure of knowledge in their area, of its inherent uncertainty, limits, and openness to revision, and of their role in knowledge creation and of the accepted standards of justification and argumentation in their field. In addition, the conceptual analyses provided by learning progression researchers should provide insight not only about the epistemic issues that are particularly important for specific big ideas (e.g. atomic-molecular theory, evolution by natural selection) but also some of the sources for those new epistemic insights, and how those ideas can be progressively constructed.

The contrasting models also provide complementary mechanisms by which epistemic thinking, metacognition, and content conceptual change may interact. Metacognitive models focus on how having more general constructivist epistemic beliefs promotes use of mastery or knowledge revision goals, metacognitive monitoring and evaluation, and the selection of strategies that lead to greater depth of processing and integration of a new idea into students' conceptual system. Of course, explicit student epistemological beliefs are not the *only* factors affecting the activation of productive learning goals and strategies. Situated cognitive models emphasize that all students have a rich range of implicit epistemic resources that can be activated by careful crafting of the situation and used to support deep processing and learning. Thus, students don't need to be aware of epistemic frames or norms in order for them to support or impede conceptual change. At the same time, they acknowledge that making students *aware* of these frames and norms through classroom discussion may speed up the process of conceptual change by supporting more consistent use of these frames and standards. Finally, content-specific models of learning progressions highlight the importance of having explicit discussion of implicit epistemic commitments underlying specific concepts as integral to the process of change. In these models, epistemic and conceptual change go hand in hand, although what epistemic issues need to be addressed can vary for different content.

One convergence across models is the recognition that some aspects of epistemic thinking may be implicit, non-symbolic, and experiential, operating below conscious awareness while other aspects are explicit, symbolically represented, and more conscious. Indeed, explicit epistemic thinking depends (in part) upon this vast implicit support structure as well as its connections with representations of conceptual content. Recognition of the importance of implicit epistemic thinking has been a mainstay of situated cognitive and learning progression models, but is increasingly recognized in metacognitive models as well. For example, Lombardi and Sinatra (Chapter 20, this volume) built on dual systems architecture to argue that plausibility judgments can be made using implicit System 1 processing and explicit System 2 processing. Further, Shea et al. (2014) recently proposed a "dual systems" framework of metacognition itself, noting that control of some processes within an individual can be accomplished implicitly with System 1 metacognition; in contrast, control of processes across different individuals may require more explicit and symbolic System 2 metacognition, a form of metacognition unique to humans. Similarly, Efklides (2008) has proposed a three-level framework for metacognition that in addition to a level of non-conscious metacognitive control of both cognitive and emotional processes and a level of personal awareness that involves integration of diverse inputs through personal metacognitive experiences also includes a higher social level of awareness that involves a more explicit, symbolic, and reflective form of monitoring and control. Her model thus brings both the role of implicit epistemic thinking and the importance of social interaction and dialog more directly into metacognitive frameworks and, like Keil, extends its function from self-regulation to effective co-regulation with others.

A second area of convergence is the recognition that increasing students' *metacognitive awareness* of epistemic thinking and *making this thinking explicit* is important in promoting conceptual change. Evidence on this point is very strong, supported by experimental studies using different ways of manipulating metacognitive awareness. For example, adding written reflective journals or self-assessment activities about one's learning and inquiry processes to innovative curricula that already include many "best practices" enhances their effectiveness (Mason & Buscolo, 2000; White & Frederiksen, 1998), as does adding in explicit discussion of underlying causal schemas (Perkins & Grotzer, 2005) or engaging students in explicit discussion of plausibility judgments and using written model-evidence link diagrams (Lombardi et al., 2013). In addition, meta-analyses of experimental studies comparing refutation texts (that make students aware of contrasting views and of arguments favoring one view over another) with expository texts (which do not) have consistently shown refutation texts to be more effective in promoting conceptual change, and that these differences are maintained on delayed post-tests up to several months later (Guzzetti, Synder, Glass, & Gamas, 1993). Studies have also found that reflective science notebooks (that highlight epistemic moves in a scientific investigation) are more effective in promoting science content learning than expository text; further, when used in the context of a larger inquiry curriculum, they enhance student understanding of inquiry itself (Magnusson & Palincsar, 2004).

What are important areas for further research?

Although there is considerable evidence that epistemic beliefs and judgments and metacognitive reflection mutually interact to support conceptual change, there are many questions to be addressed in further research. In closing, let me list four.

First, researchers need to develop assessments of a broader range of epistemological aims, beliefs, and processes, using multiple contrasting approaches to assessment. At present, most assessments have focused on explicit epistemic beliefs, rather than assessing implicit beliefs or epistemic monitoring and evaluation skills and strategies. In addition, most have considered only a limited range of general epistemic beliefs, rather than the more specific schemas for reliable processes and causal explanations. Finally, most assess students acting alone rather than in interaction with others. Richer and broader assessments would not only allow researchers to better capture how epistemic thinking varies for different conceptual content, but also how different components of epistemic thinking, including implicit and explicit aspects, relate to each other and to conceptual change.

Second, researchers need to investigate ways the interaction among epistemology, metacognition, and content-specific conceptual change *may change* over broader spans of time and for different content. At present, researchers have often investigated hypotheses about how the three interact *in similar ways* across different ages and content. This focus on developmental similarities in learning mechanisms may have served as an important antidote to rigid stage theories that suggested young children have limited logical abilities and learn in fundamentally different ways. Yet learning progressions work also suggests there may be differences in what epistemological issues need to be addressed for different content and that these issues can be addressed at different levels of sophistication for different ages. In addition, some early conceptual changes may depend more on metacognitive or metalinguistic resources than epistemic ones (see Wiser & Smith, 2016, for further discussion of these issues).

Third, researchers need to use small-scale experimental or microgenetic studies to test hypotheses about how epistemology, metacognition, and content-specific conceptual change interact, that can inform the design of longer, more complex interventions. For example, they could test the importance of addressing specific epistemological issues in refutation text by varying whether those issues are included in the text, the way Skopeliti and Vosniadou (2016) showed that including information about ontological categories in a refutation text improved its effectiveness. In addition, they can experimentally investigate the role of different representational formats (e.g. written or oral) or text types (e.g. refutation vs. reflective journal) in facilitating metacognitive reflection and conceptual change.

Finally, researchers need to examine the importance of emotion in mediating the interaction among epistemic and conceptual development, as it is a crucial part of metacognitive awareness that affects student engagement and persistence. In addition, researchers have found that epistemic trust in authorities was an important predictor of change in students' conceptual understanding (see Hofer, Chapter 19, this volume). Hence, it is important to examine how such epistemic trust in scientists can be nurtured in classroom communities, and how it may depend upon having a shared conceptual understanding of epistemic processes, standards, and virtues.

Note

1 In dual process theories, System 1 thinking is always "on" and does not demand working memory resources whereas System 2 does; System 2 is typically in "low idle" mode but springs into action when conflicts are detected that call for such resource-intensive processing (Kahneman, 2011).

References

Amin, T. G., Smith, C. L., & Wiser, M. (2014). Student conceptions and conceptual change: Three overlapping phases of research. In N. G. Lederman & S. K. Abell (Eds.), *Handbook of research on science education, Vol II* (pp. 57–81). New York: Routledge.

Barzilai, S., & Zohar, A. (2014) Reconsidering personal epistemology as metacognition: A multi-faceted approach to the analysis of epistemic thinking. *Educational Psychologist, 49*(1), 13–35.

Chinn, C. A., Rinehart, R. W., & Buckland, L. A. (2014). Epistemic cognition and evaluating information: Applying the AIR Model of epistemic cognition. In D. N. Rapp & J. L. G. Braasch (Eds.), *Processing inaccurate information: Theoretical and applied perspectives from cognitive science and the educational sciences*, Cambridge, MA: MIT Press.

Driver, R., Leach, J., Millar, R., & Scott, P. (1996). *Young children's images of science.* Buckingham: Open University Press.

Duncan, R., & Rivet, A. (2013). Science learning progressions. *Science, 339*, 396–397.

Efklides, A. (2008) Metacognition: Defining its facets and levels of functioning in relation to self-regulation and co-regulation. *European Psychologist, 13*(4), 277–287.

Evans, M. (2007). Conceptual change and evolutionary biology: A developmental analysis. In S. Vosniadou (Ed.), *International handbook of research on conceptual change* (pp. 263–294). New York: Routledge.

Flavell, J. (1979) Metacognition and cognitive monitoring: A new domain of cognitive-developmental inquiry. *American Psychologist, 34*(10), 906–911.

Guzzetti, B., Snyder, T., Glass, G., & Gamas, W. (1993). Promoting conceptual change in science: A comparative meta-analysis of instructional interventions from reading education and science education. *Reading Research Quarterly, 28*(2), 116–159.

Hammer, D., & Elby, A. (2002) On the form of a personal epistemology. In B. K. Hofer & P. R. Pintrich (Eds.), *Personal epistemology: The psychology of beliefs about knowledge and knowing* (pp. 169–190). Mahwah, NJ: Lawrence Erlbaum.

Hammer, D., Elby, A., Scherr, R., & Redish, E. (2010). Resources, framing, and transfer. In J. Mestre (Ed.), *Transfer of learning from a modern multidisciplinary perspective* (pp. 89–119). Greenwich, CT: Information Age Publishing.

Hofer, B., & Pintrich, P. (1997). The development of epistemological theories: Beliefs about knowledge and knowing and their relation to learning. *Review of Educational Research, 67,* 88–140.

Kahneman, D. (2011). *Thinking fast and slow.* New York: Farrar, Straus and Giroux.

Linnenbrink, E. A., & Pintrich, P. R. (2003). Achievement goals and intentional conceptual change. In G. M. Sinatra & P. R. Pintrich (Eds.). *Intentional conceptual change* (pp. 347–374). Mahwah, NJ: Lawrence Erlbaum Associates.

Lombardi, D., Sinatra, G. M., & Nussbaum, E. M. (2013). Plausibility reappraisals and shifts in middle school students' climate change conceptions. *Learning and Instruction, 27,* 50–62.

Lombardi, D., Brandt, C. B., Bickel, E. S., & Burg, C. (2016). Students' evaluations about climate change. *International Journal of Science Education, 38*(8), 1392–1414.

Magnusson, S. & Palincsar, A. (2004). Learning from text designed to model scientific thinking in inquiry-based instruction. In S. Magnusson & A. Palincsar (Eds.) *Crossing borders in literacy and science instruction: Perspectives on theory and practice* (pp. 316–339). Neward, DE: International Reading Association.

Mason, L. (2010). Beliefs about knowledge and revision of knowledge: On the importance of epistemic beliefs for intentional conceptual change in elementary and middle school students. In L. D. Bendixen & F. C. Feucht (Eds.), *Personal epistemology in the classroom: Theory, research, and practice* (pp. 258–291). Cambridge: Cambridge University Press.

Mason, L., & Buscolo, P. (2000) Writing and conceptual change: What changes? *Instructional science, 28,* 199–226.

Mason, L., Boscolo, P., Tornator, M., & Ronconi, L. (2013). Besides knowledge: A cross-sectional study on the relations between epistemic beliefs, achievement, goals, self-beliefs, and achievement in science. *Instructional Science, 41,* 49–79.

Palincsar, A., & Brown, A. (1984). Reciprocal teaching of comprehension-fostering and comprehension-monitoring activities. *Cognition and Instruction, 1,* 117–175.

Perkins, D., & Grotzer, T. A. (2005). Dimensions of causal understanding: The role of complex causal models in students' understanding of science. *Studies in Science Education. 41,* 117–165.

Pintrich, P. R. (1999). Motivational beliefs as resources for and constraints on conceptual change. In W. Schnotz et al. (Eds.), *New perspectives on conceptual change* (pp. 33–50). Amsterdam: Pergamon.

Qian, G., & Alvermann, D. (1995). Role of epistemological beliefs and learned helplessness in secondary school students learning science concepts from text. *Journal of Educational Psychology, 87,* 282–292.

Redish, E., & Hammer, D. (2009) Reinventing college physics for biologists: Explicating an epistemological curriculum. *American Journal of Physics, 77,* 629–642.

Ryu, S., & Sandoval, W. A. (2012). Improvements to elementary children's epistemic understanding from sustained argumentation. *Science Education, 96*(3), 488–526.

Sandoval, W. A., & Çam, A. (2011). Elementary children's judgments of the epistemic status of sources of justification. *Science Education, 95*(3), 383–408.

Schwartz, C., & White, B. (2005). Metamodeling knowledge: Developing students' understanding of scientific modeling. *Cognition and Instruction, 23*(2), 165–205.

Shea, N., Boldt, A., Bang, D., Yeung, N., Heyes, C., & Frith, V. (2014). Supra-personal cognitive control and metacognition. *Trends in Cognitive Science, 18*(4), 186–193.

Skopeliti, I., & Vosniadou, S. (2016). The role of categorical information in refutation texts. *Journal of Cognitive Science, 17*(3), 441–468.

Smith, C., Maclin, D., Houghton, C., & Hennessey, M. G. (2000). Sixth grade students' epistemologies of science: The impact of school science experiences on epistemological development. *Cognition & Instruction, 18*, 349–422.

Songer, N., & Linn, M. (1991). How do students' views of science influence knowledge integration? *Journal of Research in Science Teaching, 28*(9), 761–784.

Stathopoulou, C., & Vosniadou, S. (2007). Conceptual change in physics and physics-related epistemological beliefs: A relationship under scrutiny. In S. Vosniadou, A. Baltas, & X. Vamvakoussi (Eds.) *Reframing the conceptual change approach in learning and instruction* (pp. 145–163) New York: Elsevier.

Stewart, J., Cartier, J. & Passmore, C. (2005) Developing understanding through model-based inquiry. In Donovan, S. & Bransford, J. (Eds.), *How students learn: Science in the classroom* (pp. 515–568). Washington, DC: The National Academies Press.

Veenman, M., van Hout-Wolters, B., & Afflerbach, P. (2006). Metacognition and learning: Conceptual and methodological considerations. *Metacognition and Learning, 1*, 3–14.

White, B. Y., & Frederiksen, J. R. (1998). Inquiry, modeling, and metacognition: Making science accessible to all students. *Cognition and Instruction, 16*(1), 3–118.

Wiser, M., & Smith, C. L. (2016). How is conceptual change possible? Insights from science education. In D. Barner and A. S. Baron (Eds.) *Conceptual change and core knowledge* (pp. 25–48). Oxford: Oxford University Press.

PART V

Identity and conceptual change

Editors: Mariana Levin and Olivia Levrini

Orientation

As a way to generate new and productive directions for research, a major thread throughout the volume has been to bring constructs and ideas from conceptual change research into contact with other research traditions and agendas (e.g. metacognition, language, etc.). This section of the volume explores a novel and important, yet theoretically and methodologically thorny, research intersection: that of conceptual change and identity. The fact that conceptual change is traditionally thought of as an individual cognitive phenomenon, and identity development has usually been conceived of as a social construct involving the relationship between groups and individuals, raises important questions for how these constructs can be articulated in such a way as to be mutually illuminating.

This section of the volume explores three different approaches to forging productive connections between the research agendas of conceptual change and identity development. In the first contribution, Einat Heyd-Metzuyanim illustrates how learning events in classroom settings can be explored, viewing both identity development and disciplinary learning through a discursive (commognitive) lens (Sfard, 2008). In the second contribution, Andrea diSessa provides a meta-reflection on aspects of identity and identity development that may be approached using a knowledge-based lens. In particular, he develops four knowledge-based models of distinct kinds of identity. In doing so, he highlights some contributions of the knowledge-based approach. Finally, Olivia Levrini, Mariana Levin, and Paola Fantini present an approach based upon the operationalization of a holistic construct, *appropriation*, that considers cognitive, metacognitive, social, and epistemological layers of disciplinary learning. In particular, they explore how the construct of appropriation sheds light on the influence of content knowledge learning on identity development.

The three contributions diverge in several deep ways: they frame the relevance of investigating the nexus between identity and conceptual change within fundamentally different research programs, they choose different research approaches, they provide different definitions of identity, and they refer to different processes of conceptual change. In spite of the differences, the three approaches share a theoretical skeleton that enabled all the researchers to rigorously address the nexus between the two constructs—identity and conceptual change—that can appear very distant in their time scale, in the involved actors and in the cognitive and social processes they refer to. In the synthesis chapter, the three approaches are compared through a framework that helps identify a common theoretical structure underlying the approaches. It is argued that this framework has the potential to guide further rigorous investigations of the nexus between conceptual change and identity.

24

A DISCURSIVE APPROACH TO IDENTITY AND CRITICAL TRANSITIONS IN MATHEMATICS LEARNING

Einat Heyd-Metzuyanim

The question of whether there exists a causal relation between identity and conceptual change is an important, yet elusive one. On the one hand, there are good reasons to believe the two are related. Psychological measures such as self-efficacy in mathematics often correlate with mathematical success (e.g., Williams & Williams, 2010). So do measures of social and cultural power, which show students from disadvantaged populations to be scoring lower in mathematical assessments than those of hegemonic sections of society (e.g., Valero & Meaney, 2014). This leads us to believe that identity may indeed have an important part to play in the successes or failure of learners to advance in their mathematical learning. Also, there are good reasons to believe that the failure to achieve conceptual change in some critical mathematical domains has a lasting impact on a person's mathematical identity.

Yet, as much as this mutual relationship is plausible, it is very difficult to capture. Where can we see identity actually affect conceptual change? And how would we track the change in such a complex construct as "identity" due to an instance of mathematical learning (or failure to learn)? Moreover, even if the causal relationship can be established, we remain in the dark regarding how the causal process actually takes place. One of the reasons for these difficulties is the fact that, within the actual activity of learning, what "identity" means and what we look for when we talk about "conceptual change" is often elusive and debatable. Even more problematic, these two theoretical concepts seem to be distant and unrelated. Not only do the theoretical frameworks underlying them differ from each other, the measures for examining them are markedly different. Whereas identity is mostly examined using interviews or surveys about the self, conceptual change is usually explored in experimental settings, often using paper and pencil tools that lack any reference to the self.

The communicational framework (Heyd-Metzuyanim & Sfard, 2012; Sfard, 2008) for studying identity and mathematical learning offers a way out of this theoretical and methodological divide. Its main goal is to unify the discourse on identity and on mathematical learning. This means that the two concepts are referred to with the same vocabulary and using the same observational methods.

An important feature of the communicational framework is its avoidance of language that would objectify the phenomena being observed. The word "identity" has a connotation of being an object or a "thing," presumably located in the individual's head. So does "concept" in "conceptual change." This objectification, as helpful as it is when theorizing about human development by taking snapshots of the individual's functioning over time, is much less productive for examining how the development takes place in activity, and especially in interactions with others. To avoid it, the communicational framework moves from "identity" to the term "identifying" to refer to the *process* of constructing identity stories. Similarly, instead of talking about "concepts" that "change" it talks about mathematizing (or reasoning) at critical junctures of meta-discursive shifts. Before getting deeper into what "critical junctures" and "meta-discursive shifts" mean, let me first explain more thoroughly the use of the word "identifying."

The point of departure for "identifying" is Sfard and Prusak's (2005) definition of identity as a collection of stories, told about a person (either by herself or by others), that are significant, reifying, and endorsable. This definition leads us to look for identity in the stories (or statements) people tell about themselves and about others. I call these types of statements "subjectifying." Out of these subjectifications (which are not necessarily identity stories) we glean the reifying effect through language and symbols. Statements such as "I am a mathematician" reify a set of historical actions over a long period of time into one statement that relates a person to a community or attaches to her/him a stable attribute. These statements form the explicit (or direct) identity narratives that are often told when a person is asked to describe him/herself. Yet people identify themselves not only directly but also in many indirect ways. In other words, there are many shades of subjectifications that contribute to the reification of a story about a person. These include general statements about his/her actions ("she doesn't know her times table") and implicit or indirect statements that elicit a narrative about a person—for example, "Everybody else knew the answer" (except her).

A good source for gleaning the significance of subjectifications comes from their *positioning* effect (Harré & van Langenhove, 1999) or what they convey about the rights and duties of participants in the interaction. For instance, when one student says to her partner "listen now" and proceeds to explain her solution for a problem, she is indirectly identifying herself as having the right to lead the problem-solving effort and as having the duty to explain her thinking to her partner. Any positioning act can contribute not only to the reification of identity narratives about the actor, but also to the reification of stories about the other participants in the interaction. Thus, "listen now" concomitantly identifies the listener (or fellow student) as having the duty to listen and as having the right to receive explanations. Of course, each positioning act in itself may be insignificant, or participants may contradict each other's positioning acts. However, it is the accretion of persistent positioning acts that eventually leads to their reification as identity narratives.

So far, I have talked about my conceptualization of identity and identifying. Now I turn to conceptual change. Just as the communicational framework avoids objectifying identity, so it attempts to avoid the objectification of mental concepts (Sfard, 2008, p. 56). Learning mathematics, for instance, is not conceptualized as the process of "acquiring" certain mental concepts, but rather as discursive activity whereby the learner gradually becomes more proficient in a community-based discourse, in this case, the mathematical discourse. This discourse includes routines (such as addition and multiplication), and certain objects (such as natural numbers or functions). It also includes meta-level rules, which determine *when*, or in what context, a certain routine is appropriate. For instance, the routine of adding whole numbers is not appropriate for adding fractions. These meta-rules thus differentiate between sub-discourses (discourse of whole numbers, discourse of fractions, etc.).

Within the communicational view of mathematical learning, the phenomena which have mostly been studied under the term "conceptual change" are the processes that learners go through during the transition from one sub-discourse to another (Sfard, 2007a). In other words, if a discourse is defined by a certain set of words, routines, visual mediators, and endorsed narratives (Sfard, 2008, p. 297), then a meta-discursive shift means that some critical subset of these has changed, and in a way that has made it incommensurable with the former discourse. For instance, in the discourse of whole numbers and discourse of fractions (or rational numbers), the sign "+" signals two different routines. This meta-discursive shift entails a movement from *object-level* learning, where familiar mathematical objects (such as whole numbers) are manipulated using previously established routines, to *meta-level* learning, which involves awareness that certain routines need to be changed when manipulating new objects (such as fractions). Such a meta-discursive shift is often difficult to achieve, since, in the words of Sfard, "the rules of the discourse changed but nobody told you" (Sfard, 2007b, p. 567).

Identifying and mathematizing in problem-solving geared for conceptual change

I shall exemplify the interaction between identifying and mathematizing over a meta-discursive boundary with excerpts from a study I took part in, which examined the effects of different pairings of 9th grade students on the occurrence of conceptual change in proportional reasoning tasks (see description of the larger study in Asterhan, Schwarz, & Cohen-Eliyahu, 2014). Our close-up examination of several of the pairs participating in this study (Heyd-Metzuyanim & Schwarz, 2017) zoomed in on the processes of crossing the meta-discursive boundary

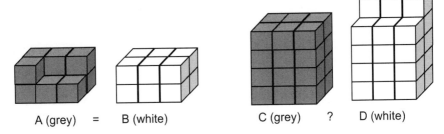

A (grey)   =   B (white)   C (grey)   ?   D (white)

FIGURE 24.1 Modified version from the Blocks Task.
Source: Aadapted from Schwarz & Linchevski (2007).

between whole-numbers discourse and multiplicative (proportional) discourse. The excerpts brought here are from a learning interaction of one pair, Dina and Peleg, in which the pair was solving the task seen in Figure 24.1.

Cubes from the A and C blocks (grey cubes) were stated to be of one (unknown) weight, while cubes from the B and D blocks (white cubes) were of another weight. The task was to determine, given that A is equal to B, what would be the relation of the weights of blocks C and D. According to their pre-tests, students were divided into those using "additive reasoning," where routines of addition applied to whole numbers were used, including comparing how many cubes are in C "more" than in A or how many cubes are "added" from A to B, and those using "proportional reasoning," where routines of multiplication and division were employed to compare products such as B/A or 27/12. The hallmark of incommensurability between discourses, where the same words are used in different ways (Sfard, 2007b), was seen here in the word "relation" (or "Yachas," which also means ratio in Hebrew). Whereas in the whole-numbers discourse, students used this word to refer to a comparison of the magnitude of a one-dimensional attribute (number of cubes or weight of the whole block), in the multiplicative discourse, it referred to a relation between relations.

Both Dina and Peleg started solving the task using routines from the whole-numbers discourse, which were also prevalent in their written pre-tests of similar tasks.

Turn	Speaker	What Is Said (What Is Done/Pointed at)
53	Dina	Alright, A and B are equal although B has two more. D has three more so D is bigger than C
54	Peleg	Yeah, this (A) is equal to this (C) and this (B) equals to this (D) and here (B) there are two more than here (A)

During the first phase of the solution process, Dina showed no hesitation about her choice of routines (comparison by addition and subtraction of whole numbers) and the endorsed narratives following them (D is bigger than C). Peleg, though from time to time asking for a moment to make sure Dina's statements

were correct, proceeded to endorse her claim that D > C. Dina was, therefore, deeply surprised when the scales, used to measure the actual weight of the
cardboard blocks, proved her statement to be wrong.

The transition between the discourse about whole numbers and proportional
discourse (or discourse about rational numbers) could be seen through Dina's
hesitant, confused words thereafter:

78a	Dina	To this (D) (they) added more (…)
b		(whispering to herself) I guess you can't know
c		You can't know if you don't know the weight
d		Listen why,
e		'Cause if (we) know the weight then you can know what the
f		relation between them (is) in their weight.
g		Like, whatever cubes that you won't add to D, then C will be
h		more until their weight will be over (something).
i		^Or that the weight (.) of this (?) with more cubes is bigger.
		And then even if you'll add to it cubes so it will grow.
		We-why did we write this answer?
		'cause we assumed that the weight is equal.
79	Peleg	Yes
80	Dina	So I think it can't be known

In the above episode, Dina is slowly realizing that the routines employed by
her in her previous solution were insufficient. From object-level discourse ("to this
they added more"), she turns into meta-level discourse ("I guess you can't know").
This is the first step in her meta-discursive transition. An even stronger indication
for this transition is seen in her attempt to explain why the previously employed
routines were unsatisfactory ("why did we write this answer?"). Moreover, Dina
pinpoints exactly the issue for which the addition/subtraction routines were insufficient: they were not taking into account the "weight" [78i]. What this "weight"
is, is not yet sufficiently explicated by her, but given her next steps, there are good
chances it refers to the weight of a single cube. Attention to the weight of a cube *in
addition* to the number of cubes is one of the necessary steps for transitioning into a
proportional discourse. Yet such attention, in itself, is not sufficient. One has to decide which calculation routine should be employed in order to take account of the
number and the weight of the cubes. This was still unclear for Dina, and therefore
she decided the answer is that the relation "cannot be known."

At that point, Peleg, who had already suggested a few times before a multiplicative routine, was able to get his idea finally registered:

85	Peleg	We can start checking if one cube in A weighs times what more
		than one cube in B
86	Dina	Times what?
87	Peleg	Look, that's six
88	Exper.	Think, you can know exactly (times how much)

Given Dina's previous dismissive reactions to Peleg's idea of using a multiplication routine (offered two times before this moment) there are good reasons to believe she was ready to dismiss this idea again, hadn't the experimenter intervened by saying "think, you can know exactly (times how much)" [88].

Now, and while Peleg was still busy counting the cubes in each block, Dina turned to her calculator and started tapping it rapidly, taking only seconds to produce a correct answer:

90	Dina	One cube of this (A) is equal to 1.2 of this (B) so 1.2 times how much is C?
92	Dina	How much are there here (C)? Here (C) 24 equals 28.8
93	Dina	How much is it here (D)?
94	Peleg	Here (D) there are 27
95	Dina	27, there
96	Peleg	So C is big

Peleg's involvement in this new solution, as well as the fact he was the one to initially offer the multiplicative idea ("times what more" [85]), may lead one to expect that he gained just as much from this interaction as Dina. Yet in his posttest, after starting with a division routine and crossing it out, Peleg reverted back to addition routines and the whole-numbers discourse, producing yet again a wrong answer. In contrast, Dina preformed the new multiplicative routine flawlessly and arrived at a correct answer. This gap led us to examine more closely the positioning acts and indirect subjectifications that occurred throughout the learning session. The analysis revealed interesting disparities between the indirect subjectifications of the two students as exemplified in Table 24.1.

TABLE 24.1 Positioning Acts and Their Interpreted Subjectifications

Positioning Act	Indirect Subjectifications
53 Dina: Alright, A and B are equal although B has two more… 54 Peleg: Yeah, ….	Dina: I am entitled to declare the solution Peleg: Dina is entitled to declare the solution My role is to endorse (or contradict) her assertions
55 Dina: Here there are two more than here… So D is bigger than C 56 Peleg: Yeah, one second 57 Dina: Get it? 'cause if when B has two more…	Peleg: My duty is to monitor Dina's assertions, I am entitled to request some time to think for myself Dina: My duty is to make sure Peleg understands my assertions
78–80 Dina: … You can't know if you don't know the weight. Listen why…. We- why did we write this answer? 'cause we assumed that the weight is equal 79–81 Peleg: Yeah… that the weight is equal	Dina: It is my duty not only to declare the right solution but also to explain why the previous solution was false. Also, my duty is to explain this to Peleg Peleg: my duty is follow and affirm Dina's assertions

It is important to clarify that interactions such as those exemplified in Table 24.1 can be interpreted as indirect subjectifications in multiple ways. For instance, the interaction in 53–54 could be, in a different context, interpreted as more egalitarian, where both participants agree on the mathematical narrative and where the order of the speaker (Dina first, Peleg second) gains less significance. It is the *repetitiveness* and *consistency* of these acts (found in the rest of the transcript but omitted due to space restrictions) that lent strength to the particular interpretations brought in the right-hand column of the table.

The examination of the implicit subjectifications of this problem-solving interaction shed light on the reason that Peleg's multiplicative ideas, as helpful as they were for the dilemma in which the students found themselves, gained footing only by the experimenter's intrusion [88]. Dina simply did not identify Peleg as a possible contributor to the solution effort, and Peleg did not show any evidence of contradicting this identity. Moreover, the fact that Dina explicated the meta-level shift, while Peleg only followed her and endorsed her statements, hints that Dina was identifying herself as entitled to make such meta-discursive shifts, while there is no evidence Peleg identified himself in a similar manner.

It seems likely that an experience such as that of Dina, where she was able to cross a meta-discursive boundary by herself, without much assistance from an external authority (such as a teacher) provided (yet another) "layer" of identification as a capable, autonomous mathematical problem-solver. Similarly, the fact that Peleg's ideas were mostly dismissed, added another "layer" (thin as it may be) on an identity of a "follower." The fact that Peleg did not resist the positioning of Dana hints that this was far from being the first time where he was identified (by himself and by others) in such a way. Thus, a plausible explanation for Peleg's hesitancy in the post-test is that he carried his story about himself as a "follower" to the post-test situation, and since in that situation, there was no one to follow, he went back to relying on the additive discourse he was more familiar with. Dina, on the other hand, had a fresh story of herself as an autonomous crosser of a meta-discursive boundary, to rely on in the post-test situation. This story was probably reinforced by the credibility of her solution, given its agreement with the rules of the multiplicative discourse.

Summary

Conceptual change is most likely the accretion of many small instances of meta-level shifts in the use of routines. Even in the case of Dina, the transition was not uniform. Her post-test still contained some problems solved using addition routines rather than multiplicative ones. Similarly, the formation of identity narratives is a continuous process of recurring subjectifications and (sometimes contradicting) positioning acts, gradually accrued into stable narratives that are applied by a person to himself or to others, and carried from one situation to another. The processes underlying the formation of stable identity narratives and lasting conceptual change in essence *co-constitute* each other. They occur concomitantly and continuously in the micro-scale of problem-solving interactions.

Identity and conceptual change interact in this way through a process of continuous layering and re-layering of positioning actions, identification narratives, and mathematical meta-discursive boundary crossings. Stable identity narratives provide the grounds for the confidence, perhaps even the courage, to cross the meta-discursive boundary, while the action of crossing a meta-discursive boundary provides a layer of identification as a capable, autonomous actor in the mathematical discourse.

References

Asterhan, C. S. C., Schwarz, B. B., & Cohen-Eliyahu, N. (2014). Outcome feedback during collaborative learning: Contingencies between feedback and dyad composition. *Learning and Instruction, 34*, 1–10.

Harré, R., & van Langenhove, L. (1999). *Positioning theory*. Oxford: Blackwell.

Heyd-Metzuyanim, E., & Sfard, A. (2012). Identity struggles in the mathematics classroom: On learning mathematics as an interplay of mathematizing and identifying. *International Journal of Educational Research, 51–52*, 128–145.

Heyd-Metzuyanim, E., & Schwarz, B. B. (2017). Conceptual change within dyadic interactions—the dance of conceptual and material agency. *Instructional Science, 45*(5), 645–677.

Schwarz, B. B., & Linchevski, L. (2007). The role of task design and of argumentation in cognitive development during peer interaction: The case of proportional reasoning. *Learning and Instruction, 17*(5), 510–531.

Sfard, A. (2007a). Reconceptualizing conceptual change. In S. Vosniadou, A. Baltas, & X. Vamvakoussi (Eds.), *Re-framing the conceptual change approach in learning and instruction* (pp. 331–337). Boston, MA: Elsevier.

Sfard, A. (2007b). When the rules of discourse change, but nobody tells you: Making sense of mathematics learning from a commognitive standpoint. *Journal of the Learning Sciences, 16*(4), 565–613.

Sfard, A. (2008). *Thinking as communicating*. New York: Cambridge University Press.

Sfard, A., & Prusak, A. (2005). Telling identities: In search of an analytic tool for investigating learning as a culturally shaped activity. *Educational Researcher, 34*(4), 14–22.

Valero, P., & Meaney, T. (2014). Trends in researching the socioeconomic influences on mathematical achievement. *ZDM-International Journal on Mathematics Education, 46*(7), 977–986. doi:10.1007/s11858-014-0638-3.

Williams, T., & Williams, K. (2010). Self-efficacy and performance in mathematics: Reciprocal determinism in 33 nations. *Journal of Educational Psychology, 102*(2), 453–466. doi:10.1037/a0017271.

25

IDENTITY AND KNOWLEDGE

Andrea A. diSessa

Introduction

The importance of identity in education is transparent. Identities projected on marginalized populations constrain their access to societal opportunities. Just as much, we need to be concerned with learners' taking on self-constructs that limit connection to mathematics and science, and limit imagining a future self in a scientific career.

Given identity's importance, I believe it is accidental and unproductive that this construct has been seen as nearly the exclusive property of sociocultural paradigms. That fact has marginalized the involvement and perspectives of those of us committed to refined, modern theories of knowledge as central to understanding education. In extreme cases, self-conscious affiliation with sociocultural views has resulted in explicit attacks on knowledge as a problematic, inaccessible, and unenlightening construct. My work here is to help reinforce recent moves that are, explicitly or implicitly, bringing the study of knowledge to the study of identity. As I explore this space, I will enumerate advantages I see in these directions. Indeed, even the idea of such inquiry brings with it the promise that engaging strong but underappreciated points of view can entail.

Advantage 0: *I seek, here, to add the resources of a theoretically and empirically well-developed alternative point of view, centering on the study of knowledge, to the study of identity.*

My genre of studying knowledge emphasizes theoretical explicitness, analytical clarity, and empirical tractability. I agree with critiques of construals of identity as often muddy, inexplicit, and empirically intractable (see Sfard & Prusak (2005) on lack of operationalization, or Gee's (2000) moves to improve the analytical state-of-the-art concerning identity).

Advantage 1: *Among the most important advantages of a move toward knowledge is precisely with respect to these dimensions: explicitness, clarity, and empirical tractability.*

My other chapter, in Part I of this volume, grounds many of the things I say here in my perspective on knowledge and its development. However, I won't have space to call them out explicitly.

Models of Identity

The essence of this innovation is *to bring human processes of interpretation* explicitly into view. This means addressing the knowledge that people have and the concomitant processes of activation and use. I focus specifically on *characterizations* that people make of themselves or other people. So, we need to know (1) the "descriptive vocabulary" that people have concerning individuals. We need to know (2) to what they attend when they characterize others, and (3) the inferences they make to get from observations to characterizations. I call item (3) the "inferential backdrop." We also need to know how people infer consequences and fitting actions from characterization, which, for simplicity, I include in the inferential backdrop.

Descriptive vocabulary, (1), includes linguistic terms, like "smart," "lazy," "good at math," and similar. We need to know what people mean by these terms and how they see them in others (i.e., items 2 and 3). However, modern conceptions of knowledge, mine in particular, emphasize inarticulate knowledge, distinct from our abilities to present ideas in words. A relevant example might be feelings of elation concerning, say, some disciplinary experience (e.g., epiphanies), or revulsion toward certain activities and people (e.g., "the intelligentsia"). Those feelings characterize the relevant action or person in senses that are operational and have definite consequences within the inferential backdrop. This is no less true if the processes that generate such characterizations are inarticulate or even opaque to our current theories.

Typical of intensive knowledge-oriented analysis, careful scrutiny of what people actually think, what knowledge they use, leads to distinctions that may be ignored at a more global level. Here, I phrase different regimes of human knowledge about identity as different models. These are not alternatives, but a multiplicity. *All* of them are enacted at different times, by different actors.

Model 1: Personal Identity

I start with the most obvious, but not obviously most important model of identity. *Personal identity* is the sum of characterizations we make of ourselves. We shouldn't make too many assumptions about the structure of personal identity—for example, that it is coherent. Persistent, even disturbing conflict among our characterizations of ourselves might be exceedingly important. On the other hand, we can assume some determinable sense of grading, separating the most consequential and frequently used characterizations from less central ones.

Model 2: Managed Identity

Managed identity is highly salient to me. I believe the social functions of this model are pervasive: We all take actions to present ourselves to others in felicitous ways (including, but not limited to, "as we see ourselves"). Such management entails a lot of knowledge. It entails analyses of all of the above categories—descriptive vocabulary, empirical strategies, likely consequences, and so on, not just with respect to ourselves, but *with respect to others*. That is, our *models of other people* (as they might characterize us) are crucial. As actors, we should optimally be flexible enough to entertain (1) possible characterizations of ourselves that we would never make on our own, and (2) consequences for those characterizations we might never assume. In response to all of this, we improvise or strategize public moves that put us in a fitting light in others' characterizations. This sometimes entails problem-solving, amenable to perhaps even traditional knowledge deployment models, such as means/ends analysis.

Model 3: Intrinsic Identity

Intrinsic identity concerns patterns inherent in our varied and distinctive ways of interacting with the world, including the social world. Although one should project some stability over time to these patterns, we must recognize that all knowledge-based action respects *contextuality*. No patterns appear in all circumstances, and every pattern will be adapted to local circumstances. Such contextualities and adaptations ("situatings") are obligatory analyses in my knowledge-based view.

A good way to construe intrinsic identity is that it concerns characterizations of people where researchers have special province. Scientific characterizations of distinctive regularities in human behavior require an explicit pedigree in respectable theory and cogent empirical grounding. And, of course, they are subject to an extended history of inquiry and public critique. We might not be far along in characterizing intrinsic identity, but there is a "there" there. People exhibit distinctive patterns in their actions. Independent of the state of the art, I project a solid scientific future for common-sense observations that some people are, say, systematically more defensive or aggressive than others, and others are prone to "look on the bright side." Intrinsic identity constitutes a hoped-for "ground truth" against which other characterizations may be compared. Unlike other kinds of identity, elements of intrinsic identity might not be cognized by anyone in the everyday (non-scientific) world. Yet, they still do work. I almost certainly have habits of mind and action that I do not cognize; others may not know me well enough nor have ready categories to describe them, either. Yet, if I fall in with a group that does things similarly, we all may recognize that things are "clicking," without any idea about why.

Model 4: Projected Identity

Managed identity implies the capacity of actors to imagine how others characterize them. How others *do, in fact*, characterize them is quite another thing. Hence, I use the term other-projected identity—briefly, *projected identity*—to describe the knowledge by someone that creates (and follows up on) characterizations of someone else. Projected identity might be insightful of things about ourselves of which we are unaware (hence, play no role in our managed identity). But, projected identity is equally likely to involve biased and presumptuous characterizations that do not withstand clear-eyed scrutiny.

Two core issues

Membership

Membership plays a significant role—even a defining role—in traditional talk about identity. But membership does not define any of these models. Instead it plays diverse roles across the various models.

- Membership might (or might not!) be a central part of personal identity.
- Whether or not it is a part of personal identity, it might constitute a cluster of goals concerning managed identity. For example, you might hide your personal identity from a group of which you are a "card-carrying member" (i.e., the group projects membership on you). Contrarily, you might want to be seen as a member for reasons that are extrinsic to the core of your personal identity—say, to receive social goods associated with a particular group (or you might be a spy!).
- Being associated with a group, you might appropriate some elements of identity that are common in the group. You might, for example, pick up their lingo in your descriptive vocabulary for identities: "tool," "bourgeois," "weak on defense." And then you might decide to leave the group and take those ideas as resources to the opposition.

I do not think any person is well-characterized by a single membership, or even a set of memberships. Some people might prize, as a core of their personal identity, that they are membership-fluid, or membership-ambiguous. In fact, it is core to my personal identity that I am *not* well-characterized by my obvious memberships. I think it is an intellectual strength and badge of honor.

Distributing membership across identity models, for me, is just the right thing to do. Its relationships to various kinds of identity are too diverse and complex to suffer a simple positioning. We need a finer grain-size to understand commonalities and contradictions in various memberships, what might be going on in multiple memberships (an underlying coherence, or a true kind of "membership schizophrenia," e.g., homosexuals who are deeply homophobic), and what exactly happens in various corners and kinds of identity when one changes membership.

Advantage 2: *Group membership is best positioned as a complex factor with multiple roles in multiple kinds of identities than as a single or defining element of identities. Knowledge-based accounts respect this.*

Diversities

The framework above makes a lot of demands on us theoretically and empirically. Every characterization demands analysis of descriptive vocabulary (especially challenging if it is non-linguistic), of the focal observations and inferences that lead to characterizations and the implications drawn from them. We must index who is doing the characterizing and who is characterized. All that we know or might find out scientifically about patterns in thinking and behavior can contribute another perspective. We might, thus, find firm grounds for saying that some characterizations are either sensible approximations, or we may find out that other characterizations are false or have nothing much to do with the reality they purport to be about. Each of these issues constitutes occasions that demand particulars.

Rough approximations can be useful, identifying some projected identities as "nativist" (implicating immutable, even genetic characterizations) or socio-structural (one "opposite" to "nativist"). I prefer starting by assuming complexity, starting with fine-grained, multi-dimensional analyses. Then, we can see if simplicities emerge. Indeed, one of my proudest accomplishments in studying conceptual change is opening secure empirical and theoretical grounds for understanding that, while we have commonalities, every individual is unique. Many sociocultural studies of identity "tack on" notice of diversity within people, groups, and across situations at the end, after general statements (see later reference); but my knowledge-based approach starts from the assumption of diversity and an empirical demand to describe or refute it.

Advantage 3: *The centrality of the idea and value of diversity in sociocultural perspectives is honored in knowledge-based analyses. Including knowledge in identity's analysis, I project, will entail more and more systematic study of diversity across people, situations, and groups with respect to various kinds of identity and their above-articulated components.*

Continuities and discontinuities with existing research

This section does more work to connect (or contrast) the perspective here with other research on identity.

Culturally specific knowledge in learning

A well-developed meme in the study of identity and learning is to argue for incorporating powerful, if unrecognized, cultural knowledge into school learning. Moll (e.g., Moll & Amanti, 2005) argues that we need to discover and incorporate culture-specific practices and "funds of knowledge" into schooling, thus harnessing the power of cultural identity. Lee (e.g., Lee, 2001) argues that specific cultural knowledge, for example, of discursive genres, can seed comprehension of the whole landscape of linguistic forms in reading and writing. Researchers such as Warren, Oganowski, and Pothier (2005) argue that the dichotomy between everyday (possibly culturally specific) concepts and scientific ones is dramatically overdone, and bringing out the continuity can allow all students, particularly disenfranchised populations, to "see themselves" in what they are learning and in possible identities as future scientists.

I heartily endorse these ideas and aim to carry them forward. Here is how I can do so: As a knowledge analyst I have spent my career focusing on unfamiliar but still powerful forms of knowledge that are rooted in everyday life and which also constitute cultural knowledge. By "turning up the microscope" on the particular elements of "disenfranchised" knowledge and on its theorization—on the very forms of such knowledge—one can achieve results like the following (for examples and references, see my contribution to Part I of this volume):

- We can chart lines of continuity from highly specific "naïve ideas" to scientific ones. Sometimes, the discovery of certain intuitive ideas has seeded particular and surprisingly successful pathways for learning that could not have been imaged or explained without such study.
- We now know that scientific understanding contains knowledge that is not only continuous with naïve ideas, but is even of *the same form*. Science is factually not categorically distinct from unschooled ideas, whatever impression is portrayed by other epistemological views.
- Knowing both the particular elements and relevant processes of change, we can focus on difficulties, also, with a much more refined lens.
- We can examine and understand how individuals vary in their learning, based on their particular out-of-school understandings. Simultaneously, we may discover (as we have in a recent project) that cultural differences often show more in the examples students will give of particular ideas, and less in the particular ideas themselves. So, multicultural classrooms may be easier to deal with than might be assumed by emphasizing obviously culturally specific tactics.

Advantage 4: *The study of knowledge provides powerful insights into the nature and form of unschooled and cultural knowledge, which can illuminate new possibilities and let us better manage both continuities and differences between everyday and scientific understanding.*

Existing work on knowledge-in-identity

Study of knowledge is already, if preliminarily, being incorporated into the study of identity. I cite here one striking case.

McGee and Martin (2011) take bold steps toward incorporating analysis of knowledge into the study of identity.[1]

They studied a group of high-achieving Black university students and how they dealt with persistent negative stereotyping concerning ability, specifically with respect to mathematics and science. What emerged from the study was strongly consistent with my discussion, above, of various kinds of identity. The authors even note the point mentioned earlier, that traditional (non-knowledge-based) analyses so far have shown characteristic limits. For example, "... most studies of differential outcomes in mathematics education begin and end their analyses of race with static racial categories and group labels used for the sole purpose of disaggregating data" (p. 1351). In addition, "... the voices of Black learners themselves are often absent from the larger discourse on achievement and persistence outcomes ..." (p. 1351). That is, researchers often don't listen to or acknowledge the rich mental life of Black students concerning racial stereotypes.

The central analytical construct of the paper is *stereotype management*, which is a specific version of managed identity that is directed toward dealing with projected identities involving racial stereotypes. The authors uncover an intricate set of ideas, beliefs, and strategic innovation concerning (1) others' projections onto these students, (2) their own personal identity, and (3) how to respond to others. Typical of knowledge-oriented analyses, the results uncover many variations both in conception and in strategic repertoire. For example, some students emulate White culture in order to promote judgments of "fitting," but others emphasize—virtually flaunt—stereotypical Blackness while simultaneously aiming to confront assumptions (i.e., the inferential backdrop of others) with high achievement.

Missing the rich interior life of managed identity also misses these students' profound agency and the non-deterministic nature of their reactions in contrast to older, well-established constructs such as "stereotype threat." The authors track individual and typical developmental trajectories—for example, from reactive self-definition (personal identities' built largely in reaction to projections of others) to relying much more on their own personal feelings about what is worthwhile to achieve.

What's left to be achieved if we move from McGee and Martin's common sense, but attentive treatment of knowledge-in-identity, to more technical model-based work, trying explicitly to connect to well-developed work on knowledge in other arenas (e.g., conceptual change of science concepts)? That's a good question, which I cannot address here. But, I am convinced that the achievements of articles like McGee and Martin's in connecting to a knowledge-based paradigm are only suggestive of great rewards to come.

Discursive theories of identity

Sfard and Prusak (2005) offer a well-developed but contrasting attempt to construct clear and operationalizable conceptions of identity,[2] while, at the same time, seeking to marginalize or eliminate talk of knowledge. To begin, I note some commonalities. Their term for identities is "narratives," which has some resonance with my term "characterizations." In addition, the authors emphasize the importance of indexing identities to who makes them and on whom they are projected.[3] However, "characterizations" are elaborated within a framework of forms and systems of knowledge, while narratives are self-described as "stories," explicitly rejecting anything (e.g., knowledge) enacting the stories, and also rejecting any reality behind the stories.

What I see as missing from their theory is, perhaps most notably, any "ground truth" with respect to identities, which I've located significantly in the scientific study of personal patterns of action (intrinsic identity). While they mention that identities can be contested, they do not identify the processes involved in such contest, for example, (1) with respect to scientifically sound construals of self or others, or (2) by examining and critiquing participants' processes of observing and then inferring characterizations.

The authors' description of the processes of development of distinctive internal resources for construing (various kinds of) identity are spare. They acknowledge, of course, that elements of identity can be drawn from others' talk, but specificity is lacking, for example, in contrast to elaborating the development and personal versions of components of identity mentioned in my models (descriptive vocabulary, elements of experiential focus, and inferential backdrop). The path to rich accounts of strategizing and gradually building individual identity are unclear to me in their account, specifically in contrast to the conceptually rich and highly strategized development of managed and personal identities described by McGee and Martin. I also believe that narrative approaches to identity are limited in handling inarticulate knowledge and affect, a backbone of intuitive and cultural knowledge, compared to modern knowledge-based views.

Notes

1 Although I find it evident, the authors don't identify any affiliation with knowledge-based analyses.
2 In contrast, I believe that Gee's (2000) framework for understanding identity is mutually illuminating, not conflicting, with that given here.
3 They also suggest indexing the audience for the story, an entirely sensible move.

References

Gee, J. P. (2000). Identity as an analytic lens for research in education. *Review of Research in Education, 25*, 99–125.

Lee, C. D. (2001). Is October Brown Chinese? A cultural modeling activity system for underachieving students. *American Educational Research Journal, 38*(1), 97–142.

McGee, E., & Martin, D. (2011). "You would not believe what I have to go through to prove my intellectual value!" Stereotype management among academically successful Black mathematics and engineering students. *American Educational Research Journal, 48*(6), 1347–1389.

Moll, L. C., & Amanti, C. (2005). *Funds of knowledge: Theorizing practices in households, communities, and classrooms.* Mahwah, NJ: Lawrence Erlbaum Associates.

Sfard, A., & Prusak, A. (2005). Telling identities: In search of an analytic tool for investigating learning as a culturally shaped activity. *Educational Researcher, 34*(4), 14–22.

Warren, B., Ogonowski, M., & Pothier, S. (2005). 'Everyday' and 'scientific': Rethinking dichotomies in modes of thinking in science learning. In R. Nemirovsky, A. Rosebery, J. Solomon, & B. Warren (Eds.), *Everyday matters in mathematics and science: Studies of complex classroom events* (pp. 119–148). Mahwah, NJ: Erlbaum.

26

PERSONAL, DEEPLY AFFECTIVE, AND AESTHETIC ENGAGEMENT WITH SCIENCE CONTENT

When disciplinary learning becomes a vehicle for identity construction

Olivia Levrini, Mariana Levin, and Paola Fantini

Introduction

In science education, the influence that students' identities have on learning and participating in science appears as a rather familiar focus (e.g., Carlone, 2003; Cobb, Gresalfi, & Hodge, 2009; Lottero-Perdue & Brickhouse, 2002; Sfard & Prusak, 2005; Varelas, 2012). However, the inverse question of how disciplinary content learning can be a vehicle for identity formation is little explored. Our approach focuses on this direction and pursues this agenda by operationally defining a theoretical construct, *appropriation*, borrowed from scholars in linguistics and education (Bakhtin, 1981; Rogoff, 1995). Appropriation implies *productive* learning, including deep conceptual understanding, but it also involves a reflexive process of populating scientific discourse with personal intentions, purposes, and tastes.

In this chapter, we first explore how the construct of appropriation sheds light on how content knowledge learning influences identity development. We then use appropriation to develop a nuanced notion of concept projection from coordination class theory, well known within the conceptual change literature (diSessa & Wagner, 2005; diSessa, Chapter 1, this volume). The chapter closes with theoretical and methodological challenges and opportunities that this approach to studying the intersection between identity and conceptual change presents.

The construct of appropriation

The starting place for our discussion of the possible relations between identity and conceptual change is Levrini, Fantini, Pecori, Tasquier, and Levin (2015), in which we analyzed data gathered from an extended intervention on thermodynamics in a class of 20 students (17 years old) from a scientifically oriented secondary school in Italy (grade 12). During the activities, students made progress in learning not only the disciplinary content of the teaching/learning path, but also in a broader, personally relevant sense. In order to better capture what happened, we started from Bakhtin's definition of appropriation that implies infusing personal meanings into words borrowed from others (Bakhtin, 1981). We then developed appropriation as an operational construct for science learning characterized by five markers able to show if and how students' discourse revealed their personal, deeply affective engagement with content knowledge.

The operational definition of appropriation built in Levrini et al. (2015) analyzes students' discourse around scientific terms/utterances for whether it is:

A   developed around a set of words or expressions repeated several times and linked together so as to express a *personal, idiosyncratic "signature" idea* with respect to physics (thermodynamics, in this case);

B   *disciplinarily-grounded*, that is, the signature idea was used by the student as a tool for focusing on pieces of disciplinary knowledge;

C   *thick*, that is, the signature idea involved a metacognitive dimension (What does learning physics mean for the student?) and an epistemological one (What sense of the discipline does the student have?);

D   *non-incidental*, that is, the signature idea was expressed in several activities throughout the students' classroom experience, not just in one interaction;

E   *carrier of social relationships*, that is, the signature idea allowed the student to play a specific role in class discussions, and this role was acknowledged by others in the classroom community.

These markers of appropriation indicate that the student is well positioned with respect to the discipline (marker B), with respect to the class (marker E), and with respect to their own personal story of who they are as a person and a learner (marker A, C, D).

The following vignettes, based on interviews with two students, Matteo and Michele, in the thermodynamics class, illustrate both the markers and how the markers indicate this tri-partite positioning—that is, with respect to the discipline, class, and self. Matteo and Michele were asked to describe how they thought about the concept of temperature. As can be seen in the vignettes, they both described correct ideas, yet their descriptions had a very different, personally inflected, character.

Matteo

Matteo systematically showed a strong interest in philosophy. At the end of the thermodynamics unit, during the interview (and in the class more generally) he repeatedly returned to the philosophical notions of "being" and "becoming" to describe the special interest he discovered in thermodynamics.

Based on a discourse analysis of the interview and class interactions, we recognized this as an idiosyncratic "signature idea" of Matteo (marker A). The idea was grounded in the discipline (marker B) for Matteo because it helped him to make sense of thermodynamics concepts themselves. For example, when discussing the concept of temperature, Matteo focused on the distinction between the temperature gradient (delta T) and temperature (T) because he could recognize, in this connection, the philosophical notions of becoming (change) and being (state). Matteo saw in the law of calorimetry ($Q = mc\Delta T$) an expression of becoming "there is a change [because of ΔT] that means everything is not stable and everything is not being, there is something that changes." In contrast, in thinking about the Ideal Gas Law ($PV = nRT$), he saw an expression of being: "[There is] absolute temperature T, that doesn't change. There is not Δ [difference in temperature], there is not the change…" When asked about what he liked most within the study of thermodynamics, he mentioned the arrow of time in the discussion of entropy because one could also see there the distinction between being and becoming. His signature idea was non-incidental (marker D) in the sense that Matteo used it repeatedly over the course of the unit. The signature idea was a carrier of social relationships (marker E) because his philosophical approach to the content was explicitly recognized by the class and valued. Lastly, Matteo's idea expressed an epistemological positioning with respect to physics seen mainly as a discipline oriented to fundamental questions about knowledge (marker C), such as "What is time?" and "What is being?"

Michele

Throughout the thermodynamics unit, Michele showed a strong interest in engines, objects, and how the world works. His personal "signature idea" (Marker A) can be recognized in his statement in the end of the unit interview: "I like Physics because it explains how reality works. That is to say, I'm very curious about how objects work and about natural events…" Michele used his signature idea to make sense of disciplinary content (marker B) as can be seen in his discussion of the concept of temperature. In the interview, he focused his attention on the temperature gradient because this is what makes engines work. As he explains, "Different temperatures are necessary … only with different bodies with different temperatures can we have a cycle and work; different temperatures induce a heat exchange—as we call it—and the heat exchange induces work; heat is turned into work." His discourse displays an expression of epistemological positioning within physics seen mainly as a discipline oriented to solving concrete problems (marker C). Michele reiterated his interest in physics because of its ability to explain "how reality works" several times during the whole unit on thermodynamics (non-incidental—marker D). In the class, Michele came to develop a social position in the class as a student who ensured that the collective discussion connected with the real world (marker E).

Notably, both Michele and Matteo discussed the concept of temperature in a way that was sound with respect to the discipline, yet not a repetition of a textbook or teacher definition of the concept. Instead, they each used their signature idea to focus attention on different pieces of knowledge related to temperature. This process of infusing a disciplinary word with personal tastes and intentions is at the heart of what the construct of appropriation captures. How identity formation, disciplinary learning, and their relations can be highlighted by appropriation will be discussed in the next two sections. We will begin by reconsidering how disciplinary content choices influence identity.

Appropriation as a lens on identity

Although there are some variations, all over the world school physics and mathematics seem to be the result of similar content choices (e.g., Duit, Niedderer, & Schecker, 2007). By referring to physics, Carlone (2003) used the term "prototypical physics" to identify the most widespread approach to the content that presents a discipline envisioned as difficult, hierarchical, objective, rigorous, and deeply elitist. These content choices are argued to be at the basis of the image of STEM disciplines as "closed and exclusive clubs" where the participants, few but satisfied, correspond to a specific, although stereotyped STEM identity (Angell, Guttersrud, Henriksen, & Isnes, 2004; Carlone, 2003).

Very seldom is there room to see these disciplines as somewhere to develop one's own identity. This view of STEM resonates with what Nasir and Hand found in their study on identity formation, in which they contrasted students' engagement in a basketball class and in a math class (Nasir and Hand, 2008). In high school basketball practice, Nasir and Hand observed three aspects that seemed to be linked to identity formation and important for engagement that, on the contrary, were not present in the math class they observed:

- access to the domain as a whole, as well as to specific skills and concepts within it;
- integral roles and accountability for carrying out those roles;
- opportunities to engage in self-expression, to make a unique contribution, and to feel valued and competent in the setting.

The points enumerated by Nasir and Hand describe an interesting process of identity formation, involving the tension between the need to express oneself and one's own subjectivity, the need to respect constraints represented by the game (the discipline), and by the social relations within the team (the class or the group of people one is a part of). This dynamic image of identity formation rejects an essentialist position according to which identity is something fixed or given. It, moreover, overcomes the sharp distinctions between different approaches to considering identity formation: (i) the psychological approach of focusing on the individual's core identity, (ii) the socio-interactionalist approach of focusing on the social discursive mechanisms of identity development, and (iii) the affiliative approach of focusing on identity as a sense of belonging to a community (Gee, 2000; Varelas, 2012). The five markers of appropriation, as well as the notion of practice-linked identity of Nasir and Hand, highlight identity as a tri-partite positioning dynamic where the personal expression of tastes and interests is sought with respect to the discipline and its rules and classroom dynamics. If recurring within discourse or actions over time, this positioning can foster identity formation, in the sense that this dynamic creates a context in which a student must engage with questions like "Who am I?", "Who do I want to become?", and "Who do I want to be perceived as?"

The approach to identity that we are suggesting here has the specific feature of focusing on disciplinary content and on the issue of how disciplinary content choices influence identity formation. Prototypical physics and mathematics promote a stereotyped idea of STEM identity and, unlike a basketball class, do not foster identity formation. Thus, the main question that motivated our design of thermodynamics materials was: What content organization can do real work to foster deep, personal engagement?

The disciplinary content in the materials in the Levrini et al. (2015) study were explicitly restructured to make the environment psychologically safe and to enable students to nurture their talents and to express themselves. This goal was reached by making the epistemological structure visible and by challenging the authoritative and exclusive image of science in which a unique point of view is legitimate (and possible) (Nasir, Rosebery, Warren, & Lee, 2006). In particular, we chose to address the same topics from different perspectives (microscopic and macroscopic) and to contrast them for their particular epistemological features. Moreover, we chose to show the polyphony of scientific discourse by presenting historical voices (for example, of Maxwell, Boltzmann, Einstein) to enable students to recognize that personal and idiosyncratic stances also exist in professional science.

Appropriation as a lens on conceptual change

In addition to enabling students to nurture their interests, the materials in Levrini et al. (2015) were designed to facilitate processes of conceptual change. To reach this goal, we were inspired by the coordination class model of conceptual change (diSessa & Sherin, 1998). Coordination class theory is situated within the Knowledge-in-Pieces epistemological perspective (diSessa, 1993; diSessa, Chapter 1, this volume), and provides a model of expert conceptual understanding in which a "concept" is seen as a complex system that has the function of "reading out" a characteristic class of information across the many contexts in which one encounters it in the world. A basic assumption is that knowing and learning involve coordinating both perceptual and inferential processes across multiple contexts. Thus, we offered students multiple contexts and definitions for exploring the same concept in a variety of circumstances.

We introduced earlier the personal and idiosyncratic ways that two students, Matteo and Michele, talked about temperature. They both talked about temperature in reasonable, scientifically correct, but, importantly, personal ways. The existence of such data gives rise to the following theoretical issue: where, in their coordination processes that led to the construction of the concept of temperature, did they infuse personal meanings?

To address this issue we draw again upon excerpts from interviews with Michele and Matteo and observe that, in thinking about the concept of temperature, both Michele and Matteo engage in two related processes of selective attention: (1) selection of a context in which to operate the concept and (2) choice of foci of attention (that is, aspects of the concept and related pieces of knowledge relevant to the concept in that context).

Michele's explanation is tightly connected to his signature idea (his interest in engines, reality, and "how things work.") With Michele, the Carnot cycle is the context he chooses ("We have seen that, in Carnot's cycle, the temperatures influence the efficiency, the process, the cycle ..."). In this context, he focuses on the *difference* in temperature, because, he explains, the difference in temperature is what makes an engine work ("Different temperatures are necessary. Only with different bodies with different temperatures can we have a cycle and work; different temperatures induce a heat exchange—we can call it so—and the heat exchange induces work; heat is turned into work."). The choice of the context leads him to focus his attention on a special piece of knowledge regarding temperature "the temperature gradient" because "only with different bodies with different temperatures can we have a cycle and work cycle."

In contrast, Matteo selects a completely different context for projecting the concept of temperature: the distinction between two relations that include temperature (i.e., the law of calorimetry and the ideal gas law). Still, the choice is consistent with his idiosyncratic idea represented by the philosophical distinction between becoming and being. The choice of the contexts leads Matteo to focus his attention on a special piece of knowledge regarding temperature: its being a state variable whose difference creates a process, a change. The distinction between change (process) and lack of change (a state) is represented by the presence and the lack of "Δ." The presence or lack of Δ become the two foci of attention where he could make his projection of the concept of temperature. It is where he could infuse his personal meaning, inspired by his idiosyncratic idea.

In the context of giving an explanation of temperature, if we refer again to the model of coordination classes, we can recognize that both Matteo and Michele generated a *concept projection* (diSessa & Wagner, 2005; diSessa, Sherin, & Levin, 2016), the parts of a full coordination class that are active in a particular explanation. What was special about the way they focused their attention and coordinated their knowledge was that their understanding was assembled around their idiosyncratic "signature" ideas. Thus, they each, in their own ways, formed what we will call a *personal concept projection* by populating a disciplinary word with their own personal intentions and tastes. To sum up, the lens of appropriation, applied to the processes of disciplinary learning, shows how coordination class theory can be extended to reveal ways that disciplinary learning and identity formation can be intimately intertwined.

Future work on the intersection between identity and conceptual change

The main thrust of our chapter has been to argue for the productiveness of viewing disciplinary learning as a site for identity formation. Through the discussion of the design of learning environments, we also indicated how disciplinary content could be changed in order to facilitate this productive kind of engagement. In looking to the future of work in this area, one issue that we see as needing innovation is how to collect explicit data on conceptual change and identity development as they unfold in classroom contexts so that they can be traced for individuals over time. An open question that remains is how we can coordinate individual level data of increasing understanding and individual processes of identity formation. Thus far, we have been able to identify whether appropriation has or has not occurred and we have been able to locate moments of classroom activity where students are animating and refining their signature ideas, but much of the data the field should be interested in with respect to both processes, increasing disciplinary competence and identity formation, are invisible.

Acknowledgments

This chapter is an elaboration of a paper presented at the symposium "The interplay between identity and conceptual change: Productive synergies and new directions for research," organized by L. Branchetti (Chair) and presented at the *9th International Conference on Conceptual Change* in Bologna, Italy, September 2014. We wish to thank Laura Branchetti and Giulia Tasquier for the work they did for the symposium and for their comments on drafts of this chapter. Thanks also to Andy diSessa and Paolo Guidoni, discussants of the symposium, for their thoughtful remarks on our presentation and their inspiring suggestions.

References

Angell, C., Guttersrud, Ø., Henriksen, E. K., & Isnes, A. (2004). Physics: Frightful, but fun. Pupils' and teachers' views of physics and physics teaching. *Science Education*, 5(88), 683–706.

Bakhtin, M. (1981). Discourse in the novel (M. Holquist & C. Emerson, Trans.). In M. Holquist (Ed.), *The dialogic imagination* (pp. 259–422). Austin, TX: University of Texas Press.

Carlone, H. B. (2003). Innovative science within and against a culture of "achievement." *Science Education*, 87, 307–328.

Cobb, P., Gresalfi, M., & Hodge, L. L. (2009). An interpretive scheme for analyzing the identities that students develop in mathematics classrooms. *Journal for Research in Mathematics Education*, 40(1), 40–68.

diSessa, A. A. (1993). Toward an epistemology of physics. *Cognition and Instruction*, *10*(2&3), 105–225.

diSessa, A. A., & Sherin, B. L. (1998). What changes in conceptual change? *International Journal of Science Education, 20*(10), 1155–1191.

diSessa, A. A., & Wagner, J. F. (2005). What coordination has to say about transfer. In J. Mestre (Ed.), *Transfer of learning from a modern multi-disciplinary perspective* (pp. 121–154). Greenwich, CT: Information Age Publishing.

diSessa, A. A., Sherin, B., & Levin, M. (2016). Knowledge analysis: An introduction. In A. A. diSessa, M. Levin, & N. J. S. Brown (Eds.), *Knowledge and Interaction: A synthetic agenda for the learning science* (pp. 30–61). New York: Taylor & Francis.

Duit, R., Niedderer, H., & Schecker, H. (2007). Teaching physics. In S. K. Abell, & N. G. Lederman (Eds.), *Handbook of research on science education* (pp. 599–629). Mahwah, NJ: Erlbaum.

Gee, J. P. (2000). Identity as an analytic lens for research in education. *Review of Research in Education, 25*, 99–125.

Levrini O., Fantini P., Pecori B., Tasquier G., & Levin, M. (2015). Defining and operationalizing "appropriation" for science learning. *Journal of the Learning Sciences*, *24*(1), 93–136. doi:10.1080/10508406.2014.928215.

Lottero-Perdue, P. S., & Brickhouse, N. W. (2002). Learning on the job: The acquisition of scientific competence. *Science Education, 86*, 756–782.

Nasir, N., & Hand, V. (2008). From the court to the classroom: Opportunities for engagement, learning, and identity in basketball and classroom mathematics. *Journal of the Learning Sciences, 17*(2), 143–179.

Nasir, N. S., Rosebery, A. S., Warren, B., & Lee, C. D. (2006). Learning as a cultural process. In K. Sawyer (ed.), *The Cambridge handbook of the learning sciences* (pp. 489–504). Cambridge: Cambridge University Press.

Rogoff, B. (1995). Observing sociocultural activity on three planes: Participatory appropriation, guided participation and apprenticeship. In J. V. Wertsch, P. del Rio, & A. Alvarez (Eds.), *Sociocultural studies of mind* (pp. 139–164). Cambridge: Cambridge University Press.

Sfard, A., & Prusak, A. (2005). Telling identities: In search of an analytic tool for investigating learning as a culturally shaped activity. *Educational Researcher, 34*(4), 14–22.

Varelas, M. (2012) (Ed.). *Identity construction and science education research*. Dordrecht: Sense Publishers.

Unpacking the nexus between identity and conceptual change

Perspectives on an emerging research agenda

Mariana Levin, Olivia Levrini, and James Greeno

Introduction

This part of the volume has explored three approaches to an emerging area of conceptual change research: the interplay between conceptual change and identity. This synthesis will situate these approaches with respect to each other and with respect to the broader literature. At the same time, we will suggest possible convergences and complementarities between them and directions for future work.

As has been documented and explored extensively throughout this volume, conceptual change research has its roots in the cognitive tradition, investigating the nature of students' ideas and asking what makes some concepts particularly difficult to learn and teach (see, for example, Sherin, Part I; Amin, Part II). Identity is a term that has been used widely across a variety of fields, and has come to have very different meanings. Especially early on, the field focused more on individual traits and characteristics like beliefs, stereotype threat, how one thinks about oneself and one's abilities (Eccles, Wigfield, Harold, & Blumenfeld, 1993). More recently and more prominently within STEM education, identity has come to be investigated from a social interactionist perspective, considering learning (and identity formation) in classrooms in terms of changing participation in a community of practice (Lave & Wenger, 1991).

The relationship between identity and conceptual change is typically construed rather implicitly, involving instead the relationship between identity and disciplinary learning (as opposed to conceptual change, per se). A typical question that research has been addressing is: "Do particular relationships between the self and the discipline (e.g. identifying, or being identified, as a 'math person' or 'science person') afford or constrain participation in mathematics and science?" The chapters in this part of the volume are framed within a scope that is at once both more specific and also broader. The scope is more specific since the focus is explicitly on conceptual change as opposed to participation in STEM fields. On the other hand, the scope of the three papers is broader because they collectively challenge the conventional way that "normative" disciplinary learning is construed, while also emphasizing the need to investigate the relationship in the other direction. That is, they explicitly take up the question "How can science and mathematics learning become an inclusive experience where students, being personally involved in processes of conceptual understanding, develop their sense of self?"

Before situating the three contributions in this part with respect to each other, a bigger picture of the landscape of the relationship between disciplinary learning and identity is outlined. The first main section will lay out different ways that disciplinary learning can come into contact with identity, and will ultimately argue that, as we consider the relationship between identity and disciplinary learning, the field needs to critically revisit dangerous and limiting assumptions about the very nature of science and mathematics as disciplines. In the second main section, we focus on the three contributions of this part and discuss the ways they build upon or react to current approaches to both identity and conceptual change in the literature. We then develop a framework for comparing the three approaches. In the last section, we recommend future directions for work on developing the nexus between conceptual change and identity.

Identity and disciplinary learning in science and mathematics education: approaches, findings, and open issues

In order to lay out a big picture of how identity and disciplinary learning come into contact, we distinguish two currently prevailing approaches to exploring this contact: (1) how the identities that students are developing and the learning practices that are available to them may favor/impede disciplinary engagement/learning; and (2) how the ways that classrooms and, indeed, the discipline itself are organized may affect identity development. We describe each of those approaches in turn.

Identities and practices for sense-making

The first way to look at the relationship between identity and disciplinary learning is expressed in the following proposition: *Efforts to achieve conceptual growth need to include the learner's commitment to participate in practices aimed at achieving sense-making and formalization of explanatory concepts.* In an early discussion, Hatano and Inagaki (1987) referred to this commitment as motivation for comprehension. Kazemi and Stipek (2001) identified a property of classroom discourse that they called a press for conceptual mathematical thinking, which involves explanatory arguments in which students engage in consideration of meanings of mathematical concepts.

Two cases that illustrate this relation between identities and conceptual understanding were reported and discussed by diSessa (1985). Two students in an introductory physics class had contrasting ways of framing their knowing of physics. One, who characterized himself as a "results man," declined to attend to derivations presented by the instructor, preferring to focus on the formulas that were derived, that is, the "results." In contrast, another student who characterized himself as someone who aimed to achieve "real understanding," scarcely ever mentioned equations while solving physics problems. "… [M]any other students like [the other student discussed] frequently say something like 'I'm trying to think of the equation' when they find themselves in a tight squeeze with a problem" (diSessa, 1985, p. 103). diSessa used "naïve epistemologies" as a theoretical term to refer to this contrast.

Hammer, Elby, Scherr, and Redish (2005) called a similar distinction a difference between "epistemological frames." They exemplified this concept with two illustrative cases. The first was a discussion in which two physics students negotiated a frame for solving a problem: one of the students proposed focusing on numerical quantities and formulas; the other student advocated reasoning more informally and kinesthetically. The second case involved an individual student, Louis, who responded to an instructor's challenging question, "What is voltage?", by changing his approach to learning in the physics course, from memorizing formulaic solutions to developing an analogical model in which flow of electricity was represented as conditions of transport by "dump trucks" (e.g. a resistor corresponded to a road accident that slows the progress of other vehicles, and resistors in parallel corresponded to splitting the road, allowing faster transport).

The student in diSessa's class who sought "real understanding" and Louis, when he included construction of a model to learn properties of circuits, were characterized (by diSessa [1985] and by Hammer et al. [2005]) as having recurrent commitments to epistemological framings that included conceptual understanding. And the "results man" and Louis (before he adopted the practice of constructing analogical models) had recurrent commitments to epistemological framings that focused on correct use of formulas and calculation.

The lesson we can learn from these and other cases is that it seems appropriate to include recurrent characterizations of a person's or group's commitment to an epistemological framing for problem-solving and reasoning in a domain, as an aspect of that person's or group's identity in his, her, or their practice in an activity. Such characterizations can also be regarded as explanations for failure to engage in problem-solving, reasoning or, more generally, in learning. Heyd-Metzuyanim and Sfard (2012) start from the assumption that these kinds of characterizations mainly originate in social interactions and focus their attention on the construct of identity just to explain how the social makes its way into processes of individual learning. In particular, they build upon definitions of identity (Gee, 2000–2001) and operationalize them in discursive terms as a set of "endorsed, reifying, and significant stories about a person." The issue of how to define identity and how to relate it to processes of learning will be unpacked in detail in the second section of this chapter where we compare the three approaches taken to this issue in this part of the volume.

Science and mathematics as exclusive clubs

As alluded to above, an important impetus for research at the nexus of identity and disciplinary learning is understanding the relationships that individuals develop with STEM disciplinary content. The personal process of sense-making in science and mathematics learning is particularly problematic because typical power dynamics, classroom, and social norms turn STEM disciplines into exclusive clubs. Unveiling these power structures, rituals, and obligations is the main goal of much research on identity in science and mathematics education (e.g. Varelas, 2012).

Many researchers analyze identity from the perspective of participating in community (classroom) practices and characterize what is called "practice-related identity." This line of research provides a situated definition of "practice" as, for example, "constituted by a patterned set of actions, typically performed by members of a group based on common purposes and expectations, with shared cultural values, tools, and meanings" (Kelly, 2008, p. 99). Accordingly, identities are assumed to be malleable, formed progressively, and changed in practice, as an "internalized positional designation" (Stryker, 1980, p. 60). Agency, even when its role is acknowledged, is assumed to be limited by historical, social, institutional, and local structures (Carlone, 2012; Holland, Lachicotte, Skinner, & Cain, 1998).

In this line, Paul Cobb, Melissa Gresalfi, and colleagues (Cobb, Gresalfi, & Hodge, 2009; Gresalfi & Cobb, 2006; Gresalfi, Martin, Hand, & Greeno, 2009) coined the phrase "normative mathematical practices" to indicate the practices that produce a *normative identity* in a mathematics class:

> Normative identity as we define it comprises both the general and the specifically mathematical obligations that delineate the role of an effective student in a particular classroom. A student would have to identify with these obligations in order to develop an affiliation with classroom mathematical activity and thus with the role of an effective doer of mathematics as they are constituted in the classroom. Normative identity is a collective or communal notion rather than an individualistic notion.
>
> *(Cobb et al., 2009, pp. 43–44)*

Carlone, after adopting Cobb and colleagues' definition and after extending it to normative *scientific* practice, stresses that, behind the idea of normative identity, there is "a situated definition of competence" (Gresalfi et al., 2009) and highlights the great importance of "making visible some of the mechanisms that maintain science as powerful, narrow, elite, and exclusive" (Carlone, 2012, p. 23).

Normative scientific or mathematical practices and the image of STEM disciplines as exclusive clubs are crucial factors that negatively influence STEM educational choices for many students and contribute to the societal problem of STEM professional shortage (Bøe, Henriksen, Lyons, & Schreiner, 2011; Regan & DeWitt, 2015). In spite of several reports and international projects (e.g. the ROSE[1] and the IRIS[2] European projects), school physics and mathematics are resistant in changing their status as disciplines where the only option available to students is to either join the club *in toto* or be left out (Carlone, 2012).

In a study on the conditions that foster identity development, Nasir and Hand (2008) contrasted students' engagement in the context of basketball and in the context of math classes. Their observations confirm that the mathematics classes, unlike the basketball class, did not foster positive practice-linked identities since they failed to provide the students: "(a) access to the domain, (b) opportunities to take on integral roles, and (c) opportunities for self-expression in the practice" (Nasir & Hand, 2008, p. 143).

In the next section, we further elaborate the implications that the results that we have reported here, such as those of Nasir and Hand, may have in reconsidering the very nature of the disciplinary experience students have.

Disciplinary learning as a site for identity construction

In order to elaborate how disciplinary learning can become inclusive and a site for identity construction, we offer as an example the approach taken by Nasir, Rosebery, Warren, and Lee (2006), according to which "culture is integral to learning." Central to Nasir et al.'s approach is the following definition of culture, focused on practices:

> [Culture is] the constellation of practices historically developed and dynamically shaped by communities in order to accomplish the purposes they value. Such practices are constituted by the tools they use, the social networks with which they are connected, the ways they organize joint activity, the discourse they use and value (i.e. specific ways of conceptualizing, representing, evaluating and engaging with the world).
>
> *(Nasir et al., 2006, p. 489)*

Consistent with this definition, science and mathematics (like every other subject matter and exactly like other social and cultural practices) are also cultures, since they have historically developed practices: they have tools, social networks, ways to organize joint activity, and discourse that is used and valued. Moreover, science and mathematics have central cultural expectations and communities that accomplish the purposes they value (at the same time as having significant variation and inhomogeneity under the surface of the culture). Accordingly, learning science and mathematics implies that students must navigate among these repertoires of tools, networks, discourses, and ways to organize joint activity.

The feeling of alienation, of not belonging to scientific/mathematical discourse ("pupils perceive school science [...] dull, authoritarian, abstract and theoretical," (Sjøberg, 2002, p. 209), can be seen as a specific case of problematic navigation among diverse repertoires for most students, independent of their cultural origin and gender. Nevertheless, as Nasir and colleagues carefully highlight, women and students from under-represented groups face an exacerbation of the navigation problem. They point out that "these youth must learn to manage multiple developmental tasks: both the ordinary tasks of life course development, as well as tasks that involve managing sources of stress rooted in particular forms of institutional stigmatization," (Nasir et al., 2006, p. 489) due, for example, to assumptions regarding gender, race, poverty, language variation.

Based on many empirical studies, Nasir et al. (2006) arrived at a set of principles for the design of learning environments that foster inclusiveness and, we would say in this context, to foster the development of students' identity through the learning of a discipline. These include (i) making a learning context "psychologically safe," i.e. attending to students' needs for a sense of belonging and identification; (ii) making epistemological assumptions about the disciplinary domain visible; and (iii) providing students with a sense of possible learning trajectories.

These principles can help situate several approaches to the design of learning environments. As an example, Levrini, Levin, and Fantini (Part V, this volume) built upon them to inform a restructuring of the *content and teaching materials* targeted to upper secondary schools (grades 12 to 13, 17- to 19-year-old students). The materials are described extensively in other papers (e.g. Levrini & Fantini, 2013; Levrini, Fantini, Pecori, Tasquier, & Levin, 2015): they concern advanced topics of physics (thermodynamics, special relativity, and quantum physics) that are part of the physics curriculum of scientifically oriented schools in Italy.

In this restructuring, Nasir et al.'s principle of providing the sense of possible learning trajectories is implemented by Levrini et al. mainly through the design principle they call *multi-perspectiveness*. Multi-perspectiveness means that the same concepts are analyzed from different perspectives (like the macroscopic and microscopic perspective in thermal phenomena) and through different "voices" (like the voice of Einstein to introduce the algebraic/operational approach in special relativity, contrasted with the voice of Minkowski presenting the geometrical approach).

As for the two roles of offering students a plurality of access points to the discipline and of fostering a sense of positioning or belonging (the first and third principles in the list of Nasir et al.), they are mainly played by the design principle that Levrini et al. call *multidimensionality*. Multidimensionality means that the content and the different perspectives are analyzed and compared at different levels: conceptual and experimental but also for their philosophical–epistemological peculiarities or, in the case of climate change, for their sociological, political, and economic implications. Multidimensionality is aimed to encourage students with different interests and tastes to find their own position within physics.

Finally, the epistemological structure of the discipline is made visible mainly through the principle called *longitudinality*. Longitudinality means that what students are learning about is framed within the entire physics curriculum, including *long-term themes* that span different scientific domains and topics. Cross-cutting ideas like modeling and argumentation are pointed out and discussed in class so as to support students in recognizing what characterizes science as a whole (Tasquier, Levrini, & Dillon, 2016).

These principles can work at multiple levels. The chapter by Levrini, Levin, and Fantini (Chapter 26, this volume) shows how students navigate across authentic scientific discourse and practices and how such a specific form of navigation fosters both identity formation and deep disciplinary learning. However, the principles can also act at the level of classroom practices, including how a teacher orchestrates classroom discussions and what participation structures are realized (Levrini, Levin, Fantini, & Tasquier, submitted).

In the next section, we contrast the three particular approaches to the nexus between identity and conceptual change represented in this part of the volume: the approaches taken by Heyd-Metzuyanim, diSessa, and Levrini et al., respectively.

Comparing the approaches to the nexus between conceptual change and identity

Before exploring how the contributions to this part address the nexus between conceptual change and identity, we recall briefly how both conceptual change and identity are taken up in the literature. Unlike in the first part of this synthesis chapter, we now focus upon approaches that are particularly amenable for guiding work on studying the relationship between identity and *conceptual change*. Given that conceptual change is the topic of this volume and is discussed extensively, we will spend more time reviewing the approaches to identity and presenting how it is defined in science and mathematics education.

Defining conceptual change and identity

Research on conceptual change has generated a wide range of data and employed a wide variety of methodologies, including clinical interviews (Sherin, Krakowski, & Lee, 2012), conceptual questionnaires (Vosniadou, 1994), and less often, highly interactional data such as problem-solving sessions between small groups of individuals (Parnafes, 2007) and classroom discussions (diSessa, 2014; Levrini & diSessa, 2008). The preponderance of individual level data stems from the fact that the unit of analysis is typically conceptual structures of individuals. However, if both conceptual change and identity development are considered, particularly informative are those perspectives on conceptual change that prioritize the collection of data that does not remove almost all of the information about the interactional context in which an individual is learning. We think that it is not by accident that the three perspectives explored in this volume all emphasize the collection of process data from clinical interviews and classroom discussions. In terms of the specific epistemological commitments of the contributions within the part, two chapters are broadly informed by the Knowledge-in-Pieces perspective (diSessa and Levrini et al.) and one is informed by Sfard's commognitive approach (Heyd-Metzuyanim).

As for how identity is taken up and defined in the literature, we already mentioned in the introduction that more recently and more prominently within STEM education, identity has come to be investigated from a social interactionist perspective, according to which learning is a process through which individuals engage with the resources (other members, artifacts, etc.) in the setting. Learning is therefore considered to be a change in participation. Within this perspective, some researchers define learning as "the construction of identities" (Lave & Wenger, 1991). Thus, "in this conceptualization, identity and learning are not simply related, but are rather inseparable" (Gresalfi, 2014). This approach leads the researchers to focus on the ways that particular designs and activity settings create opportunities for students to engage with science or mathematics. More than trying to understand what someone has learned, the researchers aim to account for how that learning took place: that is, how individuals engage with resources, interact with the teacher and classmates, and change participation patterns within the social environment of the class.

The debate on the definitions of identity in science and mathematics education is controversial since each definition is an expression of a research approach, a way of looking at science or mathematics, education and, more broadly, a "worldview." To borrow from Chinn's synthesis in Part III of this volume, each definition is consistent with a research model that has different epistemic aims, ideals and processes (Chinn, Synthesis III, this volume).

An influential piece that helped to frame the debate on the way identity should be defined is the famous article of James P. Gee (2000–2001), in which he developed a discursive approach to analyze and compare possible ways to conceptualize identities. In this piece, Gee shows how identities are tied to the workings of historical, institutional, and sociocultural forces and loosely describes "identity" as "being recognized as a certain 'kind of person,' in a given context" (p. 99).

Foundational to Gee's discursive approach to identity is his notion of d/Discourses that identifies who individuals are in various contexts. In Gee (1996), discourse is defined to be the language individuals exchange in moment-to-moment interactions. In contrast, Discourses are "ways of behaving, interacting, valuing, thinking, believing, speaking, and often reading and writing that are accepted as instantiations of particular roles (or 'types of people') by specific *groups of people*" (Gee, 1996, p. viii). Discourses identify one with

> families of a certain sort, lawyers of a certain sort, bikers of a certain sort, business people of a certain sort, church members of a certain sort, African–Americans of a certain sort, women or men of a certain sort, and so on through a very long list.
>
> *(Gee, 1996, p. viii)*

Discourse and discourse are deeply interrelated since the choice of language and patterns of behavior used in local interactions are informed by participation in particular Discourses and, on the other hand, local interactions strengthen Discourses.

Gee outlines a multifaceted perspective to address the problematic issue of defining identity. He proposes four "ways to view identity," to show both the plurality of the discursive usages of the term "identity," and the historical and social influences that the various views of identity were subjected to. The four ways are: Nature-identity (a state developed from forces in nature, such as being an identical twin), Institution-identity (a position authorized by authorities within institutions, such as being a professor), Discourse-identity (an individual trait recognized in the discourse/dialog of/with "rational" individuals, such as being charismatic), and Affinity-identity (experiences shared in the practice of "affinity groups," such as being a "Trekkie") (Gee, 2000–2001).

The individuation of these four ways to view identity has been influenced by the sociological debate on post-modernism that saw the fundamental contributions of intellectuals like Bauman (1997, 2000), Beck (1992), and Giddens (1991). Drawing upon this debate, Gee analyzes the relationship between these views of identity as a key to comparing different societies and different historical periods. The four perspectives are, however, argued to be not separate from each other and in some societies all the perspectives are present and socially act.

The most divisive point of Gee's perspective is the notion of "core identity" that he defines as follows:

> Each person has had a unique trajectory through "Discursive space." That is, he or she has, through time, in a certain order, had specific experiences within specific discourses (i.e. been recognized, at a time and place, one way and not another), some recurring and others not. This trajectory and the person's own narrativization (Mishler, 2000) of it is what constitutes his or her (never fully formed or always potentially changing) "core identity."
>
> *(Gee, 2000–2001, p. 111)*

As we will discuss, the notion of "core identity" is a point of divergence between the approaches taken by the three contributions to this part of the volume.

A framework for comparison of the three approaches

The approaches described in the three chapters of this part appear to be very different from one another. Nevertheless, if they are read carefully, a common theoretical skeleton can be pointed out, based upon shared research assumptions and methodological features. In the spirit of the whole volume and to contribute to moving the field toward a synthesis, we have focused on these common structural aspects and built a framework for comparing the different approaches. Hence, the framework that we describe now has been developed from a bottom-up analysis of the common and distinctive features of the three chapters and it will be used, afterwards, to present the approaches so as to both stress their specificities and point out their complementarities.

The first common feature of the three approaches concerns the baseline—but not trivial—assumption that identity and conceptual change are two different foci of attention but, in spite of that, they have a special relationship that is worth addressing. The baseline assumption includes the belief that identity is not something fixed and given but, rather, a dynamic construct that furthermore interacts with the *process* of conceptual change. The three contributions to this part each start by defining, from their perspective, the exact nature of the dynamic construct of identity and how it interacts with learning processes.

The second assumption underlying all the approaches in this part is that the relation between identity and conceptual change can be *rigorously investigated*. This means, as diSessa (Chapter 1, this volume) explains in his chapter on conceptual change, that the nexus is addressable through an approach characterized by: (1) theoretical explicitness, (2) analytical clarity, and (3) empirical tractability. This assumption implies the need to find a commensurate way to discuss both phenomena (identity and conceptual change) or, in other words, to move the study of identity and conceptual change onto either the same ontological level or onto a comparable level. Finally, the three approaches make explicit choices about the time and space scale of the phenomenon being analyzed when addressing the nexus between identity and conceptual change.

Following Lemke (2000), we find that the notions of time and space scales are important to understand how each contributor to this part has studied identity in contexts of disciplinary learning. Within research on cognition, the notion of time scale can be a very useful dimension to distinguish—and identify as complementary—approaches that focus respectively on: the threshold of cognition, the length of a thought sequence, the duration of a lesson and, finally, much longer time scales, like that required for substantial conceptual development to occur (Sherin, Synthesis I, this volume). Saxe (Chapter 6, this volume), for example, distinguishes changes:

> over short durations, as individuals cognize and structure solutions to problems during 'in-the-moment' activities (microgenesis); over extended periods of individual development, as individuals create new ways of thinking (ontogenesis); and, over durations in community life, as the common ground of talk and action is (often unwittingly) reproduced and altered in networks of interlocutors (sociogenesis).
>
> *(p. 51)*

The space scale is also a very useful comparative dimension and we interpret it as concerning the number and type of interactions between an individual and others. Some of the "actors" involved in an interaction under study may be hidden or implicit, like societal expectations, stereotyped projections, or implicit scientific norms. Typically, studies of conceptual change have focused on the individual as a cognizing unit. Work from the perspective of distributed cognition (Hutchins, 1995; Stevens & Hall, 1998) has encouraged us to consider the cognitive activity of units larger than the individual. Thus, the boundaries of cognition have a space dimension that depends on the chosen approach and, also when considering the study of identity, a rigorous approach, implicitly or explicitly, tracks the unit of analysis in terms of space. While studies of identity in science and mathematics education have so far focused on interactions between an individual and a small group or class on time scales ranging from moment-by-moment to years of classroom instruction, there are calls for expanding studies of identity in both time and space dimensions (Langer-Osuna & Esmonde, 2017) so as to better understand how school, community, and societal structures shape what happens within the classroom and within local interactions.

In the next three sections, we will go through each approach represented within Part V in turn and will use the same structure to report each approach. We will begin by discussing (1) the theoretical commitments of the researcher with respect to studying both identity and conceptual change; (2) how the nexus between identity and conceptual change is conceptualized—that is how the two constructs are defined, what dynamic processes are examined and how the interaction between such processes is modeled; and (3) what time and space scales are implied by the approach. This strategy will allow us both to point out a synthetic convergent picture of the field, and to frame the diversities and complementarities of the approaches.

Heyd-Metzuyanim's narrative approach to identity and conceptual change

Heyd-Metzuyanim draws upon a discursive approach to identity developed by Anna Sfard and colleagues (Sfard & Prusak, 2005). In their paper, they pointed out the proclivity of replacing talk about actions with talk about states (reifying is-statements), that is, "turning properties about actions into properties of actors" (p. 16). The process of identity formation, "identifying" in their perspective, is hence a discursive activity and identities are "collections of stories about persons or, more specifically, … those narratives about individuals that are *reifying, endorsable,* and *significant*" (p. 16). They develop a position that takes into consideration both the stories that individuals tell about themselves, and also those told about others, allowing for the possibility that what a person endorses as true about themselves may not be the narrative others would endorse. Multiple identities exist for every person. Further, there is no assumption that the stories about a person are consistent with each other. One of the main impetuses for Sfard and Prusak's narrative definition of identity is to avoid objectification (i.e. avoiding the idea that identity is a "thing," presumably located in individuals). This is one of the main ways that they react to Gee (2000–2001) and his notion of "core identity."

Heyd-Metzuyanim's approach to researching the nexus between identity and conceptual change built directly upon Sfard and Prusak's (2005) discursive approach and has built upon her own studies of identity development in mathematics classrooms (Heyd-Metzuyanim, Chapter 24, this volume). In addressing conceptual change, she likewise chose a discursive definition of conceptual change, building upon Sfard's commognitive perspective (Sfard, 2007, 2008) that allowed her to position conceptual change/learning at the same ontological level of identity, as well as at the same space and time scales:

> Conceptual change is most likely the accretion of many small instances of meta-level shifts in the use of routines. [...] Similarly, the formation of identity narratives is a continuous process of recurring subjectifications and (sometimes contradicting) positioning acts, gradually accrued into stable narratives that are applied by a person to himself or to others, and carried from one situation to another. The processes underlying the formation of stable identity narratives and lasting conceptual change in essence co-constitute each other. They occur concomitantly and continuously in the micro-scale of problem solving interactions. (Heyd-Metzuyanim, Chapter 24, this volume, p. 295)

Thus, Heyd-Metzuyanim stresses the two dynamical processes whose interaction is under investigation: on the one hand, "conceptual change is most likely the *accretion of many small instances of meta-level shifts* in the use of routines"; on the other hand, "identity formation" is meant as "the *formation of stable identity narratives*" (emphasis added). The two processes are, hence, argued to "co-constitute each other" and their interaction is worth addressing since it can help explain specific learning phenomena that can be observed, for example, in problem-solving interactions. Accordingly, within the analysis developed in her chapter in this part, Heyd-Metzuyanim's focus of research attention is *very local in time*, on the interrelation between in-the-moment disciplinary learning and in-the-moment identity formation. With respect to "space," the type of interactions considered are mainly between *two persons or even with the self.*

To sum up, we can say that the key move that Heyd-Metzuyanim describes in her chapter involves describing the two dynamical constructs of identity formation and conceptual change in terms of discourse, as well as in their contextual application to interpret problem-solving interactions. This move allows her to focus on very specific moments of learning and very specific interactions. As opposed to merely focusing on conceptual change and learning in context, her approach enables her to illuminate the role of local interactions relevant to identity development.

DiSessa's knowledge-based approach to identity and conceptual change

In contrast to Heyd-Metzuyanim, diSessa chose a knowledge-based approach to identity, like his approach to studying conceptual change (diSessa, Chapter 1, this volume), whereby it is necessary to recognize and study the nature of the knowledge that underlies what he calls one's *characterizations* of oneself and others. The knowledge-based approach to identity by diSessa, unlike the narrative approach of Heyd-Metzuyanim, foresees a stratified definition of identity that includes, following Gee, a model of "intrinsic identity." Thus, this places diSessa's model of intrinsic identity on a different ontological level when compared to Sfard and Prusak (2005) and Heyd-Metzuyanim. Whereas Gee's four types of identity draw upon an historical reconstruction of sociological changes, diSessa points out a plurality of models of identity according to their different "regimes of human knowledge." diSessa's models of identity include: personal, managed, intrinsic, and projected identity. Like Gee's identity types, they "are not alternatives, but a multiplicity. All of them are enacted at different times, by different actors" (diSessa, Chapter 25, this volume, p. 298).

The knowledge-based approach to identity allows diSessa to transfer the theoretical and methodological apparatus he has developed to study conceptual change (diSessa, Chapter 1, this volume) to the study of identity. Underlying this approach there are at least three strong assumptions: "learning is substantially a recrafting of naïve conceptual resources" (diSessa, Chapter 1, this volume, p. 9); every person is unique and diversities have to be systematically honored within any theoretical approach; regularities, commonalities and recognizable patterns are, in case one observes them, emergent properties of a complex underlying world and they have to be explained through an empirical, fine-grained, and multidimensional analytic approach.

According to assumptions like these, a knowledge-based approach aims to recognize the knowledge that individuals have—and how that knowledge is activated and used—in their processes of learning (conceptual change) and of characterizing themselves and others (identity formation and/or identity management). When this approach is transferred to the study of identity, it focuses analytic attention on the knowledge that people use to describe themselves and others (What is the "descriptive vocabulary" for forming *characterizations*?) and also on what individuals attend to when they are characterizing others (What inferences do they make when characterizing others, the *inferential backdrop*? What do people do with this information?).

As in his studies of conceptual change, diSessa points out that inarticulate sensations, such as the feeling of epiphany or joy during participating in mathematical or scientific activity (or in contrast, the feeling of revulsion toward particular activities or communities) have consequences within the inferential backdrop. This may be difficult to theorize about with our current theoretical machinery, but diSessa highlights them as important to recognize as part of the big picture. DiSessa seems particularly interested in how identity is managed by an individual, how intrinsic identity manifests itself accordingly to the principles of contextuality or adaptation and how projected identity acts in moment-by-moment interactions.

With respect to time scale, as in diSessa's approach to conceptual change (the Knowledge-in-Pieces (KiP) perspective), a distinctive methodological issue of the approach to identity study that he outlines is the accountability to moment-by-moment processes of learning. As diSessa points out, accountability to moment-by-moment process data is rare within the field of conceptual change. Yet, it is this grain size and time scale of work that produces data that can be analyzed both through the lens of conceptual change and the lens of identity formation.

With respect to the space scale (i.e. the type of interactions and relationships considered), diSessa identifies places where it may be productive to consider expanding the focus on identity research. At least with respect to the issue of considering the nexus of identity and conceptual change, he advocates analyzing the role of the individual in identity formation and management. Indeed, the foci for research identified by diSessa include the knowledge-based strategizing of individuals in managing their identities, or the role of feelings in developing identity and relationship to the discipline.

To sum up, from this perspective, identity and conceptual change are viewed as two research foci, both contributing to the same pursuit of understanding the "continuities and differences between everyday and scientific understandings" (diSessa, Chapter 25, this volume, p. 302). More precisely the knowledge-based analysis of identity appears as a crucial enrichment of the analysis of conceptual change so as to include how emotional, cultural, and social interactional factors act in students' learning.

Levrini, Levin, and Fantini's appropriation approach to identity and conceptual change

Levrini, Levin, and Fantini chose a third way to make identity and conceptual change commensurable: they developed the holistic construct of "appropriation" that already is positioned at the nexus of conceptual change and identity. In common with the emphasis on operationalization found in Gee, Heyd-Metzuyanim, and diSessa, the work on appropriation also starts from the need to carefully operationalize the construct. In this case, the process of operationalizing resulted in the individuation of five markers that can be recognized in the discourse of students who appropriated the ideas of physics that they were learning. It was possible to recognize the following markers in the discourse of these students: "(A) an expression of a personal 'signature' idea, (B) grounded in the discipline, (C) thick, in that it involves a metacognitive and epistemological dimension, (D) non-incidental, in the sense of being consistently used throughout classroom activities and (E) a carrier of social relationships, in that it positions the student within the classroom community" (Levrini et al., 2015, p. 26). As the markers show, appropriation involves different layers of learning, including conceptual, epistemological, metacognitive, and social layers. This stratification appears in students' discourse, as the emergent property of a complex dynamical process of positioning "with respect to the discipline (marker B), with respect to the class (marker E) and with respect to their own personal story of who they are as a person and a learner (marker A, C, D)" (Levrini et al., Chapter 26, this volume, p. 306).

The definition of appropriation provides a framework where disciplinary learning and identity can be compared and related. On the one hand, disciplinary learning is the grounding dimension of a broader and multidimensional process of learning (marker B). On the other hand, identity formation is seen as the recurrence over time of the tri-partite positioning dynamic, where tastes and interests are explored, sought, and managed in a confrontation with the discipline and its rules, as well as within classroom dynamics. This process of positioning is argued to foster identity formation, in the sense that this dynamic, if recurrent over time, "creates a context in which a student must engage with questions like 'Who am I?' 'Who do I want to become?' and 'Who do I want to be perceived as?'" (Levrini et al., Chapter 26, this volume, p. 309)

In their chapter in Part V, Levrini et al. contributed a particular way of thinking about the moment in conceptual change/learning where the individual is actually populating their understanding of scientific content (such as temperature, in the example given of Matteo and Michele) with their personal tastes and purposes. This leads them to introduce the notion of *personal concept projection*, which is constructed around individuals' "signature ideas." The notion of personal concept projection is an enrichment of the model of coordination class, developed by diSessa to model conceptual change (diSessa, Chapter 1, this volume) and introduces a locus, in that theoretical model, where an event contributing to identity formation can happen.

This moment-by-moment time scale of observation makes the appropriation approach adopted by Levrini et al. similar to the approaches of Heyd-Metzuyanim and diSessa. However, we note that within this approach medium and longer time scales must also be considered. Marker D [non-incidental] implies that researchers must search for several learning moments over classes to check if and how the idiosyncratic "signature" idea emerges. Moreover, the model assumes that the idiosyncratic idea identified in the discourse of students is the result of a longer and interdisciplinary process (such as the case of Matteo, where the signature idea that permeated his study of thermodynamics came from his interest in philosophy).

As for the space scale, Levrini et al.'s approach involves careful attention to the design of the disciplinary content and learning environment (through the design principles discussed earlier) and thus students are supported in interacting with the discipline in multifaceted ways that promote developing personal positioning and tastes with respect to what they are learning. As a consequence, the character of identity development and conceptual change, considered in this approach, are intimately related to the relationship of the self and others to the discipline. This line of research offers a critical perspective on the assumptions that we make about the discipline and offers a vision that includes a deep restructuring of disciplinary content in order to foster students' aesthetic and personal engagement.

Convergences and complementarities among the approaches focused on the nexus between identity and conceptual change

When we compare theories of the nexus between identity and conceptual change, the first impression is that they are so different that only a pluralistic argument can be supported, as in Sandra Mitchell's (2003) argument for integrative pluralism in biology. Mitchell argued that, because of the complexity of phenomena in biology, we will not succeed in developing a single, best theory of living systems. Instead, we will be able to develop multiple, valid explanatory analyses, each of which supports conceptual understanding of some of the important phenomena of the domain.

Indeed, the various approaches differ with regard to the notion of "core identity" in a way that is epistemically non-trivial. The discursive approach taken by Heyd-Metzuyanim (building upon Sfard & Prusak, 2005) explicitly avoided notions such as "core identity" or any objectification. In contrast, diSessa critiqued this theoretical move by Sfard and Prusak for its lack of "ground truth" and proposed the need for a model of "intrinsic identity" (among other models). Finally, the construct of appropriation that Levrini, Levin, and Fantini operationalized (in particular the idea that appropriation is related to recurrent narrativizations of students' "signature ideas") is consistent with the idea that each student searches for a unique trajectory through discursive space and, in this sense, it is consistent with Gee's notion of core identity.

Moreover, significant distinctions between the approaches concern (i) the relevance of the nexus (why it is worth analyzing), (ii) the cognitive processes of conceptual change and identity formation/management under inspection, and (iii) the space and time scales of the phenomenon under study. More evidently, there is a larger grain size distinction between approaches that originates from the vast differences in the nature of the broader research program each researcher is addressing:

- Heyd-Metzuyanim's approach to the nexus focuses on the need to consider both identity and conceptual change together when interpreting student impasses and difficulty in problem-solving interactions;
- diSessa's approach to the nexus connects with a larger program of work related to understanding the nature and form of human knowledge, including intuitive and inarticulate forms of knowledge related to identity management;
- Levrini et al. address the nexus in reference to a larger program of work aimed at understanding how learning science can support students broadly in their personal development as young people.

In spite of all these differences, to recapitulate a point that we made when we began our discussion of the contributions, all three approaches share a theoretical structure and some basic structural features: all of them consider identity and conceptual change as distinct constructs (as opposed to viewing them as one and the same thing, as is typical in a strictly sociocultural reading of learning processes) and each involves operationalizing both constructs in a way that allows for the interplay between identity and conceptual change to be studied, including coordinating both time and space scales. Heyd-Metzuyanim moved both constructs to the same ontological level (discourse). DiSessa moved the study of identity to the knowledge level, focusing on the knowledge involved in managing identity relations. Levrini et al. chose a construct, appropriation, which was already situated at the nexus of identity and conceptual change. More deeply, they all focus on pointing out *characterizations* that can indicate what discourse or knowledge elements can be recognized as related to identity when students are involved in developing conceptual understanding.

These common aspects appear robust enough to argue that the three approaches can be developed as a complementary program of work (Sherin, Part I, this volume) and not as diverse, contrasting programs. To support this claim, the future directions outlined in the single chapters can be seen as aspects of an integrated research program whose main goal is to build up a (discursive practices or knowledge) theory of the relationship between identity formation and conceptual change. The program toward such a theory implies studies where:

1 the *characterizations* of discourse and of facets of knowledge related to identity are made more and more explicit and systematically recognizable when students engage with each other and with learning science or mathematics. Such characterizations include positioning actions (with respect to the self, the others and the discipline), identification narratives, meta-discursive boundary crossings, idiosyncratic terms, or utterances, but also (more or less implicit) facets related to managed or projected identity and to feelings (joy, epiphany, revulsion, etc.);

2 the *descriptive vocabulary* involved in characterizing the self and others, including a descriptive vocabulary that may be tacit, is empirically grounded and the *inferential backdrop* tested for its explanatory power;

3 time and space scales are progressively enlarged and differentiated so as to unpack when emergent and enduring identity narratives manifest themselves in moment-by-moment learning interactions and, *vice versa*, to recognize *what* learning moments impact enduring identity formation and *how*.

4 the implications for teaching practice are systematically investigated, both for the design and management of teaching resources and activities, but also concerning how disciplinary content can be restructured.

Appropriate methodologies present several challenges. The first challenge concerns the level of consensus that the search for vocabulary and the specification of characterizations can reach (i.e. the locus where the epistemological and ontological differences can emerge and where eventual theoretical incommensurabilities can be explicitly addressed) (Sherin, Part I, this volume). Another challenge to be grappled with will emerge in pushing forward the agenda of expanding the time and space scales while also maintaining an analysis of the individual in local context. More generally, in nurturing this new line of work, methodological challenges to the field must be part of the continuing effort to make these constructs speak to each other in powerful and rigorous ways.

The most demanding challenge, however, is not methodological, but epistemological and cultural. We think we can say that all three approaches assume that personal diversities—as well as cultural and gender diversities—are central to learning and, as such, should have a place in every theory of learning and teaching practice. As a consequence, the aim to build a serious theory of the nexus between identity and conceptual change implies questioning and deeply revising cultural habits around STEM education and conventional views of science and mathematics. The image of science and mathematics as exclusive clubs must be broken down and the very nature of the discipline that students experience must be reconsidered. Although extremely tough, this challenge is worth accepting because it positions research on conceptual change at the very core of a crucial democratic debate within contemporary society: how can disciplinary teaching/learning in schools foster students' identities as capable persons and citizens in a global, fragile, and rapidly changing world?

Acknowledgments

We are deeply grateful to Tamer Amin for his careful reading and substantial suggestions on drafts of this chapter. We also thank the authors of the chapters in this part for their thoughtful and generative comments.

Notes

1 ROSE stands for "The Relevance of Science Education" (http://roseproject.no/).
2 IRIS stands for "Interests and Recruitment in Science" (http://iri.uni-lj.si/data/Projekti/IRIS/irisarhiv/about-iris/index.html).

References

Bauman, Z. (1997). *Postmodernity and its discontents*. New York: New York University Press.
Bauman, Z. (2000). *Liquid modernity*. Cambridge: Polity Press.
Beck, U. (1992). *Risk Society*. London: Sage.
Bøe, M. V., Henriksen, E. K., Lyons, T., & Schreiner, C. (2011). Participation in science and technology: Young people's achievement-related choices in late modern societies. *Studies in Science Education*, 47(1), 37–72. doi:10.1080/03057267.2011.549621.
Carlone, H. B. (2012). Methodological considerations for studying identities in school science: An anthropological approach. In M. Varelas (ed.), *Identity construction and*

science education research: Learning, teaching, and being in multiple contexts (pp. 9–25). Rotterdam: Sense Publisher.

Cobb, P., Gresalfi, M., & Hodge, L. L. (2009). An interpretive scheme for analyzing the identities that students develop in mathematics classrooms. *Journal for Research in Mathematics Education, 40*(1), 40–68.

diSessa, A. A. (1985). Knowing about learning. In E. Klein (Ed.), *Children and computers* (pp. 97–124) *New directions for Child Development no. 28.* San Francisco, CA: Jossey-Bass.

diSessa, A. A. (2014). The construction of causal schemes: Learning mechanisms at the knowledge level. *Cognitive Science, 38*(5), 795–850.

Eccles, J. S., Wigfield, A., Harold, R., & Blumenfeld, P. B. (1993). Age and gender differences in children's self and task perceptions during elementary school. *Child Development, 64,* 830–847.

Gee, J. P. (1996). *Social linguistics and literacies: Ideology in Discourses.* Philadelphia, PA: The Falmer Press, Taylor and Francis, Inc.

Gee, J. P. (2000–2001). Identity as an analytic lens for research in education. *Review of Research in Education, 25,* 99–125.

Giddens, A. (1991). *Modernity and self-identity.* Cambridge: Polity Press.

Gresalfi, M. (2014). Identity as patterns of participation. Paper contributed to the symposium. *The interplay between identity and conceptual change: Productive synergies and new directions for research* (Organizer: L. Branchetti). 9th International Conference on Conceptual Change, EARLI, August 26–29, 2014, Bologna, Italy.

Gresalfi, M. S., & Cobb, P. (2006). Cultivating students' discipline-specific dispositions as a critical goal for pedagogy and equity. *Pedagogies: An International Journal, 1*(1), 49–57.

Gresalfi, M., Martin, T., Hand, V., & Greeno, J. (2009). Constructing competence: An analysis of student participation in the activity systems of mathematics classrooms. *Educational Studies in Mathematics, 70,* 49–70.

Hammer, D. M., Elby, A., Scherr, R. E., & Redish, E. F. (2005). Resources, framing, and transfer. In J. P. Mestre (Ed.), *Transfer of learning from a modern multidisciplinary perspective* (pp. 89–120). Greenwich, CT: Information Age Publishing.

Hatano, G., & Inagaki, K. (1987). A theory of motivation for comprehension and its application to mathematics instruction. In T. A. Romberg & D. M. Stewart (Eds.), *The monitoring of school mathematics: Background papers, volume 2: Implications from psychology; outcomes of instruction* (pp. 27–46). Madison, WI: Wisconsin Center for Education Research.

Heyd-Metzuyanim, E., & Sfard, A. (2012). Identity struggles in the mathematics classroom: Learning mathematics as an interplay between mathematizing and identifying. *International Journal of Educational Research, 51–52,* 128–145.

Holland, D., Lachicotte, W., Skinner, D., & Cain, C. (1998). *Identity and agency in cultural worlds.* Cambridge, MA: Harvard University Press.

Hutchins, E. (1995). *Cognition in the wild.* Cambridge, MA: MIT press.

Kazemi, E., & Stipek, D. (2001). Promoting conceptual thinking in four upper-elementary mathematics classrooms. *The Elementary School Journal, 102*(1), 59–80.

Kelly, G. J. (2008). Inquiry, activity, and epistemic practice. In R. A. Duschl & R. E. Grandy (Eds.), *Teaching scientific inquiry: Recommendations for research and implementation* (pp. 99–117). Rotterdam: Sense Publishers.

Langer-Osuna, J., & Esmonde, I. (2017). Identity in research on mathematics education. In J. Cai (Ed.) *Compendium for research in mathematics education.* Reston, VA: National Council of Teachers of Mathematics.

Lave, J., & Wenger, E. (1991). *Situated learning: Legitimate peripheral participation.* New York: Cambridge University Press.

Lemke, J. L. (2000). Across the scales of time: Artifacts, activities, and meanings in ecosocial systems. *Mind, Culture, and Activity, 7*(4), 273–290.

Levrini, O., & diSessa, A. A. (2008). How students learn from multiple contexts and definitions: Proper time as a coordination class. *Physical Review Special Topics-Physics Education Research 4*, 010107.

Levrini, O., & Fantini, P. (2013). Encountering productive forms of complexity in learning modern physics. *Science & Education, 22*(8), 1895–1910, doi:10.1007/s11191-013-9587-4.

Levrini, O., Fantini, P., Pecori, B., Tasquier, G., & Levin, M. (2015). Defining and operationalizing 'appropriation' for science learning, *Journal of the Learning Sciences, 24*(1), 93–136, doi:10.1080/10508406.2014.928215.

Levrini, O., Levin, M., Fantini, P., & Tasquier, G. (submitted). Orchestration patterns that manage the tension between collective disciplinary understanding and personal engagement.

Mishler, E. (2000). *Storylines: Craftartists' narratives of identity.* Cambridge, MA: Harvard University Press.

Mitchell, S. D. (2003). *Biological complexity and integrative pluralism.* Cambridge: Cambridge University Press.

Nasir, N. S., & Hand, V. (2008). From the court to the classroom: Opportunities for engagement, learning, and identity in basketball and classroom mathematics, *Journal of the Learning Sciences, 17*(2), 143–179, doi:10.1080/10508400801986108.

Nasir, N. S., Rosebery, A. S., Warren, B., Lee, C. D. (2006). Learning as a cultural process. In Sawyer K. (ed.), *The Cambridge handbook of the learning sciences* (pp. 489–504). Cambridge: Cambridge University Press.

Parnafes, O. (2007). What does "fast" mean? Understanding the physical world through computational representations. *The Journal of the Learning Sciences, 16*(3), 415–450.

Regan, E., & DeWitt, J. (2015). Attitudes, interest and factors influencing STEM enrolment behaviour: An overview of relevant literature. In E. K. Henriksen, J. Dillon, J. Ryder (Eds.), *Understanding student participation and choice in science and technology education* (pp. 63–88). Dordrecht Heidelberg New York London: Springer. doi:10.1007/978-94-007-7793-4.

Sfard, A. (2007). Reconceptualizing conceptual change. In S. Vosniadou, A. Baltas, & X. Vamvakoussi (Eds.), *Reframing the conceptual change approach in learning and instruction* (pp. 331–337). Amsterdan: Elsevier.

Sfard, A. (2008). *Thinking as communicating: Human development, the growth of discourses, and mathematizing.* Cambridge: Cambridge University Press.

Sfard, A., & Prusak, A. (2005). Telling identities: In search of an analytic tool for investigating learning as a culturally shaped activity. *Educational Researcher, 34*, 14, doi:10.3102/0013189X034004014.

Sherin, B. L., Krakowski, M., & Lee, V. R. (2012). Some assembly required: How scientific explanations are constructed during clinical interviews. *Journal of Research in Science Teaching, 49*(2), 166–198.

Sjøberg, S. (2002). Science and technology education in Europe: Current challenges and possible solutions. In E. Jenkins (ed). *Innovations in science and technology education,* Vol. VIII (pp. 201–228). Paris: UNESCO.

Stevens, R., & Hall, R. (1998). Disciplined perception: Learning to see in technoscience. In M. Lampert and M. Blunk (Eds.), *Talking mathematics in school: Studies of teaching and learning* (pp. 107–149). Cambridge: Cambridge University Press.

Stryker, S. (1980). *Symbolic interactionism: A social structural version.* Menlo Park, CA: Benjamin-Cummings.

Tasquier, G., Levrini, O., & Dillon, J. (2016). Exploring students' epistemological knowledge of models and modelling in science: Results from a teaching/learning experience on climate change. *International Journal of Science Education, 38*(4), 539–563. doi:10.1080/09500693.2016.1148828.

Varelas, M. (2012). (ed.). *Identity construction and science education research: Learning, teaching, and being in multiple contexts.* Rotterdam: Sense Publisher.

Vosniadou, S. (1994). Capturing and modeling the process of conceptual change. *Learning and Instruction, 4*(1), 45–69.

Facing the challenge of programmatic research on conceptual change

Tamer G. Amin and Olivia Levrini[1]

Introduction

As suggested in the introduction to this book, research on conceptual change is currently in a state of fragmentation. We conceived this book as a response to this situation and designed it in a way that might help point the field in a more programmatic direction. Most edited volumes collecting work on conceptual change have highlighted diversity: the diversity of the theoretical perspectives, the diversity of domains in which conceptual change is explored, and the diversity of ways in which our understanding of conceptual change has been applied to instruction (e.g. Vosniadou, 2013). This volume was designed based on evidence that diverse research perspectives have converged in significant ways (Amin, Smith, & Wiser, 2014) and our belief that distinct strands of research do complement each other in ways that can be explicitly articulated. Moreover, this design rests on an epistemological assumption that programmatic scientific research on conceptual change is possible and valuable—namely, that we can describe empirical phenomena clearly and formulate empirical generalizations precisely; that we can put forward explanatory theories that can be tested empirically and that theoretical constructs elaborated within different strands of research can (and should) be identified clearly as overlapping with one another or as making conflicting claims that need to be evaluated empirically. We also believe that we will be more successful in applying our knowledge to practical problems and in contributing to school reform processes if we commit, as a community, to pursuing a more programmatic agenda. We recognize that the existence of multiple perspectives can be a source of richness in a field of inquiry, especially when these perspectives are explicitly and clearly formulated and differences rigorously discussed (Chinn, 2016). However, we also believe that excessive diversity can be harmful and that in such circumstances consolidation is needed. In our view, inquiry into conceptual change is currently in need of consolidation.

The book was structured in five parts. Part I put side-by-side a number of theoretical perspectives that are often contrasted, treatments of conceptual change in different domains, and research addressing a range of different target phenomena spanning different time scales. Six short chapters representing this range of views and areas of focus were followed by a longer synthesis chapter that articulated clearly the challenges that synthesis poses and outlined a starting point for synthesis of diverse perspectives. Each of the remaining four parts of the book addressed a key strand of empirical research on conceptual change. While there are connections between these strands, these largely complement one another. Each strand was addressed through a set of short chapters representing a range of key programs of research, which were also followed by a longer synthesis chapter. Within each strand, the researchers adopt different theoretical lenses and use different methodological approaches. Indeed, these diverse programs span different disciplines including developmental psychology, education, educational psychology, and the learning sciences. Each synthesis related the different perspectives reflected in the short chapters to one another, and situated them with respect to the literature addressing that strand more broadly. These synthesis chapters offered a view of how different programs of research within each strand both converge and complement one another.

In this concluding contribution, we engage in a second layer of synthesis, offering what we view as a number of different synthetic readings of the content of this book. In a first reading, we describe the different *ways* in which the authors of the synthesis chapters in each of the five parts of the book approached the task of synthesis. Next, we outline what we call a "Synthetic Narrative" which brings together a picture of the nature of conceptual change and its implications for instruction that emerge from the five parts of the book. We intend this narrative as a framework through which to view the various strands of research on conceptual change as parts of a larger whole; a kind of road map of the research landscape. In a third reading, we reflect on how some of the challenges to synthesis were addressed in this book and then conclude with a discussion of important challenges that we must still face as a community of researchers if we hope to move forward with a more programmatic orientation to research on conceptual change.

Approaches to synthesis

Synthesizing a diverse research literature is a demanding task. The design of the book was the first step toward synthesis: key theoretical perspectives and strands of research were identified and researchers who represent these perspectives and have made prominent contributions to these strands were invited to contribute. The synthesis chapters at the end of each part constitute the book's backbone. We provided the authors of the syntheses with broad guidelines to establish a degree of continuity across those chapters. We asked them to use the research discussed in the short chapters as a basis for offering a synthetic overview of the research in that area. That is, they were not asked to prepare "discussant's remarks" but rather to lay out a broader picture of the literature with respect to which the research described in the short chapters can be situated. Within those broad constraints, the authors of the synthesis chapters approached their task as they found appropriate. The outcome was a range of different approaches to the task of synthesis. We consider identifying and comparing these approaches to be one of the contributions of this book and so begin this chapter by describing them. We do not summarize the *results* of their syntheses in this section (i.e. what they conclude about research on conceptual change dealing with the aspect they address) but focus on their *approaches* to the task. These results are interwoven into the "Synthetic Narrative" we present in the next section.

We identified two dimensions along which we found it helpful to contrast the different approaches taken to synthesis: the first can be described as the degree to which the range of research programs were amenable to synthesis and thus forced considerable discussion of the obstacles to the synthetic task; the second is the degree to which the approach taken was "bottom-up," looking to see if multiple research programs cluster naturally into groups, as opposed to "top-down" approaches that viewed a range of research programs through the lens of a theoretical perspective selected from the outset. We describe the different approaches taken by the authors of the synthesis chapters and compare them in relation to these two dimensions.

We begin with two synthesis chapters where the authors needed to do the most work to discuss obstacles to, and conceive of possibilities for, synthesis: Bruce Sherin's synthesis for Part I, 'The Nature of Concepts and Conceptual Change,' and Mariana Levin, Olivia Levrini, and Jim Greeno's synthesis for Part V, 'Identity and Conceptual Change.'

Sherin's task was to synthesize research programs that are foundational and broad in scope. The contributions to Part I are foundational in the sense that they represent quite different theoretical perspectives: Knowledge-in-Pieces, Framework Theory, and the Ontological Shift views of conceptual change. Moreover, the contributions span domains: science, mathematics, and the social sciences. They also address widely contrasting target phenomena: learning in the context of formal instruction, development over the lifespan and conceptual change at a sociohistorical level in a community.

Given the differences between these contributions, the challenges of synthesis are formidable and Sherin engages in a meta-theoretical reflection on the nature of synthesis and obstacles to it. He discusses whether programs of research on very different target phenomena should "go their separate ways" or whether they can be seen as complementing each other with different programs (e.g. those focusing on learning at different time scales) providing boundary conditions for each other. His discussion also identifies a deeper obstacle to synthesis: the theoretical incommensurability of different theoretical perspectives. Seeing different research programs as in some sense complementary will require that they are formulated in terms that can be aligned with one another and that translation across theoretical perspectives is possible. Moreover, Sherin points out a particularly subtle problem of relating programs to one another arising from what he calls "ontological slippage." He describes ontological slippage as a process in which even the same researcher can fluctuate between the ontology of building models of learning (e.g. characterizing the construct "concept" within an explicit and well developed cognitive model of knowledge and knowledge change) and the ontology inherent in the world of practice (e.g. using the term "concept" less formally to refer to an idea as it appears in a textbook or in a curricular learning objective).

It was beyond the scope of Sherin's chapter to present a detailed discussion of the degree of theoretical incommensurability among the widely contrasting perspectives on concepts and conceptual change represented in Part I and to discuss specific cases of ontological slippage. He does, however, begin the task of synthesis, and paves the way for subsequent efforts, by recognizing the need for more generic constructs as a lens through which to view broad classes of constructs in the literature. He suggests that we make the broad distinction between elements, ensembles, and dynamic mental constructs. He also suggests that, despite the differences between the constructs appealed to by the different researchers, it is often possible to distinguish research programs by the degree of emphasis given to these different types of entities.

Levin, Levrini, and Greeno synthesize research, examining the connection between identity and conceptual change. In contrast to other strands of research on conceptual change, this area is the least developed. While a number of researchers have examined how disciplinary learning implicates students' identity in various ways, Levin, Levrini, and Greeno focus their attention on those approaches that both explicitly conceptualize identity and conceptual change and explicitly investigate their interaction. In order to compare such approaches, the authors extracted what they see as a skeletal framework of common assumptions and methodological stances. They then used this framework as a tool to analyze how the different lines of research converge and how they complement one another. They go on to argue that this theoretical skeleton can guide further rigorous investigations of the nexus between conceptual change and identity and orient researchers to more programmatic research moving forward.

Sherin grounds his synthetic proposal in a meta-theoretical discussion of the nature and possibilities of synthesis. Levin, Levrini, and Greeno choose instead to stay close to the three approaches discussed in Part V and to extract from them a theoretical framework through which the approaches themselves could be compared. Levin et al.'s strategy could be described as "bottom-up" in the sense that they examined the available approaches to arrive at a synthetic picture of that area of research.

Carol Smith's chapter, synthesizing research connecting metacognition and student epistemology to conceptual change, also used a bottom-up strategy. But a bottom-up synthesis in this area of research on conceptual change begins from a different starting point when compared to research on identity and conceptual change. A very large and rich literature on metacognition, epistemology, and conceptual change already exists. Smith's assessment of the state of the field led her to formulate explicitly what she sees as three classes of models of research in this area that share empirical focus, theoretical assumptions, and methodological approaches. One might say (but Smith does not explicitly use this term) that three *paradigms* of research have emerged in this area of research on conceptual change. Smith argues that these classes of models (or paradigms) do complement each other and converge in important ways. In order to clarify this complementarity, Smith draws on the broad AIR (Aims, Ideals, Reliable Processes) model of epistemic cognition (Chinn, Rinehart, & Buckland, 2014) that incorporates many aspects of these three classes of models she has identified (discussed below).

Unlike the bottom-up approach followed by Smith and Levin et al., Clark Chinn's synthesis of research on modeling, explanation, and argumentation in conceptual change is more top-down. Noticing some diversity in the use of key terms such as model/modeling, explanation and argument/argumentation he offers a set of working definitions that can help researchers use these terms with greater consistency. He then offers the AIR model (Chinn et al., 2014) (also used by Smith as an organizing tool) as a heuristic device to organize the different areas of focus of the different research programs in this area. Chinn orients the reader to how different programs of research can be seen as focusing on different epistemic *practices* (e.g. modeling, explanation, and argumentation) that learners engage in, different epistemic *aims* to which learners strive, and the different *ideals* that guide their engagement in these practices, also showing how these are implicated in different routes to conceptual change. Thus, the AIR model allows the reader to navigate a diverse literature. But it must be seen as a heuristic device because, by using this framework, Chinn is not claiming that the AIR model constitutes a theoretical framework with respect to which the different programs of research can be assimilated. Each of these programs has areas of focus not addressed in the AIR model.

Such a claim of theoretical assimilation is made by Tamer Amin in his top-down synthesis of research on the connection between representations and conceptual change. Amin adopts a sort of Kuhnian (Kuhn, 1962) perspective in assuming that evolution toward paradigmatic research involves one paradigm or program being selected as a basis for cumulative, programmatic work moving forward. Thus, Amin chooses Susan Carey's (Carey, 2009) view of concepts and concept acquisition as an organizing framework through which to view a diverse literature on representations, concepts, and concept learning. Not just using this framework as a heuristic device, Amin suggests that Carey's framework is sufficiently comprehensive theoretically, broadly grounded empirically, and makes many of the needed distinctions that allow us to see how different research programs address different aspects of a larger whole. He argues that we can see different programs as addressing different kinds of representations and different types of concept-learning processes. He also suggests that starkly contrasting perspectives—cognitivist and situated/discursive approaches to conceptual change—can, in fact, be seen as complementary from the perspective of Carey's view.

A synthetic narrative of conceptual change research

We have just described the different *ways* in which the task of synthesizing the diverse literature on conceptual change was approached by the authors of the synthesis chapters. We turn next to another result of this synthetic effort: a "synthetic narrative" which weaves together the strands of research addressed within each of the five parts of the book. To arrive at this narrative, we extracted key ideas that emerge from the different parts of the book, guided by the synthetic work done by the authors of synthesis chapters. Our story tries to make explicit the connections between the different strands of research and themes that cut across them. We hope that this narrative can serve as a useful road map, orienting newcomers to a rich field of research with many interrelated components and drawing practicing researchers' attention to where their work fits within the larger research landscape.

This narrative should be treated simply as the starting point of a process and must be subjected to a collective process of revision and elaboration. We should also comment on the scope of this narrative. While this book has addressed a number of important strands of research on conceptual change, we cannot claim that it is exhaustive. For example, an area that is not well represented in this volume is the role that social interaction plays in conceptual change (but see diSessa, Levin, and Brown, 2016, in which connections between interaction and changes in knowledge systems are explored). Moreover, we acknowledge that while research on conceptual change in a variety of domains has been considered in this book, work on concept learning in science has received the most attention.

We do not include specific citations to the sources of the ideas in the various aspects of the narrative but we acknowledge here that this synthetic narrative is a composite of the broad conclusions arrived at in the five chapters synthesizing work across different perspectives and different empirical strands of research on conceptual change. Given our goal of presenting a concise statement that conveys convergence, complementarity, and interrelationships between strands of research, the presentation below is necessarily a bit abstract and lacks illustrative examples. We encourage the reader to read the five synthesis chapters that are the basis of this synthetic narrative.

Synthetic Narrative

"Conceptual change" is a label used to refer to research that tries to understand changes in conceptual understanding in some domain. Across this large literature, target phenomena can vary, including changes in learners' conceptual understanding in the context of formal instruction, conceptual development across the life span, or conceptual change in a community over a sociohistorical time scale.

Research is conducted on these target phenomena from a range of different perspectives which are not always easy to articulate with one another

(Continued)

given different terminology, incommensurable theoretical constructs, and differences in ontological commitments (sometimes even within the same program of research). In spite of the variety of approaches to conceptual change, there is a coarse level of consensus that has emerged where most researchers distinguish knowledge *elements* (e.g. *p-prims*) and larger knowledge *ensembles* (e.g. *theories, coordination classes*), and possibly also *dynamic mental constructs* (e.g. *mental models*). A lot of theoretical work is still needed to arrive at a finer level of consensus regarding issues as fundamental as the nature of concepts and the process of conceptual change. Pursuing a finer level of consensus may require that we develop an explicit language and criteria for constructing, comparing, and evaluating cognitive models of "concepts" and "mechanisms of conceptual change." We might need to develop different models with particular situations and purposes in mind.

While a case could certainly be made for including other strands, four additional interwoven strands of research on conceptual change can be identified. One strand of research addresses how conceptual knowledge is represented and the roles that representations of various kinds play in knowledge change. A second looks at how knowledge construction practices—such as constructing models and explanations and developing arguments—drive knowledge change. A third examines how knowledge construction practices and knowledge change occur within the epistemic context of what learners believe about knowledge, learning, and knowledge construction and how they regulate their knowledge-building efforts. Finally, a fourth strand broadens the scope of investigation and views research on changes in conceptual understanding as a process that a *person* undergoes, whose learning is emotionally charged, and for whom a sense of self or identity is at stake.

The strand of research on the representation of conceptual knowledge and the role of representations in processes of change has not settled on a shared understanding of these foundational issues. While a variety of productive lines of research persist, the field is at a stage where researchers are exploring ways that these different lines of research might relate to each other. One approach has been to identify a broad framework that might be able to coordinate the contributions of these different lines of work and would incorporate the key insights of diverse perspectives without suppressing them.

In a proposed candidate framework, a concept per se is understood as a mental symbol; what the concept means (its content) is characterized in terms of how it refers to entities in the world and the role that it plays in thought, its inferential role. Representations of various kinds—iconic (resembling what they represent) and propositional (language-like); internal (mental) and external (public symbols)—are needed to account for both aspects of a concept's meaning. Moreover, some of these representations are implicit, intuitive knowledge elements that operate beyond the learner's awareness, whereas others are explicit and accessible to conscious reflection. When it comes to concept acquisition, this framework suggests that we distinguish "conceptual change" strictly speaking, in which new concepts are created, from what we can call "knowledge enrichment," that is better seen as drawing on existing conceptual representations, such as the revision of beliefs that express relationships between the concepts a learner already has. Mental representations and external public symbols play various roles in each of these types of knowledge change, and the roles that representations play in the different cases differ.

A mechanism that has been proposed to account for the development of new concepts is "Quinian bootstrapping," in which an external public symbol structure (e.g. a linguistically formulated principle or mathematical equation) serves as an, initially poorly, interpreted placeholder for a new concept and its relationships to others. Modeling activities support meaningful interpretation of the symbol structure, often by guiding the activation of useful internal iconic representations. Different research programs can be seen as addressing different aspects of this mechanism: describing external symbol structures and the difficulties learners have interpreting them, documenting the basic fact that iconic representations do help with concept learning, testing hypotheses about what iconic representations might be helpful, examining the interactions between internal and external representations that occur during concept learning, and explicitly describing the relevant Quinian bootstrapping episodes in some domain. The extent to which this framework succeeds in incorporating and coordinating multiple lines of research on representation, concepts, and concept learning will need to be evaluated carefully.

Some of the changes in knowledge of the kinds just described are not changes that learners deliberately seek to achieve. Not all the changes to the knowledge system that take place are available to conscious reflection. Implicit and explicit changes will often take place in the context of engaging in problem-solving or in epistemic practices of various kinds. A strand of research addresses the connection between changes in content-specific conceptions and specific epistemic practices such as modeling, explanation, and argumentation, practices central to science but relevant to other domains as well. To examine this connection, a shared understanding of the key constructs is useful: a *model* can be seen as an idealized representation of some aspect of the world, which is not judged true or false but is more or less similar to what it represents and more or less useful given some purpose; *modeling* refers to the processes of constructing, evaluating, and revising models; *explanations* provide causal accounts of phenomena or general schemas within which specific causal accounts can be elaborated; an *argument* is, minimally, a set of reasons that support a claim, and can also include justifications for why the reasons should be seen as supporting the claim; and *argumentation*

(Continued)

refers to the realization of arguments in a variety of possible formats, orally or in writing, constructed by an individual or through dialogic interaction.

Engaging in these practices is linked to changes in conceptual knowledge in various ways. Modeling can result in fundamental changes in models or one explanation can be replaced by another. Alternatively, there might be a more gradual change over time in aspects of a model or an explanation. A third case is contextual shifting, as when a model is seen to apply to a new situation. Argumentation can be involved in all of these types of knowledge change by helping learners shift their stance in relation to a model or explanation, resulting in them "accepting," or just "entertaining" an alternative or revised model or explanation, for example. So when learners engage in these practices they enact cognitive processes that result in knowledge change. Learners will see themselves as revising models or explanations and engaging in argumentation, but implicit in the knowledge change taking place will be changes that we, as researchers, might sometimes see as "conceptual change" per se, or as knowledge enrichment.

Participating effectively in epistemic *practices* is to take on their *aims* as your own and to be committed to the epistemic *ideals* that govern their use. Learners might have other epistemic aims than explaining, constructing models, or persuading. Moreover, learners might not be committed to ideals such as the fit of a model with evidence or the internal consistency and intelligibility of a theory. This means that we also need to address changes in learners' *understanding of* epistemic practices.

Another strand of research addresses this issue directly. It investigates learners' knowledge about knowledge, learning, and knowledge-building and their abilities to reflect on their knowledge and control their own thinking processes—that is, metacognition and epistemic cognition. It also examines how metacognition and epistemic cognition relate to changes in conceptual understanding in some domain. Three clusters of models for investigating these issues can be distinguished in the literature.

One class of models, metacognitive models of epistemic thinking, emphasizes the *individual* mental processes underlying self-regulated knowledge-building and focuses on identifying the *general* beliefs about knowledge and knowing that apply across a broad range of topics. Researchers developing these models tend to characterize conceptual change as belief revision in some domain and examine the impact of students' *existing* epistemic beliefs on content-specific beliefs in some domain in the context of relatively brief learning episodes. A second class of models, situated and distributed models, has focused on the social and contextual nature of epistemic thinking. Learners' knowledge resources are traced to their experiences and it is recognized that the application of these resources is highly sensitive to the contexts of learning situations. Successful learning is seen as involving the *organization of* these resources into more coherent and explicit knowledge structures. From this perspective, an individual's epistemic stances have social origins and are shaped by what is considered *normative* in some discourse community. Finally, a third class of models takes a longer-term perspective on learning, uncovering *implicit epistemic commitments* that relate to *specific* conceptual content and epistemic practices. These models assume that concepts should be characterized in terms of complex conceptual ecologies and conceptual change is seen to involve both change in specific beliefs and, more fundamentally, in the concepts themselves used to formulate beliefs. Because the latter involve changes in a network of knowledge elements of a variety of different kinds, conceptual change is often expected to be difficult and take time.

These three classes of models describe complementary mechanisms by which epistemic thinking, metacognition, and conceptual change in particular domains interact. Moreover, researchers investigating this strand agree that it is important to distinguish implicit epistemic thinking that operates below conscious awareness and explicit, symbolically represented, more conscious processes. Moreover, they all recognize that increasing students' *metacognitive awareness* of epistemic thinking and *making this thinking explicit* is important in promoting conceptual change.

We must not forget that knowledge change is something that involves a person in a broad sense. So another strand of research is united by the assumption that learners' emotional experiences and their identities should not be ignored. But what arguments explicitly motivate the need to study the interplay between identity and disciplinary learning? And how can we investigate rigorously the point of contact between identity and knowledge change? These are questions that are just beginning to be explored.

Most studies on identity in the context of STEM education focus on unpacking the effect of social interaction in classrooms on learners' identity development. Several research programs in this strand show how classroom interaction and, more generally, social and institutional practices combine to shape a "normative scientific/mathematical identity" that is narrow and elitist, an identity which excludes many students. The result is that mathematics and science classes rarely foster processes of identity formation in students who do not already perceive themselves as "science-" or "math-persons." In response, research programs have put forward design principles for inclusion and have started discussing, through empirical studies, how the implementation of such principles applies to processes of conceptual change.

The approaches that have been investigating the actual connection between identity and conceptual change differ in deep ways but they all share a number of common theoretical assumptions. First, they share the baseline belief that knowledge change and identity formation/management are two processes that interact and their interaction is worth examining: understanding

(Continued)

knowledge is assumed to contribute *something* to understanding identity and vice versa. This baseline assumption includes the belief that identity is not something fixed and given in an individual, but is a *dynamic construct* that interacts with the *process* of knowledge change. The second shared assumption is that the relationship between identity and knowledge change can be *rigorously investigated*. This should not be taken for granted: identity is usually seen as a social construct which characterizes how people position themselves (or are positioned) in a community, while knowledge and knowledge change are often considered to be internal mental phenomena. But it is possible to find a way of articulating the two phenomena where the ontologies of the two constructs are compatible and both are conceptualized at space and time scales that are well aligned.

Instruction that is particularly effective in supporting the development of conceptual understanding in learners applies the understanding we have arrived at from these various strands of research. In this instruction, learners engage in epistemic practices central to the knowledge-building practices in a domain. Teaching scaffolds learners as they carry out the various cognitive processes that constitute these practices, encouraging them to pursue domain specific epistemic aims and to be guided by the appropriate epistemic ideals. Learners do not engage in these practices alone but within communities of learners within which epistemic aims and ideals are socially shared. Larger-scale curricular design needs to balance the goals of developing specific content understandings, epistemological sophistication, and the skills of carrying out knowledge-building practices. This requires distinguishing changes in knowledge that will be particularly challenging and changes that will be more straightforward. Moreover, instruction needs to attend to the diversity of learners' sense of themselves as learners and manage the emotional implications of participating in learning environments that require understanding and beliefs to be publicly shared and evaluated.

Addressing the challenges to synthesis

In this section, we offer a third reading of the synthetic effort represented in this book. We reflect here on the strategies that were used by the authors of the synthesis chapters to address the challenges that synthesis posed. Indeed, as has been discussed, these challenges are numerous: researchers use different terminology; they draw on different theoretical constructs and it is often not clear how these relate to each other; and researchers often explicitly advocate very different meta-theoretical and methodological approaches, viewing alternatives as incompatible. So, what strategies helped in addressing these challenges?

One of the main concerns of the perceived fragmentation in the field was that it would not be possible to talk across perspectives. The twenty-six short chapters contributed to this book represent a diverse set of research programs distributed across different disciplinary traditions. Any hope of discerning order across this diversity assumed, at the very least, the ability to overcome the hurdle of the distinct "languages" used by the different research programs. As discussed at the beginning of this chapter, the authors of the synthesis chapters approached the synthetic task differently. Looking across these chapters we see a number of strategies used for talking across perspectives.

All the authors made an effort to be clear about their use of terminology and tried to help the reader navigate researchers' use of various terms for closely related constructs. One strategy for talking across perspectives was to use generic terminology to abstract away from differences across perspectives (Sherin, Part I). Another strategy was to use the language of an existing framework to view a diverse literature through a common lens (Amin, Part II; Chinn, Part III; and Smith, Part IV). These strategies help the reader map terminology across research programs. By organizing the field into three different classes of models, Smith helps the reader of the literature get a synthetic picture of the field despite the distinct languages used by different researchers. Tackling an area of research on conceptual change still in its infancy, Levin et al. (Part V) engage in a more exploratory discussion and outline a framework that captures common elements of different perspectives. This created a language to talk across the existing diversity.

Another synthetic strategy was to identify broad theoretical frameworks that seemed to be promising as tools that could help integrate diverse theoretical perspectives. Sherin makes uses of generic constructs that might offer a generic meta-theoretical envelope within which to understand how researchers differ in their focus on different aspects of a system—for example, elements, ensembles, or dynamic mental constructs. This is a theoretical move similar to that made by Brown and Hammer (2008), who offered dynamics systems theory as a coherent lens through which to view perspectives on conceptual change, typically seen as in competition with one another. Levin et al. point out a sort of theoretical skeleton that can orient and shape the search for a common approach to investigate rigorously the interaction between identity and conceptual change. Amin draws on Carey's view of concepts and concept acquisition. He suggests that this allows researchers to view their research as focusing on the roles that different kinds of representations play in concept representation and in knowledge change of different kinds. Both Chinn and Smith found that the AIR model described by Chinn et al. (2014)—which distinguishes epistemic aims, ideals, and reliable processes—offers a useful lens through which to view two overlapping literatures: one literature dealing with connections between various epistemic practices and conceptual change; and another dealing with connections between metacognition, epistemic cognition, and conceptual change.

The synthesis offered above was not hindered by a number of traditionally big fault lines in the field which did not emerge as major obstacles to this synthetic effort. The traditional cognitivist versus discursive/situated divide is one example (Mason, 2007). This distinction has not had a very strong presence in this volume and to the extent that it was discussed it has not been seen as an obstacle to synthesis. Sherin (Synthesis I, this volume) considered the possibility of seeing sociogenesis, on the one hand, and development and learning within individuals, on the other, as distinct yet compatible strands of research where the findings of one might be considered as boundary conditions of the other. Smith (Synthesis IV, this volume) identified situated perspectives on the connection between epistemic cognition and conceptual change as a distinct class of models but viewed this class as complementary to other classes of models not incompatible with them. Amin (Synthesis II, this volume) argued that the cognitivist/discursive tension of viewing concepts as internal mental constructs or as, in some sense, outside the head can be resolved when we characterize concepts in terms of both how they refer and their inferential role. Indeed, a variety of ways of synthesizing knowledge change in an individual with the dynamics of social and conversational interaction has recently been extensively explored (diSessa et al., 2016).

Another traditional fault line is methodological. Different traditions of research on conceptual change have drawn, over the years, on different methods and analytical techniques. The 1970s and 1980s witnessed a rise in interest in qualitative research methods in the social sciences generally (Morgan, 2007). This was accompanied by critiques of quantitative methods and the epistemological assumptions on which they were based, as well as by the development of strong arguments that had to defend the approach from attacks that they were not scientific. Indeed, the contributions in this volume represent a range of different methodological orientations including experimental hypothesis-testing (e.g. Chapter 8, Gelman & DeJesus; Chapter 3, Henderson et al.; Chapter 23, Keil; Chapter 9, Novack et al.; Chapter 20, Lombardi & Sinatra), correlational studies (e.g. Chapter 19, Hofer; Chapter 20, Lombardi & Sinatra), cross-sectional research (e.g. Chapter 2, Vosniadou), clinical interviews and individual student case studies (e.g. Chapter 1, diSessa; Chapter 21, Hammer; Chapter 7, Sherin), classroom discourse analysis (e.g. Chapter 16, Berland & Russ; Chapter 11, Säljö) and design-based research (e.g. Chapter 14, Lehrer & Schauble).

It is noteworthy, however, that attempts to synthesize the contributions in the different sections have not found methodological differences to be obstacles to synthesis. Instead when differences in methodological approach were addressed in the synthesis chapters, diverse methods were seen as complementary. For example, Amin sees the hypothesis generation role of qualitative methods as complemented by the hypothesis-testing role of quantitative experimental methods. Smith identifies three different classes of models used to explore connections between metacognition, epistemic cognition, and conceptual change and points out that these models are associated with different methodological approaches. Smith views these three classes of models as complementary. Her synthesis encourages us to view different methods as particularly well suited to addressing different types of phenomena. For example, correlational methods have helped research identify the link between metacognition and epistemic cognition, on the one hand, and content-specific conceptual change, on the other; whereas qualitative, discourse-oriented methods seem to be particularly well suited to identifying the social origins of learners' epistemic orientations and skills.

The situated/cognitive and methodological fault lines are broad. They have impacted conceptual change research in the past but they are not specific to it. Finally, a third fault line is specific to conceptual change research: the coherence versus fragmentation of pre-instruction understanding. This has been a lively debate in the literature (e.g. diSessa, 2013; Vosniadou & Skopeliti, 2014). However, this debate has not featured prominently in this volume, and whether explicitly referred to or implied, it does not come up as a major obstacle to synthesis. The contributions to this volume by researchers usually seen as proponents of distinct sides (see contributions to Part I by diSessa, Henderson et al. and Vosniadou) have played down the theoretical differences. Moreover, in his synthesis of contributions to Part I, Sherin treats the coherence versus fragmentation divide as an empirical disagreement on the degree of coherence of people's conceptual structures that can differ with age and by domain. In his discussion, this is seen as a relatively minor obstacle to synthesis, when compared to ontological differences and theoretical incommensurabilities. Other contributors to this volume have discussed themes that imply that this debate is not an obstacle to synthesis. For example, Chinn refers to revolutionary and evolutionary conceptual change as both varieties of knowledge revision that can be observed. Amin integrates diverse views of conceptual change, including accounts of knowledge change as theory change, and others that emphasize knowledge change as changes in the activation of experience-based intuitive knowledge elements.

The challenges of programmatic research on conceptual change

In light of this discussion of the ways to address challenges to synthesis, it is reasonable to suggest that conceptual change researchers can consider moving in a new programmatic direction that builds on the convergence and complementarity that has been identified in the field. But, corresponding to each of the positive aspects of the synthetic effort we have just described, there are challenges. Collectively, we view these as challenges associated with striving for the epistemic ideal of convergence and complementarity. We would like to unpack this idea here.

A key aspect of the epistemic ideal of convergence and complementarity is the ideal of taking theories seriously. A quick survey of edited volumes on conceptual change published over the last two or three decades shows that as a community we are happy to live with the coexistence of multiple theories (e.g. Limón & Mason, 2002; Schnotz, Vosniadou, & Carretero, 1999; Sinatra & Pintrich, 2003; Vosniadou, 2013). We commonly use the phrase "theoretical perspective" to refer to different accounts of concepts and conceptual change. The term "perspective" is associated with an attitude of theoretical pluralism: "perspectives" are different ways of looking at something with no implication that one is more accurate than another; and there is no expectation that different perspectives should cohere with one another. It is often noted that different perspectives can be particularly well suited to certain purposes, and the existence of a variety of perspectives can be a source of richness for a field of inquiry. Different lines of research on conceptual change do seem to cluster loosely in groups with similar broad commitments to styles of theorizing, and it might be argued that each cluster is particularly well suited to particular purposes. It is only a slight exaggeration, however, to say that we have almost as many perspectives as there are researchers. In our view, this kind of theoretical pluralism will not be productive and will not help develop conceptual change research in a programmatic direction since cumulative knowledge building at the level of the community of researchers as a whole will not take place. We need to take our theories of conceptual change seriously.

More specifically, what do we mean by taking our theories seriously? What we mean is to treat our theories as just that, theories: claims about how conceptual knowledge is represented and organized (or not); claims about the kinds of changes in conceptual knowledge that take place, and claims about mechanisms of change. Theoretical claims are subject to empirical test, and sustained testing of a theoretical claim on empirical grounds refines its scope. Moreover, theoretical claims are subject to judgments about the extent to which they cohere with other aspects of our knowledge to which we are committed. So, different theoretical claims that purport to have the same (or overlapping) empirical scope *should* be seen as competing with one another. Different theoretical claims that have a non-overlapping scope should be evaluated in terms of whether they cohere conceptually with one another. Internal contradictions in our theories should be something we try to avoid. Over time, as we build our empirical base and continue to evaluate theories in this way, our theories become more consistent with the evidence and more internally coherent. This is what we see as programmatic progress.

On this view, the relationships between multiple theories cannot be ignored, as is all too common in research on conceptual change as it stands. In addition, the importance of considering the scope of theoretical claims is underappreciated. Too often when theoretical claims are contrasted in the conceptual change literature they are treated as competing when it may well be that their scope is different. They may be addressing different aspects of a larger whole.

A basic aspect of this kind of programmatic commitment is the consistent use of terminology. Of course, as a community we will have to get into the habit of defining our terms carefully. Even more challenging, however, is the commitment to understand how terms are used by others and to compare different uses and to agree on a shared term for the same construct. It is fair to say that using terms consistently within the community of conceptual change researchers is not an epistemic ideal that currently characterizes this community, including key constructs such as "concept" and "conceptual change" themselves, whose different uses are not easy to unpack and contrast with one other. As discussed above, the synthesis chapter authors had to use a variety of strategies to deal with the terminological diversity found across the different strands of research: new generic terms were proposed (e.g. element, ensemble), commonly used terms were carefully defined and contrasted (e.g. model and explanation), similar constructs labeled differently by different researchers were pointed out (e.g. "core intuitions" and many "p-prims" are image schemas) and warnings about implicit problematic habits were voiced (e.g. ontological slippage). We hope that the synthesis chapters and the synthetic narrative we have presented above can serve as a kind of reference point for terminological consistency as we attempt to move in a more programmatic direction as a community. Of course, the specific terms used here, how they have been defined, and how they have been contrasted with one another can be contested. But we hope that the ideal of terminological clarity and consistency can be embraced by the community.

Another aspect of programmatic research and our commitment to an epistemic ideal of convergence and complementarity is our use of methods. At present, different research traditions gravitate toward different methods with some researchers preferring interpretive, qualitative methods and others quantitatively establishing correlational or causal links between variables. In our view, the coordination of these methodologies is necessary for a cumulative program of research on conceptual change to gather momentum. Interpretive, qualitative methods have proved to be very productive in providing rich descriptions of specific cases supporting hypothesis formulation, and in generating new models and triggering a variety of theoretical innovations. Nevertheless, when the generalizability of claims needs to be examined, quantitative methods are often required. Moreover, design-based research (Cobb, Confrey, diSessa, Lehrer, & Schauble, 2003) is needed that evaluates our knowledge in the real context of learning in classrooms and schools, and produces new hypotheses.

While most researchers will agree with what we have said about methods here, our practices do not reflect a sustained commitment to these complementary roles of research methods. What we are advocating here is a commitment to practice what we often preach when it comes to how multiple methods contribute to the larger endeavor of cumulative knowledge building. Of course, we are not suggesting that all researchers should be trying their hand at all aspects of this three-pronged agenda. Indeed, each part of it requires different research talents, abilities, intellectual interests, and professional knowledge. Because of this, it is very natural that each researcher privileges the methods that match their purposes, know-how, and inclinations. Instead, we are suggesting that we need a commitment to methodological complementarity and to promote the creation of communities of researchers to develop the qualitative, quantitative, and design aspects of larger research agendas.

Pursuing the epistemic ideal of mapping convergences and complementarity is not simply an academic exercise. Increasingly, the need has been recognized to bring conceptual change research closer to the realities of schools and classroom practice (e.g. Duschl, Schweingruber, & Shouse, 2007). An effective bridge is needed between the theoretical outcomes of research studies and practice. This means that the goal of constructing precise cognitive models of learning will have to be carefully coordinated with the practical challenges of designing curricula and classroom learning environments that are effective and inclusive. Our synthetic narrative shows that research on conceptual change has now embraced complexity. In addition to claims about mental representations and processes, our models of conceptual change now incorporate accounts of the role of public representations, knowledge-building practices, and the epistemic, emotional, and social aspects of the contexts in which conceptual change takes place. The complexity and scope of the emerging synthetic narrative bodes well for its relevance to the complex realities of learners, classrooms, and schools.

As we embrace the complexity of our models, we must be disciplined modelers and do our best to "cut nature at its joints"; embracing aspects of our models that cohere with one another and with our empirical findings, and discarding those that do not cohere well. Moreover, as we develop our models and attempt to coordinate these with practical realities, we need to be wary of what Sherin called "ontological slippage"; in our theories, it can happen that the ontology and language of modeling knowledge representation and learning does not align well with the everyday ontology and language of practitioners. This kind of theoretical inconsistency can hinder our research effort from impacting actual teaching and learning in schools. This volume has focused primarily on bringing together our theoretical accounts of the representation of conceptual knowledge and the complexities of the processes of change. While this effort puts us in a good position to apply our knowledge to practice, we have not yet engaged with the challenge of establishing a coherent interface with the world of practice. This is an important challenge for future work.

We close our book by saying that the challenges of pursuing programmatic research, while articulated conceptually here, have implications for our institutional practices and community norms. Researchers, adopting different theoretical perspectives and with different methodological preferences, have increasingly diverged institutionally and have formed different research associations and interact in different annual conferences. Research publications reflecting these different commitments appear in different journals whose editorial boards embrace distinct epistemological and methodological commitments. These trends will increase fragmentation and undermine efforts to engage in more programmatic research. Facing the challenge of programmatic research on conceptual change will require the commitment of individual researchers to the epistemic ideal of convergence and complementarity. But it will also require commitment at a more institutional level if this epistemic ideal can become the norm of our research community.

Acknowledgments

We would like to thank Clark Chinn, Mariana Levin, and Carol Smith for comments on an earlier version of this chapter.

Note

1 Both authors made equal contributions to this chapter. The names are in alphabetical order.

References

Amin, T. G., Smith, C., & Wiser, M. (2014). Student conceptions and conceptual change: Three overlapping phases of research. In N. Lederman & S. Abell (Eds.), *Handbook of research on science education* (vol. 2, pp. 57–81), New York: Routledge.

Brown, D., & Hammer, D. (2008). Conceptual change in physics. In S. Vosniadou (Ed.), *International handbook of research on conceptual change*. New York: Routledge.

Carey, S. (2009). *The origin of concepts*. Oxford: Oxford University Press.

Chinn, C. A. (2016). Outgoing editor's statement: A perspective on EP and debates in education. *Educational Psychologist, 51*(1), 3–6. DOI:10.1080/00461520.2016.1160782.

Chinn, C. A., Rinehart, R. W., & Buckland, L. A. (2014). Epistemic cognition and evaluating information: Applying the AIR model of epistemic cognition. In D. N. Rapp & J. L. G. Braasch (Eds.), *Processing inaccurate information: Theoretical and applied perspectives from cognitive science and the educational sciences*. Cambridge, MA: MIT Press.

Cobb, P., Confrey, J., diSessa, A., Lehrer, R., & Schauble, L. (2003). Design experiments in educational research. *Educational Researcher, 32*(1), 9–13.

diSessa, A. A. (2013). A bird's-eye view of the "pieces" vs "coherence" controversy (from the "pieces" side of the fence). In S. Vosniadou (Ed.), *International handbook of research on conceptual change* (2nd Ed., pp. 31–48). New York: Routledge.

diSessa, A. A., Levin, M., & Brown, N. J. S. (2016). *Knowledge and interaction: A synthetic agenda for the learning sciences*. London: Routledge.

Duschl, R. A., Schweingruber, H. A., & Shouse, A. W. (2007). *Taking science to school*. Washington, DC: National Academies Press.

Kuhn, T. (1962). *The structure of scientific revolutions*. Chicago, IL: University of Chicago Press.

Limón, M., & Mason, L. (Eds.) (2002). *Reconsidering conceptual change: Issues in theory and practice*. Dordrecht: Kluwer.

Mason, L. (2007). Bridging the cognitive and sociocultural approaches to research on conceptual change: Is it feasible? *Educational Psychologist, 42*(1), 1–7.

Morgan, D. L. (2007). Paradigms lost and pragmatism regained: Methodological implications of combing qualitative and quantitative methods. *Journal of Mixed Methods Research, 1*(1), 48–76.

Schnotz, W., Vosniadou, S., & Carretero, M. (Eds.) (1999). *New perspectives on conceptual change*. New York: Pergamon.

Sinatra, G., & Pintrich, P. R. (Eds.) (2003). *Intentional conceptual change*. Mahwah, NJ: Erlbaum.

Vosniadou, S. (2013) *International handbook of research on conceptual change* (2nd Ed.). New York: Routledge.

Vosniadou, S., & Skopeliti, I. (2014). Conceptual change from the framework theory side of the fence. *Science & Education, 23*(7), 1427–1445.

Index

Page numbers in *italic* indicate a figure on the corresponding page. Page numbers in **bold** indicate a table on the corresponding page.